oosten

Brabant, The Netherlands
ington County, Oregon
rown County, Wisconsin to:

anLanen

Brabant, The Netherlands
ington County, Oregon

Joosten
d Chute, WI
nhill, OR
boort, OR

Hermens
rence, WI
nhill, OR

Ila Hermens
oort, OR
land, OR

Hermens
boort, OR
land, OR

Hermens
oort, OR
gton Co., OR

Hermens
oort, OR
boro, OR

Hermens
oort, OR
nville, OR

Hermens
oort, OR
nville, OR

Hermens
oort, OR
nville, OR

Hermens
nville, OR
nville, OR

Hermens
nville, OR
ham, OR

Catherine Joosten
b. 27 Feb 1872 Grand Chute, WI
d. 2 Aug 1954 Appleton, WI
m. 27 Sep 1892 Little Chute, WI

William Henry Weyenberg
b. 26 Feb 1865 Grand Chute, WI
d. 3 Nov 1941 Grand Chute, WI

James William Weyenberg
b. 23 Jul 1894 Grand Chute, WI
d. 15 Feb 1929 Grand Chute, WI

Ellen Marie Weyenberg
b. 21 Jul 1896 Little Chute, WI
d. 16 Mar 1959 Appleton, WI

Joseph Peter Weyenberg Sr.
b. 24 Aug 1898 Grand Chute, WI
d. 22 Jun 1962 Appleton, WI

Albert J. Weyenberg
b. 15 Sep 1900 Grand Chute, WI
d. 2 Jun 1982 Winnebago Co., WI

Francis M. Weyenberg
b. 12 Aug 1902 Grand Chute, WI
d. 24 Nov 1973 Appleton, WI

Martin J. Joosten
b. 7 Sep 1874 Grand Chute, WI
d. 24 Jun 1925 Rudolph, WI
m. 21 Sep 1897 Little Chute, WI to:

Anna Marie VanDomelen
b. 2 Jul 1872 Oconto Falls, WI
d. 29 Jun 1950 Rudolph, WI

Mamie Joosten
b. 19 Nov 1898 Grand Chute, WI
d. 5 May 1902 Grand Chute, WI

Wilhelmina Joosten
b. 8 Sep 1900 Grand Chute, WI
d. 23 Apr 1964 Rudolph, WI

Joseph William Joosten
b. 31 Aug 1902 Grand Chute, WI
d. 23 Jun 1988 Los Alamitas, CA

Maymie Joosten
b. 5 Jul 1904 Grand Chute, WI
d. 24 Jun 1994 Rudolph, WI

William Joosten
b. 15 Apr 1907 Rudolph, WI
d. 23 Sep 1925 Rudolph, WI

Richard Simon Joosten
b. 6 Aug 1909 Rudolph, WI
d. 11 Aug 1968 Wonder Lake, IL

Rosella Joosten
b. 23 Sep 1911 Rudolph, WI
d. 29 Nov 1918 Rudolph, WI

George A. Joosten
b. 25 Jun 1914 Rudolph, WI
d. 10 Dec 1972 Wisconsin Rapids, WI

Christina J. Joosten
b. 6 Aug 1876 Grand Chute, WI
d. 23 Dec 1931 Fremont, WI
m. 6 Nov 1895 Little Chute, WI

Adrian Henry Verhagen
b. 22 Sep 1871 Little Chute, WI
d. 14 Oct 1943 Chili, WI

Edward Henry Verhagen
b. 4 Jun 1899 Chili, WI
d. 6 Jun 1953 Chili, WI

Ellen N. Verhagen
b. 24 Feb 1901 Chili, WI
d. 25 Apr 1955 Chili, WI

Joseph Albert Verhagen
b. 20 Nov 1902 Chili, WI
d. 9 Nov 1921 Chili, WI

Harriet Alice Verhagen
b. 3 Apr 1904 Chili, WI
d. 18 Feb 1987 Madera, CA

Paul Martin Verhagen
b. 14 Sep 1905 Chili, WI
d. 20 Dec 1964 Los Angeles, CA

Marie Mathilda Verhagen
b. 23 Dec 1907 Chili, WI
d. 10 Jun 1989 Waukegan, IL

Louise Elizabeth Verhagen
b. 19 Aug 1909 Wisconsin
d. 12 Dec 1973 Marshfield, WI

Bertha Lucille Verhagen
b. 11 Feb 1913 Chili, WI
d. 30 Oct 1985 Antioch, IL

Frances Josephine Verhagen
b. 10 May 1914 Chili, WI
d. 22 Oct 1994 Wisconsin Rapids, WI

Louis John Verhagen
b. 10 Feb 1917 Chili, WI
d. 17 Mar 1974 Forest Grove, OR

Howard George Verhagen
b. 22 May 1918 Chili, WI
d. 1 Apr 1965 Waukegan, IL

Mabel Phyllis Verhagen
b. 4 May 1920 Chili, WI
d. 13 Aug 2008 Medford, WI

Margaret J. Joosten
b. 8 Apr 1880 Grand Chute, WI
d. 12 Jan 1960 Verboort, OR
m. 9 May 1901 Verboort, OR

Walter VanDyke
b. 27 Sep 1876 DePere, WI
d. 8 Oct 1940 Verboort, OR

Joseph Theodore VanDyke
b. 17 Jul 1902 Verboort, OR
d. 2 Jun 1987 Forest Grove, OR

George Theodore VanDyke
b. 12 Nov 1903 Verboort, OR
d. 5 Jan 1991 Forest Grove, OR

Wilhelmina Mary VanDyke
b. 29 Mar 1905 Verboort, OR
d. 25 Jan 2007 Forest Grove, OR

Albert Martin VanDyke
b. 6 Jul 1906 Verboort, OR
d. 18 Jul 1989 Walla Walla, WA

Theodore August VanDyke
b. 14 Feb 1908 Verboort, OR
d. 2 May 1979 Forest Grove, OR

Cecilia Josephine VanDyke
b. 16 Nov 1909 Verboort, OR
d. 4 Jan 2006 Beaverton, OR

Raymond Wilfred VanDyke
b. 11 Sep 1911 Verboort, OR
d. 18 Mar 2005 Woodland, WA

Christine Margaret VanDyke
b. 29 May 1913 Verboort, OR
d. Living

Clarence George VanDyke
b. 11 Dec 1914 Verboort, OR
d. 29 Oct 2005 Forest Grove, OR

Loretta M. VanDyke
b. 7 Dec 1916 Verboort, OR
d. 21 Jan 2009 Forest Grove, OR

Howard Walter VanDyke
b. 20 Oct 1918 Verboort, OR
d. 8 Oct 2001 Cornelius, OR

Florence Walteria VanDyke
b. 13 Feb 1921 Verboort, OR
d. Living

Leona Ida VanDyke
b. 15 Jul 1922 Verboort, OR
d. Living

Ralph John VanDyke
b. 24 Jun 1924 Verboort, OR
d. Living

nts of

Petronella VanLanen

The Joostens
A Dutch Family Legacy & Genealogy

Connecting Cousins

Neven en Nichten verbinden (Dutch)

Steve Shaw

The Joostens
A Dutch Family Legacy & Genealogy

By Stephen J. Shaw

ISBN 978-0-9963913-0-6
Library of Congress Control Number: 2015940924
Print Run: 9 8 7 6 5 4 3

This book is available from:

Steve7429@hotmail.com and
www.facebook.com/SteveShawAuthor.
Any additions and corrections to the names, dates, and
facts listed in my book are welcomed, and can be
submitted to the email address above.

Printed and Bound in the United States of America
By Gorham Printing, Centralia, WA
http://www.gorhamprinting.com

Other Books Authored By Stephen J. Shaw:

Wilhelmina Mary Vanderzanden, A Biography of A Grandma's Life, 2008
(Copies available from steve7429@hotmail.com or
www.facebook.com/SteveShawAuthor)

Steve Shaw

*"We make a living by what we get,
but we make a life by what we give."*

Winston Churchill

 Please join us on the Descendants of Joseph and Nellie Joosten Facebook Page at https://www.facebook.com/groups/1496740763886656/ to stay in touch with your cousins and friends.

 Please follow me on Facebook at www.facebook.com/SteveShawAuthor

I Dedicate This Book To:

The memory and legacy of our family pioneers
Joseph and Nellie Joosten.

Acknowledgements

My sincere appreciation goes out to all of the cousins who graciously welcomed me into their homes, or talked to me on the phone. I am grateful for your kindness and help in my mission to gather names, dates, and your wonderful stories.

Many thanks to my fiancée Christi Manning for your loving support over the years in allowing me to take time to complete this massive writing journey, walking through cemeteries in search of family, and for help editing this book.

I am grateful to Christine Greenall (Schwall) for her wonderful contribution of the very nice looking Joosten family tree chart that graces the inside of the cover.

Joseph Joosten's Birth Record

Dutch Language Version: ("…" = illegible word)

Het jaar een duizend acht honderd achtendertig, den tweeentwintigsten der maand january om vier ure des namiddag verscheen voor ons Burgemeester, Beambte van den Burgerlijken Stand, der gemeente Nuenen, Gerwen en Nederwetten, provincie Noord-Braband, Martinus Joosten, oud achtendertig jaren, van beroep landbouwer wonende te Nuenen, dewelke ons heeft vertoond een Kind van het manlijk geslacht, geboren op den een en tweeentwintigsten January dezes Jaars te twaalf ure des middags van hun comparant en van Lijne huisvrouw Anna Marie Dekkers oud tweeendertig jaren, van beroep landbouwer woonend al. hier en aan hetwelk hy velklaard heeft te geven den voornaam van Joost welke verklaring en vertooning zijn geschied in bijwezen van Herman Christiaan van Hovey oud vijf en twintig jaren, van beroep particulier en van Antonie Boojakkers oud vijf en zestig jaren, van beroep landbouwer beide alhier woonachtig; nadat aan de comparanten van deze akte voorlezing is gedaan, hebben dezelve … … … nomen de … die verhlaarde niette kunnen …

English Language Translation: ("…" = translation unknown)

The year one thousand eight hundred thirty-eight, the twenty-second day of the month January at four o'clock in the afternoon appeared before our Mayor, Officer (or official) of the Civil State, the municipality of Nuenen, Gerwen and Nederwetten, province of North Braband, Martinus Joosten, aged thirty-eight years, occupation of farmer living in Nuenen, which has presented a Child of the male gender, born on the twenty first of January this year at twelve midday to/for their appearing and of housewife Anna Marie Dekkers age thirty-two years, occupation of farmer who lives here and declares to have given the forename of Joost which declaration and … were done in the presence of Herman Christiaan van Hovey age twenty five years, occupation private and Antonie Boojakkers age sixty five years, occupation farmer both local residents; after the appearing of this deed for reading is done, have them … … … except the … that … nevertheless can …

Petronella VanLanen's Birth Record

N°. 22 *[handwritten birth record certificate in Dutch]*

Dutch Language Version: ("…" = illegible word)
In het jaar een duizend acht honderd veertig, den twintigsten dag der maand Mei, is voor ons Ambtenaar van den Burgerlijken Stand, der gemeente Boekel provincie Noord-Braband, verschenen Gerardus van Lanen van beroep landbouwer oud vierendertig jaren, wonende te Boekel welke in tegenwoordigheid van twee getuigen, als van Peter van den Berg van beroep landbouwer oud zesenvijftig jaren, en Johannes Arnoldus Peters van beroep Arbeider oud veertig jaren, beide wonende binnen deze gemeente, ons heft verklaard dat Maria van den Elsen Lijne huisvrouw oud Lesentwintig jaren, van beroep Boerin wonende te Boekel Voormeld bevallen is van Ean kind van het vrouwelijk geslacht, geboren op deze dag den negentiende der maand Mei een duizend acht honderd
en veertig om negen ure des avonds welk kind zal genaamd worden Petronella van welke verklaring wij de tegenwoordige Akte hebben opgemaakt, die, na voorlezing, is geteekend door ons beneffens de comparanten voornoemd.

G V Laanen   De Ambtenaar van den Burgerlijken Stand voornoemd,
Peter VDBerg
A Peters   Herman van der Heyden

English Language Translation: ("…" = translation unknown)
The year one thousand eight hundred and forty, the twentieth Day of the month of May, before our Chief of the Civil State, the municipality of Boekel, province of North Braband, appeared Gerardus van Lanen, occupation of farmer, aged thirty-four years, living in Boekel, which in the presence of two witnesses, as Peter van den Berg
occupation farmer aged fifty-six years, and Johannes Arnoldus Peters occupation of Worker aged forty years, both residing in this municipality, has stated that Maria van den Elsen housewife aged twenty-six years, occupation farmer's wife residing in Boekel, the above-mentioned, gave birth to a child of the female gender, born on this day the nineteenth of the month of May one thousand eight hundred and forty in the ninth hour of the evening which child will be called Petronella from which we have drawn up the present statement, after reading is signed by us … the aforementioned appearing

G V Laanen   Chief of the Civil State, aforesaid,
Peter VDBerg
A Peters   Herman van der Heyden

TABLE OF CONTENTS

Washington County Donation Land Claims

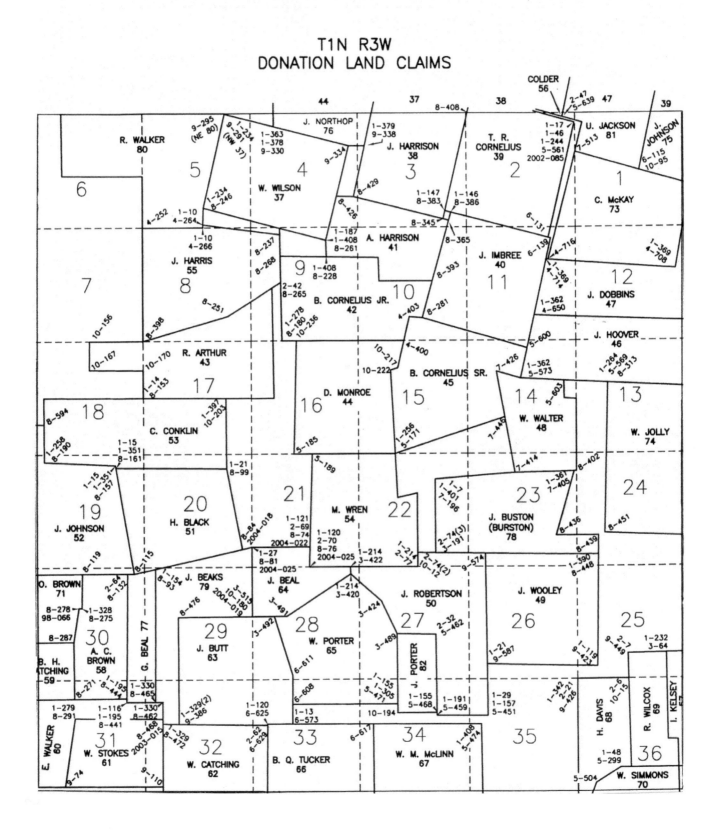

T1N R3W
DONATION LAND CLAIMS

Outagamie County 1889 Plat Map

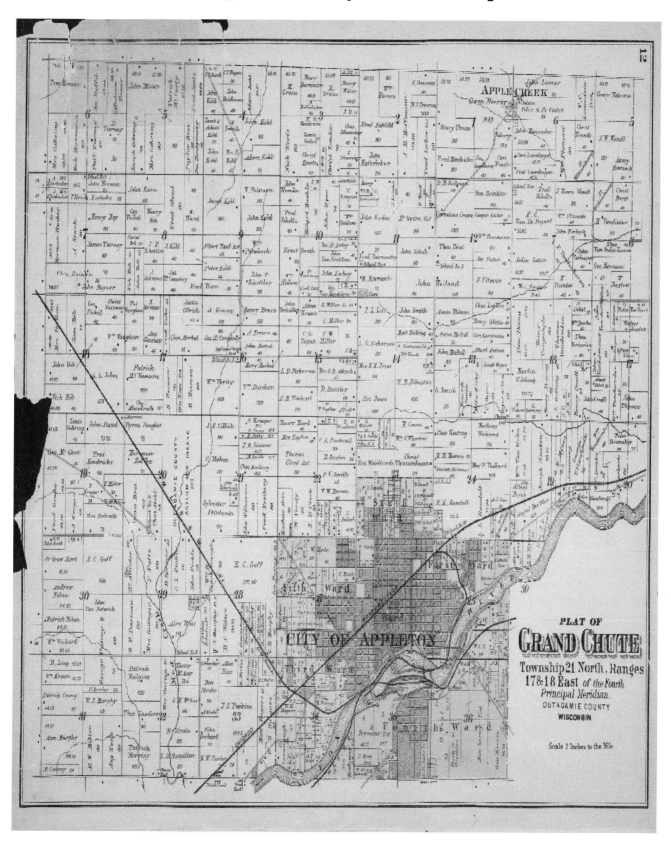

PLAT OF
GRAND CHUTE
Township 21 North, Ranges
17 & 18 East of the Fourth
Principal Meridian.
OUTAGAMIE COUNTY
WISCONSIN

Scale 2 Inches to the Mile

Preface

At some point in our lives we have a desire to know where we came from. How great would it be to imagine yourself in the shoes, and living the life, of your favorite ancestor 100 or 150 years ago? This desire has burned inside me for many years. When I started researching and learning more about Joseph and Nellie Joosten and their children, the more I became intrigued. After visiting Wisconsin, the Badger State, for the first time in the summer of 2008, I came away with a huge ambition to tell the stories of Joseph, Nellie and their family. These stories need to be told, because everyone has a story to tell about their life. There is immense historical value getting family stories documented for future generations so our descendants know more about us, and our lives as we live them today. Many of our older ancestors never had their story told. Today with technology, uncovering treasures in census records or newspapers makes finding family stories easier.

It has been more than 100 years now since the Joosten family split in half, exchanged their Badger hats for Beaver hats, and moved from Wisconsin to Oregon. In the early 20th century family would travel to Oregon or to Wisconsin for visits. Although those visits have diminished over time, my goal in writing this book is to reunite the family, and to bridge the knowledge gap of "who is who" in our vast Joosten Family. Another goal was to create a book filled with names and dates to become a valuable reference for future use.

When I started this book writing journey it became very apparent early on the Catholic faith and the priests who preached the faith were central figures in the lives of the Joosten family. There were two influential and visionary priests, first Father Theodore Vandenbroek who led the Joostens from Holland to Wisconsin, and later Father William Verboort who convinced part of the family to move to Oregon. For that reason I have dedicated chapter one to these two wonderful priests, and other priests who were close to the Joostens. I feel it is important to reveal how and why the Joostens came to America, which is captured in the early chapters.

The remainder of the book is laid out with a chapter dedicated to each of Joseph and Nellie's nine children. In all there are five complete generations of the Joosten family you will get to know and learn about. Each of these chapters comprises four parts; first there are family stories and facts, a dedication to our family members' military service, a photo and image gallery from my vast collection of memorabilia, and ends with a three-generation genealogy.

An index can be found at the end of this book containing more than 1,750 people who are named throughout this book. Incredibly Joseph and Nellie Joosten's nine children added 86 grandchildren and 387 great-grandchildren to this awesome family.

Our ancestor's grave headstones list two dates with a "dash" in between them. This book is the "dash" of the Joosten Family. In addition to the Joostens, if you are related to or know the Bernards, Hermens, VanDyke, VanHandel, Verhagen, or the Weyenberg families, this book is for you. History must be captured to be preserved for future generations of family. Enjoy my book.

❧ Chapter One ❦
Our Priests, Our Leaders

Through all generations of the Joosten family, the gift of faith was handed down from parent to child, and so on, and so on. This gift of faith grew because of many faithful priests who were an integral and spiritual part of their lives. A select few of these priests were missionary men who had visions larger than life because of their love for the Lord, the Catholic Church, and their "flock", the faithful people who they would lead. These wonderful priests led our family on long life-changing journeys, baptized the babies, fed us First Communion, joined us in matrimony, and gave us our last rites as our ancestors were mourned.

Our ancestors trusted these priests to guide them when they proclaimed a better future for them and their children. Two of the most prominent and influential priests who persuaded families to "dig up" deep roots from Holland and later from Wisconsin were Fr. Theodore Vandenbroek and Fr. William Verboort. Both are leaders in their own right and so highly revered that towns were named after them; the Town of Vandenbroek, WI, and Verboort, OR. They were simply amazing men.

Theodore J. Vandenbroek was born on November 5, 1783 in Amsterdam, Holland to Abraham Vandenbroek and Elizabeth deMeyne. His parents were considered wealthy. As a young adult he was a well-built man of 5' 10" tall, with hazel eyes, and brown hair. Theodore was a very smart and driven man who had mastered the Dutch, French, German, Greek, and Latin languages.

The Reverend Theodore J. van den Broek, O. P.

According to the book written and published by Sister Mary Alphonsa Corry in 1907 titled *"The Story of Father Van Den Broek, O.P.: A Study of Holland and the Story of the Early Settlement of Wisconsin"*, mentions that at the age of 24 Theodore was ordained a priest in 1808, possibly in Germany, into the Franciscan order. Apparently at the time Holland did not have any Bishops. In his early days as a priest, Fr. Vandenbroek was an assistant priest at a church run by Dominican priests in Groningen, a town in northern Holland not far from the North Sea. After receiving his release from the Pope, he was received into the Dominican Order and ordained on June 16, 1817. In 1819, he was appointed pastor at a church in Alkmaar, which is approximately 25 miles (40 km) north of his hometown of Amsterdam, and remained there for 11 years until 1830. While at Alkmaar, he wrote and published three large volumes titled *"Sermons for all Sundays and Holidays"*. Next, Fr. Theodore was reassigned as pastor in Tiel, a town 52 miles (83.6 km) southeast of Amsterdam. He would stay in Tiel until 1832 when he asked for and was granted permission from his Provincial (an official in charge of an ecclesiastical province acting under the superior general of a religious order), Albertus van Kampen, to leave the country to establish a missionary in America. The spirit of the Dominican Order was the salvation of souls. Fr. Vandenbroek carried out this mission in Holland and now, at the age of 49, he wanted to carry it out in the United States of America, the Land of the Free.

After leaving Antwerp for the four-week voyage at sea crossing the Atlantic, Fr. Vandenbroek and seven other missionaries arrived in Baltimore on August 15, 1832. After a few days in Baltimore, the missionaries were sent to different cities. Approximately nine weeks later Fr. Vandenbroek arrived in Springfield, Kentucky for his first assignment at the St. Rose Convent. While there he spent time studying English and the American culture. He then was called to Ohio to serve the St. Joseph Catholic Church because the Germans living there had no priest who knew their language, and of course Father was fluent in German.

A great book was published in 1900 by P. Chrysostomus Verwyst, OFM titled *"Life and Labors of Rt. Rev. Frederic Baraga"*. Fr. Verwyst emigrated from Holland on the ship Maria Magdalena in 1848 when he was a small boy of six years old, and Fr. Vandenbroek was on this same ship. In this book he dedicates some pages to other missionaries in northwest Wisconsin including Fr. Vandenbroek. The author wrote that Fr. Vandenbroek's next assignment was in Green Bay and arrived there on July 4, 1834 to serve the Native American mission, and only ten Catholic families living there at the time. The Menominee and Oneida tribes were in the area at this time. He then writes, *"Father Van den Broek labored at Green Bay, sometimes with Father S. Mazzuchelli, from 1834 till the winter of 1836. It seems he left Green Bay in December of the last named year and went to reside in Little Chute."* One of the first white settlers from the Little Chute, Wisconsin area named Charles Grignon went to Green Bay accompanied by Native Americans from the local tribe to invite Fr. Vandenbroek to come to Little Chute. He accepted their invitation, and promised to relocate there once another priest took his place in Green Bay. For a time, Father said two Masses on Sunday, the first one in Green Bay and the second in Little Chute. His mode of transportation ... by foot! Yes, apparently he would walk the 20-some odd miles between the two

towns. Fr. Verwyst offers this story about Fr. Vandenbroek's travels by foot. *"Once his feet bled profusely from the pegs in his boots, whence he was obliged to stop on his way to have them extracted. Another time he lost his boots in the mud."* Given the point in time, and the lack of developed land, Father's existence was at best meager. He lived in a wigwam measuring fifteen feet long by six feet high, and he was often hungry. Wigwams of the northeast were typically made of wood formed into a dome and covered with bark stripped from trees to provide the best shelter known from the harsh and cold winters. Fr. Vandenbroek's wigwam served as his home, the church, and school for the Menominee children

Image 1.02- Photo of sign located in St. John Nepomucene Church parking lot (2008)

and adults for the first six months in 1836. Father taught the children and adults to read by having them read Bishop Frederic Baraga's (Bishop of Green Bay) prayer books and the Catechism. In the meantime, Father and his Native American congregation were building their new church and rectory, which at the time was referred to as a "parsonage". At this time, Fr. Vandenbroek had converted 50 souls into the faith, and it did not take long before his churchgoers reached 200. With this amazing growth came the need to build a new and larger church structure. Fr. Verwyst noted that Fr. Vandenbroek was not only a missionary to the tribe he was serving, but also a civilizer. He not only converted and baptized many of the Native Americans into the Catholic faith, but he showed them how to plant crops, use carpenter tools, and the trades of mason and plasterer.

In the year 1836, Fr. Vandenbroek's congregation again stepped up and helped construct a new larger church, 30 feet long and 22 feet wide, made of logs, and they did it without any fundraising. Fr. Vandenbroek named his church in honor of St. John Nepomucene. Their new church started out with no floor and the joists served as the bench pews, and the roof was made of bark from the trees used to build the church. The following year, 1838, the floor was put in and the roof covered with boards. In 1839, the congregation had grown so much that another 20 feet was added onto the church, and a tower was also erected.

St. John Nepomucene (1345-1393) was born in Nepomuk, Bohemia, a historical region in Central Europe occupying the western two-thirds of the Czech Lands. After John Nepomucene was ordained he was sent to a parish in the city of Prague, Czechoslovakia. He became a great preacher and thousands of those who listened to him changed their way of life. Father John was invited to the court of Wenceslaus IV, King of the Romans, and King of Bohemia. John became the queen's confessor. One day, about 1393, the king asked him to tell what the queen had said in confession. When Father John refused, he was thrown into prison. A second time, he was asked to reveal the queen's confession. *"If you do not tell me,"* said the king, *"you shall die. But if you obey my commands, riches and honor will be yours."* Again Father John refused, and he was tortured. The king ordered John to be thrown into the Vltava River. A strange brightness appeared upon the water in the place where he drowned. He is known as the martyr of the "Seal of the Confessional." St. John Nepomucene was canonized by Pope Benedict

Image 1.03- St. John Nepomucene (1345-1393) Photo

XIII on March 19, 1729, 336 years following his fateful death. He is the patron saint of Czechoslovakia, and his feast day is May 16.

In the midst of Fr. Vandenbroek and his companion Native Americans from the Menominee tribe building and adding onto their church, the United States Government and the Menominee Nation were working out a land purchase deal. These negotiations concluded in the <u>Treaty of the Cedars</u> on September 3, 1836 on the Fox River just west of Little Chute at a place called Cedar Point. Under article one of this Treaty the Menominee tribe ceded 4,000,000 acres of land to the federal government for a total of just $700,000 (17 cents per acre). According to the second article of the Treaty document the Government was to:

- Pay the Tribe $23,750 in cash annually for 20 years;
- Provide the Tribe $3,000 worth of provisions annually for 20 years, including 2,000 pounds of tobacco, 30 barrels of salt, and $500 for farming utensils;
- Pay $1,000 in cash annually for 20 years to Robert Grignon, a friend of the Tribe, for his valuable service to the Nation;
- Make a $80,000 one-time payment to the Chief to be divided among the Tribes friends and relatives of mixed blood;
- Forgive $99,710.50 in debt owed by the Tribe.

The Treaty encompassed an area of land stretching from Oshkosh in the south to Marquette, Michigan in the north and from Wisconsin Rapids in the west to Green Bay in the east, and required the Tribe to move west of the Wolf River, which flows into Lake Poygan. The US Government promised the Menominee a reservation at Lake Poygan, which is about 38 miles southwest of Little Chute.

Image 1.04- Treaty of the Cedars, Page One

The fourth article of the Treaty stated annual payments of cash and goods was to be paid in "*June or July, or soon thereafter*," and the Tribe was "*to remove from the Country ceded within one year after the ratification of this Treaty.*" Nearly five months later the two parties' principal negotiators, Wisconsin Governor Henry Dodge and Menominee Chief Oshkosh, proclaimed and ratified the Treaty on February 15, 1837, which meant the Menominee Tribe had to pick up their belongings and head westward. I have read two other accounts of this story stating the Tribe moved to their new reservation at Lake Poygan in 1843. This Treaty and subsequent settlement profoundly affected the Menominee Tribe, resulting in drastic changes to their culture and lifestyle. As these people were forced off their land and to live nearby other settlers, their housing and clothing styles became anglicized, or more English in form. As the years past, they were compelled to leave behind a nomadic lifestyle and take up farming. The government strongly encouraged, sometimes through force, the Menominee to send their children to boarding schools where they were taught the white man's ways. There was a huge environmental impact to the land the Tribe left behind; canals, locks, and dams were constructed on the Fox River, and railroads were built over the land. All of this infrastructure led to the clear cutting of forests, depletion of the soil, and the change of the natural course of rivers. And I am left with a sour taste in my mouth over the deal the US Government gave the Menominee Tribe for their abundant land.

Image 1.05- Menominee Warrior

Remember the government bought the land for 17 cents an acre; well, this same land was selling for two to five dollars per acre just a short time later in the late 1850s. Probably not the first or the last time the Menominee people got a raw deal.

Around the mid to late 1840s a company by the name of Fox and Wisconsin Improvement Company was formed and commissioned to dig a canal between the Fox and Wisconsin Rivers in order to facilitate travel and commerce between the Great Lakes and the Gulf of Mexico, and to build locks along the lower Fox River. Father Theodore was aware of this effort and was in contact with two men from the company. He mentioned to them he could easily persuade many of his countrymen from Holland to come to Little Chute and help them dig the canal at Portage, WI. Hollanders were very familiar with locks and canals since much of their land is below sea level; it seemed a natural fit. It has been written in various accounts these two men from the Improvement Company were so elated and approving of Father's plan that they promised him employment for those he brought back, and offered to pay his ship fare back to Holland.

Around this same time, Fr. Vandenbroek's mother had passed away in 1844, leaving him an inheritance of 20,000 gulden and a similar sum to his only sister, Mrs. Ootmar. Also, 1844 saw the establishment of the Cathedral (or also known as "See") in Milwaukee. Bishop John Martin Henni (1805-1881) was appointed as the Archdiocese's first Bishop. This enabled many more priests to enter into the priesthood in the Milwaukee diocese. Fr. Vandenbroek was able to obtain an assistant, Rev. P. J. Mannis D'Arco, which enabled him to plan a trip back to his homeland. His goal was two-fold, to collect his inheritance, including his own savings, and convince more Hollanders to emigrate to Little Chute. In August 1847, he sailed back and arrived at Amsterdam, his birthplace, only to find that the notary he had entrusted with his inheritance and savings had stolen all of it. His money and the notary were nowhere to be found. I imagine this saddened him because I bet a portion of this money he had set aside was to help his fellow countrymen who did not have the means to pay for the voyage to Little Chute. Although his goal was to return to Little Chute that same summer, now he would have to wait because there was no way he would make the three month journey during the winter when the seas were treacherous. Besides, even the most talented and experienced ship Captain probably would not attempt the voyage across the Atlantic during this time of the year.

Never discouraged to achieve his goals, Fr. Vandenbroek wrote letters that were published in the prominent Roman Catholic newspaper called "De Tijd", or translated "The Times". The De Tijd was created and first published in 1845 in the city of Bois-le-Duc, Holland, which is the French name for 's-Hertogenbosch in the North Brabant Province. In 1846, the paper was transferred to Amsterdam and considered the chief leader of public opinion amongst Roman Catholics in Holland. In his letters Father described the fertile Wisconsin soil, the beautiful country, and as mentioned before the promise of employment. This was music to the ears of our ancestors who were tired of the high unemployment, limited farmland, the potato crop failure covering most of Europe, poor economic conditions, poverty, and a pietistic revolt of the German Lutheran Church against the Dutch Reform Church. The response to his appeal was huge. More than 300 families were ready to make their life-changing voyage to the Land of the Free. Father engaged the ship broker Hudig & Blokhuyzen, who filled three ships of Hollanders. The names of these ships, also known as barks (small three-masted sailing ships), were the "America", "Maria Magdalena", and the "Libra". All of these families brought with them all of their worldly possessions they were allowed to bring, and then boarded the bark and prepared to remain in very close quarters with the other passengers for the next six to eight weeks. All three ships departed from Rotterdam on different days in March 1848 for three different American ports.

- The Libra departed March 13th and arrived in Boston on May 6th,
- The America departed March 18th and arrived in Philadelphia, and
- The Maria Magdalena departed March 20th and arrived in New York City on May 8th. Fr. Vandenbroek was aboard this bark.

Image 1.06- Definition of "Bark" or "Barque": A three- masted sailing ship, typically with the foremast and mainmast square-rigged and the aftermast rigged fore-and-aft.

The Maria Magdalena, like most ships, encountered storms along the way across the Atlantic. In the book, "*The Story of Father Van Den Broek, O.P.*", the author describes an amazing story about Fr. Vandenbroek written by J.H. Wigman, one of his fellow passengers. A large and fearful storm was kicking up strong winds on Easter Sunday, which continued to rage with a steady and increasing wrath. By Tuesday Captain Smit had ordered all of the port holes closed, and all of the crew to remain on deck where they were tethered to it. Massive waves were crashing into and over the ship, making it rock back and forth violently where anyone would have had a hard time standing up. All passengers feared for their lives. Mr. Wigman, thinking his time had come, wondered where Fr. Vandenbroek was. And as written, he found *him kneeling in his room before a crucifix.* At this particular moment, the Captain was in search of an axe to cut away the ship's mast in order to save the ship. Upon hearing this, Father instantly left his room, exited the cabin, and safely walked onto the deck unassisted to where the

Captain was standing. His guardian angel must have been guiding him at this moment. He ordered the Captain to drop the axe and save the mast. The Captain was not sure what to make of Father's demands. Astonishingly, the storm began to subside, and suddenly the conditions became safe.

Of course the Maria Magdalena and the other two ships made it safely to their respective ports. It was common for immigrants to travel by train from the ports to Buffalo. From there a steamer boat transported them through the Great Lakes to Green Bay. After removing all their personal belongings from the steamer boat, they now loaded them onto a flatbed boat for a trip up the Fox River to Kaukauna. The final leg of the long journey was by wagon to Little Chute.

Nine families who intended to settle in Little Chute did not for a couple of different reasons, and went east to settle a new Dutch-only community of their own. They named it "Franciscus Bosch" meaning "St. Francis of the Woods"; known today as Hollandtown. Legend has it these families, including the Vandehey and Verboort families, were unhappy about the process of how the remaining land was divided up among the immigrants. Some believe those with Fr. Vandenbroek on the Maria Magdalena were given first priority to their choice of land. Another story has these families stopping part way up the Fox River to Wrightstown and heading south from there to land that had not yet been touched by mankind. They asked Fr. A. D. Godhard, who was aboard the Libra ship, to come with them, and soon the St. Francis Church was established.

Waves of Hollanders continued to flow into the Fox Valley including the Joosten family in 1851. In all, these Dutch settlers established roots in numerous communities centered around Little Chute including Freedom, DePere, Green Bay, Hollandtown, and Bay Settlement.

This period in history also saw Wisconsin become the 30th state on May 29, 1849, and the 15th "free" state, which balanced out the slave and free states. In 1851 Outagamie County was officially formed out of a western portion of Brown County.

On All Saints' Day, 1851, while speaking during Mass to his congregation of the glory and happiness of the saints, our Fr. Vandenbroek suffered a stroke (then called apoplexy) and died November 5, 1851 on his 68th birthday. His last will and testament gave all of his personal property to the church, including numerous parcels

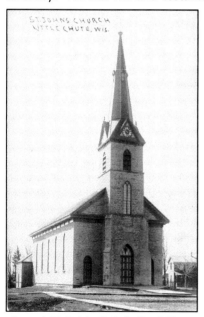

Image 1.07- St. John Catholic Church Photo

of land. This truly remarkable and visionary priest continued his zeal and passion of his faith by converting and baptizing Native Americans to Catholicism, and convincing Hollanders to the new Holland of Little Chute and Outagamie County up to the moment of his death. As told in the magnificent monument to his memory, Fr. Vandenbroek was laid to rest beneath the church he built, St. John Catholic Church at Little Chute. Clearly, Fr. Vandenbroek brought and bestowed many blessings to Little Chute and the village thrived. May the Lord bless his soul.

Following Fr. Vandenbroek's death, the St. John Parish had numerous pastors pass through, many spending one or two years serving the parishioners. They were Rev. William DeJonce, OSC (1851-1853), Rev. Francis Daems, OSC (1853-1855), Rev. William Verhoeff, OSC (1855-1856), Rev. Albert Mauclere, SM (1856-1857), Rev. Michael Peifferl (1857-1860), and then Rev. Egbert Spierings (1860-1865) who began the monumental project of building a new church. Because of the multitude of Hollanders immigrating to Little Chute, the congregation had outgrown the old wooden church so much so that a church of greater size was needed for future growth for decades to come.

Construction of a new church was started in 1860. The nearby Fox River provided a source of limestone used in the church's construction, and most of the labor was done by parishioners. Work was halted as many of the men were called to service during the Civil War. After eight years of labor a new beautiful church was finished under the direction of their pastor Fr. Anthony Verberk who served the parish, for the first of two times, from 1865-1869. The consecration ceremony was led by Bishop Melcher of Green Bay in August of 1868. The pictured cornerstone was placed near the doors at the front of the church.

Fr. Verberk was a central figure in the lives of many of the Joostens. During his second assignment from 1881 to 1890 he performed many Joosten family baptisms and marriages, including the dual wedding of Frances Joosten (this author's 2nd great-grandmother) to Walter Bernards, and Frances' older sister Elizabeth to Joseph VanHandel on July 3, 1882.

Image 1.08- St. John Catholic Church Cornerstone 1868

Anthony Joseph Verberk was born in Holland on January 17, 1832, the son of Martin Verberk, a cabinet maker and painter. Anthony was one of ten children born to his parents. The family immigrated to the USA in 1853, and landed in the New York port. He entered the St. Francis Seminary near Milwaukee on January 29, 1862 where he studied philosophy and theology. On December 27, 1863, he was ordained into the priesthood by Bishop John Henni at the Cathedral in Milwaukee. For his first assignment, he was stationed at the Town of Theresa in Dodge County, WI as the assistant to the pastor. In September 1864, Fr. Anthony was given his first parish at Freedom in Outagamie County, WI. He would remain pastor of St. Nicholas until March 1865 when, as mentioned above, he was transferred to St. John in Little Chute. He was good friends with Fr. Egbert Spierings, who was the St. John Pastor prior to Fr. Anthony's arrival. The two knew each other back in Holland, and it was Fr. Spierings who faithfully convinced Fr. Anthony to resume his theological studies back in 1861. After leaving in 1869 for assignments in Wrightstown and Chilton, Fr. Anthony was called back to St. John in May 1881 because of the fact he could speak the Dutch language, which was best understood by the Catholic Hollander congregation. He served the parish again until 1890, when he was re-assigned back to the parish in Chilton.

Reverend Verberk also knew Fr. Vandenbroek as a young man before immigrating to the USA. When Fr. Vandenbroek returned to Holland in 1847, Anthony heard about Father's desire to take his fellow countrymen back to Little Chute, and inquired with Father about making the voyage with the rest of the families to Little Chute. As we know, Anthony did not immigrate in 1848, but chose to wait a couple more years. How ironic that the young man would meet a worldly missionary priest, become a priest himself, and then builds a new church on the same hallowed ground where Fr. Vandenbroek lies in eternity.

In 1892, Fr. Verberk retired because of his failing health, and made his home in DePere. After receiving medical advice to move away from Lake Michigan, he moved to Hollandtown about a year later. Father would remain in this small farming town for the rest of his days. At the age of 69, Father contracted the flu and then came down with pneumonia. He was not able to recover from this grave illness, and heartbreakingly passed away on January 27, 1901. A very nice obituary was placed in the Chilton Times on February 02, 1901 expressing the deep love the Chilton community had for this man and priest who was a central figure of the St. Augustine Church; the headline reading *"A Good Man Is Dead"*. He will be remembered for his impressive ability to manage the construction of churches, especially the St. Augustine Church for the Chilton Catholic community. The newspaper summed up Father's ministry and personality with these thoughtful words, *"In reviewing, Father Verberk's church work in this city, the characteristics of the man that appear in bold relief are sincerity of purpose and earnestness of execution, even to austerity,--excellent qualities, both and when coupled with soundness of judgment and kindness of heart, as in this case, resultants of great and enduring good."* May Fr. Verberk's soul rest in peace.

In a long line of influential priests to serve the community of Little Chute and St. John Church, one of the more beloved was Father Theodore Knegtel (pronounced "connec-tel"). Fr. Knegtel took over the pastorate reins after Fr. Verberk left in 1890 to return to Chilton. He served until 1915, and was one of the longest serving priests at St. John, dedicating 25 years of his life to the ministries.

Theodore Joseph Knegtel was born on August 13, 1845 in Tilburg, Holland. Convinced he desired a life in the priesthood, he enrolled in seminary at Michielsgestel, a small town south of the North Brabant's province capital 's-Hertogenbosch and then at Haaren in northern Holland. After he was ordained in 1872, Reverend Knegtel served as chaplain in several parishes in Holland until 1882, and then decided he too would immigrate to the USA and settle in Little Chute. He was received on October 26th of that year into the Green Bay diocese and was appointed Pastor in Preble, WI, which today is a community in the east part of Green Bay. He spent eight years as Pastor at Preble, and then on January 21, 1890 was assigned as pastor of St. John in Little Chute. The church had grown to 1800 parishioners by the year of 1895. Much was accomplished at St. John Church during the pastorate of Reverend Knegtel. New stained glass windows were installed, a large clock and bells became part of the church steeple, and the interior received new pews and decorations. He erected three new additions to the building between 1894 and 1909, including the sanctuary and sacristies, the red brick rectory, and an addition to the school.

Another great story comes from the book of *"The Story of Father Van Den Broek, O.P."*. In 1894, during one of the remodel projects of the church, Fr. Knegtel had a crew digging under the middle of the church in front of the sanctuary for a spot to place a heating apparatus. While the laborers were at work they came upon Father Vandenbroek's grave; the day of this experience was September 8th, the Nativity of the Blessed Virgin. In their excitement, the workers did not waste any time to inform Fr. Knegtel of their glorious finding. As the author describes, there is no doubt the remains found were those of Fr. Vandenbroek. He was the only priest buried there and with his remains were his cherished rosary, his wax chalice, and pieces of stole. The passionate priest's remains were entombed once again and sealed for eternity.

As mentioned earlier, Fr. Knegtel served the parishioners of St. John for an incredible 25 years; his people loved him dearly. Up to this time he had been their longest serving priest. In 1915, the church held a nice ceremony to honor Father for his 25 years of service, and he was presented with a chalice. When June 15 of the same year came, the parishioners were shocked and saddened when they learned their favorite priest had passed away. A huge funeral was held at the church, which was packed with his faithful followers. His obituary cited 1,200 people were in attendance, including 46 priests from the region.

Image 1.10- Gravesite headstone of Fr. Theodore Knegtel, St. John Catholic Cemetery, Little Chute, WI

This small village of Hollanders was so blessed with such a wonderful priest; his accomplishments were special and plentiful. The Little Chute Historical Society reveals Fr. Knegtel performed 2269 baptisms, 760 funerals, and 418 marriages. There were a total of 1154 confirmations in his 25 years at St John. His obituary says Fr. Knegtel *"was a zealous priest, a kindly sincere man. He will be missed in his church, by his people in the village, by the children in the parish school, by his fellow priests, and by all who knew him."* He was laid to rest in the parish cemetery, being interred in the 3rd row of section 1A. The Lord definitely blessed us with a man and priest who changed our lives.

As mentioned previously, on his journey back to Little Chute, Fr. Vandenbroek sailed the Atlantic on the Maria Magdalena. There was also another important passenger on the same ship by the name of William A. Verboort who would later become Fr. William Verboort and lead some of these same Hollander immigrants to the beautiful Tualatin Valley of Oregon in 1875.

William Augustine Verboort was the second child born to his parents John and Theodora Verboort on October 23, 1835 in Uden, North Brabant, Holland. When William was a young boy of 12 years, the Verboort

Family boarded the bark Maria Magdalena at Rotterdam and headed to sea on March 20, 1848. In addition to his parents, William's older brother John Jr. (age 15), younger sister Theodora (age 11), and younger brother Albert (age 8) were also on the ship. On November 23, 1897, John Jr., wrote a letter to his friend John Smith about his memories of the journey to America, which was re-printed in page 86 in the book "Verboort Quadricentennial 1875-2000". John Jr. writes, *"After a voyage of 52 days we arrived safely at the dock in Boston on Friday May 5. The next day we left by train, in boxcars, to Buffalo. Three of the families stayed in Boston. We sailed from Buffalo to Mackinaw Island where we stayed three days until we could get a sailing ship for Green Bay. From there we proceeded up the Fox River by scow or flat boat propelled by six men who used poles. This took two entire days. From Kaukauna we were brought in two wagons, drawn by six oxen, to Little Chute where we arrived on 22 May. There we rested and laid plans for the future."*

Image 1.11- Fr. William A. Verboort

William entered the St. Francis Seminary in Milwaukee, WI. After he completed his studies he was ordained a priest, at age 28, in the Diocese of Milwaukee by Bishop John Henni on December 28, 1863. In 1864, Fr. Verboort was appointed the first resident pastor of DePere by Bishop Henni. In 1870, construction was completed on a chapel on Lewis Street in East DePere that became St. Mary Catholic Church, and Fr. Verboort became its first pastor. According to St. Mary Church, legend has it Fr. Verboort cut the cornerstone and carved the figures on it himself. The church contained 114 pews of five seats and three altars, including one main and two small altars.

In 1875, unhappy with Wisconsin's soil and harsh winters, John Verboort and five other families packed up their worldly possessions and headed west to Oregon with the promise of a milder climate and better soil. At this point in the 1870s, travel to the western United States was possible by train. So the six families from Little Chute went by train to San Francisco, next by boat north up the Pacific Ocean to Astoria, OR, and then up the Columbia River to Portland, OR. The final leg of the journey to Forest Grove, OR in Washington County was by horse drawn wagon or stagecoach. The families bought 550 acres of land and the home of Henry Black who had a land donation claim a few miles northeast of Forest Grove; today Verboort. These six families shared the large 10-bedroom house on their newly purchased land. Fr. Verboort also decided to head west to join his family. He was 40 years old when he transferred to the Archdiocese of Oregon City, Oregon. Archbishop Francis N. Blanchet sent Father Verboort to be the Pastor of the Catholic Colony of Forest Grove. He became a key figure and leader of this new Catholic mission, just as Fr. Vandenbroek did for the Little Chute community.

Image 1.12- Gravesite Headstone of Fr. William A Verboort

Soon after arriving in Forest Grove, Father Verboort began saying Mass in various homes around the area. Eventually, he moved the meeting place to an old and empty blockhouse owned by John O'Brien. An article published in the Oregon Journal in November, 1875, tells of an attempt by the Catholics to use a public schoolhouse on Barnes Road for services on November 21. It reads, *"after receiving permission to use the building, a number of the worshipers came to the school, but found the building locked. Surprised at this turn of events, there was nothing much they could do but return home. Fr. Verboort and his churchgoers later learned that a non-Catholic man, who objected to this type of activity, secured keys to the building and locked it against the intrusion of the Catholics. As it turned out, Father Verboort was unable to get to the schoolhouse because of bad weather. A date was set for the following week and there were no further complications."* In 1875, Fr. Verboort and the communities' pioneers orchestrated the construction of a small church that was consecrated as St. Francis Xavier Catholic Church on September 19th. It was not large, just 20x49 feet. A few years later, this structure was torn down and replaced with a more modern church.

In 1876, some sort of severe fever-borne illness swept the small and budding community, and tragically Father Verboort's mother, Dora Verboort, succumbed to the illness on June 23, 1876. Father had the sad duty to administer the last rites and preside at her funeral mass. Then just twelve short days later, amidst his grieving, the same grave illness claimed Fr. Verboort's father John on July 5th. It has been told Father was so ill himself that local men had to transport him by wheelbarrow to administer the last rites to his dying father. What an

awful situation for Father and his community to have to endure. Father Verboort had a terrible infection in his knee, which entered his bloodstream, and he became critically ill and developed pneumonia. A story was told how the news of Father's condition swept the countryside, and his grief-stricken people came to his bedside for a last word and for the grace of the Sacrament of Penance. He received his people with great love and gave them the words of absolution until he was no longer able to raise his hand. Then just nine days after his father's death, Father Verboort passed away on July 14th at the young age of 40. This must have just been unbelievable to these strong-faith Dutch pioneers. Archbishop Francis Blanchet traveled from Portland to offer the Solemn Requiem Mass. The community sorrowfully buried all three members of

Image 1.13- Visitation Catholic Church (2003)

the Verboort family side-by-side in the parish cemetery, which today is the Visitation Catholic Cemetery. Before long, the Archbishop declared the name of the Catholic Colony of Forest Grove be changed to "Verboort" in memory of the good Father Verboort. And so with this declaration history was made.

The Verboort community endured three months without a pastor for their church. Then Archbishop Blanchet assigned Rev. Joseph E. Hermann to Verboort. John and Albert Verboort (Fr. Verboort's brothers) donated six acres of land for church purposes. In June 1883, Father Hermann started a quest to erect a new larger and more modern church. The new 70 foot long by 37 foot wide church was raised along with a tall bell tower. The bell for the tower, which Father Verboort had purchased in Wisconsin especially for his new church, was moved from the old church and put into the new one. On October 24, 1883, the new church was blessed and named "Visitation of the Blessed Virgin Mary", which today is also known as Visitation Catholic Church. The older St. Francis Xavier chapel was converted into a two-room schoolhouse; a good choice so the landmark could still serve the community in some way. Since then the new church and the surrounding Dutch Catholic community thrived all because of the vision of Fr. Verboort.

Another very influential and gifted priest who became part of the Joosten family was Father Philip J. Wagner of the St. Philomena Church in Rudolph, WI. The exact year this story starts is not known for certain, but some time before 1910 John Joosten, a nephew of Joseph Joosten, and his wife Rose along with three of their sons (Albert, Christian, and Martin) moved from Little Chute west about 90 miles to the small Village of Rudolph. Even today there is not much around this small town, including no large population centers; it is pretty much just rural farming. So the draw to Rudolph for some members of the Joosten family could have been cheap land for farming or some other great opportunity. These opportunities also got the attention of Joseph's son Martin and his wife Anna. In 1905, they likewise picked up their possessions and moved from Grand Chute to Rudolph.

Image 1.14- Fr. Philip Wagner Standing in His Grotto

At this time, their church, St. Philomena, was located roughly one and a half miles west of town on 5th Avenue. The current building was some 30 years old, after being built in 1878. This is where Fr. Philip Wagner enters the picture. In 1917, he was appointed pastor following the retirement of Fr. Van Sever. Soon after his appointment, in 1918, the decision was made to purchase land and move the church into the Village of Rudolph. And the old land would become the parish cemetery. Plans were drawn up for construction of one large eight-room building to accommodate a new church, school, rectory and convent. The new building was erected and finished in 1921 on what today is Grotto Ave. The dedication ceremony was held on May 1, 1921.

Philip J. Wagner was born to his parents Nicholas and Katherine (Meyer) Wagner on December 23, 1882 in Festina, Winneshick County, Iowa; his parents were natives of Wisconsin and Indiana. Philip attended school in Festina, and then moved to Wisconsin to attend Campion College at Prairie du Chien, where he graduated in

1911. Yearning to become a priest and continue his studies, he spent the next four years at the University of Innsbruck in Austria. Philip graduated and was ordained into the priesthood in 1915, after which he returned to the United States. As the story has been told, while Philip was at the University he became very ill. In 1912, he stepped off a train at the Grotto of Our Lady in Lourdes, France. Amidst the grace and beauty of the Grotto, he prayed and promised should his health improve and be restored he would build a shrine in Mary's honor. After praying and bathing in the miraculous waters, his condition improved, and his strength and courage returned. His promise and resolve to build a grotto of his own would never fade and would someday become a reality.

After his return to the United States, Fr. Philip's first assignment was at St. Joseph's Cathedral in La Crosse, WI where he remained for nearly two years. Then as mentioned earlier, he became pastor of St. Philomena in 1917 where he would remain the rest of his days.

It was not long before Fr. Philip started putting his Grotto vision plans into action. As the new church was being planned and built, he was planting trees and flower beds. He also began collecting the large rocks, a rare type of lava rock, he wanted from the surrounding area. By 1928, his first shine commemorating the Lourdes Shine was finished.

Of course Fr. Wagner did not stop his grotto planning and building, and soon some of his followers would also become dedicated to helping Father carry out his vision and promise. One of these many volunteers was Edmund Rybicki, who became known as Father's right-hand-man. Over the next three decades Fr. Philip and Edmund would erect many more shrines and monuments. Some of the wonderful shrines and monuments Father would end up building himself:
- The Wayside Shrine was built during the winter of 1930.
- The Old Register monument was constructed around 1931. It contained the words "Please Register" spelled out in shells, and the book visitors signed as they entered the magnificent grotto.
- The Pillar Planter was the fourth project completed by Fr. Philip in 1931 and is formed commemorating the ruins of the ancient Greek and Roman temples.
- The St. Bernadette monument was added in the summer of 1933.
- The Soldier's Memorial Monument was built in 1934 to honor the fallen heroes of World War I.
- The Sundial, which is located on top of the Wonder Cave was added in the winter of 1934.

According to the Grotto booklet, the Wonder Cave is a 1/5 of a mile long, and created with the catacombs in mind. Each of the statues within the Cave is made of marble, except the Sacred Heart stone statue, which is made of cast stone and was donated by Simon Joosten. Simon is a nephew of our Joseph Joosten who lived in Rudolph.

Over the next several decades, when it was finally completed, more than 30 amazing shrines and monuments would fill the beautiful Grotto grounds behind St. Philomena Church with the last project being completed in 1983. In the end, the creation started by Fr. Wagner was a unique collection of marble, glass, and shells all meticulously chosen by him. The glass was from the Kokomo Opalescent Glass Company in Kokomo, Indiana. The glass was melted down in the school's coal furnace, then fused and broken again before Father placed it in the Grotto according to his master designs. Most of the rare lava rock brought to the Grotto was picked by Father from a 15-20 mile radius surrounding Rudolph. On a visit to Wisconsin, I was able to visit the Grotto Gardens in August 2012, and a few of my favorites are the Ten Commandments, the Our Lady of Fatima

Image 1.15- The Lady of Fatima Shrine

Shrine, the 14 Stations of the Cross, the Stations of the Seven Sorrows of Mary, and of course the shrine dedicated to Fr. Philip in the cemetery. If you are in the Rudolph area this is definitely a must-see to add to your list. There is nothing like it you will ever see!

In 1950 or 1951, Fr. Wagner once again found himself with a large construction project on his hands. Due to the large number of parishioners, the old church building was no longer adequate. A combination of a church and rectory was built. By this time, Father was in his upper 60s, and was experiencing heart problems.

The entire Rudolph community, I am sure, was brokenhearted when they learned Fr. Philip succumbed to his poor health and passed away on All Saints Day; November 1st 1959. How ironic and spiritual this gifted priest would depart from this life on the day that is celebrated for the very people he enshrined in his Grotto. Fr. Philip

was laid to rest in the All Souls Cemetery, located in the property right next door to the grounds of the Grotto and church. A spectacular monument dedicated to the memory of Fr. Philip lies in the center of the cemetery, which more than likely was constructed prior to Father's passing. As can be seen in the photo, Father's headstone lies right in the middle of the monument.

In an enormous tribute, the faithfully dedicated parishioners of St. Philomena, in 1961, renamed the church to St. Philip in honor of their long serving priest. He forever changed this community, may his soul rest in peace.

Image 1.16- All Souls Cemetery Monument Dedicated to the Memory of Fr. Philip Wagner

So far I have written about priests I have not had the pleasure of knowing, only our ancestors. Now it is time for some words about a priest I <u>do</u> know, and who is still living dedicating his life serving his people. This chapter and this book would not be complete if I did not dedicate some space to one of my favorite and inspirational priests, Fr. Scott Vandehey.

Scott Vandehey was the third child born to his parents Anthony and Marcella (Kalsch) Vandehey in 1939 in the Verboort/Roy Oregon area. A remarkable fact is he was one of eight sons born to his parents, and lived his childhood on the family farm just south of the Roy community. He attended St. Francis of Assisi elementary school at Roy, and graduated from Banks High School in 1957. The following school year he enrolled in the Agriculture program at Oregon State University. Being a man of faith, he was hearing the Lord's call to the priesthood, and faithfully heeded that call. In 1958, he entered the Seminary at Mt. Angel, OR to begin his studies to enter the priesthood. In 1960, he was sent to the St. Thomas the Apostle Seminary in Seattle where is earned his Bachelor of Arts Degree in Philosophy and in Theology. Next, he spent some time teaching religion at North Plains and Vernonia, OR, and counseling children at Camp Howard.

Image 1.17- Fr. Scott Vandehey Ordination Photo-1966

He was ordained into the priesthood on May 14, 1966 by Archbishop Edward D. Howard at the St. Mary Cathedral in Portland, OR. Fr. Scott celebrated his first Mass at his home parish of St. Francis of Assisi Church in Roy, OR. He also joined Fr. Ervin and Fr. Robert, both 2nd cousins to him, in the group of faithful Vandeheys in the clergy serving the church. The first ten years of his priesthood were spent in the Portland area. During his weekly visits to see his parents, he often was engaged in conversations with his dad about their deep family history. Fr. Scott was told and understood he came from a long line of deeply faithful Dutch immigrants, and his interest to gain additional knowledge about his roots from his parents grew with each conversation. As Fr. Scott wrote in his first book, his dad asked him point blank, *"why don't you write all this down in a book?"* What was Fr. Scott's response? As he wrote, *"at the time I just laughed and quipped something about the lack of time."* He then describes how he read Samuel Clemens' masterpiece "The Adventures of Tom Sawyer", which was a tribute to America's first centennial in 1876. Well, Fr. Scott wanted to produce something special for this country's bi-centennial in 1976, and so began his remarkable quest to document history and satisfy his desire to learn about his ancestors.

This remarkable quest took Father to Nebraska, Wisconsin, and to the Vandehey homeland in Zeeland, Holland in search of information and answers to his many burning questions. What he produced just a few short years later is the epic "Wooden Shoes West", published in 1979. Fr. Scott not only wrote about his great Grandfather John Henry Vandehey (1813-1888), John's children, but also an awesome historical depiction of Holland, Fr. Theodore Vandenbroek, the Dutch Catholic immigration to Wisconsin, and the move west to Oregon. As mentioned earlier in this chapter in relation to the community of Hollandtown, WI, this 347-page classic talks about how John Vandehey and his wife Ardina were part of the group of first families who created Hollandtown.

Given the amount of detail in this book it is astounding to think of the amount of research that must have been required to produce this project. All completed without the convenience of the internet or computers with the sophisticated word processing software we have today. I am awestruck.

After such a successful inaugural book writing, Fr. Scott was just getting warmed up. Now that he had written about his father's side of the family, it was time to put pen to paper about his mom's side. This new effort produced "In the Wildwood", a 283-page rendering of the Kalsch family, published in April 1988. One year earlier Fr. Scott entered into my life when he became Pastor of St. Mary Church in Eugene, OR in 1987. He and my Dad share two aunts. My Grandmother, Minnie Shaw, was a Vanderzanden from Roy, OR, and as most know the Vandeheys and the Vanderzandens are related in many ways. Two of Fr. Scott's aunts, Hannah Vandehey and Bernie Kalsch, married two of my Grandmother's brothers, Walter and Bert. Hannah married Walt in 1929, and Bernie married Bert in 1934.

Soon after his arrival to St. Mary, Fr. Scott brought long-lasting positive changes. One of the first was hiring a music director by the name of David Phillips. Now we had music at every Mass, and we still do today. I remember when Masses were being celebrated by another parish priest, Fr. Scott would be with the choir singing with them. One could tell he had a great voice and loved music a great deal. This passion for music and his collaborations with Mr. Phillips led to a lot of recorded music. I have read stories that put this number at more than 150 hymns Fr. Scott has sang and recorded.

Another big change for the St. Mary Parish was his leadership in raising millions of dollars to build a new parish center. The old school building on the parish grounds was being used as a parish center to host events and to gather for coffee and donuts. It was becoming too small to hold everyone with a growing parish, and the equipment in the kitchen and other furnishings were antiquated. What followed was the razing of the decades old convent extending between the church and old school, and then the construction of a brand new 14,500-foot parish center. Now our new parish center had an Adoration Chapel, a state of the art kitchen, lots of room for coffee and donuts, a practice room for the choir, and five classrooms for religious education; a big bonus for the children. The new addition was dedicated by Archbishop William J. Levada in 1994.

Image 1.18- Cornerstone of Parish Center

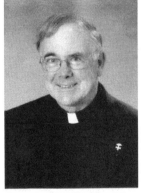
Fr. Scott Vandehey

We were blessed and happy when Fr. Scott decided to remain at St. Mary for an additional six years, but when the calendar turned to the year 1999 we knew our time with him as our pastor was drawing to a close. In June, the Archbishop transferred Fr. Scott to St. Cecilia Church in Beaverton, OR. Prior to his departure, the parishioners wanted to send him off in a big way and with something to remember his "old" parish. So a secret collection was started on his behalf. The parishioners cared for him deeply. A big party was thrown for Father, and enough money was pooled to purchase him a brand new Toyota Camry. St. Cecilia would benefit greatly from Father's experience with large parishes that have a school. After a number of blessed years spent at St. Cecilia, Fr. Scott would get, in my mind, the assignment of his dreams. Amazingly, he was transferred to the Visitation of the Blessed Virgin Mary Church in Verboort; back to his old stomping grounds, and the very church Fr. Verboort founded. And to top it off, he was only a short number of years away from retirement, and he could be closer to his Mom in the later years of her life. Now he could spend the rest of his active years as a priest in the community where he was born and raised.

During these years at Visitation Church, Fr. Scott embarked on another book project. This time he dedicated pages to Fr. William Verboort, and the four pastors who followed him at the Visitation Church along with stories and histories of 60 families who settled in Verboort between 1875-1900. Father picked the perfect title for his glorious 403 page book … "Verboort: A Priest and His People".

In 2010, Fr. Scott was 70 years old and eligible for retirement from daily life in the parish. This did not slow him down, and he decided to continue on for one more year. In June 2011, Father decided to (in baseball jargon) "hang up his cleats" after 45 years of serving so many Catholics and parishes in western Oregon. A big celebration bash was held in the Visitation parish center to honor the man who was their faith-filled leader. Today, Fr. Scott enjoys retirement in Beaverton at the residence the Archdiocese has established for our retired priests.

So there you have it. Six gifted and faith-filled priests who each touched the lives of our family past and present. These men went above and beyond their calling serving us and at the end of the day what mattered the most to them was celebrating the Eucharist with us.

☙ Photo and Image Gallery ❧

Image 1.20- St. Mary Parish Center Main Entrance

Image 1.21- St. Mary Parish Center Courtyard

Pastor to mark retirement with celebration

VERBOORT — Visitation of the Blessed Virgin Mary Parish hosts a retirement celebration for Father Scott Vandehey Sunday, June 26.

Held in the parish center, the party starts with a social hour at 11 a.m., followed by a luncheon at noon.

Guests are asked to bring written memories and photos.

"[Father] Vandehey has impacted our church and school with his deep spiritual awareness of God and great devotion to Mary," said Lisa McMullen, Visitation's secretary.

Ordained on May 14, 1966 at St. Mary's Cathedral in Portland, the priest has a deep interest in music and history.

He has recorded more than 150 hymns and has written five historical books about the ancestry of Washington County.

"He is very humble, generous, intelligent, has a great sense of humor and a voice like an angel, but most of all, he is loved by all."

Father Vandehey used all proceeds from his most recent book, *Verboort A Priest & His People*, to create a tuition assistance endowment fund for Visitation School.

All are invited to attend the celebration. A money tree with cards and envelopes will be available.

The church is at 4285 NW Visitation Road.

Father Scott Vandehey: Ordination year, 1966; today.

Image 1.22- Fr. Scott Vandehey Retirement News Article, Catholic Sentinel, 06-07-2011, page 16

Image 1.23- Grotto Gardens Entry Monument, Rudolph, WI

Image 1.24- Grotto Gardens 'Ave Maria' Monument, Rudolph, WI

Anthony J. Verberk - Chilton Times
February 2, 1901
A Good Man is Dead
Formerly Pastor of St. Augustine Church In this City-He Passed Away at Hollandtown on Sunday Last.

On Sunday, last, January 27, 1900, rev. Anthony Joseph Verberk, for many years pastor of St. Augustine's Catholic Church, of this city, died at his home in Hollandtown, Brown County, aged 69 years. He had been in poor health for years but the immediate cause of his death was pneumonia, superinduced by the grippe.

Father Verberk was born in Holland, January 17, 1832. He received his theological education at St. Francis seminary, Milwaukee, where he was ordained a priest Dec. 27, 1863. His first appointment as pastor was to Theresa, Dodge county and Freedom. Later he had charge of the congregation at Little Chute where he built the church, parsonage and school; and from 1869 to 1872 he was pastor of St. Mary's Appleton, resigning this charge for a year's travel in Europe.

After his return, in February, 1876, he was appointed rector of St. Augustine's in this city, continuing as such after the German portion of the congregation withdrew and until 1881, when he returned to Little Chute.

In 1889 he again took charge of St. Augustine's of this city, but in 1892 failing in health, he was obligated to resign the pastorate and was then relieved from further regular parish work. Since that time he has resided at Hollandtown. It was during his administration in Chilton that the present substantial church edifice was built; and the healthy condition of the affairs of the parish at the time of his first removal, in 1881, attests his successful ministry while in charge.

In reviewing, Father Verberk's church work in this city, the characteristics of the man that appear in bold relief are sincerity of purpose and earnestness of execution, even to austerity,--excellent qualities, both and when coupled with soundness of judgment and kindness of heart, as in this case, resultants of great and enduring good.

The funeral took place on Wednesday, from the Holland church, at Green Bay, Rt. Rev. Bishop Messmer conducting the services.

I thought it would be valuable to see the family histories of Fr. William Verboort and Fr. Scott Vandehey. And so here they are, the descendants of John and Theodora Verboort are up first, as I know them in 2014.

❧ Descendants of John Verboort ❧

(1= 1st generation, 2= 2nd generation, 3= 3rd generation)

1 <u>John Verboort, Sr.</u>
Born: November 06, 1806 in Uden, North Brabant, Holland
Died: July 05, 1876 in Verboort, Washington County, Oregon
Buried at: Visitation Catholic Cemetery, Verboort, OR, NW section, row 1
Married: June 23, 1832 in Uden, North Brabant, Holland
<u>Theodora Wilhelmina Van De Rayt</u>
Born: July 23, 1807 in Uden, North Brabant, Holland
Died: June 23, 1876 in Verboort, Washington County, Oregon
Buried at: Visitation Catholic Cemetery, Verboort, OR, NW section, row 1

   2 <u>John Verboort, Jr.</u>
     Born: July 31, 1833 in Uden, North Brabant, Holland
     Died: January 08, 1909 in San Luis Rey, San Diego County, California
     Buried at: Unknown

   2 <u>William Augustine "Rev." Verboort</u>
     Born: October 23, 1835 in Uden, North Brabant, Holland
     Died: July 14, 1876 in Verboort, Washington County, Oregon
     Buried at: Visitation Catholic Cemetery, Verboort, OR, NW section, row 1

   2 <u>Theodora Marie Verboort</u>
     Born: December 19, 1837 in Uden, North Brabant, Holland
     Died: May 08, 1921
     Buried at: St. Boniface Catholic Cemetery, Sublimity, OR
     Married: May 30, 1858 in Bay Settlement, Brown County, Wisconsin
     <u>Martin Hermens</u>
     Born: September 28, 1828 in Zeeland, North Brabant, Holland
     Died: December 01, 1921 in Sublimity, Marion County, Oregon
     Buried at: St. Boniface Catholic Cemetery, Sublimity, OR
     Parents: Anthony Hermens (1788-1869) Cornelia VanDijk (1792-1838)

      3 <u>Cornelius Martin Hermens</u>
        Born: March 10, 1862 in De Pere, Brown County, Wisconsin
        Died: September 26, 1948 in McMinnville, Yamhill County, Oregon
        Buried: St. James Catholic Cemetery, McMinnville, OR, west section, row 9

      3 <u>William August Hermens</u>
        Born: February 14, 1864 in De Pere, Brown County, Wisconsin
        Died: June 04, 1950 in Verboort, Washington County, Oregon
        Buried at: Visitation Catholic Cemetery, Verboort, Washington County, OR
        Married: November 03, 1891 in Verboort, Washington County, Oregon
        <u>Anna Marie Vandervelden</u>
        Born: August 24, 1872 in De Pere, Brown County, Wisconsin
        Died: December 06, 1945 in Verboort, Washington County, Oregon
        Buried at: Visitation Catholic Cemetery, Verboort, Washington County, OR
        Parents: Adrian Vandervelden (1846-1908) & Angelina Cuene (1854-1942)

3   Ann Dorothy Hermens
     Born: January 29, 1868 in De Pere, Brown County, Wisconsin
     Died: September 08, 1947 in Sublimity, Marion County, Oregon
     Buried: St. Boniface Catholic Cemetery, Sublimity, OR
     Married: October 20, 1891 in Oregon
     William W. VanHandel
     Born: 1865 in Green Bay, Brown County, Wisconsin
     Died: 1941 in Sublimity, Marion County, Oregon
     Buried: St. Boniface Catholic Cemetery, Sublimity, OR
     Parents: Arnold VanHandel & Anna VanErmen

2   Albert Verboort
     Born: March 01, 1840 in Uden, North Brabant, Holland
     Died: October 17, 1916 in Verboort, Washington County, Oregon
     Buried: Visitation Catholic Cemetery, Verboort, OR, NW row 1
     Married: 1863 in Brown County, Wisconsin
     Antonetta Jansen
     Born: November 13, 1836 in North Brabant, Holland
     Died: January 06, 1902 in Greenville, Washington County, Oregon
     Buried: Visitation Catholic Cemetery, Verboort, OR, NW row 1

     3   William Albert Verboort
          Born: April 02, 1876 in Verboort, Washington County, Oregon
          Died: September 28, 1940 in Verboort, Washington County, Oregon
          Buried: Visitation Catholic Cemetery, Verboort, OR, SW row 3
          Married: May 10, 1904 in Verboort, Washington County, Oregon
          Petronella M. VanDyke
          Born: January 24, 1892
          Died: September 21, 1954 in Verboort, Washington County, Oregon
          Buried at: Visitation Catholic Cemetery, Verboort, OR, SW row 3
          Parents: Theodore VanDyke (1847-1934) & Mary Ann Bernards (1846-1922)

     3   John Verboort
          Born: December 15, 1871 in Wisconsin
          Died: August 24, 1934 in Wisconsin
          Buried at: Mt. Calvary Catholic Cemetery, DePere, WI, sec O, row 7
          Married: Date unknown
          Petronella Aerts
          Born: December 25, 1880 in Wisconsin
          Died: September 09, 1946 in Wisconsin
          Buried at: Mt. Calvary Catholic Cemetery, DePere, WI, sec O, row 7

❧ Ancestors of Fr. Scott Vandehey ❧

Notes: 1= 1ˢᵗ generation, 2= 2ⁿᵈ generation, 3= 3ʳᵈ generation.
The year of birth is only given for individuals still living, if known.

1   <u>Cornelius Vandehey</u>
Born: December 07, 1864 in Hollandtown, Brown County, Wisconsin
Died: July 09, 1938 in Roy, Washington County, Oregon
Buried at: St. Francis Catholic Cemetery, Roy, OR, south row 7
Married: October 09, 1887 in Atkinson, Holt County, Nebraska
<u>Catherine Anne Van Domelen</u>
Born: July 21, 1869 in Little Chute, Outagamie County, Wisconsin
Died: October 21, 1947 in Forest Grove, Washington County, Oregon
Buried at: St. Francis Catholic Cemetery, Roy, OR, south row 7
Parents: Henry Van Domelen (1842-1903) and Anna Marie P. Meulemans (1848-1876)

> 2   <u>Elizabeth Vandehey</u>
> Born: July 23, 1888
> Died: Unknown
> Buried: Unknown
> Married: Edward West

> 2   <u>Henry J. Vandehey</u>
> Born: July 07, 1890
> Died: April 30, 1965 in Roy, Washington County, Oregon
> Buried at: St. Francis Catholic Cemetery, Roy, OR, south row 1
> Married: Helena M. Vanderzanden on October 6, 1914

> 2   <u>Christina Bertha Vandehey</u>
> Born: October 25, 1892 in Roy, Washington County, Oregon
> Died: January 28, 1979 in Beaverton, Washington County, Oregon
> Buried: St. Francis Catholic Cemetery, Roy, OR, west row 1
> Married: William H. Cop, Sr. on November 08, 1910

> 2   <u>August J. Vandehey</u>
> Born: February 07, 1895 in Roy, Washington County, Oregon
> Died: April 09, 1962 in Forest Grove, Washington County, Oregon
> Buried: St. Francis Catholic Cemetery, Roy, OR, north row 6
> Married: Helen J. Heynderickx on September 26, 1922

> 2   <u>George Phillip Vandehey</u>
> Born: June 01, 1897 in Roy, Washington County, Oregon
> Died: September 04, 1974 in Forest Grove, Washington County, Oregon
> Buried: St. Francis Catholic Cemetery, Roy, OR, west row 2
> Married: Mary P. Vandervelden on February 07, 1922

> 2   <u>Paulina Marie Vandehey</u>
> Born: November 08, 1899 in Roy, Washington County, Oregon
> Died: December 1990 in Forest Grove, Washington County, Oregon
> Buried: Mountain View Memorial Gardens, Forest Grove, OR
> Married: George L. Hendricks on August 24, 1920

2   Charles A. Vandehey
Born: June 19, 1902 in Roy, Washington County, Oregon
Died: October 1970 in Forest Grove, Washington County, Oregon
Buried: Visitation Catholic Cemetery, Verboort, OR
Married: Agnes C. Hermens on June 14, 1927

2   Cecilia Marie Vandehey
Born: October 18, 1904 in Roy, Washington County, Oregon
Died: September 02, 1984 in Portland, Multnomah County, Oregon
Buried: Mt. View Memorial Gardens, Forest Grove, OR, Catholic Garden, row 9
Married: George A. Vuylsteke on January 24, 1928

2   Hannah Marie Vandehey
Born: December 18, 1906 in Roy, Washington County, Oregon
Died: September 10, 1997 in Beaverton, Washington County, Oregon
Buried: St. Francis Catholic Cemetery, Roy, OR, west row 1
Married: Walter J. Vanderzanden on October 01, 1929

2   Anthony F. Vandehey
Born: November 23, 1908 in Roy, Washington County, Oregon
Died: April 21, 2003 in Forest Grove, Washington County, Oregon
Buried: St. Francis Catholic Cemetery, Roy, OR, west row 6
Married: February 09, 1935 in Forest Grove, Washington County, Oregon
Marcella G. Kalsch
Born: August 31, 1915 in Gales Creek, Washington County, Oregon
Died: November 07, 2010 in Forest Grove, Washington County, Oregon
Buried: St. Francis Catholic Cemetery, Roy, OR, west row 6
Parents: Philip A. Kalsch (1878-1958) & Barbara M. Franck (1887-1976)

     3   Gary P. Vandehey
        Born: 1936
        Died: Living

     3   Monte Vandehey
        Born: 1939
        Died: Living

     3   Scott Vandehey
        Born: 1939
        Died: Living
        Ordained: May 14, 1966

     3   Spencer Vandehey
        Born: 1944
        Died: Living

     3   Reed Vandehey
        Born: 1949
        Died: Living

     3   Philip Vandehey
        Born: 1953
        Died: Living

      3   <u>Timothy Vandehey</u>
          Born: 1954
          Died: Living

2   <u>Alfred William Vandehey</u>
    Born: March 05, 1911 in Roy, Washington County, Oregon
    Died: August 12, 1989 in Forest Grove, Washington County, Oregon
    Buried: St. Francis Catholic Cemetery, Roy, OR, south row 10
    Married: Mildred E. Hulsman on May 18, 1937

❧ Chapter Two ❧

Ocean Journey on the Leila

T he first Joosten footprints to make impressions into the soil of the undeveloped and vast flat land of Wisconsin came from Martin Joosten, Sr. and his wife Anna, a determined couple wanting a better life and opportunity for their family. There was a great migration of Dutch in the mid-19th century when approximately 250,000 Dutch peasants and rural artisans came to America. This began in the 1830s, continued into the mid-1840s when about 20,000 people emigrated en masse for a host of reasons. Among them, as mentioned earlier, the potato crop failure, poor economic conditions, poverty, and a pietistic revolt of the German Lutheran Church against the Dutch Reform Church. Many of them settled in southwestern Michigan, central Iowa and in the Fox River Valley of Wisconsin. Between 1840 and 1890, Wisconsin was a major center of Dutch immigration. Dutch immigrants in Wisconsin were easily divided into two basic groups based on religious affiliation - Protestants and Catholics. The Protestants were the first to arrive in Wisconsin and settled mainly in Sheboygan, Fond du Lac, Columbia and La Crosse counties. The Catholics preferred the Fox River Valley in communities that later became known as Appleton, Green Bay, Hollandtown, and Little Chute. The first general influx of Dutch began in 1844 with the "Seceders", Dutch who had broken from the Reformed Church of the Netherlands and came to Wisconsin seeking religious freedom. As mentioned in the first chapter, Father Theodore Vandenbroek was an early promoter of Dutch Catholic emigration to Wisconsin, and beginning in 1848 he helped to bring 40,000 Catholic Dutch to Wisconsin. Martin most likely heard of Reverend Vandenbroek whose story has been well told many times, one of the best told is in the story "Wooden Shoes West" written by the talented author Fr. Scott Vandehey in 1979.

So far we have learned of three Barks that brought our pioneer family members from Holland to Wisconsin; they were the America, the Maria Magdalena, and the Libra. I am sure these sailing ships went back and forth many times bringing hopeful immigrants from Holland to the land of opportunity. Through my research, I have found two more Barks which left Rotterdam in 1851 & 1854 with Joosten families on them bound for Little Chute via the Port of New York. The "Leila" sailed from Rotterdam, Holland in the spring of 1851 with the Martin Joosten, Sr. family, and in the spring of 1854 "The Mississippi" also set sail from Rotterdam with Henry and Catherine (Joosten) Verhagen, Simon Joosten, and the Christian Joosten family. It is my belief Martin, Christian, and Simon are 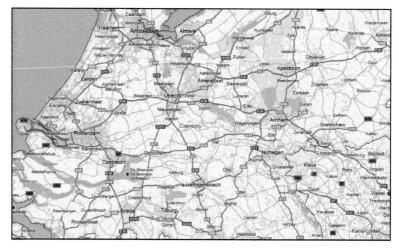 all brothers, and a good possibility Catherine is a daughter of Martin Sr. These beliefs are based on facts from the 1860 Little Chute Census and the passenger ship lists where the Joostens journeyed and lived together, which will be explained later in this chapter. Before I introduce my 4th great-grandfather, Martin, it should be known there are three consecutive generations of men with the name "Martin", and I am not sure if they all share the same middle name. So there is no confusion with which Martin I am referring to, I have added "Sr.", "Jr.", and the "III" after their names.

Martin Joosten, Sr. was born on November 25, 1799 to his parents Judocus and Maria (DeGroot) Joosten in the Province of North Brabant, Holland. In 1826, he married Anna Marie Dikkers in Holland, and they started a family and farmed their land in 's-Hertogenbosch (pronounced "sher-toe-chen-bos"), the capital city of the North Brabant Province. From what I know today in 2014, Martin and Anna had at least six children; they are:

Name	Birth Date	Birth Place
Walter	03/30/1828	Nuenen, North Brabant, Holland
William	about 1830	Nuenen, North Brabant, Holland
Catherine	1830-1831	Nuenen, North Brabant, Holland
Martin, Jr.	01/27/1833	Nuenen, North Brabant, Holland
Joseph	1/21/1838	Nuenen, North Brabant, Holland
Francis	1840	Nuenen, North Brabant, Holland

In 1851, Martin and Anna made up their minds to emigrate to America to seek the promised land of opportunity just like so many of their family and friends. Unfortunately, the Joosten Family was not lucky enough to be able to travel by ship with Fr. Vandenbroek. As we know, he had passed away in Little Chute that same year. Although I am sure Father influenced their decision to emigrate prior to his passing. Martin, Anna, Martin Jr., Joseph, and Francis made their way to Rotterdam to begin their long journey on the ship Leila.

I was able to obtain the passenger list of the Leila showing the Joosten Family along with some 220 other emigrants embarking this sailing ship. These long journeys could take anywhere from four to six weeks based on weather and favorable winds to propel the ship across the Atlantic. There were ship regulations and rules from the Captain that each family and passenger had to abide by. In another excerpt from the letter John Verboort, Jr. wrote to his friend. He recounts what he remembers about these policies. "*In those days each passenger had to buy his own provisions, and the captain was not*

Image 2.02- Port of New York Passenger List of the Ship Leila, 08/08/1851

allowed to accept any passenger who had not complied with prescribed regulations. Everything was carefully weighed, a number was put on each passenger's bag or package which the captain put under lock so that later, according to the ship's rules a fixed daily portion could be doled out. Passengers were not permitted to use as much of their provisions as they wished, but only as much as the captain allowed, in accordance with the rules. A small amount of drinking water was portioned out each day. The passengers, however, did not have to provide their own drinking water; this the shipping company brought on board at Rotterdam."

According to the ship manifest, the ship's Captain or Master, Mr. Stafford, documented 613 tons of cargo. What would be interesting to know is what the families were allowed to take onto the ship. I am sure they were limited to just a few possessions, and things like furniture or large farming tools were probably ruled out. The thought of this is a true sense of leaving everything behind and starting over. This was a very bold decision by Martin and Anna.

A passenger in the Maria Magdalena ship gave the author of the "*The Story of Father Van Den Broek, O.P.*" book the following account of their experience of the conditions on the ship, which I am sure were similar to what the Joostens and their fellow passengers on the Leila. In the back end of the ship on each side there were bunk beds two or three high. All of the passenger's possessions were in the middle. More than likely there was a priest onboard and an alter toward the stern of the vessel. Mass was said daily.

The Leila arrived at the Port of New York on August 6, 1851 after setting sail in June from Rotterdam, a good time of the year to take a long journey across the Atlantic. As can be seen from the portion of the Passenger List showing the Joosten Family, Martin is 50 and a farmer, Anna is 46, Martinus (Jr.) age 16, Joseph age 13, and Francis age 10. Such a long voyage can bring sickness and disease. The manifest also lists those who passed away during the trip, and unfortunately the excursion was very tough on the very young children. Nineteen youngsters tragically passed away, most under the age of 10, and some infants. How this must have been very difficult on their parents. All of the Joosten Family members made it safely across The Pond. I am uncertain how or when William made it to the United States from Holland or whether he emigrated or not. Catherine came over in 1854 with her husband Henry Verhagen. As for Walter, according to the *"Passenger and Immigration Lists Index, 1500s-1900s"*, he is listed as coming through an unknown port in 1850 at age 22. I am confident this was Walter based on the date of birth I listed above, and his age listed in the immigration records. According to the 1860 Census, Walter also ended his journey in Little Chute.

The quality of the Leila Passenger List is excellent as compared to the Mississippi Passenger List, in which many names are unreadable and illegible, and first names with just a single initial. So I have put together my best translation of names and ages. On May 12, 1854 the Mississippi arrived at the New York Port, meaning they left Rotterdam, Holland somewhere around early March 1854. This ship was much larger than the Leila, and carried 647 tons of cargo for the 326 passengers. Among the Hollander passengers were emigrants from Prussia and Germany. Illness and death did not escape the Mississippi with eight passengers succumbing to the harsh and dangerous conditions dying enroute to New York.

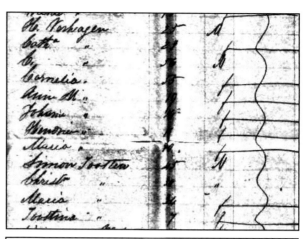

Translation of the Mississippi Passenger List	
	Age
H. Verhagen = Henry	25
Cath Verhagen = Catherine (Joosten)	24
C. Verhagen = ?	36?
Cornelia Verhagen	35?
Anna M Verhagen	19?
Johanna Verhagen	?
Illegible? Verhagen	?
Maria Verhagen	?
Simon Joosten	45
Christ Joosten	31
Maria = Johanna Maria (Schuls)	34
Joostina = Justina Christina	7

As previously mentioned, Henry and Catherine (Joosten) Verhagen are listed on the manifest as well as some other members of the Verhagen family, more than likely related to Henry, but it is not known how. Simon Joosten, a brother of Martin Sr., is listed by himself at age 45, followed by another brother Christian (31), his wife Johanna Maria (Schuls), 34 years old, and their first daughter Justina Christina at seven years old.

After arriving safely to Little Chute and surveying the land for the very first time, one could only imagine the feeling. Certainly one feeling was probably being weary from the long voyage, but another must have been elation of the new opportunities that lie ahead. The landscape was heavily wooded, trees as far as the eye could see, and there was a lot of back-breaking work that also lie ahead just to clear the land to build on, and make room for their new homes. Since it was summer, there was time to build shelter in whatever form needed before the extreme cold of winter set in. I am sure there was nothing in the form of even a meager convenience such as a wagon and a horse to travel somewhere close, like Appleton, to purchase lumber. Needless to say, their existence must have been very primitive. The men began cutting down trees to build their first log homes; the start to their new beginning, and a place to call "home sweet home".

I came across a brilliant and very old book entitled the *"Commemorative Biographical Record of the Fox River Valley"* written by J.H. Beers & Co. in 1895. It contains excellent short stories of many pioneers in Outagamie and Brown counties. As the author wrote, his purpose was *"to place in book form biographical history of representative citizens – both for its immediate worth and for its value to coming generations – is admitted by all thinking people, and within the past decade there has been a growing interest in this commendable means of perpetuating biography and family genealogy."* I praise this man's work and passion to document these biographies for a couple of reasons, first because generations, now 115 years later, are still enjoying his work, and second he wrote about Joseph and his father Martin, Sr.

On page 837 of this wonderful book, the author starts his story of Joseph Joosten, son of Martin, Sr. Within the story of Joseph, there is the following tale of Martin, Sr., which I will quote in its entirety in order to capture the true vocabulary of the time. It reads: *"Martin Joosten, his father, lived on a small farm, which was not entirely paid for. In the spring of 1851 he concluded that the United States afforded better prospects for himself and his sons, of whom three of the four were then at home, and he consequently engaged passage for himself and family on the "Lila", and sailing from Rotterdam in June, 1851, reached New York after a voyage of thirty-eight days. He had determined to come to Wisconsin, and finally arrived in this State, journeying by water from Buffalo to Milwaukee, thence to Green Bay, where the party landed in August. A quarter section of land was entered in section 8, Township 21, range 18, Kaukauna Township, Outagamie County, on which they located, and, sickness having made nearly an end of their limited means, commenced life in the wilderness in an exceedingly primitive style. A cabin was constructed of poplar poles, with a chimney in one corner; a roof of the same material was added, covered over the top with red clay, and this was the extent of the family's protection from the cold or storm. Then followed the work of clearing the land, which was all heavily timbered, the first tree being cut by then after their arrival. Then it became necessary for some of the boys to put a shoulder to the wheel and earn something to help support the family, as the early returns from the farm were but meager. By reason of his being more robust, this lot fell upon Joseph, and he succeeded in obtaining employment with the Fox River Improvement Company."* What a fantastic recounting of a true pioneer.

By 1860, Martin, Sr. and his family had been in Little Chute for about nine years now, and were settled into their farm and new life. Martin Jr., Joseph and Francis, all age 20 or older, were still living at home, more than likely helping their father on the farm to earn enough money to live on. The year 1860 was also a census year when the federal government took on the monumental task of counting everyone in the union. These served another purpose than just enumerating everybody in the country; the census also gave the government a list of people they could tax, and also a record of men who would be able to go to war, especially since the Civil War was soon to begin. After the great Abraham Lincoln was elected to office on November 6, 1860, the southern states did not like this momentous event since the Republican Party had an anti-slavery platform. On December 20, 1860, South Carolina split from the Union, and within five weeks Alabama, Florida, Georgia, Louisiana, Mississippi, and Texas had done the same naming themselves the Confederate States of America. President Lincoln made it known he had no intention of ending slavery, but this did not make a difference to the Confederacy. On April 4, 1861 the Confederacy attacked Fort Sumter in Charleston, SC, a stronghold for the Union, and the Union returned fire, and so began the Civil War. Immediately Arkansas, North Carolina, Tennessee, and Virginia left the Union for the Confederacy, followed by Delaware, Maryland, Missouri, and Kentucky making 15 states in all splitting from the Union.

At this same time, Joseph had journeyed south to Louisiana and Arkansas in the fall of 1860 looking for work, and did so cutting cordwood. After the summer harvest, it was common for the men to find work to keep money rolling in for the family until the next planting season. Working as a lumberjack cutting trees, wood, or working in a sawmill was easy work to find in those days. News spread fast about the battle at Fort Sumter to where Joseph was working, and he sensed the growing tension the Confederacy had for the Northerners. Joseph made the smart decision to head back to Little Chute. It was a good thing he left the South because he had heard some men did not see their homes in the North again, probably due to getting caught up in the war.

When taking a close look at the 1860 Outagamie County census it was surprising to see the Joostens were all essentially next door neighbors. Even though they all probably owned 100+ acre farms, they all shared property lines. Equally as surprising was the census taker, S. Ryan, Jr., must have misunderstood the Joosten name when it was pronounced to him, assuming he went door to door, and wrote down the family name as "Hoousten". This made it virtually impossible for anyone searching for "Joosten" to find the family in Little Chute, unless one looks page by page, which is how I found the family. Below I have replicated the 1860 census of Little Chute; please keep in mind I have documented the Joosten name as it was actually spelled on the census record. Though not yet incorporated as a village, Little Chute was known as a "village" versus a town or city.

Looking at my census reproduction, you can see that Martin's real estate value is much more than his son Walter, son-in-law Henry, and brother Christian. Why is this? Well, maybe he had a substantial amount of acreage compared to the others. And who valued the property? Did Martin come up with the value, or did the county? I am thinking it was probably the county, and then they taxed the real and personal property.

1860 Little Chute, Outagamie County, Wisconsin Census, page 237 and 238						
Household Number	Name	Age	Occupation	Value of Real Estate	Value of Personal Estate	Place of Birth
1779	Walter Hoousten	32	Farmer	$580	$400	Holland
	Wilhelmina	21	Housewife			Holland
	Arnold	3				Wisconsin
	Mary	1				Wisconsin
1780	Henry Verhagen	31	Farmer	$300	$300	Holland
	Catherine	29	Housewife			Holland
	Antone	3				Wisconsin
	Cornelia	1				Wisconsin
1781	Martin Hoousten	60	Farmer	$1,300	$245	Holland
	Ann	54	Housewife			Holland
	Martin	27				Holland
	Joseph	22				Holland
	Francis	20				Holland
1785	Christian Houston	37	Farmer	$400	$490	Holland
	Mary	39	Housewife			Holland
	Mary	4				Wisconsin
	Harriet	3				Wisconsin
	Ella	2				Wisconsin
	Catherine	7/12				Wisconsin

Neighbors of the Joostens included Hannah Ebben and William Ebben (Walter Joosten's mother-in law and brother-in law), Martin & Elizabeth Verhagen (Henry Verhagen's brother), Gijsbert & Cornelia Verhagen (Henry's parents), Theo VanAldenhofen, and Francis VanCamp. Some of the family names in Little Chute at this time were Ebben, Hietpas, Shoemaker, VanHandel, VanderHeyden, Verstegen, and Weyenberg. They came from the countries of Canada, Ireland, France, Scotland, and England.

Also of interest from this census were the occupations the people held besides that of a farmer and who was the oldest resident. A farmer by the name of John Tillman, who was age 80 at the time and born in Holland, held the title of oldest resident. Here is a sampling of the trade professions and who held them:

- ❖ Catholic Church Priest: Rev. Michael Peifferl, age 34, born in Prussia. (St. John Pastor 1857-1860)
- ❖ Doctor: Henry Bongers, age 43.
- ❖ Shoemakers: Martin Kemper, age 39.
    Henry Weyenberg, age 25.

- ❖ Blacksmith: Antone Johnson, age 35.
    Harlour(?) Rice, age 53
- ❖ Saloon Keeper: John Enwright, age 31
- ❖ Circuit Court Clerk: C.A. Hamer, age 47
- ❖ School Teacher: Janette Hamer, age 21
- ❖ Hotel Keeper: Tom Austin, age 29.

Ten years later, according to the 1870 Census, Martin, Sr. and his children, of course all of them were out on their own now, and all were still living in Little Chute pretty much next door to one another. This also included the Henry Verhagen family, but Catherine (daughter of Martin, Sr.) is not counted with her husband. Unfortunately, Catherine passed away on June 15, 1861 and her husband is enumerated with his new wife Henriette (VanHammond). And from information I have, it appears Henry and Henriette were married in August 1862, and had three children (Catherine, John and Albert) during the 1860s. Martin, Sr.'s real estate property value dropped by $100 to $1,200, while Henry's rose by $100 to $400 and Christian's doubled to $800. So, not much rhyme or reason to real estate values from year to year, or even over a 10 year period.

Walter and Christian were still in the neighborhood with Martin, Sr., and now Martin, Jr. had his own property in the area. It is unknown where Frances was living when the 1870 census was taken, but I found out Joseph and his family were living in Grand Chute after living in Bay Settlement for a time. Some new neighbors arrived to the neighborhood too. A couple of them were the P.W. Vanden Wildenberg and Peter DeBruin families.

By 1880, Martin, Sr. was 81 years old, and his wife Anna Maria was 74. Martin was certainly at an age well past life expectancy at that time. According to encyclopedia.com, life expectancy when Martin was born was 57 years for a 10 year old, and surprisingly 40.5 years for a 10 year old in 1880. The higher mortality rate in those days was due to epidemic diseases like measles and small pox becoming an endemic disease like pneumonia, malaria, and tuberculosis. An "endemic" disease is one that was constantly present in a population. So for Martin and Anna Maria to be alive at this point late in the 19th century was certainly a blessing because if one of these epidemics would have struck, I do not think they would have survived it.

At some point around 1880, Martin must have sold his farm and retired; it could be possible one of his children inherited or just took over the property. And since Martin and his wife were now living with his son Martin, Jr. and his family in Little Chute, my belief is Martin, Jr. moved onto the property and took over the operations of the farm. Martin, Jr. did live next door to his parents in 1870. Another clue to confirm this belief is the 1880 census record showing the Peter DeBruin family still as a next door neighbor of the Joostens. You will remember the DeBruin family was listed as neighbors in the 1870 census. As for the location of Martin's other children, none of them were in close vicinity, such as on the same road as they might have been around the 1870s. Christian and Walter were still in Little Chute, and Joseph remained in Grand Chute. Also at this time it was really nice to see in the 1880 census record two of Martin, Jr.'s children, Maria (age 7) and Simon (age 6), attending school. Though their older sister Frances, who was age 13, was not in school, and at home helping her mother tend to running the household.

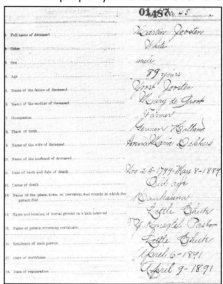

Image 3.03- Death Certificate of Martin

Just as Martin, Sr.'s daughter Catherine Verhagen could not be found in the 1870 census, her husband Henry was not enumerated in the 1880 census. Thirteen years after his first wife passed away; sadly Henry passed away in March 1873 at the young age of 43, but lived to the average age of that era. Henry left behind his six children from his two marriages; his second wife, Henriette, had passed away in December 1871.

Surprisingly and fortunately for us, the state of Wisconsin started recording births and deaths in the late 1880s. I was thrilled, for only historical purposes, when I found the death certificate of Martin, Sr. at the vital records department in Milwaukee, WI. At the amazing age of 89, Martin, Sr. passed away on May 08, 1889 at Little Chute, well beyond many others of this time, and what a blessing for his family to have him in their lives for so long. He would leave his wife of 62 years, Anna, to mourn his death, and just a short ten months later she would pass away at the age of 84. What an honorable couple of people who were true pioneers following the zealous faith of Fr. Vandenbroek, and leaving an immense legacy behind for those of us who descended from such greatness and graciousness. Both are said to be buried in St. John Catholic Cemetery in Little Chute. May they both continue to rest in peace with the Lord.

❧ Descendants of Judocus Joosten (Joseph's Grandfather) ❧

Please see Petronella's Family Genealogy below
Notes: 1= 1st generation, 2= 2nd generation, 3= 3rd generation.

1   Judocus Joosten
     Born: September 14, 1778 in Gerwen, North Brabant, Holland
     Died: November 04, 1846 in Nuenen, North Brabant, Holland
     Married: October 06, 1799 in Nuenen, North Brabant, Holland
     Maria DeGroot
     Born: February 08, 1780 in Gerwen, North Brabant, Holland
     Died: July 11, 1830 in Nuenen, North Brabant, Holland

    2   Martinus M. Joosten, Sr.
         Born: November 29, 1799 in Nuenen, North Brabant, Holland
         Died: May 10, 1889 in Little Chute, Outagamie County, Wisconsin
         Buried at: St. John Catholic Cemetery, Little Chute, WI.
         Married: August 05, 1826 in Nuenen, North Brabant, Holland
         Anna Marie Dikkers
         Born: October 01, 1805 in Gerwen, North Brabant, Holland
         Died: March 27, 1890 in Kaukauna, Outagamie County, Wisconsin
         Buried at: St. John Catholic Cemetery, Little Chute, WI.
         Parents: Walterus Dikkers (1768-1815) and Johanna Vanroij (1774-1811)

        3   Walter Joosten, Sr.
             Born: March 20, 1828 in Nuenen, North Brabant, Holland
             Died: January 08, 1914 in Little Chute, Outagamie County, Wisconsin
             Buried at: St. John Catholic Cemetery, Little Chute, WI, sec 1A, row 3
             Married: April 14, 1856 in Little Chute, Outagamie County, Wisconsin
             Wilhelmina Ebben
             Born: December 27, 1837 in 's-Hertogenbosch, North Brabant, Holland
             Died: May 07, 1927 in Little Chute, Outagamie County, Wisconsin
             Buried at: St. John Catholic Cemetery, Little Chute, WI, sec 1A, row 3
             Parents: Arnoldus Ebben (1805-1853) and Johanna Ermers (1801-1874)

        3   William Joosten
             Born: About 1830 in Nuenen, North Brabant, Holland

        3   Catherine Joosten
             Born: 1830 or 1831 in Nuenen, North Brabant, Holland
             Died: June 15, 1861
             Buried: St. John Catholic Cemetery, Little Chute, WI
             Married: August 31, 1852
             Henry Verhagen
             Born: November 30, 1829 in Nuenen, North Brabant, Holland
             Died: March 17, 1873 in Little Chute, Outagamie County, Wisconsin
             Buried: St. John Catholic Cemetery, Little Chute, WI
             Parents: Gijsbert Verhagen (1797-1883) and Cornelia VanStappen (1800-1865)

        3   Martin M. Joosten, Jr.
             Born: January 27, 1833 in Nuenen, North Brabant, Holland
             Died: February 07, 1912 in Little Chute, Outagamie County, Wisconsin
             Buried at: St. John Catholic Cemetery, Little Chute, WI.
             Married: November 18, 1866 in Little Chute, Outagamie County, Wisconsin

Mary Verhagen
Born: January 26, 1843 in Holland
Died: June 20, 1923 in Little Chute, Outagamie County, Wisconsin
Buried at: St. John Catholic Cemetery, Little Chute, WI
Parents: Gijsbert Verhagen (1797-1883) and Cornelia VanStappen (1800-1865)

3   Joseph Joosten
Born: January 21, 1838 in Nuenen, North Brabant, Holland
Died: January 09, 1907 in Verboort, Washington County, Oregon
Buried at: Visitation Catholic Cemetery, Verboort, OR, SE row 1
Married: April 04, 1861 in Bay Settlement, Brown County, Wisconsin
Petronella VanLanen
Born: May 20, 1840 in Boekel, North Brabant, Holland
Died: October 26, 1911 in Verboort, Washington County, Oregon
Buried at: Visitation Catholic Cemetery, Verboort, OR, SE row 1
Parents: Gerardus L. VanLanen (1807-1882) and Marie M. VandenElsen (1814-1879)

3   Francis Joosten
Born: July 24, 1840 in Nuenen, North Brabant, Holland
Died: February 11, 1863 in Little Chute, Outagamie County, Wisconsin
Buried: St. John Catholic Cemetery, Little Chute, WI
Married: September 16, 1862 in Little Chute, Outagamie County, Wisconsin
Mary Verhagen
Born: January 26, 1843 in Holland
Died: June 20, 1923 in Little Chute, Outagamie County, Wisconsin
Buried at: St. John Catholic Cemetery, Little Chute, WI
Parents: Gijsbert Verhagen (1797-1883) and Cornelia VanStappen (1800-1865)
Second marriage to Martin Joosten, Jr.

2   Petronella (VanAnsem) Joosten
Born: April 15, 1801 in Nuenen, North Brabant, Holland
Died: August 14, 1855 in North Brabant, Holland

2   Anna Maria (Maasackers) Joosten
Born: June 18, 1805 in Nuenen, North Brabant, Holland
Died: August 13, 1850 in Nuenen, North Brabant, Holland

2   Simon Joosten
Born: December 12, 1808 in in Nuenen, North Brabant, Holland
Died: Unknown

2   Woutrien (deGreef) Joosten
Born: about 1810 in Nuenen, North Brabant, Holland
Died: April 24, 1873 in Lieshout, North Brabant, Holland

2   Joostina Joosten
Born: about 1818
Died: September 22, 1818

2   Christian Joosten
     Born: May 19, 1823 in 's-Hertogenbosch, North Brabant, Holland
     Died: January 20, 1899 in Kaukauna, Outagamie County, Wisconsin
     Buried at: St. John Catholic Cemetery, Little Chute, WI
     Married: February 18, 1854 in Nuenen, North Brabant, Holland
     Joanna Maria Schuts
     Born: May 16, 1821 in 's-Hertogenbosch, North Brabant, Holland
     Died: April 07, 1892 in Kaukauna, Outagamie County, Wisconsin
     Buried at: St. John Catholic Cemetery, Little Chute, WI
     Parents: Unknown

          3   Justina Christina Joosten
               Born: May 06, 1845 in Gerwen, North Brabant, Holland
               Died: March 28, 1918 in Little Chute, Outagamie County, Wisconsin
               Buried: St. John Catholic Cemetery, Little Chute, WI
               Married: November 14, 1864 in Little Chute, Outagamie County, Wisconsin
               Petrus Johannes Vandenheuvel
               Born: February 20, 1840 in Uden, North Brabant, The Netherlands
               Died: September 21, 1877 in Little Chute, Outagamie County, Wisconsin
               Buried: St. John Catholic Cemetery, Little Chute, WI
               Parents: Johannes Vandenheuvel (1799-1848) & Allegonda VerHulen (1802-1864)

          3   Anna Maria Joosten
               Born: January 24, 1856 in Little Chute, Outagamie County, Wisconsin
               Died: January 26, 1869 in Little Chute, Outagamie County, Wisconsin
               Buried: Unknown

          3   Henrica Joosten
               Born: April 12, 1857 in Grand Chute, Outagamie County, Wisconsin
               Died: January 29, 1927 in Little Chute, Outagamie County, Wisconsin
               Buried: St. John Catholic Cemetery, Little Chute, WI
               Married: April 27, 1874 in Little Chute, Outagamie County, Wisconsin
               Martin Vandervelden
               Born: January 09, 1856 in Uden, North Brabant, Holland
               Died: January 12, 1926 in Little Chute, Outagamie County, Wisconsin
               Buried: St. John Catholic Cemetery, Little Chute, WI
               Parents: Johannes Vandervelden (1826-1900) and Johanna VanderWyst (1820-1893)

          3   Petronella Joosten
               Born: April 28, 1858 in Little Chute, Outagamie County, Wisconsin
               Died: March 03, 1948
               Buried at: St. John Catholic Cemetery, Little Chute, WI
               Married: June 07, 1880 in Little Chute, Outagamie County, Wisconsin
               Anton VanDeWeyer
               Born: July 21, 1855
               Died: May 14, 1913
               Buried at: St. John Catholic Cemetery, Little Chute, WI
               Parents: Anton VanDeWeyer (1827-1855) & Mary Vandenheuvel (1828-1913)

3   Catherine Joosten
Born: December 12, 1860 in Little Chute, Outagamie County, Wisconsin
Died: October 10, 1926 in Little Chute, Outagamie County, Wisconsin
Buried at: St. John Catholic Cemetery, Little Chute, WI
Married: unknown
George Hermsen
Born: August 16, 1857 in Little Chute, Outagamie County, Wisconsin
Died: August 17, 1902 in Little Chute, Outagamie County, Wisconsin
Buried at: St. John Catholic Cemetery, Little Chute, WI
Parents: Gerardus Hermsen (1821-1884) and Elisabeth Geurts (1819-1908)

❧ Descendants of Gerardus VanLanen (Nellie's Father) ❧

Notes: 1= 1st generation, 2= 2nd generation, 3= 3rd generation.
I have come across different spelling variations of the surname VanLanen, including VanLaanen, and VanLannen.

1   Gerardus L. VanLanen
    Born: January 28, 1807 n Boekel, North Brabant, Holland
    Died: August 25, 1882 in Bay Settlement, Brown County, Wisconsin
    Buried at: Holy Cross Catholic Cemetery, Bay Settlement, WI., row 26
    Married: October 03, 1835 in Boekel, North Brabant, Holland
    Marie M. VandenElsen
    Born: September 03, 1814 in Boekel, North Brabant, Holland
    Died: July 11, 1830 in Nuenen, North Brabant, Holland
    Buried at: Holy Cross Catholic Cemetery, Bay Settlement, WI., row 26
    Parents: Adriaan VandenElsden and Elisabeth Hendriks

> 2   John Adrianus VanLanen
>   Born: July 26, 1836 in Boekel, North Brabant, Holland
>   Died: February 26, 1912 in Bay Settlement, Brown County, Wisconsin
>   Buried at: Holy Cross Catholic Cemetery, Bay Settlement, WI., row 15
>   Married: 1861 in Green Bay, Brown County, Wisconsin
>   Domatil Sophia Lyonnais
>   Born: April 18, 1842 in Town of Scott, Brown County, Wisconsin
>   Died: August 14, 1907 in Green Bay, Brown County, Wisconsin
>   Buried at: Holy Cross Catholic Cemetery, Bay Settlement, WI., row 15
>   Parents: Antione Lyonnais & Julia Gamelin

>> 3   Julia Johanna VanLanen
>>   Born: July 29, 1862 in Green Bay, Brown County, Wisconsin
>>   Died: June 13, 1946 in Wrightstown, Brown County, Wisconsin
>>   Buried at: St. Paul Catholic Cemetery, Wrightstown, WI., sec 2, row 3
>>   Married (1): John Adrian VanLanen
>>   Married (2): John Cornelius Verbeten

>> 3   George A. VanLanen
>>   Born: 1865 in Bay Settlement, Brown County, Wisconsin
>>   Died: 1936 in Bay Settlement, Brown County, Wisconsin
>>   Buried at: Holy Cross Catholic Cemetery, Bay Settlement, WI., row 10
>>   Married: Clara M. Baenen

>> 3   Albert Peter VanLanen
>>   Born: 1866 in Bay Settlement, Brown Co, Wisconsin
>>   Died: 1913 in Iron Mountain, Dickinson County, Michigan
>>   Buried at: Unknown
>>   Married: Victoria Rochon

>> 3   Francis John VanLanen
>>   Born: 1868 in Bay Settlement, Brown County, Wisconsin
>>   Died: 1953 in Bay Settlement, Brown County, Wisconsin
>>   Buried at: Allouez Catholic Cemetery, Green Bay, Brown County, Wisconsin
>>   Married: Rose Garvey

3   Hugh VanLanen
Born: April 05, 1869 in Bay Settlement, Brown County, Wisconsin
Died: August 13, 1944 in Green Bay, Brown County, Wisconsin
Buried at: Holy Cross Catholic Cemetery, Bay Settlement, WI., row 15
Married: Harriet DeLeers

3   Joseph VanLanen
Born: 1870 in Bay Settlement, Brown County, Wisconsin
Died: 1940 in Town of Scott, Brown County, Wisconsin
Buried at: Unknown
Married: Unknown

3   Mary VanLanen
Born: 1872 in Bay Settlement, Brown County, Wisconsin
Died: 1951 in Bay Settlement, Brown County, Wisconsin
Buried at: Holy Cross Cemetery, Bay Settlement, Wisconsin
Married: John VanVeghel

3   Edward John VanLanen
Born: 1874 in Bay Settlement, Brown County, Wisconsin
Died: 1941 in Bay Settlement, Brown County, Wisconsin
Buried at: Unknown
Married: Unknown

3   Elisabeth VanLanen
Born: Died at birth
Died:
Buried at: Unknown
Married: n/a

3   John Adrian VanLanen
Born: 1883 in Bay Settlement, Brown County, Wisconsin
Died: 1945 in Bay Settlement, Brown County, Wisconsin
Buried at: Holy Cross Catholic Cemetery, Bay Settlement, WI., row 12
Married: Ida Louise Degrand

3   Elizabeth VanLanen
Born: 1885 in Bay Settlement, Brown County, Wisconsin
Died: 1959 in Milwaukee, Milwaukee County, Wisconsin
Buried at: Fort Howard Memorial Park, Green Bay, Wisconsin
Married: John VanEss

2 Petronella VanLanen
Born: May 20, 1840 in Boekel, North Brabant, Holland
Died: October 26, 1911 in Verboort, Washington County, Oregon
Buried at: Visitation Catholic Cemetery, Verboort, OR, SE row 1
Married: April 04, 1861 in Bay Settlement, Brown County, Wisconsin
Joseph Joosten
Born: January 21, 1838 in Nuenen, North Brabant, Holland
Died: January 09, 1907 in Verboort, Washington County, Oregon
Buried at: Visitation Catholic Cemetery, Verboort, OR, SE row 1
Parents: Martinus M. Joosten, Sr. (1799-1889) & Anna Marie Dikkers (1805-1890)

Nellie and Joseph had nine children. Please see their family at the end of chapter three.

2 Frank Laurentius VanLanen
   Born: April 02, 1842 in Boekel, North Brabant, Holland
   Died: March 21, 1894 in Stiles, Oconto County, Wisconsin
   Buried at:
   Married: Unknown
   Caroline Fisher
   Born: 1847 in Prussia
   Died: 1912 in Stiles, Oconto County, Wisconsin
   Buried at:
   Parents: Unknown

   3 Anne VanLanen
      Born: 1867 in Town of Scott, Brown County, Wisconsin
      Died: 1947 in Green Bay, Brown County, Wisconsin
      Buried at: Unknown
      Married: Joseph M. Baenen

   3 Christine VanLanen
      Born: About 1868
      Died: Unknown
      Buried at: Unknown
      Married: Henry VanVeghel

   3 Cecilia VanLanen
      Born: 1870 in Bay Settlement, Brown County, Wisconsin
      Died: 1909
      Buried at: Unknown
      Married: Martin VanEperen

   3 Eugene F. VanLanen
      Born: About 1872 in Bay Settlement, Brown County, Wisconsin
      Died: 1943 in Stiles, Oconto County, Wisconsin
      Buried at:
      Married: Mary E. Bedore

   3 Matthew VanLanen
      Born: 1875 in Bay Settlement, Brown County, Wisconsin
      Died: 1918
      Buried at:
      Married: Theresa Duca

   3 William VanLanen
      Born: About 1877 in Bay Settlement, Brown County, Wisconsin
      Died: 1933 in Outagamie County, Wisconsin
      Buried at: Unknown
      Married: Unknown

3   George VanLanen
     Born: About 1879
     Died: Unknown
     Buried at: Unknown
     Married: Unknown

2   Elizabeth VanLanen
     Born: 1848 in Boekel, North Brabant, Holland
     Died: July 1851 at sea
     Buried at: At sea
     Married: n/a

2   Johanna VanLanen
     Born: 1850 in Boekel, North Brabant, Holland
     Died: July 1851 at sea
     Buried at: At sea
     Married: n/a

❧ Chapter Three ❧

Joseph & Nellie Joosten

The fifth born child to Martin and Anna Maria was Joseph, my 3rd-great-grandfather. Joseph Joosten was born in the dead of winter on January 21, 1838 in Nuenen, North Brabant, Holland. Winters in Nuenen were pretty cold and probably very similar to the chilly, and sometimes frigid, conditions in Little Chute. Nuenen sits on the 51st parallel, not too far from the 44th parallel where Little Chute is located, and is located about 25 miles south of North Brabant's capital 's-Hertogenbosch.

I was unbelievably fortunate and lucky to obtain Joseph's birth record from a gracious and helpful genealogist in Holland. It is a wonderful document written in Dutch, of course, but as you will notice the handwritten portion is very challenging to read. So after getting some nice help from a cousin in Scotland who studied Dutch, and hours spent translating the document myself the result is a pretty good rendering of the original. The birth record reveals Martin and Anna took the baby, who didn't actually have a first name at the time (recorded as "Joost"), to a meeting with a Notary to record his birth. There were two witnesses present, Herman Christiaan van Hovey who was 21 years old and considered his occupation "private", and Antonie Boojakkers, a farmer who was 65 years old. I have included Joseph's original birth record, how the document was written in Dutch, and the English translation in the front pages of this book.

Vincent van Gogh (1853-1890), one of the all-time greatest and popular painters, was born in Holland too. He was born in 1853 in Groot-Zundert, and around 1882 his parents moved to Nuenen where his father became pastor of the Protestant Dutch Reformed Church there. It makes me wonder if the Joostens and van Goghs knew each other, even though the Joostens were long gone by then. It is in Nuenen where Vincent produced his first painting "The Potato Eaters" in 1885. He considered it his best work by depicting peasants in a non-awkward way, but in their true and natural way of life in Holland. He had a fondness and feelings of sympathy for the working class peasants. It is widely known Vincent's "models" for his masterpiece were the Cornelis and Cornelia

Image 3.01- Vincent VanGogh's "Potato Eaters"

(VanRooij) DeGroot family. This is interesting too because there are members of the DeGroot family who are in-laws of Joseph and Petronella's children. I really think his piece captures how our Holland ancestors dressed, and how the inside of their homes looked. Another interesting fact is Vincent took piano lessons from Hein Vanderzanden. The Vanderzandens are in the Joosten family too; my grandmother (Minnie Shaw) was a Vanderzanden. See chapter five for further details.

As mentioned before, Joseph journeyed across the Atlantic for America with his family in the summer of 1851 at the young age of 13 aboard the bark Leila. Also aboard this same ship was the George VanLanen family, which included his daughter Petronella (Nellie). It seems as though the Joostens and VanLanens knew one another since both families were on the Leila; this is an interesting situation as you will later read.

By the time the Joosten family arrived in Little Chute many efforts by prominent Wisconsinites and the State government had been made to increase boat travel for goods and commerce between the Great Lakes and the Gulf of Mexico. After many failed attempts due to financial and political reasons, a company by the name of Fox and Wisconsin Improvement Company was formed and commissioned to dig a canal between the Fox and Wisconsin Rivers, and build locks along the Lower Fox River. In the mid to late 1850s, Joseph went to work for the Fox and Wisconsin Improvement Company to help earn extra money to help support the family. It is my belief he assisted in the construction of the lock at Little Chute or the canal which was dug between the Wisconsin and Fox Rivers.

Image 3.02- Canal at Portage, WI

This massive project to dig a canal was in the area of what today is the city of Portage, WI. At Portage there is a one-and-a-half mile distance between the Wisconsin and Fox Rivers, and in the mid-19th century is when the effort was undertaken to dig the canal between the two rivers so boats could pass from one river to the other, thereby creating the missing link from the Gulf of Mexico to the Great Lakes. You see, with no canal boats would have to be carried or "portaged" between the two rivers in order to continue a journey to the other river. It is interesting how the town of Portage got its name from this feat. The layout of the rivers when looking at a map was like this; the Upper Fox River originates in south-central Wisconsin, where it passes close to the southerly flowing Wisconsin River before flowing northeast into Lake Winnebago. Then the Lower Fox River flows out of Lake Winnebago north and empties into Lake Michigan at Green Bay. The Wisconsin River flows south through Wisconsin and empties into the Mississippi River, and of course the Mississippi River flows south to the Gulf of Mexico.

On the Lower Fox River between Lake Winnebago and Lake Michigan, there is a 169-foot elevation drop in the 39-mile distance between the two lakes. So in order to tame or slow the river down for the benefit of boat travel, locks were built; one of which was put in and eventually opened at Little Chute in 1856. As previously mentioned, the company who was awarded the contract to build the locks was the Fox and Wisconsin Improvement Company, the same company who Joseph was employed with for probably just a couple of years.

In the fall of 1860, Joseph traveled south to Louisiana and Arkansas finding work cutting cordwood. Just as the civil war started, Joseph had made it back to Wisconsin, and returned to Kaukauna. He was reunited with Nellie VanLanen, his childhood friend. Before long their friendship turned into love, and at age 23, Joseph married Nellie, age 20, on May 4, 1861 in Bay Settlement, Brown County, Wisconsin.

Petronella (Nellie) VanLanen was the second born child to her parents Gerardus and Marie (VandenElsen) VanLanen, and came into this world on May 20, 1840 in Boekel, North Brabant, Holland. Boekel and Nuenen are only about 13.5 miles apart, so Joseph and Nellie were virtually neighbors in Holland and after both families emigrated to Wisconsin. I was equally fortunate to acquire Nellie's birth certificate, likewise written in Dutch. Her parents had her birth recorded down at city hall. The witnesses who were present and signed the certificate were Peter VandenBerg, occupation farmer and 56 years old, and Johannes Arnoldus Peters, 40 years old. Both were residents of Boekel. I have included an image of Nellie's original birth record next to Joseph's in the front pages of this book. As mentioned above, ironically and fatefully, Nellie and Joseph were on the same ship crossing the Atlantic to the United States in 1851. Nellie along with her parents and four siblings made the voyage, but so sadly Nellie's two youngest sisters, Elizabeth and Johanna, passed away while at sea. They were just age three and nine months old, respectively. The long ocean crossing was very tough on the very young and old.

As written in the wonderful story about Joseph in the Commemorative Biographical Record of the Fox River Valley, the young newly married couple had $35 to their name, and started their life together by renting a farm in Bay Settlement. It is my belief Nellie's parents and siblings who came to America also lived in Bay Settlement at this time. The Joostens lived in Brown County for six years, and then in October 1868 packed up their worldly possessions and four children and headed west to Grand Chute, which is just a few miles north from Little Chute. So now they were closer to the Joosten side of the family instead of 35 miles away, which was the distance to Bay Settlement. The story continues on by stating that Joseph and Nellie moved everything by wagon pulled by oxen and two horses with a couple of cows following behind.

Their new farm, which was only partially cleared from the trees, was situated on 99 acres in section 19 in the Grand Chute Township, which borders Appleton. As can be seen on the plat map pictured, the southern boundary of the property was bordered by tracks owned by the Chicago & Northwestern Railroad, and the farm was within yards of the Fox River. Certainly, a lot of work laid ahead for the family to get the farm in shape to be able to produce a decent living. Talk about starting over again from scratch, Joseph and Nellie surely did that, but I guess they were probably used to doing this.

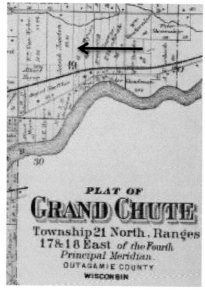

Image 3.03- Grand Chute Plat Map, 1889

The family was captured in the 1870 census, and we know Joseph, Nellie and their family were living in Grand Chute. But just as the case with the 1860 census, the census taker wrote down a different misspelling of the Joosten name; this time instead of "Hoousten", it shows "Justen", so we are getting closer to the actual spelling. Joseph is shown as a farmer with the value of the farm at $3,000, and $600 for their personal possessions. By this time, five of their nine children were born; all of them girls. They are Elizabeth (7), Frances (6), Anna (4), Mary (2), and Jane (3 months). I am sure Joseph was hoping and praying for a son at some point, not because he did not want to be the only male in the family, but for the reason of help running the farm. I believe the future success of a family farm in those days depended on sons and daughters helping out on the farm, since they did not have to be paid. In those days, once the children finished grade school they were put to work on the farm, or someone else's farm to earn money to support the family. The majority of the children's earnings automatically went to their parents and some to the savings piggy bank. We know Joseph and Nellie ran a successful farm. I am sure their daughters were a big part of this success because it sure showed in the thriving family farms in later generations.

Just like Little Chute, Grand Chute was a farming community. All of the Joosten's neighbors were farmers, and the average value of the land according to the census of the farms nearby was about $2,000. The Joosten farm was valued higher, but their farm might have been larger. And instead of having neighbors all from Holland, some were born in Prussia and Canada.

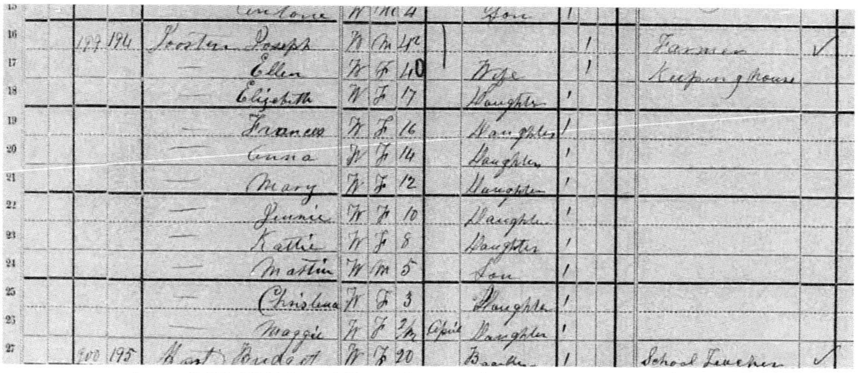

Image 3.04- 1880 Grand Chute, Outagamie County, WI ED126, sheet21

As the 1880 census was taken it can be seen from the image of the page showing the Joosten family that all nine children of Joseph and Nellie have been blessed to the family. There was certainly a full house now, and the lone son, Martin, had eight sisters!! That must have been fun for him. Joseph was age 42 and listed as a farmer, and Nellie 40 at this time. Interestingly, the family living next door to the Joosten family were also Joostens and listed as being born in Bavaria, but I do not believe they are related to our Joostens.

Like many families living in Outagamie County who followed Fr. William Verboort to Oregon in the early 1870s, more families did so like the Joosten family members, from word received from other family and friends. It is known three of Joseph and Nellie's daughters, Frances, Johanna, and Jane decided to pick up their roots and made the journey to Oregon. The beautiful Tualatin Valley of the northwestern region of Oregon, just west of Portland, promised better soil for the crops. More than likely they all left Grand Chute at the same time, which is apparent from the following dates of marriage and children birth dates:

- ❖ Frances and her husband Walter Bernards were in Verboort, OR in 1888 when their second child Martin was born in December.
- ❖ Johanna and her husband Antone Hermens were in Verboort, OR in 1889 when they were married in June of that year.
- ❖ Jane and her husband Cornelius Hermens were in Verboort, OR in 1889 when they were married in November of that year.

Joosten Jos. 99a, 19, 18, Gr. Chute, Appleton.
Joosten Martin, 130a, 17, 18, Kau. Little Chute.
Joosten Walter, 70a, 8, Kau. Little Chute.

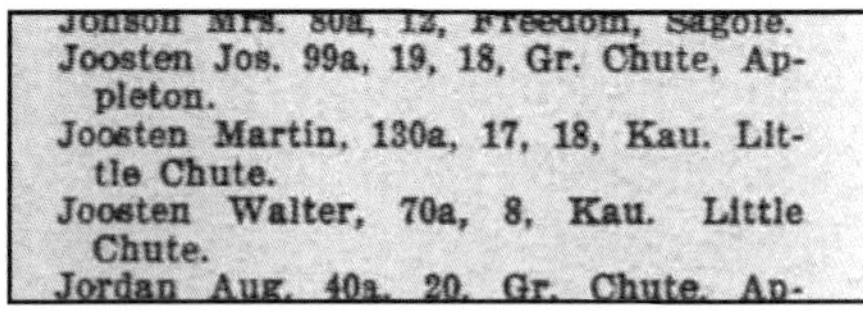

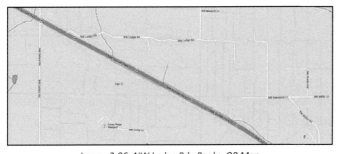

Image 3.05- 1897-1898 Outagamie County City Directory, page 344

Joseph, Nellie, and their youngest daughter Margaret would later follow their other three family members some years later out to Verboort, OR. It was not likely in the late 1880s since at the time the youngest four children were still at home and would have been too young to leave behind. For example, in 1890 Catherine was 18, Martin was 16, Christina was 14, and Margaret was only 10 years old; all besides Margaret would remain in Wisconsin as adults. There is some indication Joseph lived in Verboort, though it is possible Joseph traveled back and forth. Another interesting fact is Outagamie County issued the 1897-1898 city directory showing Joseph and family living in Grand Chute on their 99-acre farm. The number "19" shown is the township where the Joosten's lived in Grand Chute, and Appleton was the official post office for Grand Chute. My best guess is Joseph and Nellie "officially" moved out to Verboort around 1896, as mentioned in their daughter Margaret's obituary. On July 12, 1899 they purchased 40 acres from Antone and Gertrude Meeuwsen for $450. The legal description of this piece of land reads "the northeast quarter of the northeast quarter of section 30 of Township Two North and Range Three West", which is located two miles northeast of Banks, OR, and just north of the Sunset Highway (Hwy 26) today. Of course, back then the highway was not yet constructed; that would begin in 1933. So my belief is this property ran somewhere very close to the east-west stretch of NW Lodge road just before it turns north (see pictured map). In addition, I do not believe Joseph and Nellie lived on this property. They more than likely leased the land to a local farmer to farm the land. Then about a year later on May 29, 1900, they purchased one acre of land for $200 in Verboort. This property is said to lie on the corner of Porter and Verboort roads, and it is where they made their home.

Image 3.06- NW Lodge Rd., Banks, OR Map

What is interesting though is Joseph was captured in the 1900 census in Verboort and in Grand Chute. Joseph and Nellie were listed in the Verboort census with Margaret, and only Joseph was shown living with his son Martin in Grand Chute. In the Verboort census, Joseph is noted as owning his farm. The Grand Chute census reveals Martin is renting the farm he and his family are living on, presumably the 99-acre farm his parents owned. An interesting detail is found in the Verboort census relating to Nellie. The 1900 census asked the woman of the household how many children they gave birth to and how many are still living. In Nellie's case, the document shown reveals she had given birth to ten, but only eight were living. This is illustrated in the columns on the right side. As we know, Nellie and Joseph had nine children, and as mentioned in a later chapter their daughter Mary (Verhagen) passed away at the early age of 26 in 1895. But... what about the 10th child? My best guess is Nellie unfortunately must have lost a child at birth around 1878. The last two children born were Christina and Margaret. At this time Nellie was in her late 30s, a high-risk age for pregnancies. Christina was born in August 1876 and Margaret in April 1880, leaving a nearly four year gap in between the two children, especially when Nellie was giving birth to healthy and happy babies every 18 to 24 months. I believe this is where an infant baby was sadly lost. As a reference, the other columns show name, relationship to head of

Joosten Joseph	Head	W	M	Jan	1838	62	M	38			Holland
— Nellie	Wife	W	F	May	1840	60	M	38	10	8	Holland
— Margaret	Daughter	W	F	Apr	1880	20	S				Wisconsin

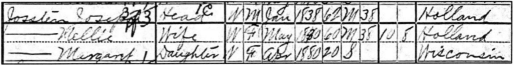

Image 3.07- 1900 Cornelius, Washington County, OR ED150, sheet 9B

household, race, gender, month and year of birth, age, marital status, years married, children born, children living, and place of birth.

Just before the turn of the century a historic moment arrived for the village of Little Chute. In 1899, Outagamie County was petitioned to grant the incorporation of Little Chute. The petition was approved and signed by Judge John Goodland on April 1st making Little Chute official; the quaint little community was now a Village. Elections were promptly held and John Kilsdonk was elected as the first President, John Hammen was voted in as Treasurer, and John DeBruin was chosen as the first Clerk (I think the town folk liked the name John ☺). More milestones continued to come to Little Chute which included the streetcar being extended more than likely from Appleton through the Village to Kaukauna in 1900, the Bank of Little Chute was incorporated in 1906, and the first newspaper came off of the presses as "The Valley Advocate" in 1920.

During this new decade of the new century, Joseph and Nellie were now well into their 60s. They continued to live in Verboort on Porter Rd., which is just a short walk from the Visitation Church. Back in Grand Chute, their son Martin moved west about 90 miles to the town of Rudolph in Wood County. In October 1906, Joseph and Nellie sold their Grand Chute farm to their daughter Catherine and her husband William Weyenberg. According to the land sales contract from Outagamie County, the 99-acre farm was sold for $9,500 with $2,000 down at closing with the remaining $7,500 payable over the next 15 years at 4% interest. Unfortunately at this time Joseph's health was starting to decline. He had developed cancer on his face, most likely as a result of all the sun he had taken in from his farming days. Back then we did not know the full extent of what the beautiful sun could do to our skin, and certainly sunscreen with 50 SPF had not been invented. Just as the new year of 1907 came, Joseph sadly passed away on January 9th; 12 days shy of his 70th birthday. Although Joseph's

> Joseph Jootsen died at his home in Verboot last week Wednesday of cancer, aged 69 years. The deceased went to Forest Grove from Wisconsin some ten years ago and was classed as one of the wealthiest and progressive farmers in Washington county, his wealth being estimated at $100,000. He left a wife and seven children.

Image 3.08- Obituary of Joseph Joosten. Published in the Hillsboro Independent, 01/18/1907, page 4.

death certificate has many fields left blank (death certificates were not required to be recorded by law until 1910), it does list an incorrect date of birth; the correct one is on his gravesite headstone, both are pictured below. It was just a few short years later when Nellie's health would get the best of her. And on October 26, 1911 at the age of 71 she sadly passed away.

Summary of Final Accounting of The Estate of Petronella Joosten	
➢ William Weyenberg Land Sale Contract ...	$6,656
➢ 16 Loans to Family and Friends ...	$4,351.99
➢ Cash from Bank ...	$1,066.66
➢ Sale of Buggy ...	$7.50
➢ Chickens and eggs ...	$3.85
Subtotal of Assets on Hand (+) ...	**$12,086**
➢ Martin Joosten ...	$1,752
➢ Jane and Cornelius Hermens ...	$1,749
➢ Charles and John Herb ...	$348
➢ John and Fred Narup ...	$252
➢ Scotia Developing Co. ...	$557
Loans to Others (+) ...	**$4,658**
➢ John M Wall, Attorney ...	$150
➢ Antone Hermens, Administrator ...	$50
➢ Inheritance Tax ...	$147
➢ Other Expenses ...	$299
Expenses (-) ...	**$646**
Total	**$16,098**

Of course at Joseph's death all of his possessions and assets went to his wife, but when Petronella (Nellie) passed away, she had no will. So it appears both of them did not formally plan how they wished their estates to be handled and distributed, and to my surprise their estate was quite large. As can be seen in Joseph's obituary pictured above someone estimated the value at $100,000; this may have been a little high. A probate was opened at the Washington County Courthouse for Petronella's estate, and fortunately I was able to obtain a copy of the 40-plus page document from the Oregon State Archives in Salem.

On November 11, 1911, Petronella's son-in-law Antone Hermens (husband of Johanna) was named as the Administrator of the estate by the probate court judge. Antone's first order of business was to inventory the possessions, list bank account assets, and sell real estate among many other tasks. Joseph and Nellie had loaned large sums of money to some of their children, which included the remaining balance of a loan note for the farm property in Grand Chute to their daughter Catherine and her husband William Weyenberg for $6,600.

The final accounting of the estate did not include personal possessions, like jewelry and china, and household furnishings, so the estate would have been valued much higher. Remarkably, with personal possessions excluded, the size of the estate was valued at a whopping $16,098. Now, this was a lot of money in 1911. And according to the Bureau of Labor's Consumer Price Index (CPI) calculator this tighty sum is worth $352,338 in today's dollars in 2010; quite a large amount of money and it is clear Joseph and Nellie worked hard for every penny. Displayed on the previous page is a summary of the final accounting as shown in Nellie's probate document. Interestingly, most of the Joosten assets were tied up in loans to family and a few friends totaling in excess of $15,000.

At the time of Nellie's death seven of her nine children survived her, while her eldest daughter Elizabeth (VanHandel) passed away on June 6, 1903 at the young age of 40, and Mary Verhagen (4th born) who passed away on March 25, 1895 at age 26 were both called to home to Heaven early. As mentioned earlier, Nellie died without a will so the probate court ordered her estate be split equally among all her nine children (or heirs), living or not, and so each would share one-ninth of the estate; this included the children of Elizabeth and Mary too. Sadly, during the process of settling the estate, Johanna (Hermens) passed away, so her one-ninth of her mother's estate was divided among her husband and nine children, as was the case for the children of Elizabeth and Mary; everything was split equally. Therefore each child or the heirs would each receive $1,788.75.

The probate court document detailed it this way:

> *"Frances Bernards; Jennie Hermens; Katie Weyenberg; Martin Joosten; Christine Verhagen; Margaret VanDyke, $1,788.75 each; one-ninth.*
>
> *To the eight children of Elizabeth VanHandel, deceased, Joseph, Mary, Cora, Christine, George, Martin, Albert Henry and Nellie VanHandel $223.60 each; one-eighth of one-ninth.*
>
> *To the two children of Mary Verhagen, deceased, Harry and Joseph Verhagen, $894.37 each; one-half of one-ninth.*
>
> *To the heirs of Anna M. Hermens, deceased, Antone Hermens, husband, $894.37 one-half of one-ninth; and to the children William M., Petronella, Pauline, Mary, Josephine, Martin, George, Christine and Ernest Hermens, $99.37 each; one-ninth of one-half of one-ninth."*

In March and April of 1913, Antone had each family member, who received money, sign a proof of payment document just like the one pictured that my 2nd great-grandmother Frances Bernards signed. Interestingly, for some unknown reason each person received a small sum less than what was ordered in the probate document. In Frances' case she received $1,785.50 instead of $1,788.75.

After a year and a half of settling Nellie's estate, and distributing the remaining cash assets to the family, Antone went back to the probate court to present the final accounting, and to have the estate closed. On April 29, 1913, the Honorable Judge D.B. Reasoner signed a court document thereby closing the estate.

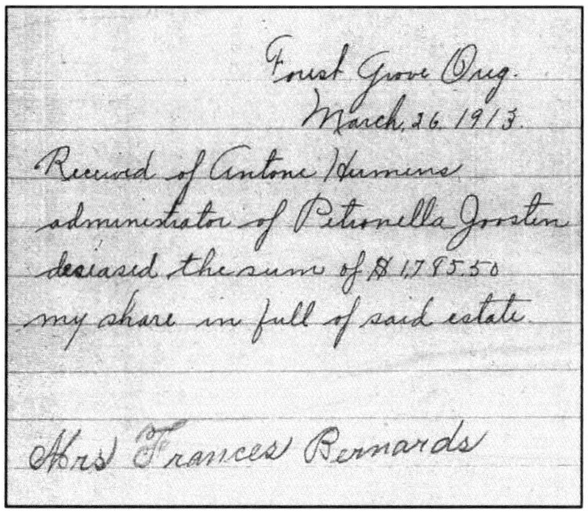
Forest Grove Oreg.
March 26. 1913.
Received of Antone Hermens
administrator of Petronella Joosten
deceased the sum of $1785.50
my share in full of said estate.

Mrs Frances Bernards

Image 3.09- Estate Proof of Payment Document Signed by Frances.

Remember, these were two remarkable people who endured weeks at sea as a young children, grew up facing the harsh winters of Wisconsin with meager shelter at best, raised nine children, and then blazed a trail to Oregon. It was Joseph who set out as a young man and journeyed south deep into the American land finding work in Louisiana. It was Joseph whose wonderful life story was told by a great author who felt compelled to include Joseph among other memorable Fox Valley pioneers in his book.

They leave behind seven of their nine children, and a whopping 86 grandchildren. What's better is Joseph and Nellie's legacy continues on with their 387 great-grandchildren. What an amazing large number of descendants. Both are buried in the beautiful and serene Visitation Catholic Cemetery in Verboort in the first row of the southeast section. An interesting life, in my book, filled with a legacy that continues to live on. May the good Lord continue to bless their souls as they rest in peace in Heaven.

☙ Photo and Image Gallery ❧

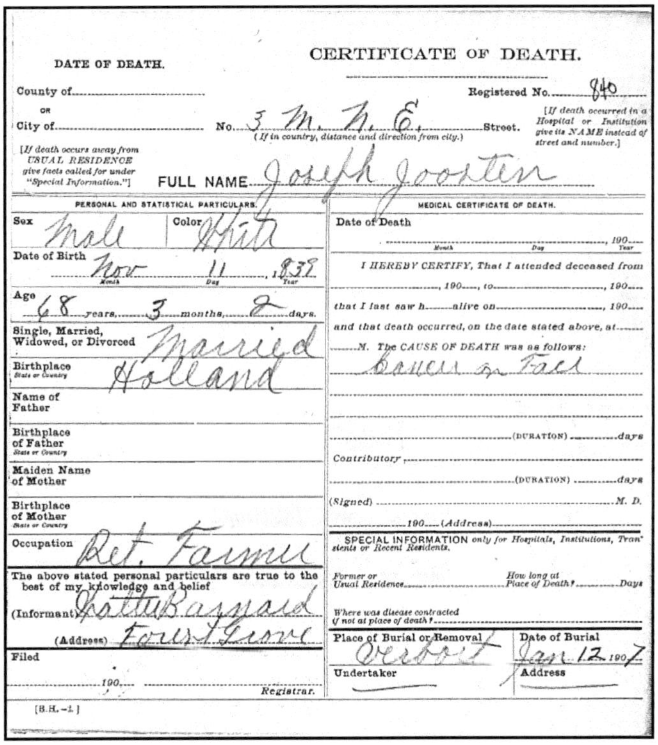

CERTIFICATE OF DEATH.

DATE OF DEATH.

County of............ Registered No. 840

OR

City of............ No. 3 M. N. E. ....Street. [If death occurred in a Hospital or Institution give its NAME instead of street and number.]

(If in country, distance and direction from city.)

[If death occurs away from USUAL RESIDENCE give facts called for under "Special Information."]

FULL NAME Joseph Joosten

PERSONAL AND STATISTICAL PARTICULARS.

Sex Male Color White

Date of Birth Nov 11 1838 (Month Day Year)

Age 68 years 3 months 2 days

Single, Married, Widowed, or Divorced Married

Birthplace (State or Country) Holland

Name of Father

Birthplace of Father (State or Country)

Maiden Name of Mother

Birthplace of Mother (State or Country)

Occupation Ret. Farmer

The above stated personal particulars are true to the best of my knowledge and belief

(Informant) Kattie Bernard

(Address) Forest Grove

Filed ....190.... ....Registrar.

MEDICAL CERTIFICATE OF DEATH.

Date of Death ...., 190.... (Month Day Year)

I HEREBY CERTIFY, That I attended deceased from ...., 190...., to ...., 190....

that I last saw h.... alive on ...., 190....

and that death occurred, on the date stated above, at ....M. The CAUSE OF DEATH was as follows:

Cancer on Face

............(DURATION) ....days

Contributory ....

............(DURATION) ....days

(Signed) ....M. D.

............190.... (Address)............

SPECIAL INFORMATION only for Hospitals, Institutions, Transients or Recent Residents.

Former or Usual Residence............ How long at Place of Death? ....Days

Where was disease contracted if not at place of death?............

Place of Burial or Removal Verboort | Date of Burial Jan 12 1907

Undertaker | Address

[B.H.—1.]

Image 3.10- Death Certificate of Joseph Joosten. Source: Oregon State Archives

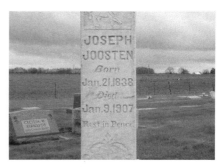

Image 3.11- Gravesite Headstone of Joseph Joosten

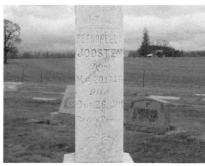

Image 3.12- Gravesite Headstone of Nellie Joosten (VanLanen)

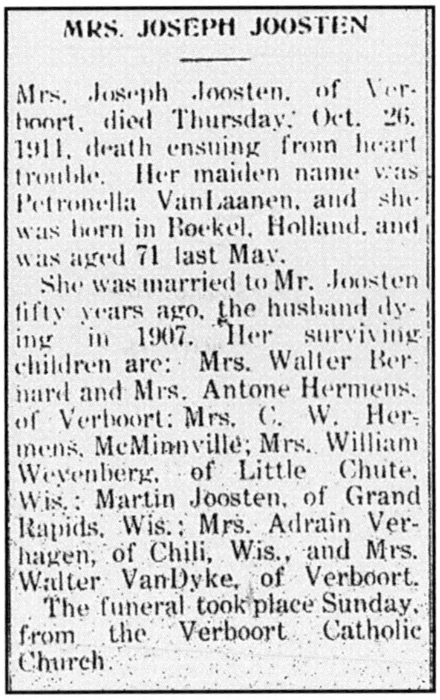

MRS. JOSEPH JOOSTEN

Mrs. Joseph Joosten, of Verboort, died Thursday, Oct. 26, 1911, death ensuing from heart trouble. Her maiden name was Petronella VanLaanen, and she was born in Boekel, Holland, and was aged 71 last May.

She was married to Mr. Joosten fifty years ago, the husband dying in 1907. Her surviving children are: Mrs. Walter Bernard and Mrs. Antone Hermens, of Verboort; Mrs. C. W. Hermens, McMinnville; Mrs. William Weyenberg, of Little Chute, Wis.; Martin Joosten, of Grand Rapids, Wis.; Mrs. Adrain Verhagen, of Chili, Wis., and Mrs. Walter VanDyke, of Verboort. The funeral took place Sunday, from the Verboort Catholic Church.

Image 3.13- Obituary of Nellie Joosten (VanLanen). Source: Hillsboro Argus; 11/02/1911, page 3

PATER NOSTER

PRAY FOR THE SOUL OF

JOSEPH JOOSTEN,

HUSBAND OF

PETRONELLA VAN LAANEN,

born at Gerven, Holland, January 21, 1838, and after timely receiving the last Sacraments died at Verboort, Washington Co., Oregon, January 9, 1907.

Blessed is the man that shall continue in wisdom and in his mind shall think of the all seeing eye of God. ECCLES. XIV, 22d.

He was a just and perfect man in his generations, he walked with God. From his childhood he was upright and fearing God, departing from evil and keeping his innocence.

The sweetest consolation taken to the grave is the thought of having been an irreproachable husband and father, a true friend who leaves for us an inheritance of christian virtues.

Beloved wife, death separates us now, but once we will live forever with Christ. My dear children, forget not the law of God, let your heart receive his words, keep his commandments and you shall live. Pray for me.

Good bye, you all, who loved me, that we may see again one another in Heaven at the feet of Jesus and Mary. ST. ALPH. DE LIG.

OUR FATHER; HAIL MARY!

HEYRMAN & SUYPERS, DE PERE, WIS.

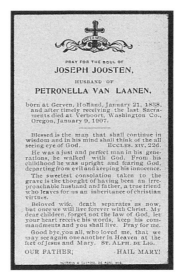

Image 3.14- Prayer Card of Joseph Joosten

PATER NOSTER

PRAY FOR THE SOUL OF

PETRONELLA VAN LAANEN,

WIFE OF

JOSEPH JOOSTEN,

born at Boekel, Holland, May 20, 1840, and after timely receiving the last Sacraments died at Verboort, Oregon, Oct. 26, 1911.

As she had learned from her early youth to fear God and to abstain from all evil, she persevered afterwards in a good and edifying life. JOB. 16-17.

She had looked well to the paths of her house, and hath not eaten her bread idle. PROV.

By her faith in God, her devotion to Mary, her devotedness to her family, her meekness towards all, she became a model for christian wives and mothers; therefore she will have the eternal reward with God in the glories of heaven.

Beloved husband, death separates us now, but once we will live forever with Christ. My dear children, forget not the law of God, let your heart receive his words, keep his commandments and you shall live. Pray for me

Jesus, Mary and Joseph, may I breathe forth my soul in peace with you. Amen. (300 days indulgence.)

Sweet Hearts of Jesus and Mary, be my refuge. 300 Days Indulgence.

Our Father. **Hail Mary.**

R. I. P.

HEYRMAN & SUYPERS, DE PERE, WIS.

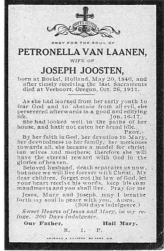

Image 3.15- Prayer Card of Petronella Joosten (VanLanen)

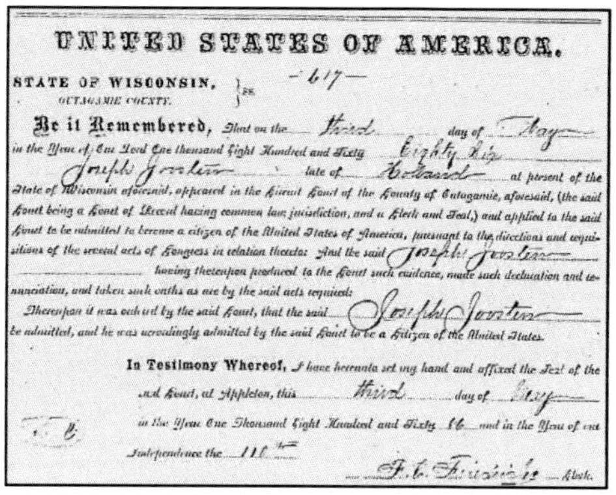

UNITED STATES OF AMERICA.

STATE OF WISCONSIN, } ss. -617-
OUTAGAMIE COUNTY. }

Be it Remembered, That on the third day of May in the Year of Our Lord One thousand Eight Hundred and Sixty Eighty Six Joseph Joosten late of Holland at present of the State of Wisconsin aforesaid, appeared in the Circuit Court of the County of Outagamie, aforesaid, (the said Court being a Court of Record having common law jurisdiction, and a Clerk and Seal,) and applied to the said Court to be admitted to become a citizen of the United States of America, pursuant to the directions and requisitions of the several acts of Congress in relation thereto: And the said Joseph Joosten having thereupon produced to the Court such evidence, made such declaration and renunciation, and taken such oaths as are by the said acts required:

Thereupon it was ordered by the said Court, that the said Joseph Joosten be admitted, and he was accordingly admitted by the said Court to be a Citizen of the United States.

In Testimony Whereof, I have hereunto set my hand and affixed the Seal of the said Court, at Appleton, this third day of May in the Year One Thousand Eight Hundred and Sixty 86 and in the Year of our Independence the 110th

F. C. Friedrich Clerk.

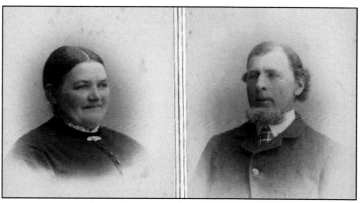

Image 3.16- Joseph Joosten Naturalization Document
Signed by Joseph May 03, 1886

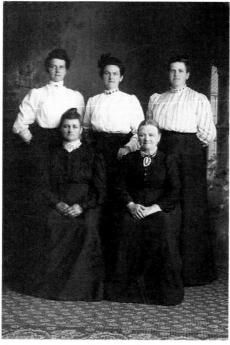

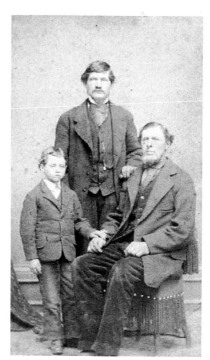

Image 3.17- Petronella and Joseph Joosten

Image 3.18- Petronella Joosten (VanLanen) with Four Daughters (L to R): Margaret VanDyke, Frances Bernards, Johanna Hermens, Petronella, Jane Hermens.

Image 3.19- Three Generations of Joostens (L to R): Joseph W., Martin, and Joseph about 1906

❧ Descendants of Joseph and Petronella Joosten ❧

Notes: 1= 1ˢᵗ generation, 2= 2ⁿᵈ generation, 3= 3ʳᵈ generation.

1   Joseph Joosten
     Born: January 21, 1838 in Nuenen, North Brabant, Holland
     Died: January 09, 1907 in Verboort, Washington County, Oregon
     Buried at: Visitation Catholic Cemetery, Verboort, OR; SE row 1
     Married: April 04, 1861 in Bay Settlement, Brown County, Wisconsin to
     Petronella VanLanen
     Born: May 20, 1840 in Boekel, North Brabant, Holland
     Died: October 26, 1911 in Verboort, Washington County, Oregon
     Buried at: Visitation Catholic Cemetery, Verboort, OR; SE row 1
     Parents: George VanLanen (1807-1882) and Anna Marie VandenElsen (1814-1879)

     2   Elizabeth Joosten
          Born: December 08, 1862 in Bay Settlement, Brown County, Wisconsin
          Died: June 06, 1903 in Little Chute, Outagamie County, Wisconsin
          Buried at: St. John Catholic Cemetery, Little Chute, WI, sec 4, row 2
          Married: July 03, 1882 in Little Chute, Outagamie County, Wisconsin
          Joseph VanHandel III
          Born: February 03, 1858 in Little Chute, Outagamie County, Wisconsin
          Died: January 26, 1936 in Little Chute, Outagamie County, Wisconsin
          Buried at: St. John Catholic Cemetery, Little Chute, WI, sec 4, row 2
          Parents: Judocus VanHandel (1774-1832) and Johanna Verstegen (1776-1845)

     2   Frances Joosten
          Born: June 12, 1864 in Little Chute, Outagamie County, Wisconsin
          Died: June 10, 1924 in Forest Grove, Washington County, Oregon
          Buried at: Visitation Catholic Cemetery, Verboort, Washington County, OR, SE row 2
          Married: July 03, 1882 in Little Chute, Outagamie County, Wisconsin
          Walter Bernards
          Born: April 29, 1858 in Reek, North Brabant, Holland
          Died: September 08, 1908 in Portland, Multnomah County, Oregon
          Buried at: Visitation Catholic Cemetery, Verboort, Washington County, OR, SE row 2
          Parents: Johannes Bernards (1812-1892) and Anna Vandenbroek (1814-1887)

     2   Johanna Marie Joosten
          Born: December 21, 1865 in Little Chute, Outagamie County, Wisconsin
          Died: December 10, 1912 in Oakland, Alameda County, California
          Buried at: Visitation Catholic Cemetery, Verboort, OR.
          Married: June 04, 1889 in Verboort, Washington County, Oregon to
          Antone Hermens
          Born: January 24, 1864 in De Pere, Brown County, Wisconsin
          Died: February 19, 1937 in Verboort, Washington County, Oregon
          Buried at: Visitation Catholic Cemetery, Verboort, OR.
          Parents: William Hermens (1830-1916) and Catharine N. Meulemans (1840-1911)

     2   Mary Joosten
          Born: June 08, 1868 in Bay Settlement, Brown County, Wisconsin
          Died: March 25, 1895 in Little Chute, Outagamie County, Wisconsin
          Buried at: St. John Catholic Cemetery, Little Chute, WI.
          Married: September 18, 1888 in Little Chute, Outagamie County, Wisconsin to

John Verhagen, Sr.
Born: December 22, 1866 in Little Chute, Outagamie County, Wisconsin
Died: 1935 in Little Chute, Outagamie County, Wisconsin
Buried at: St. John Catholic Cemetery, Little Chute, WI.
Parents: Henry Verhagen (1829-1873) and Henriette Van Hammond (1846-1871)

2   Jane Margaret Joosten
Born: March 31, 1870 in Little Chute, Outagamie County, Wisconsin
Died: October 16, 1940 in McMinnville, Yamhill County, Oregon
Buried at: St. James Catholic Cemetery, McMinnville, OR; 11 rows NE of Flag.
Married: November 30, 1889 in Verboort, Washington County, Oregon to
Cornelius William Hermens
Born: April 25, 1867 in Lawrence, Brown County, Wisconsin
Died: April 09, 1946 in McMinnville, Yamhill County, Oregon
Buried at: St. James Catholic Cemetery, McMinnville, OR; 11 rows NE of Flag.
Parents: William Hermens (1830-1916) and Catharine N. Meulemans (1840-1911)

2   Catherine Joosten
Born: February 28, 1872 in Grand Chute, Outagamie County, Wisconsin
Died: August 02, 1954 in Appleton, Outagamie County, Wisconsin
Buried at: St. John Catholic Cemetery, Little Chute, WI, sec 1, row 17.
Married: September 27, 1892 in Little Chute, Outagamie County, Wisconsin
William Henry Weyenberg
Born: February 26, 1865 in Grand Chute, Outagamie County, Wisconsin
Died: November 03, 1941 in Grand Chute, Outagamie County, Wisconsin
Buried at: St. John Catholic Cemetery, Little Chute, WI, sec 1, row 17.
Parents: Martin Weyenberg (1834-1908) and Ellen Maria Hayden (1837-1874)

2   Martin J. Joosten
Born: September 08, 1874 in Little Chute, Outagamie County, Wisconsin
Died: June 24, 1925 in Rudolph, Wood County, Wisconsin
Buried at: St. Phillip Catholic Cemetery, Rudolph, WI.
Married: September 21, 1897 in Little Chute, Outagamie County, Wisconsin to
Anna Marie Van Domelen
Born: July 02, 1872 in Oconto, Oconto County, Wisconsin
Died: June 29, 1950 in Rudolph, Wood County, Wisconsin
Buried at: St. Phillip Catholic Cemetery, Rudolph, WI.
Parents: William Van Domelen (1839-1893) and Mary VenRooy (1845-1926)

2   Christina Joosten
Born: August 07, 1876 in Little Chute, Outagamie County, Wisconsin
Died: December 23, 1931 in Fremont, Clark County, Wisconsin
Buried at: St. Stephen Catholic Cemetery, Chili, WI., row 3
Married: November 06, 1895 in Little Chute, Outagamie, Wisconsin
Adrian Henry Verhagen
Born: September 22, 1871 in Little Chute, Outagamie County, Wisconsin
Died: October 14, 1943 in Chili, Clark County, Wisconsin
Buried at: St. Stephen Catholic Cemetery, Chili, WI., row 3
Parents: Henry Verhagen (1829-1873) and Henriette VanHammond (1846-1871)

2 <u>Margaret Joosten</u>
Born: April 08, 1880 in Little Chute, Outagamie County, Wisconsin
Died: January 12, 1960 in Verboort, Washington County, Oregon
Buried at: Visitation Catholic Cemetery, Verboort, OR; SW row 3
Married: May 09, 1901 in Verboort, Washington County, Oregon
<u>Walter VanDyke</u>
Born: September 27, 1876 in De Pere, Brown County, Wisconsin
Died: October 08, 1940 in Verboort, Washington County, Oregon
Buried at: Visitation Catholic Cemetery, Verboort, OR; SW row 3
Parents: Theodore VanDyke (1847-1934) and Mary Ann Bernards (1846-1922)

⁊ Chapter Four ⤫

Elizabeth VanHandel

T he first bundle of joy came a little more than a year and a half after Joseph and Nellie were united in marriage. Their first born child Elizabeth was born on December 4, 1862 in Bay Settlement, WI located in Brown County. After the family moved west to Grand Chute, Elizabeth may have had some formal education, but probably not much back in those days. Since she was the oldest of the family much responsibility was given, and she was expected to assist in running the farm and household.

As Elizabeth reached her teen years I am sure she was helping her mother raise her youngest siblings. By the time she legally attained adulthood, she and a dashing man by the name of Joseph VanHandel had met.

Image 4.01- Elizabeth & Joseph VanHandel

At this time in the early 1880s, Joseph was living in Kaukauna working and earning his living on his parent's farm. Elizabeth's love for Joseph grew and at the young tender age of 19, they were united in marriage on July 3, 1882 at St. John Catholic Church in Little Chute. Also unique about this day was the fact that it was a double wedding. Elizabeth and Joseph were married alongside Elizabeth's next youngest sister Frances, who wed Walter Bernards. John Joosten served as best man and Dina VanHandel was maid of honor. John was a first cousin of Elizabeth and the son of Walter & Minnie Joosten. Dina was a younger sister of Joseph. Fr. Anthony Verberk was the celebrant of these nuptials. Please see page 71 for the marriage certificate and translation.

Joseph VanHandel III was born February 3, 1858 in Little Chute to his parents Joseph Jr. and Mary (Vandenheuvel). On a side note, Joseph's father and grandfather's names were also Joseph, and it appears they did not have middle names. So in order to distinguish who this author is referring to, the Joseph who is the spouse of Elizabeth I will refer to as "Joseph III".

Over the next six years three children were born to Elizabeth and Joseph III. The first born was a son named, true to VanHandel tradition, Joseph (referred to as Joseph IV) who was born July 10, 1883. He was the second grandchild of Joseph and Nellie. Next was Mary born January 10, 1885, and then Nellie who was born October 8, 1888. One may conclude Elizabeth may have experienced a miscarriage since there was more than three years in between the births of Mary and Nellie. Unfortunately, I feel it likely did happen given over the next 15 years eight more children were blessed to Elizabeth and Joseph each about two years apart; bringing a total of 11 children to the VanHandels. These next eight children were Martin, Cornelia (Cora), Martin John, Christine, George, Albert Henry, Petronella (Nellie), and finally Katherine born in 1903.

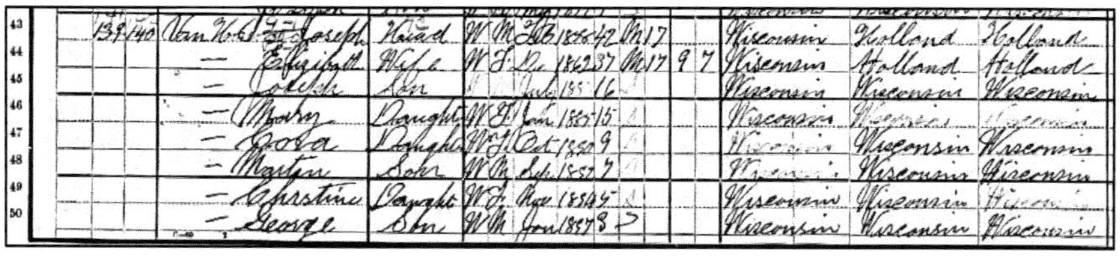

Image 4.02- 1900 Kaukauna, Outagamie County, WI Census, ED 89, sheet 9A

Sadly heartbreak struck the family with the loss of two children, both departing this life early in childhood. According to a reliable website source, the first to pass away was Martin, the fourth child, born in 1889 and died in 1892. Next was Nellie, the third child, who passed away in 1896 just a couple weeks shy of her eighth birthday. True to an old tradition, Joseph III and Elizabeth named their next born son and daughter after the children who passed away and this is why the family has two Martins and Nellies. The untimely deaths of the young children is confirmed in the 1900 census of Kaukauna as Elizabeth or Joseph III told the census taker they had nine children born to them, but only seven were living at the time. This census record also reveals the occupations of Joseph and his son Joseph IV as farmers. Even though Joseph IV was 16 years old at this time, it looks like he was out of school and working full time with his father. The document also shows the VanHandels owned their farm free and clear, which was good for them because most residents in the area had a mortgage. Their son Albert was not missed in the census; he was listed at the top of the next page (9B).

As previously mentioned Joseph III and Elizabeth welcomed their last child Katherine into this world on May 24, 1903, but something must have went horribly wrong with the birth. Poor little Katherine did not survive and passed away the same day. And then to make these dreadful matters worse, Elizabeth passed away just 13 days later at the young age of 40 (although her obituary says 42, this is not correct). What awful circumstances for this family to face. Now Joseph was faced to raise the rest of the children himself, four of which were under the age of ten. Mary was 18 at this time, unmarried, and must have been at home, so I would imagine she gave a willing helping hand to support her father raising her younger brothers and sisters. Elizabeth was laid to rest in the 2nd row of section four in the St. John Catholic Cemetery. May she be resting in peace in Heaven.

LITTLE CHUTE.

Mrs. Joseph Van Handel died here last Saturday at the age of 42, leaving a sorrowing husband and a large family of children to mourn her loss. Deceased was buried from St. John's church last Monday, followed by a large number of friends and relatives.

Image 4.03- Obituary of Elizabeth VanHandel from the Appleton Post-Crescent 06/13/1903, page 1.

By the year 1910, the family was still living on Holland Road in the Town of Vandenbroek and living near, or were next door neighbors to, the William Vandenheuvel and Henry Coenen families. George and Albert (now going by his middle name "Henry") were the only children living in the VanHandel household. Joseph IV was now out on his own and renting part of the farm owned by John Kreissen, which was next door to his uncle John VanHandel. But the interesting thing is Cora, Christine, and Nellie were living with Joseph IV, most likely helping him on his farm. What is not known though is where Mary and Martin were living. Mary was now 25 still unmarried, and old enough to be living on her own, but Martin was 17, so he was either missed when the census was taken or he was living with another relative.

It has been six years now since the passing of Elizabeth, and Joseph III made the decision to remarry. The lucky lady was Mary Hietpas (Ebben) who lost her first husband Peter Hietpas on March 21, 1902. Joseph and Mary were married on June 29, 1909, and his house was once again full of children because Mary brought with her her four children Albert, William, Bernard, and Annie. This brought the count to six children in the new VanHandel household, and Joseph III and Mary would add one more with the birth of their son Peter on March 20, 1911.

Just 11 months after Joseph III remarried, Joseph IV married Elizabeth Hietpas on May 5, 1910 in Little Chute. This was just the first of many weddings taking place over the next few years. Next was Cora who married John J. Hammen on June 17, 1913 in Little Chute, and then Mary who tied the knot with John H. Spierings on May 20, 1914 also in Little Chute. I imagine each of these weddings took place at St. John Catholic Church and was presided over by Rev. Theodore Knegtel. Sadly, Joseph III was not able to live out the rest of his days with his spouse, Mary passed away on September 30, 1913, only four years following their marriage. She was laid to rest in the 2nd row of the old section in St. John Catholic Cemetery.

A NARROW ESCAPE FROM DEATH

Mr. Joseph Van Handel, of Little Chute, Route 1, was badly injured last week and barely escaped being trampled to death by a bull which he was leading by a rope to water. The bull had always been of a gentle disposition and Mr. Van Handel was wholly unconscious of any danger when the bull suddenly turned on him, and threw him to the ground, breaking his leg and inflicting a number of bruises about the body.

Mr. Van Handel would have been killed without a doubt if he had not been fortunate enough to work his way to the stable door, crawl inside the barn and lock the door on the maddened animal.

The injured man was taken to the hospital where he received proper attention.

Image 4.04- Joseph VanHandel IV Accident, Kaukauna Times 05/12/1921, page 1

Following Mary's death, it is my guess Joseph III sold the farm he owned and operated for decades. Fortunately, he was able to keep the farm in the family by selling it to his eldest son Joseph IV and his wife Elizabeth. This theory is supported by the 1920 census when Joseph III was captured living in Little Chute on North Monroe St. He was now 62, retired, and had two sons Peter (age 9) and Henry (age 21) living with him in his house he owned free and clear. In addition, his daughter Mary Spierings, her husband John, and son Edward were also part of this household.

An interesting but frightening story comes out of the Kaukauna Times about one scary run-in Joseph IV had with one of his bulls. Since Joseph IV now owned the farm, and his father Joseph III lived in the city, I am fairly certain this article was written about Joseph IV. As written in the newspaper article pictured on the previous page, Joseph was leading the bull with a rope to water when suddenly the normally tame bull turned on him, throwing him to the ground and breaking his leg. He had the presence of mind to crawl inside the barn and lock the door before the bull inflicted further injury to him. After a trip to the hospital, I am sure he came out from the experience fine, other than a few bumps and bruises.

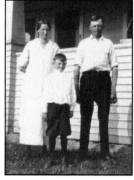

Image 4.05- John & Mary Spierings with Edward (1925)

As mentioned earlier, Mary married John Spierings in 1914. I learned from a very reliable source all but one of the babies blessed to them died as newborns, but were old enough to be baptized. The one surviving child was Edward Henry who was born February 20, 1917 in Little Chute. Edward was used to challenges in life, as a teen he regrettably lost both of his parents in the short span of two years. Following a lingering illness, Mary passed away on May 5, 1928 at the very young age of 43. John died even earlier in life, only reaching the age of 40. He died on May 20, 1930 in Appleton. John and Mary are buried side-by-side in the third row of section three of the St. John Cemetery.

Their son Edward grew to become a great public servant to the residents of Little Chute becoming one of the longest serving Village Presidents. His service to the Village began in 1962 when he was elected to a Trustee seat in the Village Board of Trustees; a position he held for three years. In 1965, Little Chute residents elected Edward as Village President, a title he retained for 16 years until he retired from the Board. Assuming each Board position had two year terms as they do today, Edward was re-elected to his seat eight times. During his presidency the Village experienced a boom in population and new housing, each increasing 40% and 60% respectively.

When 1930 rolled around, Henry was out of his father's house by this time. The 1930 census indicates Joseph III was still living on North Monroe Street in Little Chute with his son Peter, who was 18 at the time. He owned his home in Little Chute, and its estimated value was $3,500. Joseph's next door neighbors were Anton & Margaret Vandenheuvel on one side and Arnold & Annie VanAsten on the other.

Joseph Van Handle, 78, Dies at Little Chute

Special to Post-Crescent

Little Chute—Joseph Van Handle, 78, died Sunday evening at his home here after a short illness. Surviving are three daughters, Mrs. William Vanden Heuvel, Mrs. John Vanden Heuvel and Mrs. John J. Hammen, Little Chute; five sons, George and Peter, Little Chute; Joseph, Vandenbrock; Martin, Grand Chute; Henry, Freedom; two sisters, Mrs. Cornelius Ebben and Mrs. Henry Evers, Little Chute; three brothers, Albert, John and Martin, Little Chute. Twenty-nine grandchildren also survive. Funeral services will be conducted at 9 o'clock Wednesday morning at St. John church. A solemn requiem high mass will be sung by the Rev. John J. Sprangers assisted by the Rev. C. Luke Leiterman and the Rev. James Geyer. Members of the Senior Holy Name society of St. John church, of which the decedent was a member, will attend the funeral in a body. Burial will take place in the parish cemetery.

Image 4.06- Obituary of Joseph VanHandel III; Appleton Post-Crescent, 01/28/1936, page 15

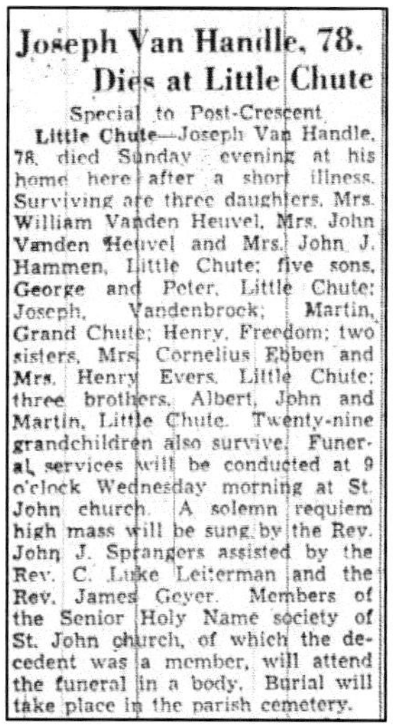

At the end of 1935, Joseph III's health condition was not the best. On January 26, 1936, Joseph departed this life and into the next after a short illness at the age of 77, only about a week shy of his 78th birthday. His funeral service was held at St. John Catholic Church, and he was buried next to his first wife Elizabeth in the 2nd row of section four in the St. John Cemetery.

In my research effort to find birth, death and burial locations of this family, when I came to Henry (Albert) VanHandel, the youngest son of Joseph III and Elizabeth. My curiosity was piqued when I saw Henry's death year was 1943. I thought maybe he was killed in action in World War II. But after finding no military records for Henry, tracing his path became a little more challenging as to why he died in 1943 at the young age of 43. After following up on a lead he was buried at St. Joseph Catholic Cemetery in Appleton, I was given confirmation that indeed he was buried there when I located his grave marker, which included the day he passed away. Next, I started looking through microfilm of the Appleton Post-Crescent and found an article about Henry reporting his tragic demise. The February 24th edition gave details of how Henry was at a tavern in Apple Creek and used the tavern owner's truck to take a friend home. It was very late at night, and somewhere along County Road E the truck he was driving broke down. It was an early model truck with a hand crank on the front of the vehicle to turn over the engine in order to start it. The newspaper article reveals Henry mistakenly left the truck in gear and when he turned the hand crank the truck rolled over him. After Henry did not return to the tavern, the tavern owner must have gone out looking. What he found was an awful scene; Henry was pinned under a wheel of the truck. The injuries were just too severe and Henry passed away that night on February 23rd. Henry was never married, did not have any children, and lived in Freedom as a farmer. He was laid to rest in section J of the St. Joseph Cemetery.

Elizabeth and Joseph left a wonderful legacy in their wake. Of their 11 children, the next generation brought 31 grandchildren, and dozens of great-grandchildren.

There were a large number of good men and women of the VanHandel Family who served our fine country in the military. They are:

- Orville J. Bongers - Captain in the Medical Service Corp US Army in World War II.
- Carl W. Hammen – Private First Class US Army in Korea.
- Eugene M. Hammen – Storekeeper (SK2) US Coast Guard in Korea.
- Roger J. Hammen - Sergeant US Army in World War II.
- Theodore L. Heid - Served as a Corporal in the US Marine Corps during World War II.
- Harold H. Vandenheuvel - Sergeant US Army in World War II.
- John T. Vandenheuvel - Sergeant E5 US Army in Vietnam, 1st Calvary Airmobile Division during Tet Offensive. Bronze Star Medal recipient.
- Leo J. Vandenheuvel - Private First Class US Marine Corp in World War II.
- George J. VanHandel - Private US Army Battery E 68th Field Artillery in World War I.
- Martin J. VanHandel - Private Company A, 150th Machine Gun Battalion, US Army in World War I.
- Robert J. VanHandel – Technician Fifth Grade (TEC 5) US Army in World War II in South Pacific
- Robert E. Woldt - Served in the US Navy.

❧ **Photo and Image Gallery** ❧

Image 4.07- John and Cora Hammen Family (l to r):
Barbara, Grace, Marian, Roger, Gordon, Eugene, John,
Jane, Cora, Carl, and Elizabeth

Image 4.08- Edward H. Spierings Family in 1964 (l to r):
Back: Virgie, Helen, Jack, Mary, Janice.
Front: Lois, Marjorie, Edward, Jim.

Image 4.09- Gravesite headstone of Joseph (III) & Elizabeth VanHandel
and Joseph (IV) & Elizabeth VanHandel. St. John Catholic Cemetery,
section 4, row 2.

Image 4.10- John and Petronella
(VanHandel) Vandenheuvel Wedding
Photo in 1919

Image 4.11- Joseph & Elizabeth VanHandel Homestead about 1906.

Image 4.12- Joseph & Elizabeth VanHandel Children about 1910

❧ Descendants of Elizabeth & Joseph VanHandel ❧

Notes: 1= 1ˢᵗ generation, 2= 2ⁿᵈ generation, 3= 3ʳᵈ generation.
The year of birth is only given for individuals still living, if known.

1   Elizabeth Joosten
    Born: December 04, 1862 in Bay Settlement, Brown County, Wisconsin
    Died: June 06, 1903 in Little Chute, Outagamie County, Wisconsin
    Buried at: St. John Catholic Cemetery, Little Chute, WI, sec 4, row 2
    Married: July 03, 1882 in Little Chute, Outagamie County, Wisconsin
    Joseph VanHandel III
    Born: February 03, 1858 in Little Chute, Outagamie County, Wisconsin
    Died: January 26, 1936 in Little Chute, Outagamie County, Wisconsin
    Buried at: St. John Catholic Cemetery, Little Chute, WI, sec 4, row 2
    Parents: Joseph VanHandel, Jr. (1810-1895) and Mary Vandenheuvel (1828-1913)

    2   Joseph J. VanHandel IV
        Born: July 10, 1883 in Little Chute, Outagamie County, Wisconsin
        Died: March 04, 1974 in Little Chute, Outagamie County, Wisconsin
        Buried at: St. John Catholic Cemetery, Little Chute, WI, sec 4, row 2
        Married: May 25, 1910 in Little Chute, Outagamie County, Wisconsin
        Elizabeth Hietpas
        Born: February 10, 1890 in Little Chute, Outagamie County, Wisconsin
        Died: April 10, 1966 in Little Chute, Outagamie County, Wisconsin
        Buried at: St. John Catholic Cemetery, Little Chute, WI, sec 4, row 2
        Parents: Arnold Alphonse Hietpas (1864-1923) and Mary VanGompel (1867-1934)

        3   Josephine VanHandel
            Born: February 16, 1911 in Town of Vandenbroek, Outagamie County, Wisconsin
            Died: April 20, 2002 in Appleton, Outagamie County, Wisconsin
            Buried at: St. Nicholas Catholic Cemetery, Freedom, WI.
            Married: November 19, 1936 in Little Chute, Outagamie County, Wisconsin
            Martin A. VanAsten
            Born: July 20, 1911 in Freedom, Outagamie County, Wisconsin
            Died: December 11, 2003 in Little Chute, Outagamie County, Wisconsin
            Buried at: St. Nicholas Catholic Cemetery, Freedom, WI.
            Parents: Henry J. VanAsten (1887-1969) and Caroline Daul (1886-1974)

        3   Edward J. VanHandel
            Born: February 02, 1912 in Town of Vandenbroek, Outagamie County, Wisconsin
            Died: March 29, 1997 in Appleton, Outagamie County, Wisconsin
            Buried at: St. John Catholic Cemetery, Little Chute, WI, sec 8, row 3
            Married: November 25, 1937 in Freedom, Outagamie County, Wisconsin
            Helena Blanche VanAsten
            Born: March 31, 1910 in Freedom, Outagamie County, Wisconsin
            Died: August 23, 1982 in Appleton, Outagamie County, Wisconsin
            Buried at: St. John Catholic Cemetery, Little Chute, WI, sec 8, row 3
            Parents: Henry J. VanAsten (1887-1969) and Caroline Daul (1886-1974)

        3   Cora R. VanHandel
            Born: February 15, 1913 in Town of Vandenbroek, Outagamie County, Wisconsin
            Died: October 17, 1996 in Little Chute, Outagamie County, Wisconsin
            Buried at: St. John Catholic Cemetery, Little Chute, WI.
            Married: Never married

3   Anna Isabella VanHandel
Born: May 21, 1914 in Town of Vandenbroek, Outagamie County, Wisconsin
Died: May 11, 2010 in Outagamie County, Wisconsin
Buried at: St. John Catholic Cemetery, Little Chute, WI, sec 4, row 4
Married: July 10, 1934 in Little Chute, Outagamie County, Wisconsin
Joseph J. Paalman
Born: September 22, 1909 in Utrecht, Utrecht Province, Netherlands
Died: October 08, 1961 in Little Chute, Outagamie County, Wisconsin
Buried at: St. John Catholic Cemetery, Little Chute, WI, sec 4, row 4
Parents: Henry T. Paalman (1888-1979) and Anna Marie VandenWyngaard (1885-1945)

3   Martha Marie VanHandel
Born: August 30, 1915 in Town of Vandenbroek, Outagamie County, Wisconsin
Died: July 25, 2014 in Ogdensburg, Waupaca County, Wisconsin
Buried at: Highland Memorial Park Cemetery, Appleton, WI.
Married: June 15, 1939 in Little Chute, Outagamie County, Wisconsin
Raymond R. Woldt
Born: March 13, 1916 in Appleton, Wisconsin
Died: August 25, 2008 in Appleton, Wisconsin
Buried at: Highland Memorial Park Cemetery, Appleton, WI.
Parents: Herman Woldt (1890-1952) and Hulda Plamann

3   Four infant children died at birth or in infancy named Richard (about 1918), Theodore (about 1921), Barbara (about 1923), and Raymond (about 1925).

3   Barbara VanHandel
Born: Between 1928 and 1929 in Wisconsin
Died: Living
Buried at:
Married: Unknown
Gene Sprague
Born: Unknown
Died: Living
Buried at:
Parents: Unknown

3   Earl J. VanHandel
Born: April 04, 1931 in Vandenbroek, Outagamie County, Wisconsin
Died: September 21, 2009 in Appleton, Outagamie County, Wisconsin
Buried at: St. John Catholic Cemetery, Little Chute, Wisconsin
Married: April 22, 1952 in Freedom, Outagamie County, Wisconsin
Audrey Regina Gerrits
Born: June 19, 1931 in Little Chute, Outagamie County, Wisconsin
Died: January 31, 1988 in Little Chute, Outagamie County, Wisconsin
Buried at: St. John Catholic Cemetery, Little Chute, Wisconsin
Parents: John Peter Gerrits (1898-1990) and Geraldine Mueller (1903-1963)

3   Raymond J. VanHandel
Born: 1935 in Vandenbroek, Outagamie County, Wisconsin
Died: Living
Buried at:
Married: Unknown

Margaret C. Ulrich
Born: 1937
Died: Living
Buried at:
Parents: Kenneth J. Ulrich (1912-1989) and Johanna W. Stienen (1914-1981)

2   Mary VanHandel
Born: January 10, 1885 in Town of Vandenbroek, Outagamie County, Wisconsin
Died: May 05, 1928 in Little Chute, Outagamie County, Wisconsin
Buried at: St. John Catholic Cemetery, Little Chute, WI, sec 3, row 2[
Married: May 20, 1914 in Little Chute, Outagamie County, Wisconsin
John H. Spierings
Born: May 05, 1890 in De Pere, Brown County, Wisconsin
Died: May 20, 1930 in Appleton, Outagamie County, Wisconsin
Buried at: St. John Catholic Cemetery, Little Chute, WI, sec 3, row 2
Parents: Henry Spierings (1849-1906) and Bernadina Meggelaars (1858-1909)
   Note: Mary and John had numerous babies born who died in childhood. Edward was their only
child who lived into adulthood.

   3   Edward Henry Spierings
Born: February 20, 1917 in Little Chute, Outagamie County, Wisconsin
Died: October 20, 2000 in Appleton, Outagamie County, Wisconsin
Buried at: St. John Catholic Cemetery, Little Chute, WI, sec 3, row 2
Married (1): June 06, 1939 in Wrightstown, Brown County, Wisconsin
Married (2): 1975
Marjorie Rose Berken (1)
Born: August 13, 1918
Died: March 10, 1974 in Little Chute, Outagamie County, Wisconsin
Buried at: St. John Catholic Cemetery, Little Chute, WI, sec 3, row 2
Parents: Hubert Berken (1888-1934) and Virginia Ann Milton (1892-1964)
Dorothy G. (Luedtke) King (2)
Born: July 13, 1916
Died: December 27, 2009 in Appleton, Outagamie County, Wisconsin
Buried at: Holy Cross Catholic Cemetery, Kaukauna, WI
Parents: Edward King (1889-1971) and Margaret Skahen (1893-1986)

   3   Gerald Spierings
Born: 1923
Died: in childhood
Buried at: Unknown
Married: n/a

2   Nellie VanHandel
Born: October 08, 1888 in Town of Vandenbroek, Outagamie County, Wisconsin
Died: September 18, 1896
Buried at: Unknown
Married: n/a

2   Martin VanHandel
Born: 1889
Died: 1892
Buried at: St. John Catholic Cemetery, Little Chute, WI
Married: n/a

2   Cornelia (Cora) VanHandel
    Born: October 02, 1890 in Little Chute, Outagamie County, Wisconsin
    Died: February 04, 1946 in Little Chute, Outagamie County, Wisconsin
    Buried at: St. John Catholic Cemetery, Little Chute, WI, sec 1, row 5
    Married: June 17, 1913 in Little Chute, Outagamie County, Wisconsin
    John J. Hammen
    Born: May 05, 1888 in Little Chute, Outagamie County, Wisconsin
    Died: March 20, 1951 in Little Chute, Outagamie County, Wisconsin
    Buried at: St. John Catholic Cemetery, Little Chute, WI, sec 1, row 5
    Parents: Joseph Hammen (1856-1896) and Georgiana Vandehey (1857-1939)

    3   Barbara Georgiana Hammen
        Born: on March 26, 1915 in Little Chute, Outagamie County, Wisconsin
        Died: September 10, 1997 in Appleton, Outagamie County, Wisconsin
        Buried at: St. John Catholic Cemetery, Little Chute, WI, sec 2, row 3
        Married: August 05, 1944 in Little Chute, Outagamie County, Wisconsin
        Orville J. Bongers
        Born: March 12, 1916 in Little Chute, Outagamie County, Wisconsin
        Died: February 09, 2012 in Little Chute, Outagamie County, Wisconsin
        Buried at: St. John Catholic Cemetery, Little Chute, WI, sec 2, row 3
        Parents: Henry W. Bongers (1883-1972) and Petronella Bergman (1887-1958)

    3   Elizabeth Josephine Hammen
        Born: February 15, 1917 in Little Chute, Outagamie County, Wisconsin
        Died: August 22, 2010 in Appleton, Outagamie County, Wisconsin
        Buried at: St. John Catholic Cemetery, Little Chute, WI, sec 2, row 3
        Married: November 15, 1980 in Little Chute, Outagamie County, Wisconsin
        Joseph Roman VanThiel
        Born: September 08, 1918 in Little Chute, Outagamie County, Wisconsin
        Died: October 18, 1987 in Little Chute, Outagamie County, Wisconsin
        Buried at: St. John Catholic Cemetery, Little Chute, WI, sec 2, row 3
        Parents: Theodore A. VanThiel (1894-1954) and Harriet M. Wydeven (1895-1973)

    3   Grace Theodora Hammen
        Born: 1919
        Died: Living
        Buried at:
        Married: October 08, 1949 in Little Chute, Outagamie County, Wisconsin
        Elmer J. Hoffman
        Born: November 14, 1921 in Grantsburg, Burnett County, Wisconsin
        Died: July 19, 1997 in Little Chute, Outagamie County, Wisconsin
        Buried at: St. John Catholic Cemetery, Little Chute, WI.
        Parents: Anton Joseph Hoffman (1907-1965) and Virginia Joan Hager (1914-1999)

    3   Marian Martha Hammen
        Born: 1922
        Died: Living
        Buried at:
        Married: June 14, 1947 in in Little Chute, Outagamie County, Wisconsin

Harold H. Vandenheuvel
Born: March 22, 1924 in Little Chute, Outagamie County, Wisconsin
Died: October 20, 2010
Buried at: St. John Catholic Cemetery, Little Chute, WI, sec 10, row 6
Parents: John H. Vandenheuvel (1897-1969) and Gertrude Williamson (1898-1955)

3   Roger John Hammen
Born: May 15, 1926 in Little Chute, Outagamie County, Wisconsin
Died: May 10, 1987 in Little Chute, Outagamie County, Wisconsin
Buried at: St. John Catholic Cemetery, Little Chute, WI, sec 2, row 3
Married: July 14, 1954 in New Holstein, Calumet County, Wisconsin
Betty A. VanderPutten
Born: 1930
Died: Living
Buried at:
Parents: Theodore VanderPutten and Ann Smits

3   Gordon Leonard Hammen
Born: 1927
Died: Living
Buried at:
Married: November 06, 1952 in Little Chute, Outagamie County, Wisconsin
Margaret Verstegen
Born: 1929
Died: Living
Buried at:
Parents: Lester A. Verstegen (1903-1962) and Margaret Brill (1906-1984)

3   Carl William Hammen
Born: August 18, 1929 in Little Chute, Outagamie County, Wisconsin
Died: March 08, 1997 in Little Chute, Outagamie County, Wisconsin
Buried at: St. John Catholic Cemetery, Little Chute, WI, sec 2, row 3
Married: Did not marry

3   Eugene Martin Hammen
Born: July 30, 1931 in Little Chute, Outagamie County, Wisconsin
Died: June 21, 2002 in Little Chute, Outagamie County, Wisconsin
Buried at: St. John Catholic Cemetery, Little Chute, WI, sec 2, row 3
Married: June 03, 1961 in Oshkosh, Winnebago County, Wisconsin
Josephine Steckbauer
Born: 1936
Died: Living
Buried at:
Parents: William J. Steckbauer (1900-1974) and Mary Binder (1904-1962)

3   Jane Mary Hammen
Born: 1931
Died: Living
Buried at:
Married: Did not marry

2   Martin John VanHandel
     Born: September 16, 1892 in Kaukauna, Outagamie County, Wisconsin
     Died: October 25, 1957 in Appleton, Outagamie County, Wisconsin
     Buried at: St. John Catholic Cemetery, Little Chute, WI, sec 4, row 2
     Married: October 21, 1919
     Mary Johanna Berghuis
     Born: December 29, 1895 in Combined Locks, Outagamie County, Wisconsin
     Died: October 30, 1973 in Appleton, Outagamie County, Wisconsin
     Buried at: St. John Catholic Cemetery, Little Chute, WI, sec 4, row 2
     Parents: Bernard John Berghuis (1860-1930) and Petronella Marie Vanderaa (1870-1953)

        3   Robert J. VanHandel
             Born: October 10, 1920 in Appleton, Outagamie County, Wisconsin
             Died: November 08, 1988 in Appleton, Outagamie County, Wisconsin
             Buried at: St. John Catholic Cemetery, Little Chute, WI, sec 8, row 4
             Married: October 19, 1946
             Marion L. Vandehey
             Born: January 14, 1923 in Kimberly, Outagamie County, Wisconsin
             Died: July 11, 1999 in Appleton, Outagamie County, Wisconsin
             Buried at: St. John Catholic Cemetery, Little Chute, WI, sec 8, row 4
             Parents: Martin Vandehey (1890-1978) and Esther Lang (1895-1932)

        3   Harold Aloysius VanHandel
             Born: May 26, 1922 in Grand Chute, Outagamie County, Wisconsin
             Died: November 12, 1994 in Appleton, Outagamie County, Wisconsin
             Buried at: Highland Memorial Park Cemetery, Appleton, WI.
             Married: Unknown
             Jule VanDinter
             Born: 1928 in Milwaukee, Milwaukee County, Wisconsin
             Died: Living
             Buried at:
             Parents: Peter J. VanDinter (1898-1967) and Bessie C. Halloran (1898-1997)

        3   Theresa E. VanHandel
             Born: February 26, 1924 in Grand Chute, Outagamie County, Wisconsin
             Died: December 07, 2003 in Freedom, Outagamie County, Wisconsin
             Buried at: St. Nicholas Catholic Cemetery, Freedom, WI.
             Married: Unknown
             Norbert A. Techlin
             Born: 1923 in Freedom, Outagamie County, Wisconsin
             Died: Living
             Buried at:
             Parents: Otto Techlin (1882-1967) and Hattie Krueger (1881-1948)

        3   Donald J. VanHandel
             Born: July 04, 1926 in Grand Chute, Outagamie County, Wisconsin
             Died: January 09, 1994 in Appleton, Outagamie County, Wisconsin
             Buried at: Highland Memorial Park Cemetery, Appleton, WI.
             Married: Unknown

Joan Witt
Born: 1932 in Wisconsin
Died: Living
Buried at:
Parents: Robert Witt (1890-1948) and Myrtle McFaul (1895-?)

3   Rosemary VanHandel
Born: July 13, 1929 in Grand Chute, Outagamie County, Wisconsin
Died: July 08, 1992 in Mackville, Outagamie County, Wisconsin
Buried at: St. Edward Catholic Cemetery, Mackville, WI.
Married: Unknown
Delmar Edward Schmeichel
Born: 1930 in Grand Chute, Outagamie County, Wisconsin
Died: Living
Buried at:
Parents: Harold F. Schmeichel (1907-1964) and Rosanna Winters (1905-1985)

3   Richard B. VanHandel
Born: 1932
Died: Living
Buried at: St. Joseph Catholic Cemetery, Appleton, WI, section N, row 3
Married: May 29, 1954
Alice A. Woods
Born: 1931
Died: Living
Buried at: St. Joseph Catholic Cemetery, Appleton, WI, section N, row 3
Parents: Michael L. Woods (1894-1961) and Cecelia M. Thompson (1896-1990)

2 Christine VanHandel
Born: November 08, 1894 in Little Chute, Outagamie County, Wisconsin
Died: June 22, 1981 in Little Chute, Outagamie County, Wisconsin
Buried at: St. John Catholic Cemetery, Little Chute, WI, sec 6, row 3
Married: May 01, 1918 in Little Chute, Outagamie County, Wisconsin
William A. Vandenheuvel
Born: January 26, 1897 in Little Chute, Outagamie County, Wisconsin
Died: April 20, 1974 in Little Chute, Outagamie County, Wisconsin
Buried at: St. John Catholic Cemetery, Little Chute, WI, sec 6, row 3
Parents: Anton Vandenheuvel (1860-1938) and Margaret Vosters (1865-1935)

3   Margaret Elizabeth Vandenheuvel
Born: July 18, 1918 in Little Chute, Outagamie County, Wisconsin
Died: February 02, 1998 in Appleton, Outagamie County, Wisconsin
Buried at: St. John Catholic Cemetery, Little Chute, WI, sec 3, row 1
Married: Unknown
Cleborne A. Vandervelden
Born: May 29, 1917 in Kimberly, Outagamie County, Wisconsin
Died: April 29, 1983 in Kimberly, Outagamie County, Wisconsin
Buried at: St. John Catholic Cemetery, Little Chute, WI, sec 3, row 1
Parents: Peter Vandervelden (1887-1927) and Hattie Van Hammond (1885-1976)

3   Leo John Vandenheuvel
Born: September 04, 1920 in Little Chute, Outagamie County, Wisconsin
Died: February 06, 1991
Buried at: Holy Name Catholic Cemetery, Kimberly, WI, sec 1, row 25
Married: April 24, 1946
Dolores G. Harrison
Born: March 04, 1923 in Lena, Oconto County, Wisconsin
Died: September 04, 2006 in Appleton, Outagamie County, Wisconsin
Buried at: Holy Name Catholic Cemetery, Kimberly, WI, sec 1, row 25
Parents: Alphonse Harrison (1886-1965) and Ida Gerondale (1891-1926)

3   Theodora Ann Vandenheuvel
Born: February 22, 1922 in Little Chute, Outagamie County, Wisconsin
Died: December 22, 1995 in Kimberly, Outagamie County, Wisconsin
Buried at: Holy Name Catholic Cemetery, Kimberly, WI.
Married: January 22, 1948 in Los Angeles, Los Angeles County, California
Theodore Louis Heid
Born: March 11, 1922 in Appleton, Outagamie County, Wisconsin
Died: January 14, 2000 in Kimberly, Outagamie County, Wisconsin
Buried at: Holy Name Catholic Cemetery, Kimberly, WI.
Parents: Theodore L. Heid (1888-1938) and Rose Elizabeth Rossmeissl (1892-1990)

3   Alice May Vandenheuvel
Born: June 17, 1927 in Little Chute, Outagamie County, Wisconsin
Died: February 26, 1963 in Little Chute, Outagamie County, Wisconsin
Buried at: St. John Catholic Cemetery, Little Chute, WI, sec 7, row 2
Married: Unknown
Paul H. Hermsen
Born: 1927
Died: Living
Buried at:
Parents: George M. Hermsen (1888-1969) and Johanna M. Gloudemans (1889-1991)

3   Mary Jane Vandenheuvel
Born: 1929 or 1930 in Little Chute, Outagamie County, Wisconsin
Died: Living
Buried at:
Married: May 11, 1950 in Little Chute, Outagamie County, Wisconsin
Cornelius Anthony Verbruggen
Born: June 13, 1927 in Little Chute, Outagamie Co, Wisconsin
Died: May 04, 2001 in Pickerel, Langlade County, Wisconsin
Buried at: St. John Catholic Cemetery, Little Chute, WI
Parents: Henry F. Verbruggen (1891-1971) and Caroline M. VanRhijn (1893-1946)

3   Joan Margaret Vandenheuvel
Born: 1936 or 1937 in Little Chute, Outagamie County, Wisconsin
Died: Living
Buried at:
Married: June 21, 1958 in Little Chute, Outagamie County, Wisconsin

Joseph W. Verbrick
Born: November 01, 1935 in Keshena, Menominee County, Wisconsin
Died: October 16, 2009 in Little Chute, Outagamie County, Wisconsin
Buried at: St. John Catholic Cemetery, Little Chute, WI
Parents: Willard C. Verbrick (1900-1957) and Grace R. Doyle (1908-2004)

2 George J. VanHandel
Born: January 27, 1897 in Town of Vandenbroek, Outagamie County, Wisconsin
Died: March 14, 1969 in Little Chute, Outagamie County, Wisconsin
Buried at: St. John Catholic Cemetery, Little Chute, WI, sec 4, row 2
Married: May 06, 1918
Mary VanDyke
Born: April 21, 1894 in Wrightstown, Brown County, Wisconsin
Died: April 27, 1976 in Little Chute, Outagamie County, Wisconsin
Buried at: St. John Catholic Cemetery, Little Chute, WI, sec 4, row 2
Parents: Matthew J. VanDyke (1868-1952) and Petronella VanDyke (1869-1955)

2 Albert Henry VanHandel
Born: March 31, 1899 in Little Chute, Outagamie County, Wisconsin
Died: February 23, 1943 in Appleton, Outagamie County, Wisconsin
Buried at: St. Joseph Catholic Cemetery, Appleton, WI, section J, lot 53
Married: Never married

2 Petronella (Nellie) VanHandel
Born: May 24, 1901 in Little Chute, Outagamie County, Wisconsin
Died: November 09, 1988 in Little Chute, Outagamie County, Wisconsin
Buried at: St. John Catholic Cemetery, Little Chute, WI, sec 6, row 3
Married: December 29, 1919
John A. Vandenheuvel
Born: November 01, 1894 in Little Chute, Outagamie County, Wisconsin
Died: December 23, 1965
Buried at: St. John Catholic Cemetery, Little Chute, WI, sec 6, row 3
Parents: Anton Vandenheuvel (1860-1838) and Margaret Vosters (1865-1935)

2 Katherine VanHandel
Born: May 24, 1903
Died: May 24, 1903
Buried at: Unknown
Married: n/a

❧ Chapter Five ❧

Frances Bernards

At the start of the summer season, in the small village of Bay Settlement, Wisconsin along the beautiful shores of Lake Michigan, Frances was the second born to her parents Joseph and Nellie on June 12, 1864. First a little side note of disclosure for the record, since birth certificates were not required to be filed with the State of Wisconsin back then, there is an anomaly with the year of Frances' birth. Different sources from books to websites list her year of birth as 1863 or 1864. Her death certificate lists her year of birth as 1864, as given by her son Martin, the informant, but her gravestone is engraved with 1863. So based on the best information I have at the writing of this book, I will list Frances' year of birth as 1864. This also fits with the date of birth with her older sister Elizabeth, which is December 4, 1862. So if Frances was born in 1863, there would have only been six months difference in age between the two, which really is not possible, especially back in those days.

Now with our facts straight, let's talk more about Frances. She is my 2nd great-grandmother, and was the second of nine children to this budding family of girls with just one boy. In this image of the 1880 census,

Image 5.01- 1880 Grand Chute, Outagamie County, WI ED126, sheet 21

the family lived in Grand Chute, which borders Appleton, WI. At age 16, Frances was not shown as attending school. An 8th grade education was typical in that day and then you went to work on your parent's farm; as I am sure that was the case with Frances since her father was a farmer.

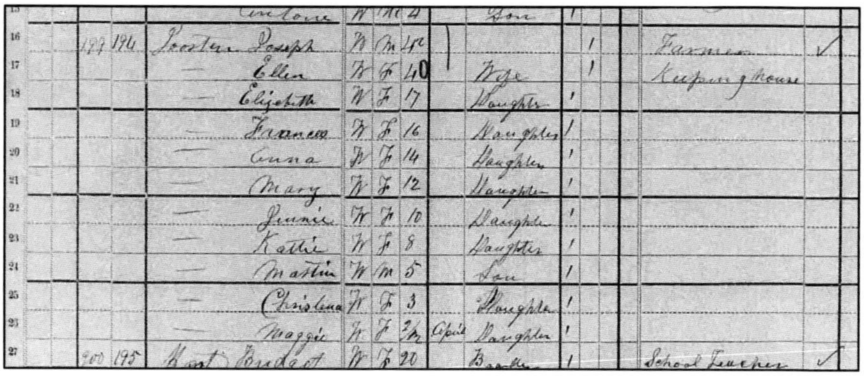

A wonderful man by the name of Walter Bernards entered into Frances' life. Love was in the air. And as mentioned in the previous chapter, Frances' older sister Elizabeth and her fiancé Joseph VanHandel agreed a double wedding would be a joyous occasion. Both couples were married on July 3, 1882 in Little Chute at the St. John Catholic Church. Fr. Anthony Verberk presided over the jubilant ceremony with Peter Schumacher and Anna Joosten standing in as the witnesses. Walter Bernards was born on April 29, 1858 in Reek, North Brabant, Holland and came to the United States aboard the SS United Kingdom with his family on April 29, 1867. At age 22, he is shown with his parents, John and Anna, in the 1880 Wisconsin census living in DePere, Brown County.

During a visit I made to Little Chute in 2008, I made a noble effort to locate Frances and Walter's marriage certificate, but unfortunately, I was not able to track it down. The Outagamie and Brown County courthouses had no trace or recording of either Frances' or Elizabeth's marriage; vital recordings of births, marriages, and deaths were not yet required by law. Then during another trip to Little Chute in 2012, I learned there was a double wedding at St. John Church. After making a search request for the marriage record from St. John with the Archdiocese of Green Bay, I was elated when the Archivist confirmed with me he had found it (see image 5.24 in the Photo & Image Gallery). How wonderful it is these precious records have been preserved for so long; microfilm is a godsend for us genealogists. Back in those days all of the sacramental records were written in Latin by the priest. Fr. Verberk recorded marriages in the same book and separated them by date, so

Frances' and Elizabeth's marriages appear on the same page. Of the amount of research required to develop a body of work such as this, this discovery was one of the best and most meaningful for me.

But wait, there is another delightful story to go along with these marriages. It all starts in 2011 when I first made contact with Anne Weiland (Bongers), a 3rd cousin-once removed of mine.

You might be asking yourself, why is this significant? Well, Frances and Elizabeth each received a beautiful covered compote dish from their parents as a wedding gift. Amazingly, this compote dish was then handed down in each family through multiple generations. One day Anne sent me an email with a photo of the compote dish asking if I knew of a matching dish that was also in her hands. She had heard through passed down stories two compote dishes were in existence. Anne's aunt Betty VanThiel (Hammen) inherited the dish even though she was not the oldest child in VanHandel family. My best guess is Betty inherited it from her mother Cornelia Hammen (VanHandel). Although Elizabeth passed away in 1903, I believe the dish remained in the Joseph's possession. Then unfortunately Cornelia's oldest sister, Mary Spierings (VanHandel), passed away in 1928, and Cornelia may have inherited the coveted dish after her father's death in 1936 since she was the next oldest child in the family.

After receiving Anne's email and photo I wondered if my family had this treasured family heirloom because my great-grandmother Anna was the oldest daughter of the Bernards family, my grandmother Minnie was the oldest daughter of the Vanderzanden family, and my father was an only child. Well, come to find out an identical compote dish had also made it down from generation to generation in my family too! It has been sitting in my Mom's china hutch all these years and we did not even know what kind of treasure we had on our hands. It is very beautiful and cherished all the more knowing its history. These two compote dishes, typically used for holding fruit, nuts, or candy, have a slight pink hue in the glass, and as can be seen in the picture, there is a lion on top of the cover and one etched into the glass on its base. How amazing these two priceless 130-year old heirlooms still exist today.

In ten months following their marriage, Frances and Walter welcomed their first child into their family. Anna Marie was born on May 5, 1883 in Appleton, Wisconsin. Anna was Joseph and Nellie's first grandchild. Then in the late-1880s, as mentioned in chapter three, the Bernards family decided to pick up their roots and make a long journey west just as both sets of their parents did, except this would be over land rather than the vast Atlantic Ocean. As previously mentioned Frances and Walter moved out to Oregon and landed in Verboort in Washington County. Along for the ride were Johanna and Jane Joosten, younger sisters of Frances. It is my belief Walter heard just how great Oregon was from his older brother Theodore. Theodore and his wife Catherine relocated to Cornelius, Oregon which is just a few miles south of Verboort. It is believed Theodore's family made the long trek from Wisconsin between the births of their first two children. This point is supported by their first child, John W., who was born in Wisconsin in September 1878, and their second child, Anna C., who was born in Oregon in May 1880. It is not known how exactly these families made their journey or what the traveling accommodations were. Other stories have been written of families boarding a train to San Francisco, and then a steamer ship from San Francisco north up the Pacific Ocean, then up the Columbia River to Portland, and finally by horse drawn wagon to the Verboort area. It is likely the Bernards and the young Joosten girls made their journey by these means. It is here in Verboort where Walter and Frances farmed the land and added onto their family. Over the next 18 years, nine more children would be blessed to them. They are Martin Joseph, Josephine Petronella, Martin John, Margaret Mary, Wilhelmina Frances, William August, Cecilia Marie, Christina Rosalia, and Frances Marie.

In the middle and late 1880s Frances and Walter were renting some farm land in the Verboort area, and purchased and sold their first farm southwest of Greenville. In 1899, the growing family purchased 167.70 acres less than one mile southeast of the Visitation Catholic Church in Verboort, on what today is NW Martin Rd., from F.J. Stapleton. This huge farm was located in the NE corner of the Silas Jacob Niles Beeks Donation Land Claim (DLC) #79, which lies in section 29 of Township 1 north, Range 3 west (the well-known Henry Black DLC is adjacent to the north of the Beeks DLC). The farm touched the SE corner of the Henry Black DLC, the Theodore M. Bernards (Walter's brother) farm to the west, and the J. Butts DLC #63 to the south. I have learned that this beautiful home was entered into the National Register of Historic Places in March 1984 because of its fine and rare early Oregon architecture. The property owner at the time, Gary Senko, filed the nomination form. This nomination form provides many excellent details about this home the Bernards lived in for decades. The home was originally built by Mr. Beeks in 1848 as a one-story, two room, timber framed structure. Beeks was a horse breeder and racer, and even had a race track on his property. In 1860, a 1½-story Carpenter Gothic style farmhouse, inspired by an Andrew Jackson Downing design, was built that incorporated the existing structure, and increased the total square footage to 2,172 sq. ft. The new house was built with a steep pitched roof with a large dormer in the center of the front-side roof that has a pointed arch door opening up onto a balcony enclosed by a wooden railing above a large front porch. The body of this house was painted in a muted yellow with white trim, which was common in Downing style homes. Sometime around 1908 the home was remodeled and a double chimney located in the center of the home was removed, leaving a single chimney on the right side of the house.

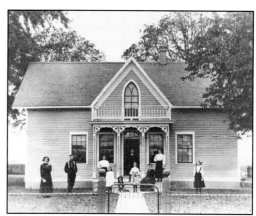

Image 5.02- Bernards Family in front of their home on NW Martin Rd., Verboort

The property also had interesting outbuildings. There was a water tower, which Walter built around 1900; a machine shed, which was partly used as a pig sty, and is believed to have been built prior to 1900; a smokehouse; and an aviary used to house canaries, constructed about 1910. It seems as though the Bernards family loved canaries, how interesting.

There is a popular photo of the Bernards family in front of their Verboort home, and it appears to have been taken around 1910. The picture was submitted to the National Register of Historic Places, and is the feature snapshot for the house. The oldest daughter, Anna, is not pictured in this photo, but interestingly there is a gentleman standing on the steps of the farmhouse. Story has it, handed down from generation to generation this gentleman is Herman Ostermann, a hired hand of the family. The others pictured left to right are: Josephine, Martin, Wilhelmina, Frances, Christina, Frances (seated), Margaret, and Cecilia.

At some point most of the acreage was sold off to other buyers from the family members who inherited their portion of the large farm. According to Washington County Assessment & Taxation records the two-story historic residence, with the address 3869 NW Martin Rd., remains on 1.61 acres, and is owned (ironically) by Silas Beeks, LLC.

13	369	378	Bernards Walter	Head	W	M	Apr	1858	42	M	18			Holland	Holland	Holland
14			—— Frances	Wife	W	F	June	1864	35	M	18	8	7	Wisconsin	Holland	Holland
15			—— Anna	Daughter	W	F	May	1883	17	S				Wisconsin	Holland	Wisconsin
16			—— Josephine P.	Daughter	W	F	Nov	1890	9	S				Oregon	Holland	Wisconsin
17			—— Martin J.	Son	W	M	May	1892	8	S				Oregon	Holland	Wisconsin
18			—— Maggie M.	Daughter	W	F	Apr	1894	6	S				Oregon	Holland	Wisconsin
19			—— Minnie	Daughter	W	F	Nov	1895	4	S				Oregon	Holland	Wisconsin
20			—— William	Son	W	M	Apr	1897	3	S				Oregon	Holland	Wisconsin
21			—— Cecilia	Daughter	W	F	Dec	1898	1	S				Oregon	Holland	Wisconsin

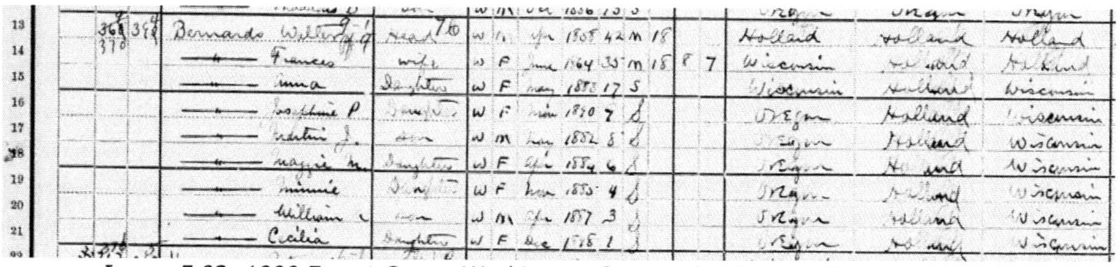

Image 5.03- 1900 Forest Grove, Washington County, OR Census ED 155, page 17A

The Bernards family was enumerated in the 1900 Forest Grove census. Verboort residents were written in with city of Forest Grove since Verboort is just a couple of miles north of Forest Grove. At this time, the Bernards family lived next door to the Peter Hermens family who also came from Wisconsin and are of Dutch descent. From my experience with census records, what was common in smaller towns and communities was for families to live next to or near other families of the same religion or having emigrated from the same country. I know there were other families of Dutch descent in Verboort during this period of time, but they did not live near the Bernards family. It just shows that Verboort was diverse in the country of origin of its great residents.

At this time during the turn to the new century, the census record shows Walter as a farmer, and he had been in the United States for 33 years after obtaining his citizenship in 1867. Anna was 17 and at home, and not going to school, while Josephine, Martin, and Margaret are shown as attending school. Of course the youngest three children were not yet of school age. By now you may have noticed that Martin Joseph (the first Martin born) is not listed with the family in the 1900 census pictured. Sadly, Martin passed away as a newborn on January 28, 1889, only one month old. This, I believe, just added to the family's grief after years of trouble Frances had with her newborn children. An indication of this comes from the 1910 census. This particular census

Image 5.04- Headstone of William A. Bernards at Visitation Cemetery

year required an interesting piece of information. Each mother listed how many children were born, and how many were still living. Well, in Frances' case she stated that she had 13 children born, and sadly only 8 were living. By looking the dates of birth of the children, early in the marriage of Walter and Frances there was a gap of 5½ years in between Anna, the 1st born, and Martin the 2nd born. So it appears there were more than likely other newborn babies to the Bernards family who sadly perished. But after Josephine was born in 1890, Walter and Frances were blessed many more healthy children.

Among these healthy children at birth was a bouncing baby boy named William August born on January 19, 1897. Heartbreak would strike the Bernards family again, and tragically William passed away on December 07, 1900, just a month shy of his fourth birthday. His loving parents buried "Willie" in the Visitation Catholic Cemetery, and he is located in the 2nd row of the northwest section.

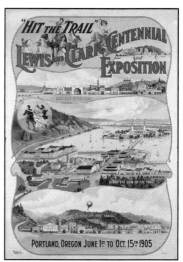

As the Bernards family said goodbye to the 19th century and hello to the 20th century, nearby Portland was conceiving plans to host the 1905 World's Fair. Oregon's most populous city at the time was of course the hub of all activity whether economic, advanced medicine, or entertainment. The city had a solid track record of economic growth since its incorporation in 1845. But with the decision to host the Fair it would take Portland to new heights and growth never seen before. The idea was to commemorate the centennial of when Lewis and Clark stayed in Portland toward the end of their journey. As seen in the poster pictured, Portland branded the World's Fair as "Hit the Trail, the Lewis and Clark Centennial Exposition".

The setting for the Fair was at Guild's Lake (pronounced "guile"), which no longer exists but was in northwest Portland and just yards away from the Willamette River; today Hwy 30 runs next to what used to be Guild's Lake. The 250 acre lake was a marsh from the collection of rainwater run-off from the west hills of Portland and overflow from the Willamette River. Brilliant landscaping began on a 400-acre site that included building exhibition halls on a bluff overlooking Guild's Lake creating an ominous scene. The backdrop of the green west hills of the city with the white exhibition hall produced a splendid sight Portland's Mayor George H. Williams called *"a diamond set in a coronet of emeralds"*. It was the first such celebration held in a Western state.

The four-and-a-half month long extravaganza ran from June 1st to October 15th, and attracted anywhere from 1.5 million visitors to twice that; interesting when census records show the population of Portland only had 100,000 citizens at the turn of the century. I am certain the Bernards, and other families like the Vanderzandens, the Joostens, the Vandeheys, the Jesses, and many other families from the Verboort and Roy communities made their way into Portland to attend the World's Fair. The spectacular event met one its long term goals and increased recognition of the city, which contributed to a doubling of the population of Portland, from 90,426 in 1900 to 207,214 in 1910.

A couple of years after the World's Fair of Portland ended, heartbreak entered the Bernards family again with the death of another family member. This time it was not another child, but the father of the family, and I am sure his death was very heart-wrenching. As we know by now, Walter was a farmer. On this fateful day in September 1908, Walter and his hired hands were harvesting the clover crop when something with the clover huller machine went wrong.   According to Walter's obituary, he *"climbed up on the huller to fix it, when he slipped in some manner and fell* (into the machine)*, his right leg getting into the machinery".*   Well, as you can imagine what followed was an awful sight, Walter's leg was in mangled critical condition, and the crisis of this incident must have been terribly harrowing for all involved.   I cannot imagine there were phones to call the doctor at this time out in Verboort, but as the story in his obituary unfolds, doctors from Forest Grove and Hillsboro were rushed to the scene.   This must have taken a very long time, and certainly Walter must have lost a lot of blood by the time the doctors arrived.   Walter was transported to St. Vincent's Hospital in Portland by train where his right leg was amputated the next day.   Sadly the loss of blood and the shock to his body proved to be too much for Walter and he passed away just two days after the surgery on September 08, 1908.

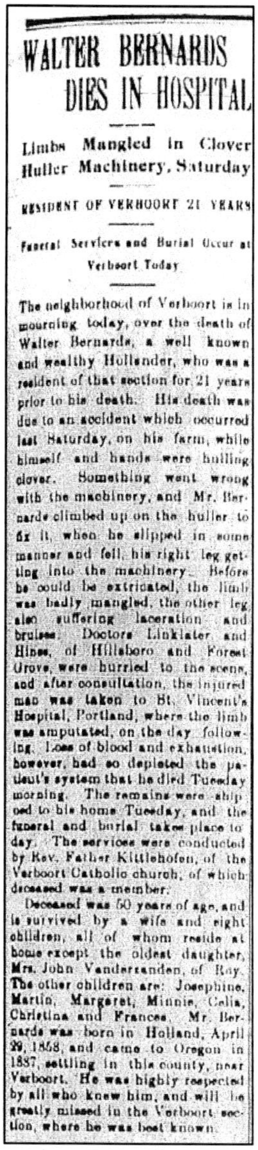

Image 5.05- Obituary of Walter Bernards

As mentioned earlier, Walter was born in Reek, North Brabant, Holland, the fifth child blessed to his parents John and Anna (Vandenbroek) Bernards.   Walter and his family came to America, and first landed in DePere, WI before coming out to Oregon.   The man who was my 2nd great-grandfather lived only a short 50 years, and his passing came so tragically.   He was laid to rest in the 2nd row of the southeast section of the Visitation Catholic Cemetery in Verboort.   May Walter rest in peace in Heaven with the Lord.

In 1910, the federal census captured the Bernards family living in Washington County in the city of Cornelius, though I believe the family did not move, my presumption is Verboort was just part of the enumeration district of Cornelius similar to what it was with Forest Grove back in 1900.   The census shows the family at the time lived next to Frances' sister Margaret VanDyke. Frances' mother, Nellie Joosten, was living with them along with a 24-year old boarder by the name of John Weyland, who is listed as a farmer and most likely was hired to tend to the farm since Walter had recently passed away.   Also nearby was the John and Cornelia Peters family.   Cornelia was the sister-in-law of Jane Hermens, Frances' sister.   Definitely a small world, but in the small communities around Cornelius and Verboort everyone knew everyone.   At this time, all the children were still at home with the exception of Anna, my great-grandmother, who was married to John Vanderzanden in 1903, and they were living in Roy.   And when the next census came around ten years later in 1920, the oldest and the youngest of the kids were at home, while the middle two daughters, Margaret and Minnie were now out on their own.   Martin was now 27 years old, and was at home doing the farming with the help of Martin J. Jansen, who was 22 years old at the time and is shown earning a wage from Martin.   The census also reveals Martin as the "employer" of the farm, and his sister Christina as taking care of the housework.   The other two children in the home, Cecilia and Frances Marie, were attending school.   At this moment in time, Frances was 56 years old and must have needed assistance around the home and farm to keep it operating efficiently. I think the reason for this was mostly because her diabetes condition had taken its toll on her body, which she had now for the better part of 10 years.

Having diabetes in the early 1900s was pretty much like receiving a death sentence.   The statistics for survival were grim since insulin had not yet been invented.   The average duration of life of a person with diabetes was only about five years.   The numbers also show that a diabetic coma was responsible for all juvenile diabetic deaths, and about 70% of adult diabetic deaths.   Frances had clearly been blessed and beaten the odds, and was one of the lucky few.   People with diabetes could only control the condition through their diet by eliminating all sugars and starches.   This type of diet was very low in calories, so low most diabetics lost weight if there was too much physical activity.   Therefore work and activities were limited to slow the burn of calories.   So this makes sense that Christina was still at home taking care of home and farm since Frances could probably no longer continue the extra physical work required.

Although insulin had been invented in 1921 by two doctors in Canada, I do not believe this groundbreaking medicine made its way down to Verboort to help Frances. Unfortunately her condition continued to worsen, and it appears living on the farm became too much of a burden. Washington County Courthouse records reveal she purchased a residence at 310 4th St. South in Forest Grove from D.C. & Mabel Giltner on October 25, 1920 for $1,800. The size of the lot was the typical 50ft x 100ft as seen inside the city.

The next task was to try to locate the actual house to see if it was still standing. A degree of difficulty was apparent from the beginning of my quest because numbered streets in Forest Grove were "streets" and "avenues" that intersected one another. For instance, 4th St. South intersected with 4th Ave. To my dismay, the 310 4th St. South address no longer exists. To make matters more complicated, in 1950 Forest Grove renamed some of the numbered city streets. Through a reliable source at the City of Forest Grove, I was able to obtain a conversion chart of sorts, and so we now know that 4th St. South is "Douglas St.", 3rd Ave is currently "17th Ave.", and 4th Ave. was renamed to "16th Ave". So the old address from 1920 is more than likely to be located on Douglas St. between 16th and 17th avenues.

A true treasure coming from the Bernards family is this portrait of the family. Though it is unknown exactly when it was taken, my best guess would to be around 1910 because noticeably Walter is not in the photo, and the youngest girl, Frances, cannot be older than seven or eight years of age (based on her size), and she was born in 1903. To help you identify who is pictured in this portrait, starting with the front row, from left to right are Frances Marie, Frances, Christina, and Cecilia. And in the back row are Margaret, Josephine, Martin, Anna, and Wilhelmina (Minnie); though not being able to confidently identify Margaret and Josephine, they could be interchanged.

Image 5.06- Bernards Family Portrait, taken about 1910

Given the details I have written about from the 1920 census, there is some significance in the timing of the decision by Frances to move away from the farm and three of her children feeling comfortable to move forward with their lives and get married. Frances was mother of the bride or groom three times in a short span of just one year. Martin tied the knot with Angelena Duyck on September 29, 1920; Frances was wed to Edward VanLom on January 12, 1921; and Josephine was married to William Lepschat on August 31, 1921. Whew!! That must have been a lot of planning for Frances to be involved in. Bear in mind when the three siblings were married Martin was 28, Frances was 17, and Josephine was 31. It certainly was not common for people to marry in their late 20s or in their 30s. As you can well imagine, it took many people to run a farm. My feeling is since Martin was running the farm, Josephine more than likely felt obligated to pitch in to help him and care for their mother. And then after their mother was moved to Forest Grove Martin, Frances and Josephine then felt free to marry. Thankfully Frances was able to experience all of her children getting married; that is those who did (Christina and Cecilia did not marry).

Image 5.07- Minnie and Edward Sohler Wedding Portrait, September 12, 1917

All the recent happy nuptials though started a few years earlier with Wilhelmina (Minnie) when she was married to Edward Sohler on September 12, 1917. Edward was the son of Gabriel and Mary (Cop) Sohler, and part owner of the Banks Garage with his brother Tony. In the wonderful portrait shown of the happy couple and their wedding party, Minnie is seated with Edward standing to her right. The best man was obviously one of Edward's brothers, though I am uncertain which one; he had many brothers, and the resemblance between the two is remarkable. The matron of honor may have been Minnie's sister Josephine, and unfortunately the two young ladies on the left

Frances & Walter Bernards

hand side of the picture are unknown.

As we all know when the year 1917 came around, World War I was in full swing in Europe with Germany declaring war on United States allies, such as Britain and France, and invading these countries. On April 2, 1917 President Woodrow Wilson asks Congress for a declaration of war against Germany, arguing that *"the world must be made safe for democracy."* On April 6, 1917, the United States declared war against Germany, which soon set the stage for the first wave of the draft for men ages 21 to 31; those born between June 6, 1886 and June 5, 1896. These brave men were required to register by June 5, 1917. At this time Edward was 25 years old, which made him the prime age for the draft. Well, Edward also had two brothers who met the age requirements for the draft. So Edward and his brothers Anthony (27) and John (23) went down to the office in Banks, OR and carried out their duty by completing their registration cards (Edward's signed draft card is pictured). The following year two more waves of the war draft were enacted by Congress with required sign up dates of June 5, 1918 and September 12, 1918. The second draft was for those men who had turned age 21 since the first draft registration, and the third for men ages 18 to 21 and 31 to 45. This act of Congress incredibly swept up four more Sohler brothers, Wendelin (36), Henry (33), William (21) and George (19) into the draft registration. I mention this phenomenon because this was truly a "band of brothers." And how these men's parents must have felt at the time by having seven of their sons drafted into the war and potentially go into harm's way. Since Armistice Day occurred on November 11, 1918 we can safely assume the latter-drafted Sohler brothers never saw action. John did see action as a Private First Class (PFC) in Company F of the 8th Infantry of the US Army, and it is not known if Anthony saw action or not; neither his obituary nor his gravesite headstone mentions military service.

104 REGISTRATION CARD No. 54

1 Edward Sohler 25
2 Banks Ore
3 September 25th 1892
4 Natural-born
5 Verbourt Oregon U.S.
6
7 Mechanic
8 Sohler Bros
Banks Ore.
9 None
10 Single Caucasian
11 No
12 No

Edward Sohler

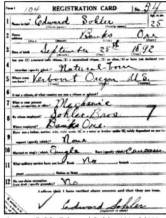

Image 5.08- Edward Sohler World War 1 Draft Registration Card

Within months after his marriage, Edward was called to duty and soon enlisted in the US Army to fight for his country. He started his training at Benson Polytechnic in Portland, and in August 1918 was shipped out for additional training at Camp Zachary Taylor in Louisville, KY. At this time, the flu epidemic was sweeping across this nation, and descended upon Louisville and unfortunately did not spare Edward. He soon contracted the flu which turned into pneumonia, and tragically he passed away on October 20th. What a heartbreaking situation for the Sohler and Bernards families. Minnie was now a widow after only one year of marriage, and to add to the sorrow Edward also leaves behind his newborn son Stanley who was born just two weeks after Edward left for Louisville. Sadly, Edward probably never got to meet his son. After Edward's body was transported home, he was laid to rest in the Visitation Catholic Cemetery in Verboort in the second row of the southeast section.

MRS. WALTER BERNARD

Mrs. Walter Bernard died at her home in Forest Grove, Jun 10.

Mrs. Bernard was born at Little Chute, Wisconsin, June 12, 1864. Her husband died at Verboort in 1908.

The following children survive: Mrs. J. M. Vanderzanden of Roy, Mrs. F. W. Lepschat of Forest Grove, Martin Bernard of Verboort, Miss Margaret Bernard of North Dakota, Mrs. E. Sohler of Forest Grove, Cecelia and Christine at home, Mrs. E. VanLom of Forest Grove.

Of her immediate family she is survived by the following sisters and brother: Mrs Walter Van-Dyke of Verboort, Mrs. C. W. Hermens of McMinnville, Mart'n Josten, Mrs. E. Verhagen and Mrs. W. Weyenberg, all of Wisconsin.

Mrs. Bernard was a woman of splendid character and beloved by all who knew her.

Image 5.09- Obituary of Frances Bernards (Joosten), Hillsboro Argus, 06/12/1924, page 5

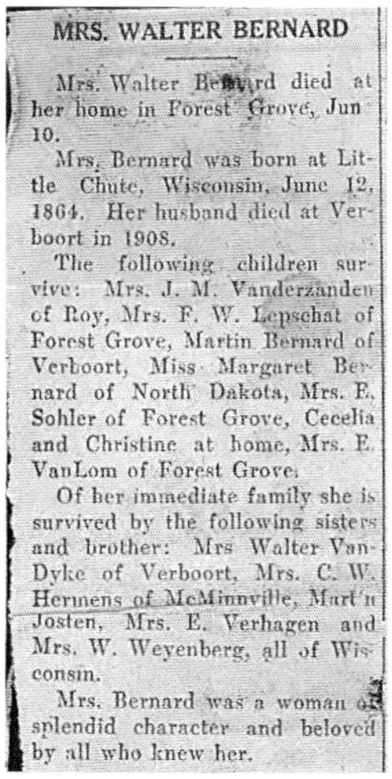

So what happened to Aunt Minnie? I was able to locate Minnie and her son Stanley in the 1920 and 1930 census years. Minnie moved to Forest Grove and purchased a home in the city at 218 2nd St. South (this address was changed when the city of Forest Grove re-named street names in 1950), which the census schedules indicate she owned free and clear. In addition, the schedules also show she was not employed during this time, so it can be safely presumed she was receiving survivor benefits from the federal government following Ed's death. Then around the early 1940s, Minnie and Stan moved to the Los Angeles, CA area living in the cities of Manhattan Beach, Santa Monica, and LA for many decades. She worked for the May Company at the famous open-air Crenshaw shopping mall in Santa Barbara in the furniture retail department for many years. Aunt Minnie returned to Oregon in 1985, moving to the Beaverton area where she lived out the rest of her days.

In 1924, Frances was still living in her much smaller home in Forest Grove. And by June 1924 Frances was now experiencing a diabetic coma. A diabetic coma is the result of very high levels of sugar in the blood after the buildup of fatty acids in the body which poisons the system leading to a condition known as acidosis. D.W. Ward, a doctor from Forest Grove, was tending to Frances in her final days, and sadly Frances passed away on June 10th. My great-great grandmother must have been a strong and tough woman to have lived during this time in history, and to have raised the eight successful children who survived her. And I will echo the eloquent sentiment given by her obituary writer who said she was *"a woman of splendid character and beloved by all who knew her."* She was laid to rest in the Visitation Catholic Cemetery in Verboort in the 2nd row of the southeast section right next to her husband. May Frances be blessed by our Lord's eternal peace.

On March 20, 1917, Frances appointed her brother-in-law Theodore M. Bernards (Walter's brother) as the administrator of her estate, and signed a land deed giving the 167 acre farm to him with the instructions it will be split evenly among her surviving children. Following Frances' death, the old farmhouse on NW Martin in Verboort remained in the Bernards family. It appears as though Martin and his new wife Lena may have stayed on the farm. According to the 1930 census they are shown as renting the land they lived on, and list Martin's employment as a farmer. Sadly, Christina passed away on March 8, 1935 at the young age of 34. So when Frances' estate was settled, the acreage was split evenly seven ways among the surviving children.

At some point, the property with the farmhouse on it was transferred to Josephine and her husband William Lepschat. The Lepschat's owned the home until William passed away in 1976 when it was sold to Gary Senko, and as mentioned previously is owned today by Silas Beeks, LLC.

Walter and Frances left a wonderful legacy. Of their 10 children, the next generation brought 31 grandchildren, and dozens of great-grandchildren.

* * *

There were a large number of good men and women of the Bernards Family who served our fine country in the military. They are:

- ❖ John A. Forsythe - Served in the US Air Force as a Colonel during World War II.
- ❖ Ruth J. (Lepschat) Forsythe - Admitted into the World War II US Cadet Nurse Corps in 09/11/1944. Promoted to Colonel in Nov. 1975 with the Air Force, served 30 years.
- ❖ Norbert J. Lepschat – Served in the US Army as a Private 1st Class in Korea.
- ❖ Robert F. Lepschat - Served in the Merchant Marines during World War II in the Pacific Theater.
- ❖ Walter J. Lepschat – Served in the US Coast Guard between 1951 and 1959.
- ❖ William A. Lepschat – Served in the US Navy as gunner during World War II.
- ❖ William C. Lepschat – Served in the US Army, Machine Gun Co., 18th Infantry during World War I. Discharged 09/03/1919.
- ❖ Adolph "Al" P. Rauch - Served as a Merchant Marine during World War II.
- ❖ George J. Steeves – Served in the US Army with the 92nd Field Artillery Battalion during World War II in Europe Theater.
- ❖ Clarence J. Vanderzanden – Served in the U.S. Army during World War II.
- ❖ Raymond J. Vanderzanden – Served as a Lieutenant in the US Navy on the USS Crockett during World War II.
- ❖ Melvin J. VanLom - Served in the US Army as a TEC 4 during World War II.

Photo and Image Gallery

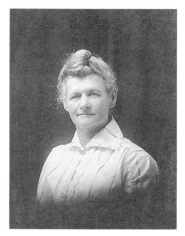

Image 5.10- Frances Bernards

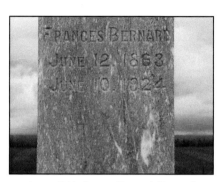

Image 5.11- Frances Bernards (Joosten) Gravesite Headstone, Visitation Cemetery, Verboort

Jesus! Mary! Joseph!

Have pity on me, have pity on me, at least you, my friends. Job. XIX

IN PIOUS MEMORY OF

FRANCES BERNARDS

nee JOOSTEN.

Born June 12th, 1860, at Bay Settlement, Wis.

Died June 10th, 1924, at ForestGrove, Oregon, after a protracted illness.

PRAYER.

O Gentlest Heart of Jesus, ever present in the Blessed Sacrament, ever consumed with burning love for the poor captive souls in purgatory, have mercy on the soul of Thy servant FRANCES, be not severe in Thy judgments, but let some drops of Thy Precious Blood fall upon the devouring flames; and do Thou, O merciful Saviour, send Thy angels to conduct her to a place of refreshment, light and peace. Amen.

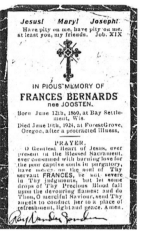

Image 5.12- Frances Bernards (Joosten) Prayer Card

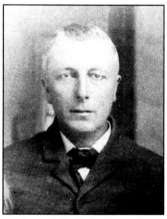

Image 5.13- Walter Bernards

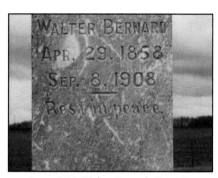

Image 5.14- Walter Bernards Gravesite Headstone, Visitation Cemetery, Verboort

WALTER BERNARDS,

FRANCINA JOOSTEN,

born at Reek, Holland, April 29, 1858, and after receiving the last Sacraments died at Portland, Oregon, September 8, 1908.

The human life is as a smoke or as a leaf that drops from a tree. Therefore, don't boast of to-morrow, for you know not what the day of to-morrow will bring you.

Book of Proverbs.

Not a sudden death is dreadful, but such a one, which is both sudden and unprepared for.

He was just before God, walking in all the commandments and justifications of the Lord without blame. Luc. I, 6.

Beloved wife, death separates us now, but once we will live forever with Christ. My dear children, forget not the law of God, let your heart receive his words, keep his commandments and you shall live. Pray for me.

We have loved him in life, let us not abandon him in death until we have conducted him into the house of the Lord by our prayers. St. Ambrose.

Sweet Heart of Mary, be my salvation. (300 days indulgence.)

OUR FATHER. HAIL MARY.

R. I. P.

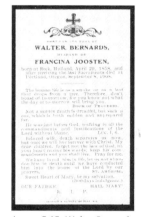

Image 5.15- Walter Bernards Prayer Card

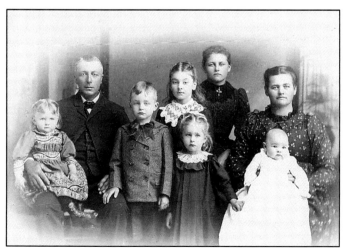

Image 5.16- Bernards Family: (L to R): Wilhelmina, Walter, Martin, Josephine, Margaret, Anna, Frances, and William (baby). Taken circa 1897.

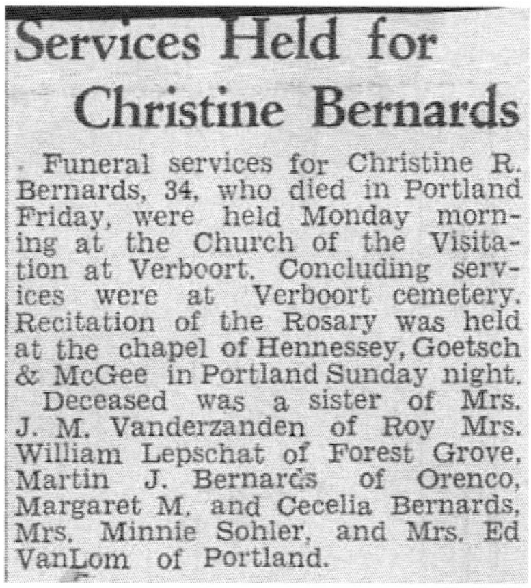

Services Held for Christine Bernards

Funeral services for Christine R. Bernards, 34, who died in Portland Friday, were held Monday morning at the Church of the Visitation at Verboort. Concluding services were at Verboort cemetery. Recitation of the Rosary was held at the chapel of Hennessey, Goetsch & McGee in Portland Sunday night. Deceased was a sister of Mrs. J. M. Vanderzanden of Roy Mrs. William Lepschat of Forest Grove, Martin J. Bernards of Orenco, Margaret M. and Cecelia Bernards, Mrs. Minnie Sohler, and Mrs. Ed VanLom of Portland.

Image 5.17- Christina R. Bernards Obituary

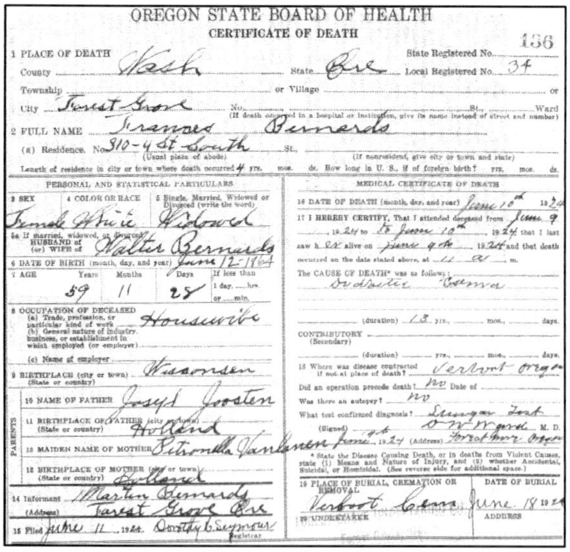

OREGON STATE BOARD OF HEALTH
CERTIFICATE OF DEATH

State Registered No. 136
1 PLACE OF DEATH
County Wash State Ore Local Registered No. 34
City Forest Grove
2 FULL NAME Frances Bernards
(a) Residence. No. 310-4 St South
Length of residence in city or town where death occurred 4 yrs.

PERSONAL AND STATISTICAL PARTICULARS
3 SEX Female 4 COLOR OR RACE White 5 Single, Married, Widowed or Divorced Widowed
5a If married, widowed, or divorced HUSBAND of (or) WIFE of Walter Bernards
6 DATE OF BIRTH (month, day, and year) June 12-1864
7 AGE Years 59 Months 11 Days 28
8 OCCUPATION OF DECEASED Housewife
9 BIRTHPLACE (city or town) (State or country) Wisconsin
10 NAME OF FATHER Joseph Joosten
11 BIRTHPLACE OF FATHER (State or country) Holland
12 MAIDEN NAME OF MOTHER Petronella VanLeenen
13 BIRTHPLACE OF MOTHER (State or country) Holland
14 Informant Martin Bernards
(Address) Forest Grove Ore
15 Filed June 11 1924 Dorothy C. Seymour Registrar

MEDICAL CERTIFICATE OF DEATH
16 DATE OF DEATH (month, day, and year) June 10th 1924
17 I HEREBY CERTIFY, That I attended deceased from June 9 1924 to June 10th 1924 that I last saw her alive on June 9th 1924 and that death occurred on the date stated above, at 11 a m.
(duration) 13 yrs.
18 Where was disease contracted if not at place of death? Verboort Oregon
Did an operation precede death? No
Was there an autopsy? No
(Signed) O W Ward M. D.
June 1924 (Address) Forest Grove Oregon
19 PLACE OF BURIAL, CREMATION OR REMOVAL Verboort Cem. DATE OF BURIAL June 18 1924

Image 5.18- Frances Bernards Death Certificate

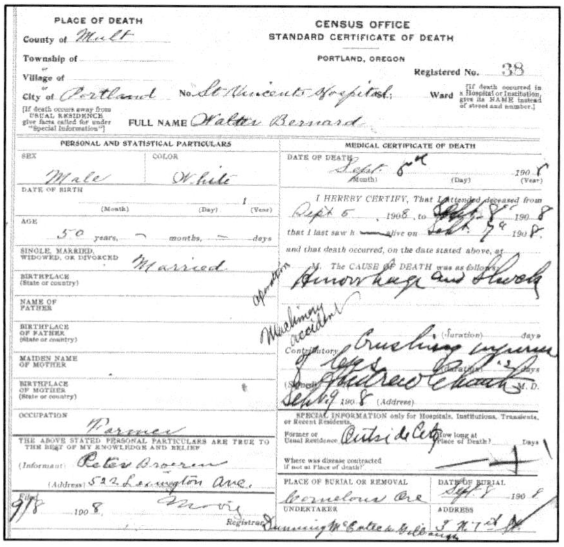

PLACE OF DEATH
County of Mult
CENSUS OFFICE
STANDARD CERTIFICATE OF DEATH
PORTLAND, OREGON
Registered No. 38
City of Portland No. St Vincents Hospital
FULL NAME Walter Bernard

PERSONAL AND STATISTICAL PARTICULARS
SEX Male COLOR White
AGE 50 years
SINGLE, MARRIED, WIDOWED, OR DIVORCED Married
OCCUPATION Farmer
THE ABOVE STATED PERSONAL PARTICULARS ARE TRUE TO THE BEST OF MY KNOWLEDGE AND BELIEF
(Informant) Peter Brouwer
(Address) 522 Lexington Ave.
Filed 9/8 1908

MEDICAL CERTIFICATE OF DEATH
DATE OF DEATH Sept. 8th 1908
I HEREBY CERTIFY, That I attended deceased from Sept 5 1908, to Sept 8 1908
SPECIAL INFORMATION only for Hospitals, Institutions, Transients, or Recent Residents.
Former or Usual Residence Outside City
PLACE OF BURIAL OR REMOVAL Cornelius Ore DATE OF BURIAL Sept 8 1908

Image 5.19- Walter Bernards Death Certificate

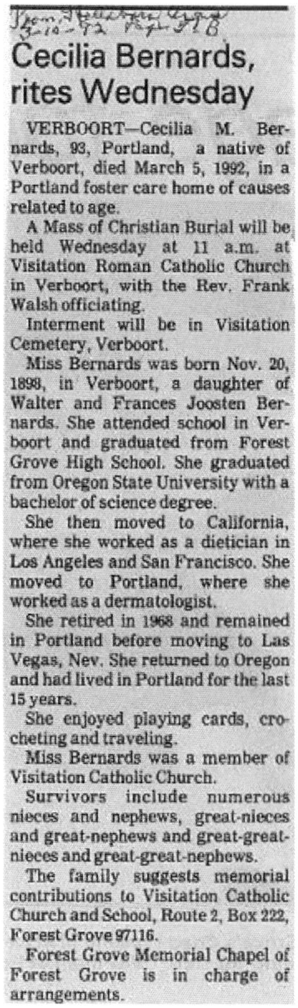

From Hillsboro Argus 3-10-92 Page 12B

Cecilia Bernards, rites Wednesday

VERBOORT—Cecilia M. Bernards, 93, Portland, a native of Verboort, died March 5, 1992, in a Portland foster care home of causes related to age.

A Mass of Christian Burial will be held Wednesday at 11 a.m. at Visitation Roman Catholic Church in Verboort, with the Rev. Frank Walsh officiating.

Interment will be in Visitation Cemetery, Verboort.

Miss Bernards was born Nov. 20, 1898, in Verboort, a daughter of Walter and Frances Joosten Bernards. She attended school in Verboort and graduated from Forest Grove High School. She graduated from Oregon State University with a bachelor of science degree.

She then moved to California, where she worked as a dietician in Los Angeles and San Francisco. She moved to Portland, where she worked as a dermatologist.

She retired in 1968 and remained in Portland before moving to Las Vegas, Nev. She returned to Oregon and had lived in Portland for the last 15 years.

She enjoyed playing cards, crocheting and traveling.

Miss Bernards was a member of Visitation Catholic Church.

Survivors include numerous nieces and nephews, great-nieces and great-nephews and great-great-nieces and great-great-nephews.

The family suggests memorial contributions to Visitation Catholic Church and School, Route 2, Box 222, Forest Grove 97116.

Forest Grove Memorial Chapel of Forest Grove is in charge of arrangements.

Image 5.20- Cecilia Marie Bernards Obituary

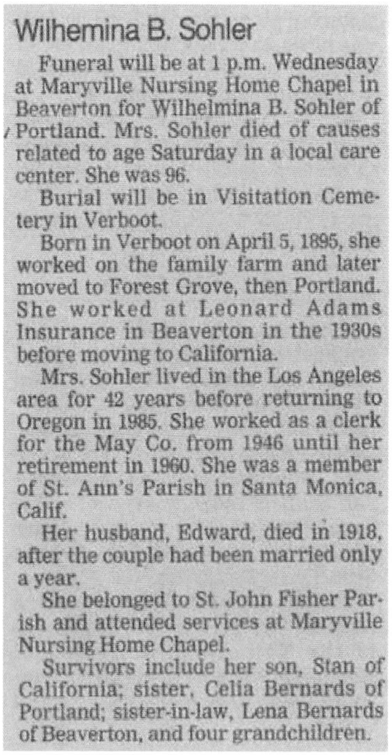

Wilhemina B. Sohler

Funeral will be at 1 p.m. Wednesday at Maryville Nursing Home Chapel in Beaverton for Wilhemina B. Sohler of Portland. Mrs. Sohler died of causes related to age Saturday in a local care center. She was 96.

Burial will be in Visitation Cemetery in Verboot.

Born in Verboot on April 5, 1895, she worked on the family farm and later moved to Forest Grove, then Portland. She worked at Leonard Adams Insurance in Beaverton in the 1930s before moving to California.

Mrs. Sohler lived in the Los Angeles area for 42 years before returning to Oregon in 1985. She worked as a clerk for the May Co. from 1946 until her retirement in 1960. She was a member of St. Ann's Parish in Santa Monica, Calif.

Her husband, Edward, died in 1918, after the couple had been married only a year.

She belonged to St. John Fisher Parish and attended services at Maryville Nursing Home Chapel.

Survivors include her son, Stan of California; sister, Celia Bernards of Portland; sister-in-law, Lena Bernards of Beaverton, and four grandchildren.

Image 5.21- Wilhelmina Frances Sohler (Bernards) Obituary

Martin Bernards Services Held

Martin John Bernards, former resident of the Verboort community, died in Salem June 17 following an illness of the past eight years. Holy Rosary was recited Friday evening in the chapel of Prickett's Mortuary, Forest Grove, by the Rev. William R. Killion of Visitation Catholic church, Verboort. Requiem Mass was offered by the Rev. Killion at Visitation church Saturday morning with interment in Visitation Catholic cemetery.

Casket bearers included Jerry Pool, James Monaghan, Walter Lepschat, Melvin VanLom, William A. Lepschat and Dale Vanderzanden.

Mr. Bernards was born in Forest Grove November 15, 1891, and had devoted his entire life to farming until ill health forced his retirement.

He is survived by his widow, Mrs. Lena Bernards of Portland; three sons, Walt of Beaverton, Robert of St. Paul, Minn., and Ralph of Battle Creek, Mich.; four daughters, Mrs. Evelyn Shealy of San Clemente, Cal., Mrs. Patricia Winczewski of San Diego, Barbara Bernards of Burbank, and Arlene Bernards of Portland. Two children died in infancy. He was brother of Mrs. Margaret Ehrsan and Mrs. Francis VanLom of Portland, Mrs. Minnie Sohler of Los Angeles and Cecelia Bernards of San Jose. He had 10 grandchildren.

Image 5.22- Martin John Bernards Obituary

Image 5.23- Bernards Family: (L-R) Margaret, Frances, Minnie, & Martin

Latin Translation

Die 3rd Julii

Josephum van Handel, filius Joseph van Handel
et Mary van den Heuvel, natus in Little Chute
die 3rd Februarii 1858, ?? Elisabeth Joosten
filia Joseph Joosten et Petronella van Lanen natus
in Bay Settlement die 3rd December 1863.
Testes: Johannes Joosten et Dina van Handel.
Walterus, filius Johannes Bernards et Anna van den
Broek natus in Reek, Hollandie die 29th April 1853,
cum Francisca Joosten filia de pra dictorum natus in
Bay Settlement die 12th Junii 1864.
Testes: Petrus Schumacher et Anna Joosten.

A J Verberk, Pastor

English Translation

Day 3rd July

Joseph van Handel, son of Joseph van Handel
and Mary van den Heuvel, born in Little Chute
day 3rd February 1858, ?? Elizabeth Joosten
daughter of Joseph Joosten and Petronella van Lanen born
in Bay Settlement day 3rd December 1863.
Witnesses: John Joosten and Dina van Handel.
Walter, son of John Bernards and Anna van den
Broek born in Reek, Holland day 29th April 1853,
with Frances Joosten daughter of the afore mentioned, born in
Bay Settlement day 12th June 1864.
Witnesses: Peter Schumacher and Anna Joosten.

A J Verberk, Pastor

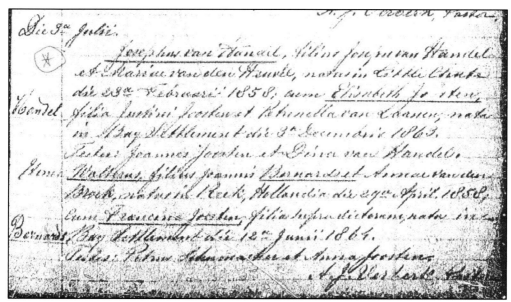

Image 5.24- Frances & Walter Bernards and Elizabeth & Joseph VanHandel Marriage Certificate

❧ Descendants of Frances & Walter Bernards ❦

Notes: 1= 1st generation, 2= 2nd generation, 3= 3rd generation.
The year of birth is only given for individuals still living, if known.

1   Frances Joosten
    Born: June 12, 1864 in Little Chute, Outagamie County, Wisconsin
    Died: June 10, 1924 in Forest Grove, Washington County, Oregon
    Buried at: Visitation Catholic Cemetery, Verboort, OR; SE row 2
    Married: July 03, 1882 in Little Chute, Outagamie County, Wisconsin
    Walter Bernards
    Born: April 29, 1858 in Reek, North Brabant, Holland
    Died: September 08, 1908 in Portland, Multnomah County, Oregon
    Buried at: Visitation Catholic Cemetery, Verboort, OR; SE row 2
    Parents: Johannes Bernards (1812-1892) and Anna Vandenbroek (1814-1887)

    2   Anna Marie Bernards
        Born: May 05, 1883 in Appleton, Outagamie County, Wisconsin
        Died: December 30, 1953 in Roy, Washington County, Oregon
        Buried at: St. Francis of Assisi Catholic Cemetery, Roy, OR; south row 1
        Married: November 25, 1903 in Verboort, Washington County, Oregon
        John Martin Vanderzanden
        Born: December 16, 1875 in De Pere, Brown County, Wisconsin
        Died: March 09, 1960 in Hillsboro, Washington County, Oregon
        Buried at: St. Francis of Assisi Catholic Cemetery, Roy, OR; south row 1
        Parents: Martin Vanderzanden (1840-1922) and Maria Anna VanDyke (1844-1894)

        3   Joseph Martin Vanderzanden
            Born: December 12, 1904 in Roy, Washington County, Oregon
            Died: June 15, 1984 in Hillsboro, Washington County, Oregon
            Buried at: St. Francis of Assisi Catholic Cemetery, Roy, Oregon, west row 1
            Married: April 09, 1929 in Roy, Washington County, Oregon
            Elizabeth Marie Meeuwsen
            Born: September 08, 1906 in Roy, Washington County, Oregon
            Died: July 19, 1994 in Aloha, Washington County, Oregon
            Buried at: St. Francis of Assisi Catholic Cemetery, Roy, Oregon, west row 1
            Parents: Antone Meeuwsen (1867-1933) and Gertrude Heesacker (1868-1948)

        3   Walter John Vanderzanden
            Born: January 02, 1906 in Roy, Washington County, Oregon
            Died: June 17, 1991 in Beaverton, Washington County, Oregon
            Buried at: St. Francis of Assisi Catholic Cemetery, Roy, OR; north row 1
            Married: October 01, 1929 in Roy, Washington County, Oregon
            Hannah Marie Vandehey
            Born: December 18, 1906 in Roy, Washington County, Oregon
            Died: September 10, 1997 in Beaverton, Washington County, Oregon
            Buried at: St. Francis of Assisi Catholic Cemetery, Roy, OR; north row 1
            Parents: Cornelius Vandehey (1864-1938) and Catherine Anne Van Domelen (1869-1947)

        3   Wilhelmina ("Minnie") Marie Vanderzanden
            Born: March 06, 1907 in Roy, Washington County, Oregon
            Died: September 22, 2002 in Portland, Multnomah County, Oregon
            Buried at: Mt. Calvary Catholic Cemetery, Portland, OR, sec V, row 12
            Married: June 19, 1938 in Portland, Multnomah County, Oregon

Benjamin Franklin Shaw
Born: September 12, 1900 in Mountain Grove, Wright County, Missouri
Died: June 11, 1957 in Portland, Multnomah County, Oregon
Buried at: Mt. Calvary Catholic Cemetery, Portland, OR, sec V, row 12
Parents: John Shaw (1847-1903) and Elsie Coward (1876-?)

3   Henrietta ("Sis") Anna Vanderzanden
Born: April 19, 1909 in Roy, Washington County, Oregon
Died: January 18, 2002 in Banks, Washington County, Oregon
Buried at: Union Point Cemetery, Banks, OR; section 2, row J
Married: March 22, 1937 in Stevenson, Skamania County, Washington
Archie G. Jesse
Born: July 04, 1901 in Banks, Washington County, Oregon
Died: December 14, 1977 in Banks, Washington County, Oregon
Buried at: Union Point Cemetery, Banks, OR; section 2, row J
Parents: Claus F. Jesse (1857-1926) and Wilhelmina Dorothea Banks (1863-1936)

3   Henry ("Hank") John Vanderzanden
Born: April 19, 1909 in Banks, Washington County, Oregon
Died: November 21, 1991 in Hillsboro, Washington County, Oregon
Buried at: St. Francis of Assisi Catholic Cemetery, Roy, OR; west row 5
Married: September 27, 1933 in Roy, Washington County, Oregon
Lena Elizabeth Cop
Born: June 11, 1912 in Banks, Washington County, Oregon
Died: October 21, 1996 in Banks, Washington County, Oregon
Buried at: St. Francis of Assisi Catholic Cemetery, Roy, OR; west row 5
Parents: William Henry Cop (1888-1965) and Christina Bertha Vandehey (1892-1979)

3   Albert Francis Vanderzanden
Born: June 30, 1911 in Roy, Washington County, Oregon
Died: October 17, 1987 in Roy, Washington County, Oregon
Buried at: St. Francis of Assisi Catholic Cemetery, Roy, OR, south row 1
Married: June 30, 1934 in Forest Grove, Washington County
Rose ("Bernie") Bernardine Kalsch
Born: February 15, 1910 in Crabtree, Oregon
Died: May 04, 2004 in Hillsboro, Washington County, Oregon
Buried at: St. Francis of Assisi Catholic Cemetery, Roy, OR, south row 1
Parents: Philip Albert Kalsch (1878-1958) and Barbara Mary Franck (1887-1976)

3   Raymond James Vanderzanden
Born: December 14, 1912 in Roy, Washington County, Oregon
Died: October 07, 1999 in Beaverton, Washington County, Oregon
Buried at: Willamette National Cemetery, Portland, OR., sec Y, grave 2140
Married: August 12, 1950 in Portland, Multnomah County, Oregon
Geraldine Claire Mangas
Born: October 20, 1916 in Akron, Montgomery County, Ohio
Died: July 11, 2009 in Portland, Multnomah County, Oregon
Buried at: Willamette National Cemetery, Portland, OR., sec Y, grave 2140
Parents: George E. Mangas (1863-1945) and Rova Edythe Hays (1886-1922)

3   Clarence Joseph Vanderzanden
    Born: January 14, 1915 in Roy, Washington County, Oregon
    Died: December 23, 1993 in Banks, Washington County, Oregon
    Buried at: Mt. Calvary Catholic Cemetery, Portland, OR, sec P, row 89
    Married: May 29, 1951 in Portland, Multnomah County, Oregon
    Mary Claire Joy
    Born: October 25, 1912 in Huron, Beadle County, South Dakota
    Died: September 12, 1985 in Hillsboro, Washington County, Oregon
    Buried at: Mt. Calvary Catholic Cemetery, Portland, OR, sec P, row 89
    Parents: William Reid Joy and Madeline Cashman

3   Martha Mary Vanderzanden
    Born: April 18, 1917 in Roy, Washington County, Oregon
    Died: October 09, 1996 in Portland, Multnomah County, Oregon
    Buried at: Mt. Calvary Catholic Cemetery, Portland, OR, sec V, row 12
    Married: November 25, 1939 in Roy, Washington County, Oregon
    Orval William Harty
    Born: October 12, 1910 in Buxton, Washington County, Oregon
    Died: September 19, 1996 in Portland, Multnomah County, Oregon
    Buried at: Mt. Calvary Catholic Cemetery, Portland, OR, sec V, row 12
    Parents: Fred Harty (1879-1953) and Lena Tolke (1887-1978)

3   Agnes Francis Vanderzanden
    Born: October 11, 1919 in Roy, Washington County, Oregon
    Died: September 06, 2012 in Pasco, Franklin County, Washington
    Buried at: City View Cemetery, Pasco, WA
    Married: July 03, 1943 in Atlanta, Fulton County, Georgia
    George James Steeves
    Born: February 13, 1919 in Moosejaw, Saskatchewan, Canada
    Died: April 11, 2003 in Pasco, Franklin County, Washington
    Buried at: City View Cemetery, Pasco, WA
    Parents: Charles Steeves and Lalia Verge

2   Martin Joseph Bernards
    Born: December 21, 1888 in Verboort, Washington County, Oregon
    Died: January 28, 1889 in Verboort, Washington County, Oregon
    Buried at: Visitation Catholic Cemetery, Verboort, OR, NW row 2
    Married: n/a

2   Josephine Petronella Bernards
    Born: May 15, 1890 in Verboort, Washington County, Oregon
    Died: November 19, 1952 in Forest Grove, Washington County, Oregon
    Buried at: Visitation Catholic Cemetery, Verboort, OR, SE row 3
    Married: August 31, 1921 in Forest Grove, Washington County, Oregon
    William Carl Lepschat
    Born: March 31, 1891 in Gonzales, Gonzales County, Texas
    Died: April 18, 1976 in Forest Grove, Washington County, Oregon
    Buried at: Visitation Catholic Cemetery, Verboort, OR, SE row 3
    Parents: Fredrick Wilhelm Lepschat (1850-1936) and Bertha Louise Quast (1864-1962)

3   Ethel L. Lepschat
Born: December 13, 1921 in Porterville, Tulare County, California
Died: September 05, 1986 in Seaside, Clatsop County, Oregon
Buried at: Mt. View Memorial Gardens, Forest Grove, OR, mausoleum
Married: Unknown
Earl Marvin Nordgren
Born: February 14, 1917 in Hillsboro, Washington County, Oregon
Died: November 15, 2012 in Hillsboro, Washington County, Oregon
Buried at: Unknown
Parents: Alfred Nordgren (?-1953) and Hildur Thorin (?-1955)

3   William August Lepschat
Born: June 17, 1923 in Forest Grove, Washington County, Oregon
Died: November 08, 1981 in Portland, Multnomah County, Oregon
Buried at: Visitation Catholic Cemetery, Verboort, OR, SE row 3
Married: October 25, 1947 in Portland, Multnomah County, Oregon
Mary Claire Heywood
Born: January 12, 1927 in Oregon
Died: December 25, 2002 in Multnomah County, Oregon
Buried at: Visitation Catholic Cemetery, Verboort, OR, SE row 3
Parents: Herbert J. Heywood (1895-1969) and Bernetta Heywood (1899-1972)

3   Ruth Josephine Lepschat
Born: March 28, 1925 in Forest Grove, Washington County, Oregon
Died: October 05, 2012 in Beaverton, Washington County, Oregon
Buried at: Willamette National Cemetery, Portland, OR; Sec S, site 1475
Married: September 03, 1971 in Sacramento, Sacramento County, California
John Adelbert Forsythe
Born: June 13, 1920 in Oregon
Died: May 20, 1988 in Otis, Lincoln County, Oregon
Buried at: Willamette National Cemetery, Portland, OR; Sec S, site 1475
Parents: Unknown

3   Robert Frederick Lepschat
Born: April 19, 1928 in Banks, Washington County, Oregon
Died: August 13, 2008 in Forest Grove, Washington County, Oregon
Buried at: Visitation Catholic Cemetery, Verboort, OR, niche
Married: December 27, 1951 in Verboort, Washington County, Oregon
Jeannine Marie Kemper
Born: 1932 in Kansas City, Oregon
Died: Living
Buried at:
Parents: William T. Kemper (1909-1995) and Dorothy M. Vandervelden (1912-1997)

3   Norbert Joseph Lepschat
Born: July 06, 1930 in Hillsboro, Washington County, Oregon
Died: January 11, 2011 in Portland, Multnomah County, Oregon
Buried at: Mt. View Memorial Gardens, Forest Grove, OR
Married: January 15, 1955 in Hillsboro, Washington County, Oregon
Norma Jane McMahon
Born: 1934 in Huron, Beadle County, South Dakota
Died: Living
Buried at:
Parents: Robert J. McMahon (1906-1969) and Rosalia F. Wellner (1905-1976)

3　Walter James Lepschat
Born: September 12, 1932 in Forest Grove, Washington County, Oregon
Died: April 27, 2010 in Verboort, Washington County, Oregon
Buried at: Visitation Catholic Cemetery, Verboort, OR, SW row 5
Married (1): February 05, 1955 in Verboort, Washington County, Oregon
Married (2): December 31, 1998 in Forest Grove, Washington County, Oregon
Rosella Mary Kemper (1)
Born: June 15, 1930 in Washington County, Oregon
Died: October 28, 1995 in Forest Grove, Washington County, Oregon
Buried at: Visitation Catholic Cemetery, Verboort, OR, SW row 5
Parents: Stephen Kemper (1887-1968) and Elizabeth A. Kemper (1898-1971)
Judith Estelle Donaldson (2)
Born: Unknown
Died: Living
Buried at:
Parents: Unknown

3　Frances Louise Lepschat
Born: October 31, 1926 in Banks, Washington County, Oregon
Died: Living
Buried at:
Married: November 03, 1951 in Verboort, Washington County, Oregon
John Frederick Koehnke
Born: July 30, 1928 in Cornelius, Washington County, Oregon
Died: Living
Buried at:
Parents: John Koehnke (1892-1978) and Martha L. Schulenberg (1894-1975)

2　Martin John Bernards
Born: November 15, 1891 in Verboort, Washington County, Oregon
Died: June 17, 1959 in Salem, Marion County, Oregon
Buried at: Visitation Catholic Cemetery, Verboort, OR, SE row 2
Married: September 29, 1920 in Forest Grove, Washington County, Oregon
Angelena Genevieve Duyck
Born: February 27, 1895 in Roy, Washington County, Oregon
Died: January 03, 1995 in Beaverton, Washington County, Oregon
Buried at: Visitation Catholic Cemetery, Verboort, OR, SE row 2
Parents: Camiel C. Duyck (1866-1920) and Lucy Crop (1872-1952)

3　Arlene Bernards
Born: 1921 in Oregon
Died: Living
Buried at:
Married: June 09, 1966 in Vancouver, Clark County, Washington
Adolph Paul Rauch
Born: July 20, 1919
Died: January 07, 2006 in Washington County, Oregon
Buried at: Willamette National Cemetery, Portland, OR., sec Y, site 1058
Parents: Unknown

3   <u>Robert J. Bernards</u>
Born: 1924 in Oregon
Died: Living
Buried at:
Married: July 18, 1953 in Multnomah County, Oregon
<u>Delores E. Bodine</u>
Born: 1925 or 1926
Died: March 06, 2013 in St Paul, Ramsey County, Minnesota
Buried at: Roselawn Cemetery, Roseville, MN
Parents: Unknown

3   <u>Wilbur Bernards</u>
Born: 1925
Died: 1928
Buried at: Visitation Catholic Cemetery, Verboort, OR, SE row 2
Married: n/a

3   <u>Mildred Evelyn Bernards</u>
Born: March 06, 1927
Died: April 16, 1927
Buried at:
Married: n/a

3   <u>Evelyn M. Bernards</u>
Born: 1931 or 1932 in Oregon
Died: Living
Buried at:
Married: October 04, 1958 in Los Angeles County, California
<u>Luther F. Shealy</u>
Born: 1932 or 1933
Died: Living
Buried at:
Parents: Unknown

3   <u>Ralph M. Bernards</u>
Born: 1932 in Oregon
Died: Living
Buried at:
Married (1): February 19, 1955 in Multnomah County, Oregon
Married (2): Unknown
<u>Virginia Ann Loken (1)</u>
Born: February 08, 1933 in Minneapolis, Hennepin County, Minnesota
Died: January 13, 2014 in Portland, Multnomah County, Oregon
Buried at: Riverview Cemetery, Portland, OR
Parents: Leonard A. Loken (1902-1981) and Blanche J. Loken (1907-1996)
<u>Patricia Bernards (2)</u>
Born: Unknown
Died: Living
Buried at:
Parents: Unknown

3 Walter Camiel Bernards
   Born: December 14, 1933 in Oregon
   Died: Living
   Buried at:
   Married: July 14, 1956 in Tigard, Washington County, Oregon
   Jerry Jean Myers
   Born: Unknown
   Died: Living
   Buried at:
   Parents: Unknown

3 Patricia B. Bernards
   Born: 1934 in Oregon
   Died: Living
   Buried at:
   Married: April 18, 1954 in San Diego County, California
   Donald Winczewski
   Born: 1932
   Died: Living
   Buried at:
   Parents: Unknown

3 Barbara Ann Bernards
   Born: 1939 in Oregon
   Died: Living
   Buried at:
   Married: February 09, 1964 in Clark County, Nevada
   Matthew Miovac, Jr.
   Born: Unknown
   Died: Living
   Buried at:
   Parents: Unknown

2 Margaret Mary Bernards
   Born: November 13, 1893 in Verboort, Washington County, Oregon
   Died: February 12, 1981 in Beaverton, Washington County, Oregon
   Buried at: Riverview Abbey, Portland, OR; Acacia-E4
   Married (1): Abt. August 1956
   Married (2): August 28, 1971 in Bend, Deschutes County, Oregon
   Holmes K. Ehrsam (1)
   Born: December 14, 1889 in Clay Center, Clay County, Kansas
   Died: February 13, 1963 in Portland, Multnomah County, Oregon
   Buried at: Riverview Cemetery, Portland, OR; Sec 123, lot 55
   Parents: Unknown
   Jesse Ellsworth Brokaw (2)
   Born: February 17, 1893
   Died: May 15, 1981
   Buried at: Riverview Abbey, Portland, OR; Acacia-E4
   Parents: Unknown

2   Wilhelmina Frances Bernards
     Born: April 05, 1895 in Verboort, Washington County, Oregon
     Died: June 01, 1991 in Portland, Multnomah County, Oregon
     Buried at: Visitation Catholic Cemetery, Verboort, OR, SE row 2
     Married: September 12, 1917 in Verboort, Washington County, Oregon
     Edward W. Sohler
     Born: September 25, 1891 in Verboort, Washington County, Oregon
     Died: October 20, 1918 in Louisville, Jefferson County, Kentucky
     Buried at: Visitation Catholic Cemetery, Verboort, OR, SE row 2
     Parents: Gabriel Sohler (1853-1908) and Mary Cop (1858-1941)

     3   Stanley Edward Sohler
          Born: 1918
          Died: Living
          Buried at:
          Married (1): Unknown
          Married (2): July 03, 1962 in Orange County, California
          Margaret H. Sohler (1)
          Born: Unknown
          Died:
          Buried at:
          Parents: Unknown
          Ellen Lavina Fairchild (2)
          Born: July 28, 1934 in Hutchinson, Reno County, Kansas
          Died: January 29, 1992 in Los Angeles County, California
          Buried at: Forest Lawn Memorial Park, Glendale, CA
          Parents: Stephen J. Fairchild (1897-1971) and Rachel I. Davis (1897-1964)

2   William August Bernards
     Born: January 19, 1897 in Verboort, Washington County, Oregon
     Died: December 07, 1900 in Verboort, Washington County, Oregon
     Buried At: Visitation Catholic Cemetery, Verboort, OR, NW row 2

2   Cecilia Marie Bernards
     Born: November 20, 1898 in Verboort, Washington County, Oregon
     Died: March 05, 1992 in Portland, Multnomah County, Oregon
     Buried At: Visitation Catholic Cemetery, Verboort, OR, SE row 2
     Married: n/a

2   Christina Rosalia Bernards
     Born: December 18, 1900 in Verboort, Washington County, Oregon
     Died: March 08, 1935 in Verboort, Washington County, Oregon
     Buried At: Visitation Catholic Cemetery, Verboort, OR, SE row 2
     Married: n/a

2   Frances Marie Bernards
     Born: February 02, 1903 in Verboort, Washington County, Oregon
     Died: October 10, 1977 in Portland, Multnomah County, Oregon
     Buried At: Visitation Catholic Cemetery, Verboort, OR, SE row 2
     Married (1): January 12, 1921 in Forest Grove, Washington County, Oregon
     Married (2): December 08, 1956 in Stevenson, Skamania County, Washington

Edward David VanLom (1)
Born: September 03, 1898 in Centerville, Oregon
Death: December 21, 1965 in Portland, Multnomah County, Oregon
Buried At: Visitation Catholic Cemetery, Verboort, OR, SW row 5
Parents: John H. VanLom (1852-1929) and Mary A. VanGrunsven (1857-1931)
Joel Sloan Miller (2)
Born: February 02, 1906
Died: April 08, 1969 in Portland, Multnomah County, Oregon
Buried At:
Parents: Unknown

3   Melvin John VanLom
    Born: April 27, 1921 in Forest Grove, Washington County, Oregon
    Died: June 12, 1996 in Portland, Multnomah County, Oregon
    Buried at: Willamette National Cemetery, Portland, OR
    Married: June 22, 1949 in Portland, Multnomah County, Oregon
    Eloise Marie Carpenter
    Born: 1927
    Died: Living
    Buried at:
    Parents: Unknown

3   Lorraine F. VanLom
    Born: 1925
    Died: Living
    Buried at:
    Married: August 15, 1968 in Multnomah County, Oregon
    Barton M. Hess
    Born: 1918
    Died: Living
    Buried at:
    Parents: Unknown

3   Kenneth Bernard VanLom
    Born: September 13, 1926 in Portland, Multnomah County, Oregon
    Died: October 19, 2005 in Multnomah County, Oregon
    Buried at: Visitation Catholic Cemetery, Verboort, OR, niche eastside
    Married: November 19, 1955 in Stevenson, Skamania County, Washington
    Joanne Rose Mitchell
    Born: December 28, 1929
    Died: February 15, 1989 in Portland, Multnomah County, Oregon
    Buried at:
    Parents: Unknown

3   Darrell E. VanLom
    Born: February 24, 1927
    Died: December 27, 2007 in Portland, Multnomah County, Oregon
    Buried at: Lincoln Memorial Park Cemetery, Portland, Oregon
    Married: August 27, 1954 in Multnomah County, Oregon
    Virginia Elaine Carlson
    Born: November 10, 1930 in Oshkosh, Winnebago County, Wisconsin
    Died: February 08, 2012
    Buried at: Lincoln Memorial Park Cemetery, Portland, Oregon
    Parents: Einar E. Carlson

~ Chapter Six ~

Johanna Hermens

The third child blessed to Joseph and Nellie was Johanna ("Anna") Marie. Anna was born on December 21, 1865 in Bay Settlement, Wisconsin. And I have noticed a pattern in the births within this family, there is an 18 month age difference between Anna and Frances, just as there is between Frances and Elizabeth. If you have been counting, Joseph and Nellie now have a house full of girls, and this is only the beginning.

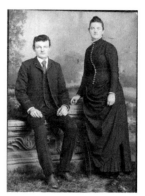

Image 6.01- Antone & Johanna Hermens (1889)

As written in Anna's obituary, she came out to Oregon with Frances and Walter, and her younger sister Jane in 1888. By the end of this decade Anna was married to Antone Hermens, who she married on June 4, 1889 in Verboort. Antone was born on January 24, 1864 in DePere, Wisconsin, which is just west of Green Bay. He is the oldest son of William and Natalie (Meulemans) Hermens. Antone's family came to Oregon at the end of 1883 when he was 19 years old, and settled on a farm located on NW Martin Rd. in Verboort.

After a little more than one year, Anna and Antone would welcome their first child into this world. William Martin was born on November 23, 1890. And then over the next nine years they welcomed their next six children, about every 18 to 24 months, who are Petronella Marie, Pauline Nathalia, Mary Antoinette, Josephine Adelia, Martin Joseph, and finally Peter George in 1899. Also at this time Antone and Anna purchased the 100 acre farm on NW Martin Rd. in Verboort from his parents in 1899. This property must have been very close to the Bernards farm, which Walter and Frances also bought in 1899.

In 1900, the Hermens family was enumerated in the Washington County census in the town of Cornelius. Verboort was considered part of Cornelius at the time. Interestingly, as can be seen in the image, John M. Vanderzanden is listed as a "domestic" and was helping Antone with the farming duties. I think this is extremely interesting because just down the road was the Frances and Walter Bernards family. Their oldest daughter Anna married John in 1903. In other words, John ended up marrying the niece of Antone and Anna, and later became my great-grandfather.

88	9/1 [illegible]	Hermens Anton [illegible]	Head	W	M	Jan	1864	36	M			Wisconsin	Holland	Belgium
89		— Johanna M.	Wife	W	F	Dec	1865	34	M	7	7	Wisconsin	Holland	Holland
90		— William M.	Son	W	M	Nov	1890	9	S			Oregon	Wisconsin	Wisconsin
91		— Petronella M.	Daughter	W	F	Dec	1891	8	S			Oregon	Wisconsin	Wisconsin
92		— [illegible]	Daughter	W	F	Mar	1893	7	S			Oregon	Wisconsin	Wisconsin
93		— M[illegible] A.	Daughter	W	F	May	1895	5	S			Oregon	Wisconsin	Wisconsin
94		— [illegible] A.	Daughter	W	F	Nov	1896	3	S			Oregon	Wisconsin	Wisconsin
95		— Martin J.	Son	W	M	Jan	1898	2	S			Oregon	Wisconsin	Wisconsin
96		— Peter G.	Son	W	M	July	1899	10/12	S			Oregon	Wisconsin	Wisconsin
97	9/12 [illegible]	Vanderzanden John M.	Domestic	W	M	Dec	1875	24	S			Wisconsin	Holland	Holland

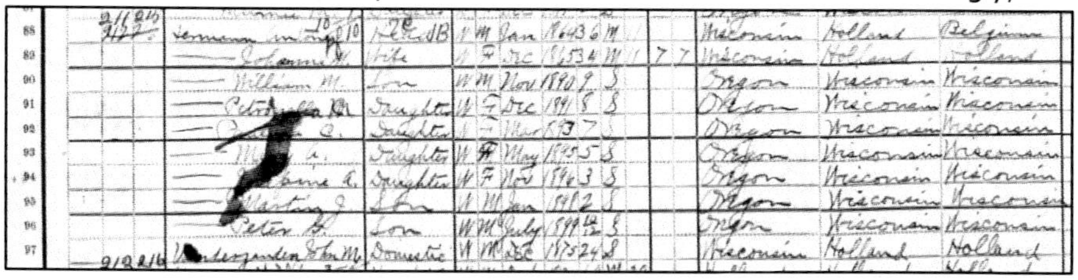

Image 6.02- 1900 Cornelius, Washington County, OR Census, ED 150, sheet 10B, line 88

This census also reveals that the farms on Martin Rd. were pretty much "all in the family"; meaning the Hermens family owned most of the land. Because neighboring Antone and Anna were his parents William and Natalie, Uncle Louis and Aunt Minnie Hermens, and Aunt Cornelia and Uncle John Peters. Pauline's (Anna & Antone's daughter) future husband William VanLoo, who was 13 at this time, lived right down the street.

Over the next ten years the couples' last two of their nine children were born. Christine Elizabeth came in 1905, and Ernest Anthony in 1910. As can be seen, there is a considerable time period in between George and Christine, and Christine and Ernest. This indicates Antone and Anna may have had to deal with miscarriages, but after being blessed with nine children Anna was 44 years old after Ernest was born, and was at an age where most women were finished having children. By 1910 all of the kids were still living in the house. William, the oldest, was 19 now, and helping his dad on the farm. Ernest was not listed in this census because he would come later in the year in October.

At some point around this time Anna had developed a bad case of goiter (a visible enlargement of the thyroid gland in the neck), which prompted her toward the end of 1912 to make travel plans to go to Oakland, CA to see a doctor to have it removed. Apparently there were no doctors specializing in this type of delicate surgery in Oregon. Anna made the journey south by herself. As the story has been told, Anna had the surgery performed on December 10th to have the gland removed. Excessive bleeding could not be stopped. The surgeon was not able to save her, and sadly Anna passed away. The very heartbreaking news came back to the family and the Verboort community that Anna had unfortunately passed away. Arrangements were made to bring her body home. Passing away at age 46, Anna left her husband of 23 years, and her nine children, with Ernest aged only two years, mourning her loss. The journalist who wrote her obituary described the type of wonderful person Anna was with eloquent kindness by writing, *"Anna had been a factor of the womanhood of Verboort, and the Hermens home was always the center of social activity. She was a woman of kindly disposition, generous charity, and her loss is a severe loss to the community."* Anna's obituary was published in the Hillsboro Argus on page five of the December 26, 1912 edition. She was laid to rest in the 2nd row of the southwest section of Visitation Catholic Cemetery in Verboort.

MRS. ANTON HERMENS

Mrs. Anna Joosten Hermens, wife of Anton Hermens, died at Oakland, Cal., December 10, and the remains were brought to Verboort, north of Cornelius, for interment in the cemetery, near her home for years. She was born in Bay Settlement, Wisconsin, Dec. 21, 1865, the daughter of Joseph and Petronella Joosten. The family moved to Oregon twenty-four years ago, and settled at Verboort. She was married to Mr. Hermens June 4, 1889, and the husband and nine children survive: William, Petronella, Paulina, Mary, Josephine, Martin, George, Christine, and Ernest, the youngest, aged about two years.

The funeral was held at the Verboort Catholic Church, and the services were under charge of Rev. Father John Bernard, of McMinnville. One of the largest gatherings ever witnessed in that section was in attendance at the funeral, Mrs. Hermens being a

universal favorite. The following brothers and sisters survive: Mrs. Walter Bernards, Verboort; Mrs. C. W. Hermens, McMinnville; Mrs. Wm. Weyenberg, Little Chute, Wisconsin; Martin Joosten, Rudolph, Wis.; Mrs. Adrian Verhaagen, Chili, Wis., and Mrs. Walter VanDyke, Verboort. The husband and children have the sympathy of a large circle of friends.

For twenty-four years Mrs. Hermens had been a factor in the womanhood of Verboort, and the Hermens home was always the center of social activity. She was a woman of kindly disposition, generous charity, and her death is a severe loss to the community.

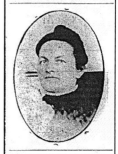

Image 6.03- Obituary of Anna Hermens (Joosten)

Although Anna was not able to experience any of the marriages of her children, four marriages would take place in each of the next four years. First was Petronella's marriage to Antone Evers in 1913, then William to Wilhelmina Bernards in 1914, next was Pauline to William VanLoo in 1915, and finally Mary to Albert Evers in 1916. As can be seen, Petronella and Mary both had new last names of Evers; they ended up marrying brothers. But this was not the first pair of siblings to marry into the Hermens family. Martin and Christine also married siblings, marrying Anna Marie and Antone Vandeberg the son and daughter of Henry and Petronella Vandeberg. Martin married in 1921, and Christine in 1924, both in Verboort. It is ironic how their spouse's names are the same as Martin and Christine's parents.

In 1920 the census taker captures Antone and his family still living in Verboort. Two sons and two daughters were living with him at this time. Josephine was now 23, Martin was 21, Christine was 14, and Ernest age 9. Also living with Antone to help with the farming was his nephew Joseph W. Hermens son of Jane and Cornelius Hermens. One might wonder where George (Peter) was, and why he was not living with his father too. He is shown in the census living with his oldest brother William, and they both were "milk wagon" drivers.

51	Fm	84	90	Hermans Antone	Head	1	O	F	M	W	55	Wd		Yes	Yes	Wisconsin
52	✓			— Josephine A	Daughter				F	W	23	S		Yes	Yes	Oregon
53	✓			— Martin J.	Son				M	W	21	S	No	Yes	Yes	Oregon
54	✓			— Christina E.	Daughter				F	W	14	S	Yes	Yes	Yes	Oregon
55	✓			— Ernest A	Son				M	W	9	S	Yes			Oregon
56	✓			— Joseph W	Nephew				M	W	21	S	No	Yes	Yes	Oregon

Image 6.04- 1920 Verboort, Washington County, OR Census, ED 435, sheet 5B

The other big news from 1920 was, after nearly eight years following the death of Anna, Antone decided to remarry at age 56. On September 07, 1920, he married Bridget Crunican (Gilroy) in McMinnville, OR. Bridget's first husband Matthew Crunican passed away on April 16, 1917 after only about ten years of marriage leaving Bridget with their four children. In 1930, three of the four Crunican children (twins Madeline and Mary, and Dorothy) were still living with Antone and Bridget on Martin Rd. Antone's son George and his family were living very close to the Hermens property, and another neighbor was his nephew Martin Bernards, who was living on the Bernards farm following the passing of his mother Frances, Antone's sister-in-law.

Some very sad news rocked the Hermens family through the first two months of 1937. Antone and Anna's oldest daughter Petronella Evers contracted influenza and passed away of pneumonia at the Jones Hospital in Hillsboro, OR on January 20th; she was only 45 years old. As if that was not enough, Antone departed this life on February 20th at age 73. According to his death certificate, an image of which I have included in the photos and images section below, reveals he died from "cerebral sclerosis", or otherwise known as a stroke. Father and daughter were interred in the Visitation Catholic Cemetery. Both their final resting places are located in the 2nd row of the southwest section.

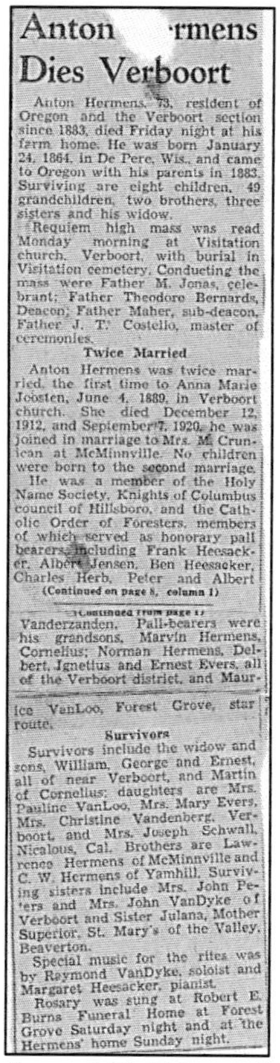
Anton ·rmens Dies Verboort

Anton Hermens, 73, resident of Oregon and the Verboort section since 1883, died Friday night at his farm home. He was born January 24, 1864, in De Pere, Wis., and came to Oregon with his parents in 1883. Surviving are eight children, 49 grandchildren, two brothers, three sisters and his widow.

Requiem high mass was read Monday morning at Visitation church, Verboort, with burial in Visitation cemetery. Conducting the mass were Father M. Jonas, celebrant; Father Theodore Bernards, Deacon; Father Maher, sub-deacon, Father J. T. Costello, master of ceremonies.

Twice Married

Anton Hermens was twice married, the first time to Anna Marie Joosten, June 4, 1889, in Verboort church. She died December 12, 1912, and September 7, 1920, he was joined in marriage to Mrs. M. Crunican at McMinnville. No children were born to the second marriage.

He was a member of the Holy Name Society, Knights of Columbus council of Hillsboro, and the Catholic Order of Foresters, members of which served as honorary pall bearers, including Frank Heesacker, Albert Jensen, Ben Heesacker, Charles Herb, Peter and Albert

(Continued on page 8, column 1)

(Continued from page 1)

Vanderzanden. Pall-bearers were his grandsons, Marvin Hermens, Cornelius; Norman Hermens, Delbert, Ignetius and Ernest Evers, all of the Verboort district, and Maurice VanLoo, Forest Grove, star route.

Survivors

Survivors include the widow and sons, William, George and Ernest, all of near Verboort, and Martin of Cornelius; daughters are Mrs. Pauline VanLoo, Mrs. Mary Evers, Mrs. Christine Vandenberg, Verboort, and Mrs. Joseph Schwall, Nicalous, Cal. Brothers are Lawrence Hermens of McMinnville and C. W. Hermens of Yamhill. Surviving sisters include Mrs. John Peters and Mrs. John VanDyke of Verboort and Sister Julana, Mother Superior, St. Mary's of the Valley, Beaverton.

Special music for the rites was by Raymond VanDyke, soloist and Margaret Heesacker, pianist.

Rosary was sung at Robert E. Burns Funeral Home at Forest Grove Saturday night and at the Hermens' home Sunday night.

Image 6.05- Obituary of Antone Hermens

Antone's son George became the administrator of his father's estate. After reviewing the probate document filed with the Washington County Courthouse there are some very interesting tidbits of information regarding the property and assets Antone and Anna amassed over the years, including some worthless investments. At the time of his death, Antone had the following assets:

- Two tracts of land that he was farming. One was 100 acres, and the second 55 acres. Value: $15,490
- About two tons of cow feed and six tons of hay. Value: $104
- 1929 Ford Model A. Value: $55
- 25 shares of Occident Rubber Company, a State of Washington Corporation, par value $10 each. Value: $0
- Six promissory notes to Silver Peak Copper Company with face values totaling $590, purchased in 1936 and 1937. Value $0

The probate document, which was filed with the county in 1944, also describes in great detail the houses and structures that were sitting on the farm. It is amazing to think about how many structures it took to run a successful farm, and Antone probably built all of them himself. The structures were fairly large too, especially the chicken house. If you have been adding it up, the total value listed here is over $6,900.

Structure Type	Size	Value
House #1, 50 years old	10 rooms	$1,500 to $1,800
House #2, 50 years old	9 rooms	$1,500 to $1,800
Barn #1	42 x 48 feet	$1,000
Barn #2*	42 x 70 feet	$1,000
Barn #3	24 x 40 feet	$500
Potato Cellar	14 x 18 feet	$150
Woodshed	14 x 18 feet	$100
Garage	14 x 18 feet	$100
Chicken House	20 x 46 feet	$125
Granary	20 x 30 feet	$135
Pump House	16 x 16 feet	$50
Hog Pen	14 x 24 feet	$100
Machine Shed	20 x 40 feet	$50

**includes two silos and a milk house*

In my mind a legacy is created through family and marriage, and Anna and Antone exemplified these values. Some interesting fun facts about the Hermens family legacy include… of the nine children blessed to Anna and Antone came 62 grandchildren. Although Antone's obituary states 49 grandchildren, the additional thirteen came after his passing. Who had the largest family? This honor goes to Mary and Albert Evers who had 15 children, and a close 2nd goes to Pauline and William VanLoo with 12 children. Who lived the longest? Mary Evers lived to 100! Who had the longest marriage? Ernest and Ida Hermens were married a remarkable 62 years, and Mary and Albert Evers were close with their 60 years of marriage. What is equally as incredible is the average length of marriage of the nine Hermens children, a whopping 49.5 years. All of these fun facts demonstrate just how much the Hermens family values marriage and family. A simply amazing legacy indeed.

A nice story comes out of the other Evers family, that of Petronella and Antone. The husband of their daughter Margaret, Rudy Landauer was a very honorable man. First of all he and Margaret shared 64 years of marriage before he passed away at age 98 in August 2013, but he also served in the US Army during World War II, and was awarded a Purple Heart. Even though he probably did not have the opportunity to graduate from high school in Kansas, he took that opportunity later in life ... much later. Rudy attended high school at Forest Grove, and earned his high school diploma in 2007 at age 92!! That's right, age 92. That is truly amazing.

So far I have come across two amazing stories of survival from the Evers family, and both are about a pair of siblings! The 15 children who came from the Mary and Albert Evers family definitely had some grit and perseverance.

The first astounding story of survival came out of the Evers family from Norma Peters (Evers) who wrote an article that looks like it appeared in a magazine. What follows is a summary of Norma's work. Fred Evers, Norma's brother, suffered a horrific hunting accident, survived, and lived to tell about it. In the early 1980s, Fred and his hunting companions, Fritz and Dave, were hunting deer on a chilly November day in the Tillamook National Forest, which is located in the Oregon Coastal mountain range; a short drive from Tillamook, OR. Dave set his sights on a four-point deer across a canyon, and put the deer down. The three men field-dressed the deer, and dragged it by the horns through the brush toward the road. They reached a ridge and heard two shots ring out in front of them. Instantly Fred felt a bullet rip through his neck, throwing him to the ground. With blood gushing from the bullet wound, he put three of his fingers from his right hand into his throat and wrapped them around his windpipe so he could breathe and avoid choking to death on the vast amounts of blood. After seeing what happened Dave shouted *"Don't shoot! You've shot this man!"* Soon a young teenage boy comes out of the brush to see what he had done. Dave told the boy to stay with Fred, and Dave ran for help. The closest phone was at a prison work camp less than a mile away. Fred's guardian angel was with him on this fateful morning. Two hunters they had passed on their way out arrived. One of them thankfully had been a paramedic in Vietnam, and knew instantly what to do. This man immediately put his hand on the artery at the base of Fred's neck to slow the tremendous flow of blood, told his hunting partner to prop his feet up, and covered Fred to keep him warm. Soon the teenager's father appeared on the scene. After seeing Fred's bleak condition, he urgently told his son *"let's go."* Apparently the father said they were headed to their car for some blankets, but unfortunately they never returned. On their way out they ran across Fritz, who had split off from Fred and Dave with the hope of bagging a deer sooner, and told him a gentleman had been shot. Fritz ran the rest of the way up the hill, and was overpowered by his level of shock. All he could mutter was *"you're going to be ok"*, and then added his jacket with the others covering Fred at the time.

Soon a young medic arrived from the prison work camp with a small first aid kit. After quickly assessing Fred's condition and his massive open wound, the medic shook his head and said there was nothing he *"could do with an open wound like that."* Just as this dire situation got bleaker, Dave and two men, also from the work camp, arrived with a stretcher. All of the men on the scene worked as a team to get Fred tied down to the stretcher while Fred kept his grip on his throat. The six men carried him feet-first down two hundred yards of steep terrain and thick brush.

The road was now within sight and the ambulance could be heard pulling up. Knowing Fred had made it this far was encouraging, but now that the ambulance was there, a little more optimism was in the air. The odds were still heavily stacked against him. He was loaded into the ambulance, and Fritz jumped in for the 30-mile ride to the hospital in Tillamook. As the ambulance hurried off, Fred noticed there were no lights and sirens blaring. He pointed upward with a twirling motion, which Fritz caught wind of and told the driver to turn on the siren and get moving faster.

Once arriving in the hospital emergency room, the doctor removed Fred's hand from his neck and inserted a tracheostomy tube into his windpipe. In disbelief after seeing the remarkable damage the doctor said *"you were dead two hours ago."* Fred was then immediately wheeled upstairs into surgery. While waiting outside the operating room a priest arrived to give Fred the Sacrament of Last Rites. Thinking he did not need his Last Rites, Fred tried to wave off the kind priest. But the priest continued anyway as a precaution. Fred's surgery was successful, and after coming out he found his wife Margie, mother Mary, and other family members waiting to see him. Thankfully, Fritz had called them while he was at the prison camp. The doctor briefed them on his condition by telling them he was very lucky, and added *"if he lives, he will never talk again."*

Johanna & Antone Hermens

Over the next 24 hours, Fred's condition became stronger, and the doctor felt he could endure the 80-mile ride to Portland. He was loaded into an ambulance again and sped off to Good Samaritan Hospital in Portland where a throat specialist was waiting to perform another surgery on Fred. After coming out of another successful surgery, the doctor told him the bullet pierced his windpipe and blew out his voicebox, taking out his vocal cords. The miracle that occurred on that fateful day was the bullet did not touch Fred's jugular artery. This is just amazing, and we all know if this artery were even slightly hit, Fred would have bled out and would have never made it out of the forest alive.

After thirty days and six surgeries, Fred's tracheostomy tube was removed and he was sent home. Even though he was fifty pounds lighter, he was able to breathe and eat on his own. He could now start to put this awful ordeal behind him, and try to get back to some sort of normal life. Certainly many adjustments would need to be made, including a new way to communicate. Fred mentioned he thinks often of the young boy who shot him, and hopes the teen is not carrying a heavy burden of guilt. One has to wonder if the boy learned that Fred survived this accident. If not, I feel it is unfortunate the boy could not experience closure, and move forward with his life, as Fred was able to do.

The second remarkable and inspiring story I have ever heard from the years of family history research I have done is the story of Eugene "Gene" Evers. Gene was a POW survivor of the Korean War, an imprisonment lasting 14 long and harrowing months. Once I heard the Portland, OR newspaper (The Oregonian) printed Gene's story, I was intrigued and immediately read it. Here is an excerpt from the March 30, 2013 article.

"Sixty years ago, Evers lived those 14 months as a prisoner of war in isolation, his human contact limited almost exclusively to a squad of Chinese guards and an interrogator. He carried shrapnel and burns from the attack on his doomed aircraft, was beaten repeatedly, kept on a frigid ledge where he was forced to remain seated at attention, given meager servings of water and rice gruel, allowed to relieve himself in a hole in the ground once a day and suffered a broken vertebrae. Somehow, when the war was over, he came out whole on the other side.

The hell of it is, Evers wasn't even supposed to be in Korea. His job was to inspect cameras carried by aircraft. He was stationed in Japan, far from the fighting on the Korean peninsula.

But one day, complaints about a balky camera led him to join the crew of a B-29 bomber on a reconnaissance mission over Korea. He knew the names of two members of the crew, who regarded him as a ride-along guest. On the way, he said, the cameras were working as they were supposed to.

Four hours into the flight, the high-flying Superfortress encountered a squadron of Russian MiGs. Their firing with 37-millimeter magnesium rounds killed members of the crew and set the plane ablaze. Evers was knocked unconscious, and when he came to the plane was empty except for the dead and careening toward a crash landing. The others had parachuted out, apparently assuming Evers was dead, too.

Evers scrambled for the opening, exiting the plane headfirst, rather than feet-first, as aviators are trained to do. He was wearing a parachute, but the only instruction he had ever been given was when he was a teenager in Oregon, when a pilot explained to him that he had to be sure to pull the handle fully away from the pack. He did so and the chute opened.

On the long way down, 'I said some pretty loud prayers,' he said. He aimed for a river, but missed, landing face-first in a rice paddy. It was around midnight, July 3, 1952.

He smeared iodine on his wounds and struggled to stay hidden and to walk. He covered about two miles, but Chinese troops found him on July 5 and took him prisoner.

Back home, his parents got a telegram from the Defense Department, informing them that their son had been killed. Three days later, they got another telegram, revising the message to say he was missing. He was never reported as a prisoner of war. And while Evers schemed about ways to get word to them, he never succeeded.

Evers' time as a prisoner was divided almost exactly in half by two extreme forms of captivity. For the first seven months, he was held in isolation in far northern Korea, spending his time in the open, never seeing the interior of a building. For most of the time, the guards forced him to sit on a concrete ledge under the eaves of an adobe house, keeping his eyes open and focused upward. He was clothed in a simple, navy-blue prison uniform. The only people he interacted with were his guards, who rotated shifts, and sometimes, an interrogator. He was always cold.

The Chinese apparently didn't know what to make of him. Other captured members of the B-29 crew didn't know his name. His story about being a camera inspector never convinced the interrogator he wasn't a spy -- an idea that Evers found ludicrous. He towered over most Chinese, has a northern European appearance and, after a while, a stout red beard. He couldn't possibly be inconspicuous in Korea.

After seven months, he was thrown into a Russian truck, blindfolded, forced to bend his head between his knees, and covered up with a tarp so he would be hidden. He rode that way for 28 hours and the constant pressure from guards sitting on him cracked a vertebrae in his neck -- a diagnosis that wasn't confirmed until more than 25 years later, when he had a scan at Oregon Health & Science University.

From the feeling of a smooth crossing over a bridge, Evers figured he had crossed into Chinese Manchuria. When he was taken out of the truck, he saw a three- or four-story concrete building. 'I'm going inside,' he thought, then passed out.

The day of his release was the first time Evers shared space with any other Americans -- two members of the B-29 crew who had been held separately. It was Sept. 6, more than five weeks after the armistice ended the war and divided Korea between the North and South. They were among the very last prisoners released.

The men were bundled together and driven to an American outpost. The general who received them didn't expect them. 'Who the hell are you guys?' he demanded. 'But welcome back.'"

The newspaper reporter ended this amazing story with a quote from Gene: *"'I'm not a hero,' he said, adding simply, 'I survived.'"* I think Gene is a hero in all of our minds.

* * *

Johanna & Antone Hermens

There were a large number of good men and women of the Hermens Family who served our fine country in the military. They are:

- ❖ Albert J. Coussens – Served in US Army during World War II.
- ❖ Edmund J. Evers - Served in the US Army as a Corporal during Korean War.
- ❖ Ernest P. Evers - Served in the US Army in New Guinea and the Philippines during World War II.
- ❖ Eugene E. Evers - Served in US Air Force in Korean War as an aircraft camera inspector. Chinese POW for 14 months.
- ❖ Frederick A. Evers - Served in the US Army during Korean War.
- ❖ Harold J. Evers - Served as a Corporal in the US Army during the Korean War.
- ❖ Ignatius A. Evers - Served in the 41st Division of the US Army during World War II.
- ❖ Neon D. Evers - Served in the US Army during Korean War.
- ❖ Robert J. Evers - Served in US Navy as a Motor Machinist 2nd Class during World War II.
- ❖ John J. Herinckx - Served in US Army as a Private during World War II. Awarded the Bronze Star medal for "heroic service in connection with military operations against the enemy at Saipan".
- ❖ Bertram J. Hermens – Served in the US Navy in the Pacific during World War II.
- ❖ Martin J. Hermens - Served in the US Army during World War I.
- ❖ Marvin J. Hermens - Served in the US Navy as an Aviation Machinist's Mate 2nd Class (AMM2) during World War II.
- ❖ John E. Hulsman, Jr. – Served in the US Marine Corp as a Corporal during World War II.
- ❖ Kenneth J. Kelly - Served in US Navy as a Fire Controlman 2nd Class during World War II.
- ❖ Richard J. La Haie - Served as a Private First Class in the 162nd Infantry, 41st Division for the US Army during World War II, and was killed in action.
- ❖ Rudolph F. Landauer - Served in the US Army during World War II. Received the Purple Heart.
- ❖ Vernon N. Maller - Served in US Navy during World War II.
- ❖ Homer E. Oblander - Served for the Coast Guard from 1942-1946.
- ❖ Stanley H. Schmidlkofer - Served in US Army during World War II.
- ❖ Lawrence A. Schwall – Served in the US Army during World War II.
- ❖ Arthur W. VanLoo - Served in the US Army as a Sergeant during World War II.
- ❖ Clifford A. VanLoo – Served in the US Army as a Private during World War II.
- ❖ Donald E. VanLoo - Served in the US Navy as a Seaman 1st Class (S1) during World War II.
- ❖ Vernon L. VanLoo - Served in the US Army during World War II.

MEDAL WINNER—Pvt. John J. Herinckx, son of Mr. and Mrs. Frank Herinckx of Banks, is entitled to wear the Bronze Star medal for "heroic service in connection with military operations against the enemy at Saipan." Pvt. Herinckx was home recently on a 30-day furlough.

Image 6.06- John Herinckx Military News Article

❧ **Photo and Image Gallery** ❧

Image 6.08- William Hermens

Image 6.07- Hermens Family about 1912. (back-L to R) Martin, Josephine, Mary, William, Pauline, Petronella, Peter. (front-L to R) Antone, Ernest, Christine, Johanna.

Image 6.09- Martin J. Hermens

Image 6.10- William & Pauline VanLoo Wedding Day Photo 1915

Image 6.11- Josephine Hermens & Albert Schwall Wedding 1920

Image 6.12- William and Minnie (Bernards) Hermens, 50th Anniversary Photo

*Image 6.13- Christine Hermens
and Antone Vandenberg
Wedding Photo 1924*

*Image 6.14- Ernest A & Ida M (Smith)
Hermens 50th Anniversary Photo*

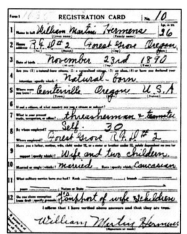

*Image 6.15- William M. Hermens, WW1
Draft Card*

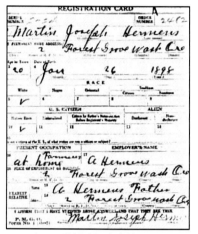

*Image 6.16- Martin J. Hermens
WW1 Draft Card*

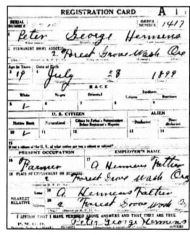

*Image 6.17- Peter G. Hermens
WW1 Draft Card*

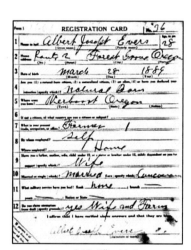

*Image 6.18- Albert J. Evers
WW1 Draft Card*

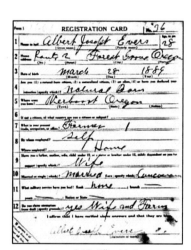

*Image 6.19- Albert J. Schwall
WW1 Draft Card*

*Image 6.20- Antone H. Evers
WW2 Draft Card*

*Image 6.21- William F. VanLoo
WW1 Draft Card*

Image 6.22- Anna Marie Hermens (Joosten) Headstone. Visitation Catholic Cemetery, SW section, row 2

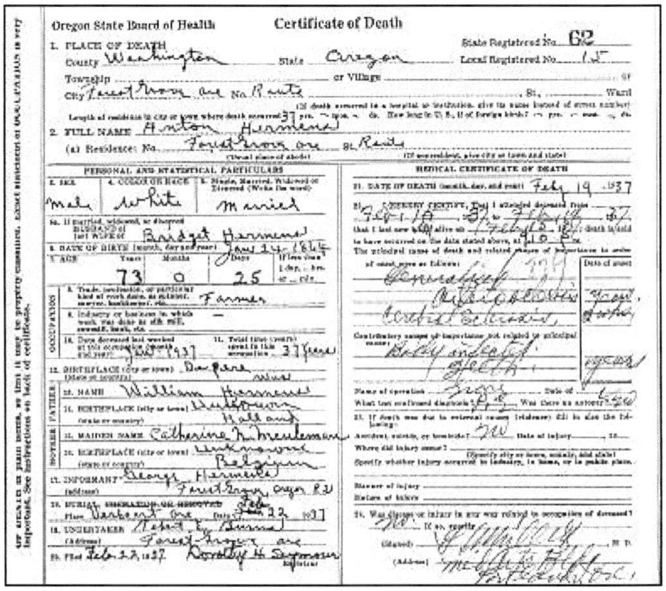

Image 6.24- Antone Hermens Death Certificate

Image 6.23- Antone Hermens Headstone. Visitation Catholic Cemetery, SW section, row 2

Image 6.25- Antone & Johanna (Joosten) Hermens Marriage Certificate 06-04-1889

❧ Descendants of Johanna Marie and Antone Hermens ❧

Notes: 1= 1st generation, 2= 2nd generation, 3= 3rd generation.
The year of birth is only given for individuals still living, if known.

1   Johanna Marie Joosten
    Born: December 21, 1865 in Bay Settlement, Brown County, Wisconsin
    Died: December 10, 1912 in Oakland, Alameda County, California
    Buried at: Visitation Catholic Cemetery, Verboort, OR, SW row 1
    Married: June 04, 1889 in Verboort, Washington County, Oregon
    Antone Hermens
    Born: January 24, 1864 in De Pere, Brown County, Wisconsin
    Died: February 19, 1937 in Verboort, Washington County, Oregon
    Buried at: Visitation Catholic Cemetery, Verboort, OR, SW row 2
    Parents: William Hermens (1830-1916) and Catharine N. Meulemans (1840-1911)

   2   William Martin Hermens
       Born: November 23, 1890 in Schefflin, Oregon
       Died: October 30, 1973 in Forest Grove, Washington County, Oregon
       Buried at: Visitation Catholic Cemetery, Verboort, OR, SW row 2
       Married: October 13, 1914 in Verboort, Washington County, Oregon
       Wilhelmina Apollonia Bernards
       Born: April 17, 1892 in Verboort, Washington County, Oregon
       Died: February 24, 1978 in Beaverton, Washington County, Oregon
       Buried at: Visitation Catholic Cemetery, Verboort, OR, SW row 2
       Parents: Theodore Mathias Bernards (1852-1936) and Catherine DeGroot (1859-1937)

      3   Bertram Joseph Hermens
          Born: March 27, 1915 in Verboort, Washington County, Oregon
          Died: January 27, 2006 in Banks, Washington County, Oregon
          Buried at: St. Francis of Assisi Catholic Cemetery, Roy, OR
          Married: February 12, 1947 in Roy, Washington County, Oregon
          Rita Catherine Duyck
          Born: May 30, 1920 in Roy, Washington County, Oregon
          Died: November 19, 2011
          Buried at: St. Francis of Assisi Catholic Cemetery, Roy, OR
          Parents: Henry Duyck (1869-1948) and Helen Catherine Spiering (1882-1970)

      3   Muriel Ann Hermens
          Born: 1917 in Verboort, Washington County, Oregon
          Died: March 27, 2014 in Tigard, Washington County, Oregon
          Buried at: St. Francis of Assisi Catholic Cemetery, Roy, OR, west row 1
          Married (1): February 28, 1942 in Tacoma, Pierce County, Washington
          Married (2): May 12, 1979 in Clackamas County, Oregon
          Patrick Joseph Moore (1)
          Born: March 18, 1912 in Forest Grove, Washington County, Oregon
          Died: November 15, 1971 in Lake Grove, Clackamas County, Oregon
          Buried at: St. Francis of Assisi Catholic Cemetery, Roy, OR, west row 1
          Parents: Hugh E. Moore (1873-1954) and Wilhelmina B. Vanderzanden (1880-1926)
          Thomas E. Petty (2)
          Born: March 19, 1916
          Died: February 03, 2003 in Washington County, Oregon
          Buried at:
          Parents: Unknown

3   Robert William Hermens
Born: May 13, 1918 in Verboort, Washington County, Oregon
Died: May 15, 1918 in Verboort, Washington County, Oregon
Buried at: Visitation Catholic Cemetery, Verboort, OR, SW row 2
Married: n/a

3   Eugenia Catherine Hermens
Born: December 05, 1923 in Verboort, Washington County, Oregon
Died: February 19, 2015 in Hillsboro, Washington County, Oregon
Buried at: Visitation Catholic Cemetery, Verboort, OR
Married (1): November 23, 1942 in Roy, Washington County, Oregon
Married (2): November 18, 1947 in Verboort, Washington County, Oregon
Richard Joseph La Haie (1)
Born: April 21, 1921 in Verboort, Washington County, Oregon
Died: May 29, 1944 in Biak, Papua, Indonesia
Buried at: Manila American Cemetery, Manila, Philippines
Parents: Amos Z. La Haie (1890-1982) and Wilhelmina A. Vandervelden (1890-1980)
Albert J. Coussens (2)
Born: March 01, 1922 in North Plains, Washington County, Oregon
Died: August 07, 1994 in Hillsboro, Washington County, Oregon
Buried at: Visitation Catholic Cemetery, Verboort, OR, SW row 7
Parents: Benjamin H. Coussens (1890-1964) and Mary J. Coussens (1893-?)

3   Dorothy Marie Therese Hermens
Born: 1925 in Hillsboro, Washington County, Oregon
Died: Living
Buried at:
Married: n/a

3   Theresa Geraldine Hermens
Born: April 25, 1927 in Hillsboro, Washington County, Oregon
Died: April 25, 1927 in Hillsboro, Washington County, Oregon
Buried at: Visitation Catholic Cemetery, Verboort, OR, SW row 2
Married: n/a

3   Anna Margaret Hermens
Born: 1929 in Hillsboro, Washington County, Oregon
Died: Living
Buried at:
Married: April 26, 1949 in Verboort, Washington County, Oregon
Stanley Howard Schmidlkofer
Born: June 05, 1926 in Banks, Washington County, Oregon
Died: January 13, 2004 in Portland, Multnomah County, Oregon
Buried at: Visitation Catholic Cemetery, Verboort, OR, SW row 7
Parents: Joseph C. Schmidlkofer Sr. (1899-1988) and Patronella Cropp (1902-1958)

3   Frances Mary Hermens
Born: 1931 in Hillsboro, Washington County, Oregon
Died: Living
Buried at:
Married: Unknown

Kenneth Joseph Kelly
Born: October 09, 1917 in New Albin, Allamakee County, Iowa
Died: September 30, 2007 in Walnut Creek, Contra Costa County, California
Buried at: Willamette National Cemetery, Portland, OR, sec KK, site 123
Parents: Unknown

2   Petronella Maria Hermens
Born: November 27, 1891 in Verboort, Washington County, Oregon
Died: January 20, 1937 in Hillsboro, Washington County, Oregon
Buried at: Visitation Catholic Cemetery, Verboort, OR, SW row 2
Married: June 25, 1913 in Verboort, Washington County, Oregon
Antone Henry Evers
Born: September 16, 1886 in Verboort, Washington County, Oregon
Died: November 20, 1978 in Beaverton, Washington County, Oregon
Buried at: Visitation Catholic Cemetery, Verboort, OR, SW row 2
Parents: Peter Evers (1851-1937) and Antonia Vandehey (1858-1891)

    3   Ernest Peter Evers
Born: July 14, 1914 in Crabtree, Washington County, Oregon
Died: May 28, 1976 in Portland, Multnomah County, Oregon
Buried at: Visitation Catholic Cemetery, Verboort, OR, SW row 2
Married: n/a

    3   Lucille A. Evers
Born: September 29, 1915 in Crabtree, Linn County, Oregon
Died: March 05, 2012 in Hillsboro, Washington County, Oregon
Buried at: Mt. View Memorial Gardens, Forest Grove, OR
Married: February 11, 1947 in Verboort, Washington County, Oregon
Francis Wilbert Kempen
Born: June 20, 1914 in Hollandtown, Brown County, Wisconsin
Died: October 23, 2000 in Hillsboro, Washington County, Oregon
Buried at: Mt. View Memorial Gardens, Forest Grove, OR
Parents: Henry Kempen (1862-1947) and Hannah Kempen (1878-1936)

    3   Anna L. Evers
Born: April 20, 1919 in Verboort, Washington County, Oregon
Died: January 27, 2013 in Beaverton, Washington County, Oregon
Buried at: Sisters of St. Mary of Oregon Cemetery, Beaverton, OR
Professed Vows: Sr. Mary Anna, SSMO in 1940 with Sisters of St. Mary of Oregon

    3   Francis Antone Evers
Born: March 29, 1922 in Verboort, Washington County, Oregon
Died: November 05, 2000 in Verboort, Washington County, Oregon
Buried at: Visitation Catholic Cemetery, Verboort, OR, SE row 4
Married: January 11, 1958 in Verboort, Washington County, Oregon
Louella Mary Vandenberghe
Born: April 13, 1925 in Butler, Ottertail County, Minnesota
Died: November 28, 2009 in Hillsboro, Washington County, Oregon
Buried at: Visitation Catholic Cemetery, Verboort, OR, SE row 4
Parents: Raymond VandenBerghe (1898-1961) and Elizabeth Schaeffer (1898-1967)

3   Robert Joseph Evers
Born: July 10, 1923 in Verboort, Washington County, Oregon
Died: December 29, 1986 in Portland, Multnomah County, Oregon
Buried at: Willamette National Cemetery, Portland, OR, sec D, site 2502
Married: n/a

3   Willis Albert Evers
Born: February 16, 1925 in Verboort, Washington County, Oregon
Died: August 08, 2007 in Portland, Multnomah County, Oregon
Buried at: Mt. Calvary Catholic Cemetery, Portland, OR, sec U, lot 504
Married: June 02, 1951 in Forest Grove, Washington County, Oregon
Eileen M. Morris
Born: June 27, 1924 in Tiskilwa, Bureau County, Illinois
Died: April 07, 1999 in Hillsboro, Washington County, Oregon
Buried at: Mt. Calvary Catholic Cemetery, Portland, OR, sec U, lot 504
Parents: Samuel R. Morris (1878-1960) & Elsie B. Spriggle (1884-1934)

3   Margaret Mary Evers
Born: 1927 in Verboort, Washington County, Oregon
Died: Living
Buried at:
Married: April 20, 1949 in Washington County, Oregon
Rudolph Frank Landauer
Born: November 23, 1914 in Klamath Falls, Klamath County, Oregon
Died: August 29, 2013 in Verboort, Washington County, Oregon
Buried at: Visitation Catholic Cemetery, Verboort, OR
Parents: Carl A. Landauer (1884-1943) and Philomena Gaschler (1887-1970)

3   Barbara Jean Evers
Born: November 23, 1930 in Verboort, Washington County, Oregon
Died: August 14, 2008 in Hillsboro, Washington County, Oregon
Buried at: Visitation Catholic Cemetery, Verboort, OR, SW row 2
Married: October 18, 1958 in Verboort, Washington County, Oregon
Vernon Edward Meeuwsen
Born: November 05, 1931 in Roy, Washington County, Oregon
Died: July 10, 2010 in Hillsboro, Washington County, Oregon
Buried at: Visitation Catholic Cemetery, Verboort, OR, SW row 2
Parents: William A. Meeuwsen (1895-1974) and Mary A. Vanderzanden (1896-1988)

3   Janice Marie Evers
Born: 1935 in Verboort, Washington County, Oregon
Died: Living
Buried at:
Married (1): August 29, 1959 in Washington County, Oregon
Married (2): January 24, 1992 in Washington County, Oregon
Richard Ernest Spath, Sr. (1)
Born: August 30, 1936 in Oregon
Died: August 24, 1987 in Warrenton, Clatsop County, Oregon
Buried at:
Parents: Ernest R. Spath (1909-1971) and Helen Stephen (1915-1983)

Richard John Duyck (2)
Born: 1933 in Oregon
Died: Living
Buried at:
Parents: Julius C. Duyck (1906-1984) and Geraldine M. VanDomelen (1910-1984)

2 Pauline Nathalia Hermens
Born: March 14, 1893 in Verboort, Washington County, Oregon
Died: May 30, 1964 in Beaverton, Washington County, Oregon
Buried at: Visitation Catholic Cemetery, Verboort, OR, SW row 2
Married: June 16, 1915 in Verboort, Washington County, Oregon
William Francis VanLoo
Born: May 14, 1887 in Verboort, Washington County, Oregon
Died: April 18, 1971 in Portland, Multnomah County, Oregon
Buried at: Visitation Catholic Cemetery, Verboort, OR, SW row 2
Parents: Augustine VanLoo (1857-1911) and Petronella Evers (1857-1932)

   3 Maurice Augustine VanLoo
   Born: July 20, 1916 in Forest Grove, Washington County, Oregon
   Died: May 25, 2014 in Hillsboro, Washington County, Oregon
   Buried at: St. Francis of Assisi Catholic Cemetery, Roy, OR, north row 4
   Married: August 29, 1939 in Roy, Washington County, Oregon
   Clara Marie Kemper
   Born: September 12, 1912 in Roy, Washington County, Oregon
   Died: January 20, 1985 in Portland, Multnomah County, Oregon
   Buried at: St. Francis of Assisi Catholic Cemetery, Roy, OR, north row 4
   Parents: Frank Kemper (1885-1942) & Anna M. Vandehey (1891-1990)

   3 Arthur William VanLoo, Sr.
   Born: August 17, 1918 in Forest Grove, Washington County, Oregon
   Died: September 14, 1993 in Cloverdale, Tillamook County, Oregon
   Buried at: Sacred Heart Catholic Cemetery, Tillamook, OR
   Married: June 03, 1943 in Rapid City, Pennington County, South Dakota
   Agnes Cecelia VonEuw
   Born: May 04, 1918 in Cloverdale, Tillamook County, Oregon
   Died: December 29, 2008 in Beaverton, Washington County, Oregon
   Buried at: Sacred Heart Catholic Cemetery, Tillamook, OR
   Parents: Frank VonEuw (1886-1966) and Josephine Hurliman (1896-1975)

   3 Mildred Anne VanLoo
   Born: January 22, 1920 in Forest Grove, Washington County, Oregon
   Died: February 05, 2001
   Buried at: Mt. Calvary Catholic Cemetery, Portland, OR, sec L, lot 1219
   Married (1): 1942
   Married (2): February 04, 1954 in Stevenson, Skamania County, Washington
   Joseph Edward Oglesby (1)
   Born: August 03, 1915 in Roy, Washington County, Oregon
   Died: October 12, 1951
   Buried at: Mt. Calvary Catholic Cemetery, Portland, OR, sec L, lot 1219
   Parents: Unknown

Bernard Henry Van Meltebeke (2)
Born: June 13, 1928
Died: November 03, 2004
Buried at: Willamette National Cemetery, Portland, OR, Sec. Y, Site 2417
Parents: Bernard Van Meltebeke (1897-?) and Bertha Van Meltebeke (1901-?)

3   Donald Edward VanLoo
Born: August 12, 1921 in Forest Grove, Washington County, Oregon
Died: July 26, 1999 in Concord, Contra Costa County, California
Buried at: Willamette National Cemetery, Portland, OR, sec MB, site 144
Married (1): Unknown
Married (2): Unknown
Georgia Mable Mays (1)
Born: Unknown
Died: August 25, 1962 in Pittsburg, Contra Costa County, California
Buried at:
Parents: Unknown
Rachel Maude Asher (2)
Born: September 13, 1913 in Tennessee
Died: July 22, 1984 in Pittsburg, Contra Costa County, California
Buried at: Memory Gardens Cemetery, Concord, CA
Parents: Unknown

3   Edna Pauline VanLoo
Born: 1923 in Oregon
Died: Living
Buried at:
Married: Unknown
Wesley Warren Lee, Sr.
Born: May 19, 1923 in Gales Creek, Washington County, Oregon
Died: July 31, 1989 in Forest Grove, Washington County, Oregon
Buried at: Gales Creek Cemetery, Gales Creek, OR
Parents: William D. Lee (1869-1935) and Dora B. Smith (1879-1953)

3   Clifford Anthony VanLoo
Born: April 07, 1925 in Forest Grove, Washington County, Oregon
Died: December 08, 2012 in Forest Grove, Washington County, Oregon
Buried at: Gales Creek Cemetery, Gales Creek, OR
Married: November 23, 1949 in Forest Grove, Washington County, Oregon
Janice Rose Eastwood
Born: 1929 or 1930 in Oregon
Died: Living
Buried at:
Parents: Clarence J. Eastwood, Sr. (1906-1987) and Emma R. Eastwood (1907-1999)

3   Doris Ella VanLoo
Born: November 27, 1926 in Forest Grove, Washington County, Oregon
Died: December 20, 1928 in Forest Grove, Washington County, Oregon
Buried at: Visitation Catholic Cemetery, Verboort, OR, SW row 2
Married: n/a

3   Vernon Leon VanLoo
    Born: July 13, 1928 in Forest Grove, Washington County, Oregon
    Died: August 13, 2007 in Hillsboro, Washington County, Oregon
    Buried at: Unknown
    Married: August 29, 1955 in Stevenson, Skamania County, Washington
    Florence Marie Perdew
    Born: December 15, 1934 in Gemmell, Minnesota
    Died: October 28, 2012 in Dilley, Washington County, Oregon
    Buried at: Forest View Cemetery, Forest Grove, OR
    Parents: Bert F. Perdew (1900-1998) and Pearl C. Tindell (1907-1976)

3   Beryl Cecilia VanLoo
    Born: October 24, 1929 in Forest Grove, Washington County, Oregon
    Died: February 26, 1978 in Cornelius, Washington County, Oregon
    Buried at: Mt. View Memorial Gardens, Forest Grove, OR.
    Married: October 17, 1953 in Washington County, Oregon
    LeRoy Edwin Reynolds
    Born: Unknown
    Died: Living
    Buried at:
    Parents: Unknown

3   Irene R. VanLoo
    Born: 1931 in Oregon
    Died: Living
    Buried at:
    Married (1): August 18, 1956 in McMinnville, Yamhill County, Oregon
    Married (2): June 28, 1968 in Washington County, Oregon
    Ralph Mahlon Williams (1)
    Born: October 30, 1922 in Cornelius, Washington County, Oregon
    Died: August 10, 1966 in Hillsboro, Washington County, Oregon
    Buried at: Willamette National Cemetery, Portland, OR
    Parents: Ralph I. Williams and Lydia Herr
    Dean A. Ritchey (2)
    Born: 1934
    Died: Living
    Buried at:
    Parents: Unknown

3   George Herman VanLoo
    Born: September 03, 1934 in Forest Grove, Washington County, Oregon
    Died: October 11, 2006 in Portland, Multnomah County, Oregon
    Buried at:
    Married (1): June 26, 1954 in Washington County, Oregon
    Married (2): October 17, 1994 in Washoe, County, Nevada
    Mildred Williams (1)
    Born: Unknown
    Died: Living
    Buried at:
    Parents: Unknown

Valentina Marie Oberson (2)
Born: Unknown
Died: Living
Buried at:
Parents: Unknown

3   Louise M. VanLoo
Born: 1935 in Oregon
Died: Living
Buried at:
Married: May 31, 1957 in Washington County, Idaho
Franklin Dale Nemeyer
Born: March 12, 1934 in Forest Grove, Washington County, Oregon
Died: February 27, 2011 in Hillsboro, Washington County, Oregon
Buried at:
Parents: Charles A. Nemeyer (1886-1974) and Malinda C. Rauert (1893-1967)

3   Earl Joseph VanLoo
Born: July 28, 1937 in Forest Grove, Washington County, Oregon
Died: August 16, 1990 in Portland, Multnomah County, Oregon
Buried at: Gales Creek Cemetery, Gales Creek, OR
Married: May 31, 1957 in Weiser, Washington County, Idaho
Theola Adelle Hatfield
Born: 1937
Died: Living
Buried at:
Parents: Unknown

2   Mary Antoinette Hermens
Born: May 01, 1895 in Verboort, Washington County, Oregon
Died: October 03, 1995 in Beaverton, Washington County, Oregon
Buried at: Visitation Catholic Cemetery, Verboort, OR., SW row 2
Married: May 24, 1916 in Verboort, Washington County, Oregon
Albert Joseph Evers
Born: March 28, 1889 in Verboort, Washington County, Oregon
Died: December 26, 1976 in Verboort, Washington County, Oregon
Buried at: Visitation Catholic Cemetery, Verboort, OR., SW row 2
Parents: Peter Evers (1851-1937) and Antonia Vandehey (1858-1891)

3   Anna Marie Evers
Born: April 12, 1917 in Verboort, Washington County, Oregon
Died: May 01, 1917 in Verboort, Washington County, Oregon
Buried at: Visitation Catholic Cemetery, Verboort, OR, SE row 2
Married: n/a

3   Ignatius Aloysius Evers
Born: 1918 in Verboort, Washington County, Oregon
Died: Living
Buried at:
Married: August 22, 1948

Marcella Leona DeClerk
Born: July 11, 1929 in Perham, Ottertail County, Minnesota
Died: May 04, 2014 in Forest Grove, Washington County, Oregon
Buried at: Visitation Catholic Cemetery, Verboort, OR
Parents: August DeClerk (1885-1965) and Mary I. VandenBerghe (1890-?)

3 Adelbert Ernest Evers
Born: June 25, 1920 in Verboort, Washington County, Oregon
Died: June 23, 1998 in Forest Grove, Washington County, Oregon
Buried at: St. Francis of Assisi Catholic Cemetery, Roy, OR, south row 14
Married: November 08, 1944 in Roy, Washington County, Oregon
Florence Elizabeth Vanderzanden
Born: September 22, 1915 in Banks, Washington County, Oregon
Died: March 29, 2006 in Beaverton, Washington County, Oregon
Buried at: St. Francis of Assisi Catholic Cemetery, Roy, OR, south row 14
Parents: Theodore M. Vanderzanden (1880-1967) and Margaret Van Domelen (1893-1922)

3 Florence Mary Evers
Born: 1922 in Verboort, Washington County, Oregon
Died: Living
Buried at:
Married: November 23, 1944 in Vancouver, Clark County, Washington
John Joseph Herinckx
Born: March 28, 1918 in Mountaindale, Washington County, Oregon
Died: May 21, 2007 in Cornelius, Washington County, Oregon
Buried at: St. Francis of Assisi Catholic Cemetery, Roy, OR
Parents: Frank Herinckx (1888-1947) and Nettie C. Vanaudenhaegen (1890-1985)

3 Peter Ralph Evers
Born: 1924 in Verboort, Washington County, Oregon
Died: Living
Buried at:
Married (1): February 10, 1953 in Clackamas County, Oregon
Married (2): February 09, 1993 in Reno, Washoe County, Nevada
Mary Suzanne Miller (1)
Born: Unknown
Died: Living
Buried at:
Parents:
Genevieve Mary Vanderzanden (2)
Born: 1922 in Verboort, Washington County, Oregon
Died: Living
Buried at: St. Francis Catholic Cemetery, Roy, OR, south row 12
Parents: Peter H. Vanderzanden (1886-1972) and Wilhelmina B. Vandehey (1892-1967)

3 Agnes Dorothy Evers
Born: 1926 in Verboort, Washington County, Oregon
Died: Living
Buried at:
Married: September 11, 1947 in Verboort, Washington County, Oregon

Homer Eugene Oblander
Born: May 05, 1923 in Kansas
Died: October 04, 2007 in Washington County, Oregon
Buried at: Visitation Catholic Cemetery, Verboort, OR
Parents: Jacob G. Oblander (1896-1965) and Ellen E. Morse (1896-1986)

3   Edmund Justin Evers
Born: April 12, 1928 in Verboort, Washington County, Oregon
Died: September 16, 1956 in Forest Grove, Washington County, Oregon
Buried at: Visitation Catholic Cemetery, Verboort, OR, SW row 1
Married: n/a

3   Alvin A. Evers
Born: 1929 in Verboort, Washington County, Oregon
Died: Living
Buried at:
Married: January 02, 1950 in Washington County, Oregon
Janice Caroline Meeuwsen
Born: 1933 in Oregon
Died: Living
Buried at:
Parents: Edward A. Meeuwsen (1903-1983) and Josephine Van Domelen (1904-1980)

3   Eugene Ernest Evers
Born: 1931 in Verboort, Washington County, Oregon
Died: Living
Buried at:
Married (1): October 18, 1954 in Washington County, Oregon
Married (2): July 01, 1997 in Washington County, Oregon
Deloris May Rierson
Born: Unknown
Died: Living
Buried at:
Parents: Andrew Rierson and Frances Meyers
Janice Fay Sherburne
Born: 1936 or 1937 in Oregon
Died: Living
Buried at:
Parents: George Sherborne (1913-1957) and Mildred G. Anderson (1917-2007)

3   Harold Joseph Evers
Born: March 19, 1933 in Verboort, Washington County, Oregon
Died: December 30, 2010 in Hillsboro, Washington County, Oregon
Buried at: Evers Family Cemetery, Verboort, OR.
Married (1): July 15, 1957 in Texas
Married (2): July 03, 1980 in Verboort, Washington County, Oregon
Catherine Lavern Braden (1)
Born: July 22, 1933 in Tillamook, Tillamook County, Oregon
Died: July 31, 1978 in Forest Grove, Washington County, Oregon
Buried: Visitation Catholic Cemetery, Verboort, OR, SW row 7
Parents: Unknown

Betty Louise Bernards (2)
Born: January 24, 1927 in North Plains, Washington County, Oregon
Died: August 06, 2010 in North Plains, Washington County, Oregon
Buried at: Evers Family Cemetery, Verboort, OR.
Parents: Joseph Bernards (1887-1978) and Emma K. Achen (1889-1976)

3 Vern Clair Evers
Born: October 30, 1934 in Verboort, Washington County, Oregon
Died: February 23, 2012 in Portland, Multnomah County, Oregon
Buried at:
Married: December 03, 1953 in Hillsboro, Washington County, Oregon
Dixie Rochelle Baughman
Born: 1937 in Oregon
Died: Living
Buried at:
Parents: Richard E. Baughman (1913-1971) and Elma L. Gottlieb (1915-1997)

3 Neon Donovan Evers
Born: 1936 in Verboort, Washington County, Oregon
Died: Living
Buried at:
Married: April 21, 1979 in Multnomah County, Oregon
Bac Thi Tuan
Born: 1946
Died: Living
Buried at:
Parents: Unknown

3 Joseph Albert Evers
Born: 1938 in Verboort, Washington County, Oregon
Died: Living
Buried at:
Married: May 07, 1960 in Verboort, Washington County, Oregon
Beverly Johanna Boogard
Born: 1939
Died: Living
Buried at:
Parents: Cornelius Boogard and Alfreda DeClerk

3 Frederick Allen Evers
Born: 1941 in Verboort, Washington County, Oregon
Died: Living
Buried at:
Married: February 19, 1966 in Roy, Washington County, Oregon
Margaret Ann Van Domelen
Born: 1944
Died: Living
Buried at:
Parents: Oliver H. Van Domelen (1907-1993) and Frances E. Kearn (1911-1993)

3   Norma Sue Evers
Born: 1943 in Verboort, Washington County, Oregon
Died: Living
Buried at:
Married: January 06, 1979 in Waterloo, Black Hawk County, Iowa
Timothy John Peters
Born: 1950
Died: Living
Buried at:
Parents: Unknown

2   Josephine Adelia Hermens
Born: November 27, 1896 in Verboort, Washington County, Oregon
Died: January 08, 1992 in Sacramento, Sacramento County, California
Buried at: Nicolaus Cemetery, Nicolaus, CA
Married: June 02, 1920 in Verboort, Washington County, Oregon
Albert Joseph Schwall
Born: December 22, 1896 in Nicolaus, Sutter County, California
Died: August 30, 1973 in Yuba City, Sutter County, California
Buried at: Nicolaus Cemetery, Nicolaus, CA
Parents: Martin Schwall (1865-1937) and Josephine K. Albert (1867-1954)

3   Robert Francis Schwall, Sr.
Born: April 21, 1921 in Nicolaus, Sutter County, California
Died: January 05, 1996 in Marysville, Yuba County, California
Buried at: Nicolaus Cemetery, Nicolaus, CA
Married: August 19, 1945 in Nicolaus, Sutter County, California
Barbara Jean Sears
Born: December 22, 1926 in Grass Valley, Nevada County, California
Died: July 16, 1996 in Sacramento, Sacramento County, California
Buried at: Nicolaus Cemetery, Nicolaus, CA
Parents: Frank H. Sears (1888-1969) and Lydia Sears (1890-?)

3   Anna Mary Schwall
Born: October 15, 1922 in Nicolaus, Sutter County, California
Died: June 16, 2008 in Sacramento, Sacramento County, California
Buried at: Nicolaus Cemetery, Nicolaus, CA
Married: n/a

3   Deloris Agnes Schwall
Born: 1925 in Nicolaus, Sutter County, California
Died: Living
Buried at: n/a
Professed Vows: Sr. Mary Alberta, SSMO on August 15, 1951 with Sisters of St. Mary of Oregon

3   Lawrence Albert Schwall
Born: May 04, 1926 in Nicolaus, Sutter County, California
Died: March 23, 1974 in Marysville, Yuba County, California
Buried at: Nicolaus Cemetery, Nicolaus, CA
Married: June 14, 1953 in Nicolaus, Sutter County, California

Claire June Darrach
Born: 1934 in Pleasant Grove, Sutter County, California
Died: Living
Buried at:
Parents: George N. Darrach (1895-1968) and Maud C. Darrach (1902-1985)

3　Evelyn Elizabeth Schwall
Born: 1927 in Nicolaus, Sutter County, California
Died: Living
Buried at:
Professed Vows: Sr. Mary Evelyn, SSMO on August 15, 1959 with Sisters of St. Mary of Oregon

3　Harold Joseph Schwall
Born: 1930 in Nicolaus, Sutter County, California
Died: Living
Buried at: n/a
Married: January 10, 1954 in Nicolaus, Sutter County, California
Betty Ann Borg
Born: September 09, 1931 in Paintersville, Sacramento, County, California
Died: June 19, 2012 in Sacramento, Sacramento County, California
Buried at: Nicolaus Cemetery, Nicolaus, CA
Parents: Olaf R. Borg (1886-1935) and Elsa M. Nilsson (1900-1978)

3　Ralph Joseph Schwall
Born: February 28, 1932 in Nicolaus, Sutter County, California
Died: February 27, 1941 in Nicolaus, Sutter County, California
Buried at: Nicolaus Cemetery, Nicolaus, CA
Married: n/a

2　Martin Joseph Hermens
Born: January 26, 1898 in Verboort, Washington County, Oregon
Died: October 29, 1969 in White City, Josephine County, Oregon
Buried at: Fir Lawn Cemetery, Hillsboro, OR
Married (1): May 21, 1921
Married (2): November 06, 1950 in Washington County, Oregon
Anna Marie Vandeberg (1)
Born: February 04, 1902 in Verboort, Washington County, Oregon
Died: September 30, 1978 in Forest Grove, Washington County, Oregon
Buried at: Mt. View Memorial Gardens, Forest Grove, OR
Parents: Henry Vandeberg (1872-1904) and Petronella Vandeberg (1877-1904)
Celia N. Mawhirter (2)
Born: 1908
Died: 1956 in Washington County, Oregon
Buried at: Fir Lawn Cemetery, Hillsboro, OR
Parents: Unknown

3　Marvin J. Hermens
Born: July 23, 1922 in Oregon
Died: May 11, 1992 in Sisters, Deschutes County, Oregon
Buried at: Deschutes Memorial Gardens, Bend, OR
Married: April 13, 1947 in Coos County, Oregon

Virginia Lee Wilson
Born: September 06, 1926
Died: August 31, 2003 in Sisters, Deschutes County, Oregon
Buried at: Deschutes Memorial Gardens, Bend, OR
Parents: Unknown

3   Eleaner Ann Hermens
Born: 1925 in Oregon
Died:
Buried at:
Married (1): November 15, 1947 in Cornelius, Washington County, Oregon
Married (2): July 29, 1995 in Washington County, Oregon
John E. Hulsman, Jr. (1)
Born: May 28, 1925 in Cornelius, Washington County, Oregon
Died: March 03, 2009 in Tualatin, Washington County, Oregon
Buried at: Fern Hill Cemetery, Cornelius, OR
Parents: John E. Hulsman, Sr. (1886-1975) and Charlotte E. Hamelman (1892-1975)
William Eberhart Fitzgerald (2)
Born: Unknown
Died: Living
Buried at:
Parents: Unknown

2   Peter George Hermens
Born: July 23, 1899 in Verboort, Washington County, Oregon
Died: March 01, 1966 in Portland, Multnomah County, Oregon
Buried at: Visitation Catholic Cemetery, Verboort, OR, SE row 2
Married: February 01, 1921 in Roy, Washington County, Oregon
Rose Margaret Cop
Born: April 03, 1900 in Roy, Washington County, Oregon
Died: December 18, 1980 in Hillsboro, Washington County, Oregon
Buried at: Visitation Catholic Cemetery, Verboort, OR, SE row 2
Parents: Henry Cop (1856-1944) and Elizabeth Spiering (1863-1911)

3   Norman Frances Hermens
Born: July 13, 1922 in Oregon
Died: March 17, 2001 in Beaverton, Washington County, Oregon
Buried at: Mt. Calvary Catholic Cemetery, Portland, OR
Married: June 26, 1948 in Multnomah County, Oregon
Elsie Regina Schachner
Born: April 23, 1925 in Bensheim, Bergstrasse, Hesse, Germany
Died: January 05, 2011 in Beaverton, Washington County, Oregon
Buried at: Mt. Calvary Catholic Cemetery, Portland, OR
Parents: Frank H. Schachner (1901-1990) and Eva L. Treffert (1902-1990)

3   Aileen E. Hermens
Born: 1926 in Oregon
Died:
Buried at:
Married: May 05, 1949 in Washington County, Oregon

Vernon Nicholas Maller
Born: November 12, 1928 in Banks, Washington County, Oregon
Died: March 09, 1987 in Vernonia, Columbia County, Oregon
Buried at: St. Francis of Assisi Catholic Cemetery, Roy, OR
Parents: Harry J. Maller (1883-1968) and Marie L. Winkler (1893-1973)

3   Donna Ann Hermens
Born: February 28, 1932
Died: December 21, 1932
Buried at: Visitation Catholic Cemetery, Verboort, OR., NW row 4
Married: n/a

2   Christine Elizabeth Hermens
Born: July 16, 1905 in Verboort, Washington County, Oregon
Died: March 27, 1995 in Beaverton, Washington County, Oregon
Buried at: Visitation Catholic Cemetery, Verboort, OR, SW row 4
Married: November 18, 1924 in Verboort, Washington County, Oregon
Antone Henry Vandeberg
Born: September 28, 1898 in Centerville, Washington County, Oregon
Died: April 18, 1977 in Forest Grove, Washington County, Oregon
Buried at: Visitation Catholic Cemetery, Verboort, OR, SW row 4
Parents: Henry Vandeberg (1872-1904) and Petronella Vandeberg (1877-1904)

2   Ernest Anthony Hermens
Born: October 24, 1910 in Verboort, Washington County, Oregon
Died: February 29, 1996 in Hillsboro, Washington County, Oregon
Buried at: Visitation Catholic Cemetery, Verboort, OR, SW row 1
Married: August 23, 1933 in Verboort, Washington County, Oregon
Ida Marian Smith
Born: December 11, 1908 in Verboort, Washington County, Oregon
Died: November 07, 2000 in Hillsboro, Washington County, Oregon
Buried at: Visitation Catholic Cemetery, Verboort, OR, SW row 1
Parents: William Smith (1873-1940) and Wilhelmina Kersten (1876-1961)

3   Richard A. Hermens
Born: 1935 in Oregon
Died: Living
Buried at:
Married: June 17, 1961 in Latah County, Idaho
Maxine Louise Kinzer
Born: 1938
Died: Living
Buried at:
Parents: Unknown

3   Ernest Joseph Hermens
Born: December 23, 1938 in Verboort, Washington County, Oregon
Died: December 23, 1938 in Verboort, Washington County, Oregon
Buried at: Visitation Catholic Cemetery, Verboort, OR, NW row 4
Married: n/a

3   Leanne M. Hermens
     Born: 1939 in Oregon
     Died: Living
     Buried at:
     Married: June 18, 1960 in Washington County, Oregon
     Louis A. LaBonte
     Born: 1940
     Died: Living
     Buried at:
     Parents: Unknown

3   Louann M. Hermens
     Born: 1948 in Oregon
     Died: Living
     Buried at:
     Married: September 12, 1970 in Washington County, Oregon
     Sidney Y. Bone
     Born: 1948
     Died: Living
     Buried at:
     Parents: Unknown

3   Louine Anne Hermens
     Born: 1948
     Died: Living
     Buried at:
     Married (1): July 02, 1971 in Washington County, Oregon
     Married (2): November 21, 1992 in Multnomah County, Oregon
     Michael Vandecoevering (1)
     Born: 1948
     Died: Living
     Buried at:
     Parents: Antone J. Vandecoevering (1913-1979) and Cecilia M. Pranger (1916-1984)
     Richard Douglas Warren (2)
     Born: Unknown
     Died: Living
     Buried at:
     Parents: Unknown

ɞ Chapter Seven ɷ

Mary Verhagen

Mary was the fourth child blessed to Joseph and Nellie. She was born on June 11, 1868 in Bay Settlement, WI, 18 months following the birth of Anna. The parents now had four children under the age of five. And the pattern in the births within this family continues, as I mentioned in the last chapter. There is also an 18 month age difference between Mary and Anna, just as there is between Anna and Frances, and Frances and Elizabeth. Ironically, Nellie's first four daughters were born like clockwork, either December or June. Elizabeth in December, Frances in June, Anna in December, and as we now know Mary in June. How interesting is that?!

At some point after Mary was born, it is believed, in October of the same year, Joseph and Nellie decided to move west to Grand Chute, and this is when they bought their 99-acre farm. In 1870 the family was captured in the Grand Chute census (see chapter 3, page 37).

In 1888, Mary became enamored with a gentleman by the name of John Verhagen. Fascinating though is that John's father, Henry Verhagen, was first married to Catherine Joosten who is a sister of our Joseph Joosten. John and his family lived in the Little Chute village at this time. At the young tender age of 20, Mary and John (age 21) were married on September 18, 1888 at the St. John Catholic Church in Little Chute. The ceremony was performed by Rev. Anthony J. Verberk. Cornelius VanOudenhoven was the best man and Jane Joosten (Mary's sister) the matron of honor.

Image 7.01- John and Mary (Joosten) Verhagen (1888)

John H. Verhagen was born on December 22, 1866 to his parents Henry and Henriette (VanHammond) Verhagen in Little Chute. Like most Little Chute residents, John's parents emigrated from Holland in 1854, and made their journey aboard the Ship Mississippi. They traveled with Simon and Christian Joosten who are uncles of our Joseph Joosten.

Following three and a half years of marriage, Mary and John welcomed their first child into the family. Henry J. (aka "Harry") was born March 28, 1892 in Grand Chute, and then two years later almost to the day their second child came. Joseph was born on March 22, 1894 in the Town of Vandenbroek (note: even though Henry and Joseph were probably born in the same town, I am stating their birth towns as documented in the World War I draft cards they both filled out in 1918). And just as the young couple was celebrating the third and first birthdays of their children, Mary came down with diphtheria and sadly passed away on March 25, 1895 from this disease at the young age of 26. Diphtheria is a potentially fatal disease involving the nose, throat, airway, and may also infect the skin. The disease is spread through the air from infected persons. Today there is an immunization for this disease in the diphtheria, tetanus, pertussis (DPT) vaccine, which has essentially eradicated this disease from the United States and other developed countries.

> Mrs. John Verhagen died with diphtheria Monday night. She leaves a husband and two children. Burial took place Tuesday. The bereaved husband and children have the sympathy of their many friends.

Image 7.02- Obituary of Mary Verhagen (Joosten)

Mary was laid to rest in fifth row of the third section in the St. John Catholic Cemetery in Little Chute. A young mother called home to Heaven much too soon. Mary's obituary (pictured) was printed in the Kaukauna Sun-Times on page A8 of the March 29, 1895 edition.

Soon after Mary's death, John married Elizabeth Schumacher later in either 1895 or in 1896. I am not certain of the exact date. In the 1900 census, John and Elizabeth are shown living in Grand Chute very near the Joosten farm occupied by Martin Joosten at this time. The census record also reveals John and Elizabeth had three children, but only two were living. Hattie was born on February 08, 1897, and William on June 08, 1898. The third unnamed child must have been stillborn between 1898 and 1900. Over the next five years the couple would welcome three more children. John Jr. born in 1901-1902 (exact date unknown), Martin born on September 13, 1902, and finally Mary K. born on November 04, 1905.

More tragic news came to the Verhagen house when Elizabeth became ill and passed away on May 09, 1906. Her cause of death is unknown to me. Like Mary, Elizabeth passed away at such a young age too, only 33. She was laid to rest in the St. John Catholic Cemetery. This must have been an awful set of circumstances for John now losing his second wife, and left to raise seven children ranging in age from twelve years to seven months all by himself. But he made do. And two years later John married his third wife Johanna ("Anna") VandenBoogart in August 1908 in Little Chute. They did not have any children together.

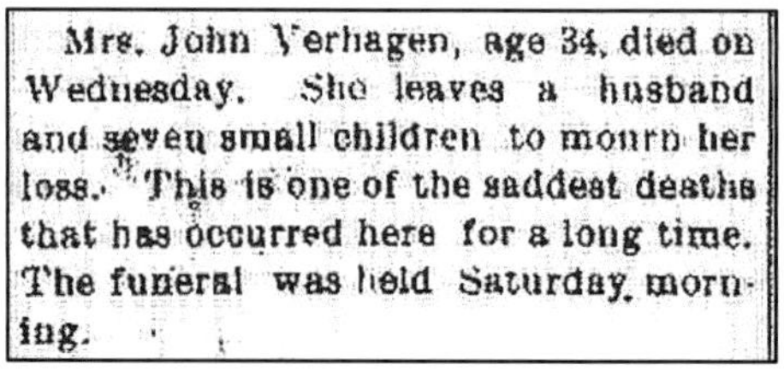
Mrs. John Verhagen, age 34, died on Wednesday. She leaves a husband and seven small children to mourn her loss. This is one of the saddest deaths that has occurred here for a long time. The funeral was held Saturday morning.

Image 7.03- Obituary of Elizabeth Verhagen (Schumacher)

After the next decade passed, Henry and Joseph Verhagen were now old enough to get married, and each did within a year or two of each other. Henry's marriage to Christine Vandenheuvel came first in 1914 or 1915 (date unknown). Christine Vandenheuvel was the oldest child of John P. and Mary (Hermsen) Vandenheuvel. And then on June 19, 1916 Joseph married Christina Justina DeGroot in Little Chute at the St. John Catholic Church. Fr. John J. Sprangers performed the ceremony with Mary K. Verhagen, John's sister, as maid of honor, and Henry DeGroot, Christina's brother, as the best man. Christina was the sixth child born to Joseph and Allegonda (Vandenheuvel) DeGroot. At this time Joseph worked for the Little Chute Pulp Mill.

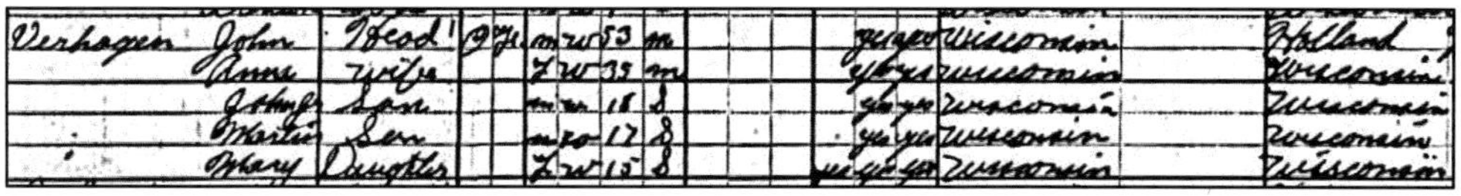

Verhagen	John	Head	O	M	W	53	M	yes yes	Wisconsin	Holland
	Anna	Wife		F	W	35	M	yes yes	Wisconsin	Wisconsin
	John Jr	Son		M	W	18	S	yes yes	Wisconsin	Wisconsin
	Martin	Son		M	W	17	S	yes yes	Wisconsin	Wisconsin
	Mary	Daughter		F	W	15	S	yes yes yes	Wisconsin	Wisconsin

Image 7.04- 1920 Grand Chute, Outagamie County, WI Census ED 209, sheet 2A

Four years later John Sr. and Anna appear in the 1920 census residing in Grand Chute, and living with them are the youngest three children John Jr. (18), Martin (17), and Mary K. (15). John Sr. and Martin were working on the farm together while John Jr. was employed at the paper mill.

As for the rest of the children, Joseph and Christina were captured in the 1920 census in Little Chute, which reveals they owned their own home, and Joseph working as a laborer for the "Kimberly Mill", which more than likely was the Kimberly-Clark Mill. Henry and Christine are in the Town of Vandenbroek living next door to Christine's brother George Vandenheuvel and his wife Annie and their children. Henry ("Harry") was noted as a farmer, and owned and mortgaged the land they were living on. Hattie was now married and living with her husband George G. Weyenberg in the Town of Vandenbroek on a farm, which was mortgaged. Also living in this household was their first child Elizabeth Maria, George's mother Anna (maiden name Gloudemans), and sister Rosella "Rosie" (married name Hietpas).

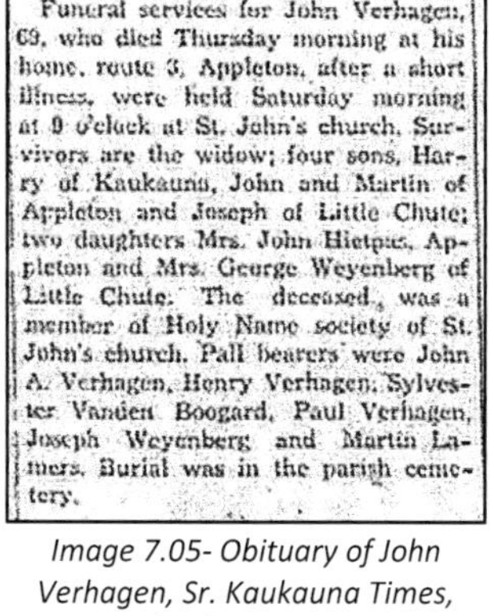
Funeral Saturday

Funeral services for John Verhagen, 69, who died Thursday morning at his home, route 3, Appleton, after a short illness, were held Saturday morning at 9 o'clock at St. John's church. Survivors are the widow; four sons, Harry of Kaukauna, John and Martin of Appleton and Joseph of Little Chute; two daughters Mrs. John Hietpas, Appleton and Mrs. George Weyenberg of Little Chute. The deceased, was a member of Holy Name society of St. John's church. Pall bearers were John A. Verhagen, Henry Verhagen, Sylvester Vanden Boogard, Paul Verhagen, Joseph Weyenberg and Martin Lamers. Burial was in the parish cemetery.

Image 7.05- Obituary of John Verhagen, Sr. Kaukauna Times, 06/11/1935, page 2

In the mid-1930s, John Sr. had reached his mid-60s. He and Anna were living on Appleton Rd. in Grand Chute, and their home was worth $4,200. His daughter Mary and husband John Hietpas, along with their newborn daughter, were living with them and paying $12 per month in rent, and possibly farming the land. John Sr.'s son Joseph changed employment and went to work for a local grocery

store as a merchant. The saddest news though was John Sr.'s health was not so good. At age 68, John passed away on June 6, 1935 after a short illness as mentioned in his obituary appearing in the Kaukauna Times. His funeral service was celebrated at St. John Church, and he was buried in the fifth row of the third section of the church cemetery. John and his three wives are all buried in the same plot, and share a headstone, which is pictured in the photo gallery below.

During World War II, Joseph J. Verhagen, the son of Henry and Christine, was sent to Germany by the US Army as part of the 10th Tank Battalion. He quickly obtained the Staff Sergeant rank. Tragic news came to the Verhagen house, Joseph had been killed in action on December 6, 1944 in Bergstein, Germany. He was only 25 years old. But this is not the end to Joseph's heroic story serving our country. In 1945, Major General Lunsford E. Oliver, commanding General of the 5th Armored Division awarded Joseph the renowned Bronze Star posthumously for his bravery. What a happy moment this must have been for the Verhagen family. A wonderful story was published in the Appleton Post-Crescent on April 18, 1945 giving some details about Joseph's heroism. As revealed in the newspaper article, after the tank platoon's leader was wounded, Joseph took command and *"performed many heroic feats, showed exceptional qualities of leadership and command, unusual coolness under fire and displayed exceptional personal courage."* Joseph's tank platoon was engaged in many offensives against the Germans from August 12 to September 17, 1944. In the latter battle, Joseph was in command of an outpost near Hommerdingen, Rhineland-Palatinate, Germany. His platoon was engaged in a heavy artillery barrage with 25 tanks and a company of infantry from the enemy, but they held their position with determination. After knocking out four German tanks, Joseph ordered the platoon to move to the top of a nearby hill. From their new position the platoon knocked out six more enemy tanks and attacked the infantry with so much machine gun fire that the remaining enemy tanks and troops retreated and were destroyed.

An official government document from the War Department, named the Distinguished Unit Citations, is given to the survivors or their families when awards are given. This document was given to many units of the 5th Armored Division, including the 10th Tank Battalion, for three fierce battles fought from November 28 to December 8, 1944. These battles took place six months after D-Day (06/06/1944). This is the period of time Joseph valiantly lost his life. In the bloody battle to capture the Hurtgen Forest the 5th Armored Division played a vital and heroic role in the operation to seize three dams on the Ruhr (Roer) River in Germany. In the three fierce battles the 5th Armored Division seized Kleinhau on November 29th, Brandenburg on December 3rd, and Bergstein on December 5th. In each battle, Joseph's armored tank division was sent out in front to capture the fortified town and hold it until the allied infantry forces could clear the adjacent woods. As revealed in this document, it says, *"Under extremely unfavorable weather conditions and over terrain emphatically not suited to armored action, this command gallantly attacked through deadly mine fields against a determined enemy, well-trenched, fortified, and supported by intense artillery and mortar fire."* Bergstein was a very important and strategic town, and the Germans did not let their town go down without an epic fight. With only eight of 56 tanks and 70 of 750 infantry troops left, the Americans heroically fought continuous combined armored and infantry counterattacks for 36 hours. Their outstanding courage and tenacity helped them to capture and hold the important heights which dominated the Rohr River dams.

I have also learned Joseph was awarded the Purple Heart posthumously. We thank Joseph for his service to our country and fighting for our freedom. He was buried in the third row of the fifth section in St. John Catholic Cemetery, and is in the same burial plot with his parents.

There were a large number of good men and women of the Verhagen family who served our fine country in the military. They are:

- ❖ Gerald J. Hietpas - Served as a Sergeant in the US Army during World War II.
- ❖ Frederick B. Vandehey – Served as a Private First Class in the US Army during World War II.
- ❖ Earl H. Verhagen – Served in the US Air Force during World War II.
- ❖ Joseph J. Verhagen - Served in the US Army 10th Tank Battalion 5 A. Killed in Action in Bergstein, Germany during World War II. Awarded Bronze Medal posthumously for heroism.
- ❖ Mark J. Verhagen, Sr. – Served as a Sergeant in the US Army during the Korea War.
- ❖ Martin Verhagen – Served as a Private First Class in the US Army during World War II.
- ❖ Clarence H. Weyenberg – Served as a Sergeant in the US Army during the Korea War.
- ❖ Lester J. Weyenberg – Served as a Private First Class in the US Army during World War II.

Photo and Image Gallery

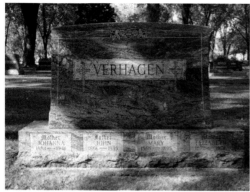

Image 7.06- Gravesite Headstone of John Verhagen, Sr., Mary Verhagen (Joosten), Elizabeth Verhagen (Schumacher), and Johanna Verhagen (VandenBoogart). St. John Catholic Cemetery section 3, row 5.

PRAY FOR THE SOUL OF

MARY JOOSTEN,

WIFE OF

JOHN H. VERHAGEN,

Born at Bay Settlement, Brown Co., Wis., June 11th, 1868, died at Little Chute, Wis., March 25th, 1895.

Behold, I come quickly: hold fast, that which thou hath, that no man take thy crown. AP. III. 11.

Behold now I shall sleep in the dust, and if thou seek me in the morning, I shall not be. JOB. VII. 21.

And at mid-night there was a cry made: the bridegroom cometh, go ye forth to meet him. MAT: XXV. 6.

Mary hath chosen the best part which shall not be taken away from her. LUKE X. 42.

Farewell, my husband and children all,
From you a mother Christ doth call.
Weep not for me for it is in vain
To call me to your sight again.

R. I. P.

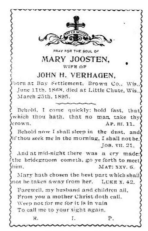

Image 7.07- Mary Verhagen (Joosten) Prayer Card

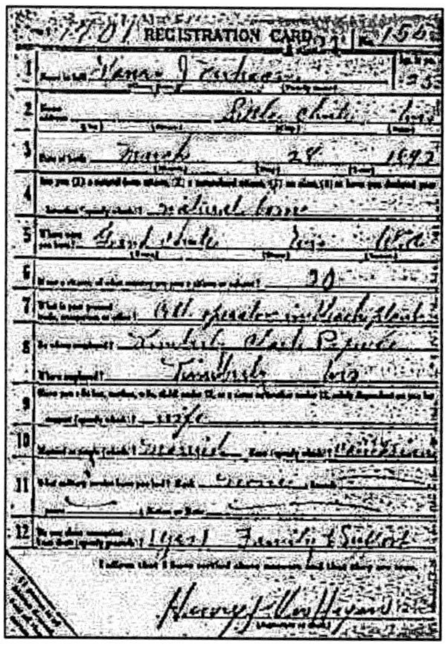

Image 7.08- Henry J. Verhagen World War I Draft Card.

Harry J. Verhagen

Rt. 1, Kaukauna

Age 79, passed away unexpectedly at the Darboy Club at 12:15 a.m. Sunday. He was born March 28, 1892 in the Town of Grand Chute and was a life resident of the Kaukauna area. He was a farmer at Rt. 1, Kaukauna, a member of the Holy Name Society of Holy Cross Catholic Church. Survivors are his wife, Christine; three daughters, Mrs. Ervin (Ruth) Rosin, Mrs. Leone Vande Hey, Little Chute, Mrs. Eugene (Mary Jean) Van Lanen, Rt. 1, Kaukauna; three sons, Earl, Richard, and Paul, all of Rt. 1, Kaukauna; two sons Joseph and Mar, preceded him in death; two brothers, Joseph, Little Chute, John, Seymour; two sisters, Mrs. George Weyenberg, Rt. 1, Kaukauna, Mrs. John Hietpas, Appleton; 35 grandchildren; 7 great-grandchildren. Funeral services will be held at 10 a.m. Tuesday morning at Holy Cross Catholic Church with Rev. Roy Crain officiating. Interment will be in St. John Cemetery, Little Chute. Friends may call at the Fargo Funeral Home after 3 p.m. Monday and there will be a prayer service at 8 p.m. Monday evening.

Image 7.09- Obituary of Henry ("Harry") J. Verhagen, Appleton Post-Crescent, 03/20/1972, page B9

Mrs. Harry Verhagen

(Christine Vanden Heuvel)
370 Malone Rd. Kaukana

Age 94, died Friday morning at her home after an extended illness. She was born April 2, 1890 in Little Chute. She was the oldest resident of the Town of Vanden Broek. She and her husband farmed at Route 1, Kaukauna for 62 years, all their married life. She was a member of the Christian Mothers of Holy Cross; Holy Cross Catholic Church, and the Gold Star Mothers. Survivors include two daughters and sons-in-law: Ruth and Ervin Rosin, Little Chute; Mary Jean and Eugene Van Lanen, Kaukauna; three sons and two daughters-in-law: Earl, Richard and Blanche, Paul and Theresa, all of Route 1, Kaukauna; a brother, Martin Vanden Heuvel, Little Chute; three sisters: Mrs. John C. (Elizabeth) Hietpas, Little Chute; Mrs. Bernard (Rose) Van Eperen, Greenleaf; Mrs. John (Helen) Lamers, Route 3, Kaukauna; 37 grandchildren; 49 great-grandchildren. She was preceded in death by her husband, Harry; three sons and a daughter. Funeral services will be 10:30 a.m. Monday at Holy Cross Catholic Church, with Father Mike Hoffmann officiating. Interment will be in St. John Cemetery, Little Chute. Friends may call at the Fargo Funeral Home, from 4 until 9 p.m. Sunday and after 9 a.m. Monday until the time of service. There will be a 7 p.m. prayer service Sunday evening at the funeral home.

Image 7.10- Obituary of Christine Verhagen (Vandenheuvel), Appleton Post-Crescent, 03/24/1985, page D10.

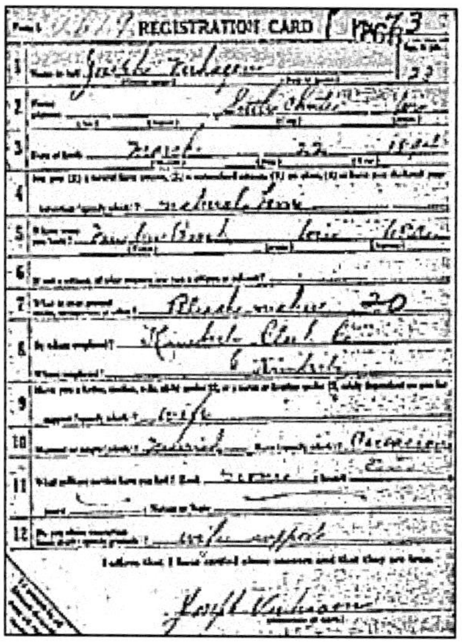

Image 7.11- Joseph Verhagen World War I Draft Card.

Joseph Verhagen

424 West Main St., Little Chute
Age 78, passed away at 3:30 p.m. Sunday following a brief illness. He was born March 22, 1894 in the Town of Vanden Broek. He was in the grocery business until 1944 and then he worked for the Oudenhoven Construction Co. until his retirement in 1959. He was a member of the Catholic Order of Foresters. Survivors are his wife, Christine; a brother, John, Seymour; two sisters, Mrs. Hattie Weyenberg, Little Chute; Mrs. Jary Hietpas, Appleton. Two brothers, Harry and Martin, preceded him in death. Funeral services will be held at 10 a.m. Wednesday from St. John Catholic Church, Little Chute, with Rev. Norbert VandeLoo officiating. Interment will be in the parish cemetery. Friends may call at the Verkuilen Funeral Home after 3 p.m. Tuesday and there will be a prayer service at 7:30 p.m. Tuesday evening.

Image 7.12- Obituary of Joseph Verhagen, Appleton Post-Crescent, 01/02/1973, page B4.

Mrs. Joseph Verhagen

(Justina De Groot)

424 W. Main St., Little Chute

Age 83, died at 5:30 a.m. Friday. She was born June 27, 1896 in Little Chute. She and her husband had operated Verhagen's Grocery from 1935 to 1945. She was a member of the Catholic Order of Foresters. Survivors include her brother, Henry De Groot, Little Chute; a sister, Mrs. Marie Retzlaff, Yermo, California. She was preceded in death by her husband, two infant children, five brothers, and two sisters. The funeral will be at 10 a.m. Monday from St. John Catholic Church, Little Chute, with the Rev. Richard Klingeisen officiating. Interment will be in the parish cemetery. Friends may call from 4 to 9 p.m. Sunday at Verkuilen Funeral Home, Little Chute, and from 9 a.m. Monday until time of the service. There will be a prayer service at 7:30 p.m. Monday.

Image 7.13- Obituary of Christina Justina Verhagen (DeGroot), Appleton Post-Crescent, 12/21/1979, page B12.

Martin Verhagen

Milwaukee, Wis.

Age 64, passed away Friday. Mr. Verhagen is survived by his wife, Marge; three brothers, Harry, Kaukauna; Joe, Little Chute; John, Seymour; two sisters, Mrs. Hattie Weyenberg, Kaukauna; Mrs. Mary Hietpas, Appleton. Funeral services will be held at 9 a.m. Monday in Milwaukee.

Image 7.14- Obituary of Martin Verhagen, Appleton Post-Crescent, 07/16/1966, page B3.

Mrs. George Weyenberg

Hattie Verhagen

Riverview Health Center Kaukauna

Age 85 was born into eternal life at 6:30 p.m. Tuesday after an extended illness. She was born February 9, 1897 in the Town of Grand Chute. She was a member of St. John's Catholic Church and the St. Elizabeth Society. Survivors include five daughters and two sons-in-law: Mrs. Betty Schumacher, Mrs. Mary Dietrick, Sister Catherine Ann, all of Appleton; Irene and Owen Hietpas, Julia and Gerald Hietpas, all of Leesburg, Florida; two sons and daughters-in-law: Lester and Elaine, Clarence and Shirley, all of Kaukauna; a sister, Mrs. Mary Hietpas, Appleton; 18 grandchildren and 16 great grandchildren. She was preceded in death by her husband, George. Funeral services will be 11 a.m. Friday from St. John's Catholic Church with the Rev. John Becker officiating. Interment will be in the parish cemetery. There will be no visitation. The Verkuilen Funeral Home assisted the family with arrangements.

Image 7.15- Obituary of Hattie Weyenberg (Verhagen), Appleton Post-Crescent, 05/11/1983, page A5.

George G. Weyenberg

Route 1, Kaukauna

Age 79, passed away suddenly at his home Saturday evening at 6 p.m. He was born in the town of Vanden Broek October 8, 1888. Survivors include his wife, the former Hattie Verhagen; five daughters, Mrs. Betty Schumacher, Appleton; Mrs. Mary Diederich, Appleton; Sister Mary Dorothy, Cape Guarden, Missouri; Mrs. Owen (Irene) Hietpas, Appleton; Mrs. Gerald (Julia) Hietpas, Kaukauna; two sons, Lester and Clarence, both of Kaukauna; one sister, Mrs. John Stoop, Little Chute; 17 grandchildren. Mr. Weyenberg was a member of the Holy Name Society. Until his retirement 10 years ago he owned and operated a farm in the town of Vanden Broek. Funeral services will be held at St. John Catholic Church, Little Chute, Tuesday at 10 a.m. with the Rev. Martin Vosbeek officiating. Interment will be in the parish cemetery. Friends may call at the Verkuilen Funeral Home, Monday after 3 p.m. The rosary will be prayed at 8 p.m. Monday.

Image 7.16- Obituary of George G. Weyenberg, Appleton Post-Crescent, 06/10/1968, page B12.

Mary K. Hietpas

St. Paul Home, Kaukauna

Age 87, passed away Friday, June 5, 1992 in a local nursing home. She was born Nov. 5, 1904 in Appleton, daughter of the late John and Elizabeth (Schumacher) Verhagen. She married John N. Hietpas, who preceded her in death in 1957. Mary was a longtime member of St. Thomas More Catholic Church and its ladies society. Survivors include two daughters, Christine (Daniel) Mayer, Appleton, and Judy (Pat) Kenney, Kaukauna; a son, Orville "John" (Antoinette) Hietpas, Prospect Heights, Ill.; two sisters-in-law, Marge Verhagen, Milwaukee, and Irene Verhagen, Seymour; seven grandchildren and six great-grandchildren. She was preceded in death by her husband, John; four brothers, John, Joseph, Martin and Harry, and a sister, Hattie Weyenberg. The Mass of the Resurrection will be held at 11 a.m. Monday, June 8, 1992, at ST. THOMAS MORE CATHOLIC CHURCH, 1825 N. McDonald St. with Father Gerald Falk officiating. Interment will be in St. John Cemetery, Little Chute. Friends may call Sunday from 4-8 p.m. at the WICHMANN FUNERAL HOME, 537 N. Superior St., and again Monday from 8 a.m. until the cortege leaves for the church. There will be a prayer and scripture service at 7:30 p.m. Sunday at the funeral home.

Image 7.17- Obituary of Mary K Hietpas (Verhagen) Appleton Post-Crescent, 06/06/1992, page B4.

◈ Descendants of Mary and John Verhagen ◈

Notes: 1= 1st generation, 2= 2nd generation, 3= 3rd generation.
The year of birth is only given for individuals still living, if known.

Since Mary's children (Henry and Joseph) were raised with John and Elizabeth's children for virtually all of their lives, I have included all of the children born to John Verhagen.

1   John H. Verhagen Sr.
Born: December 22, 1866 in Little Chute, Outagamie County, Wisconsin
Died: June 06, 1935 in Appleton, Outagamie County, Wisconsin
Buried at: St. John Catholic Cemetery, Little Chute, WI, section 3, row 5
Parents: Henry Verhagen (1829-1873) and Henriette VanHammond (1846-1871)
Married (1): September 18, 1888 in Little Chute, Outagamie County, Wisconsin
Married (2): 1895 or 1896
Married (3): August 1908 in in Little Chute, Outagamie County, Wisconsin
Mary Joosten (1)
Born: June 11, 1868 in Bay Settlement, Brown County, Wisconsin
Died: March 25, 1895 in Little Chute, Outagamie County, Wisconsin
Buried at: St. John Catholic Cemetery, Little Chute, WI, section 3, row 5
Elizabeth Schumacher (2)
Born: March 1873 in Wisconsin
Died: May 09, 1906
Buried at: St. John Catholic Cemetery, Little Chute, WI, section 3, row 5
Parents: John Schumacher (1818-1890) and Wilhelmina Vandenheuvel (1832-1908)
Johanna VandenBoogart (3)
Born: November 02, 1884 in Wisconsin
Died: May 08, 1941
Buried at: St. John Catholic Cemetery, Little Chute, WI, section 3, row 5
Parents: John VandenBoogart (1859-1938) and Ardina Ebben (1861-1937)

Children of Mary and John Verhagen:
2   Henry J. Verhagen
Born: March 28, 1892 in Grand Chute, Outagamie County, Wisconsin
Died: March 19, 1972 in Darboy, Calumet County, Wisconsin
Buried at: St. John Catholic Cemetery, Little Chute, WI, section 5, row 3
Married: 1914-1915
Christine Vandenheuvel
Born: April 02, 1890 in Little Chute, Outagamie County, Wisconsin
Died: March 22, 1985 in Little Chute, Outagamie County, Wisconsin
Buried at: St. John Catholic Cemetery, Little Chute, WI, section 5, row 3
Parents: John P. Vandenheuvel (1865-1941) and Mary Hermsen (1865-1950)

3   Joseph J. Verhagen
Born: March 08, 1916 in Wisconsin
Died: March 25, 1917
Buried at: St. John Catholic Cemetery, Little Chute, WI, section 1A, row 8
Married: n/a

3   Ruth Verhagen
Born: June 30, 1917 in Kaukauna, Outagamie County, Wisconsin
Died: April 25, 2015 in Kaukauna, Outagamie County, Wisconsin
Buried at: St. John Catholic Cemetery, Little Chute, WI
Married: October 26, 1945 in Kaukauna, Outagamie County, Wisconsin

Ervin T. Rosin
Born: November 23, 1917 in Wrightstown, Brown County, Wisconsin
Died: July 08, 2001 in Appleton, Outagamie County, Wisconsin
Buried at: St. John Catholic Cemetery, Little Chute, WI
Parents: Albert A. Rosin (1889-1971) and Elsie J. Zuelke (1895-1991)

3   Joseph J. Verhagen
Born: January 1919 in Town of Vandenbroek, Outagamie County, Wisconsin
Died: December 06, 1944 in Bergstein, Duren, North Rhine-Westphalia, Germany
Buried at: St. John Catholic Cemetery, Little Chute, WI, section 5, row 3
Married: n/a

3   Leone Elisabeth Verhagen
Born: November 06, 1920 in Town of Buchanan, Outagamie County, Wisconsin
Died: November 02, 1983 in Little Chute, Outagamie County, Wisconsin
Buried at: St. John Catholic Cemetery, Little Chute, WI, sec 6, row 3
Married: Unknown
Frederick Barney Vandehey
Born: February 05, 1916 in Wrightstown, Brown County, Wisconsin
Died: May 27, 1955
Buried at: St. John Catholic Cemetery, Little Chute, WI, sec 6, row 3
Parents: Peter J. Vandehey (1873-1937) and Mary Timmers (1879-1958)

3   Earl Henry Verhagen
Born: July 08, 1922 in Town of Vandenbroek, Outagamie County, Wisconsin
Died: September 30, 1989 in Forest County, Wisconsin
Buried at: St. John Catholic Cemetery, Little Chute, WI, section 5, row 3
Married: n/a

3   Richard G. Verhagen
Born: March 06, 1924 in Kaukauna, Outagamie County, Wisconsin
Died: April 23, 2010 in Appleton, Outagamie County, Wisconsin
Buried at: Holy Cross Catholic Cemetery, Kaukauna, WI, section 1, row 2
Married: May 06, 1947 in Kimberly, Outagamie County, Wisconsin
Blanche B. Verhagen
Born: October 12, 1928 in Wisconsin
Died: January 12, 2013 in Kaukauna, Outagamie County, Wisconsin
Buried at: Holy Cross Catholic Cemetery, Kaukauna, WI, section 1, row 2
Parents: Louis R. Verhagen (1899-1967) and Mary M. Ducat (1903-1979)

3   Mark J. Verhagen Sr.
Born: December 11, 1926 in Kaukauna, Outagamie County, Wisconsin
Died: March 10, 1968 in Little Chute, Outagamie County, Wisconsin
Buried at: St. John Catholic Cemetery, Little Chute, WI, section 5, row 3
Married: October 12, 1957 in Little Chute, Outagamie County, Wisconsin
Irene C. Dercks
Born: August 26, 1932 in Little Chute, Outagamie County, Wisconsin
Died: June 03, 2012
Buried at: St. John Catholic Cemetery, Little Chute, WI, section 5, row 3
Parents: Nicholas Dercks (1896-1976) and Rose Jansen (1900-1986)

3   Mary Jean Verhagen
Born: 1927 or 1928 in Wisconsin
Died: Living
Buried at:
Married: Unknown
Eugene P. VanLanen
Born: November 22, 1930 in Kaukauna, Outagamie County, Wisconsin
Died: July 02, 1996 in Madison, Dane County, Wisconsin
Buried at: Highland Memorial Park Cemetery, Appleton, WI.
Parents: Albert P. VanLanen (1893-1980) and Delia M. Peters (1895-1995)

3   Paul P. Verhagen
Born: 1930 in Wisconsin
Died: Living
Buried at:
Married:
Theresa F. Pynenberg
Born: 1931
Died: Living
Buried at:
Parents: Unknown

2   Joseph Verhagen
Born: March 22, 1894 in Town of Vandenbroek, Outagamie County, Wisconsin
Died: December 31, 1972 in Little Chute, Outagamie County, Wisconsin
Buried at: St. John Catholic Cemetery, Little Chute, WI, section 3, row 5
Married: June 19, 1916 in Little Chute, Outagamie County, Wisconsin
Christina Justina DeGroot
Born: June 27, 1896 in Little Chute, Outagamie County, Wisconsin
Died: December 21, 1979 in Little Chute, Outagamie County, Wisconsin
Buried at: St. John Catholic Cemetery, Little Chute, WI, section 3, row 5
Parents: Joseph DeGroot (1861-1942) and Allegonda Vandenheuvel (1867-1929)

Children of John Verhagen and Elizabeth Schumacher:
2   Hattie Verhagen
Born: February 08, 1897 in Grand Chute, Outagamie County, Wisconsin
Died: May 10, 1983 in Kaukauna, Outagamie County, Wisconsin
Buried at: St. John Catholic Cemetery, Little Chute, WI, section 6, row 3
Married: May 14, 1918 in Little Chute, Outagamie County, Wisconsin
George G. Weyenberg
Born: October 08, 1888 in Town of Vandenbroek, Outagamie County, Wisconsin
Died: June 08, 1968 in Kaukauna, Outagamie County, Wisconsin
Buried at: St. John Catholic Cemetery, Little Chute, WI, section 6, row 3
Parents: George Weyenberg (1840-1912) and Anna Maria Gloudemans (1845-1939)

3   Elizabeth Maria Weyenberg
Born: March 31, 1919 in Town of Vandenbroek, Outagamie County, Wisconsin
Died: May 17, 1996 in Appleton, Outagamie County, Wisconsin
Buried at: St. John Catholic Cemetery, Little Chute, WI
Married: May 21, 1947 in Little Chute, Outagamie County, Wisconsin

Peter J. Schumacher
Born: March 31, 1917 in Town of Vandenbroek, Outagamie County, Wisconsin
Died: June 30, 1963 in Appleton, Outagamie County, Wisconsin
Buried at: St. John Catholic Cemetery, Little Chute, WI
Parents: John P. Schumacher (1889-1961) and Henrica N. Williamsen (1896-1986)

3   Mary Weyenberg
Born: June 10, 1921 in Town of Vandenbroek, Outagamie County, Wisconsin
Died: December 09, 2010 in Appleton, Outagamie County, Wisconsin
Buried at: St. Mary Catholic Cemetery, Appleton, WI
Married: August 21, 1940
Woodrow A. Diederich
Born: October 12, 1916 in Freedom, Outagamie County, Wisconsin
Died: May 21, 1964 in Appleton, Outagamie County, Wisconsin
Buried at: St. Mary Catholic Cemetery, Appleton, WI
Parents: Phillip J. Diederich (1882-1950) and Gertrude Arnoldussen (1891-1959)

3   Catherine Weyenberg
Born: 1922-1923 in Wisconsin
Died: Living
Buried at:
Professed Vows as Sr. Mary Dorothy

3   Irene N. Weyenberg
Born: 1925 in Wisconsin
Died: Living
Buried at:
Married: August 21, 1946 in Little Chute, Outagamie County, Wisconsin
Owen N. Hietpas
Born: May 09, 1925 in Town of Vandenbroek, Outagamie County, Wisconsin
Died: February 21, 2014 in Leesburg, Lake County, Florida
Buried at: St. John Catholic Cemetery, Little Chute, WI
Parents: William P. Hietpas (1898-1955) and Margaret Verhagen (1899-1994)

3   Julia Hattie Weyenberg
Born: September 16, 1928 in Town of Vandenbroek, Outagamie County, Wisconsin
Died: October 23, 2005 in Leesburg, Lake County, Florida
Buried at: Florida National Cemetery, Bushnell, FL., section 201, site 2363
Married: October 18, 1947 in Little Chute, Outagamie County, Wisconsin
Gerald J. Hietpas
Born: August 30, 1925 in Kaukauna, Outagamie County, Wisconsin
Died: December 10, 1994 in Leesburg, Lake County, Florida
Buried at: Florida National Cemetery, Bushnell, FL., section 201, site 2363
Parents: Bernard J. Hietpas (1899-1984) and Mathilda Romenesko (1901-1975)

3   Lester J. Weyenberg
Born: November 08, 1926 in Town of Vandenbroek, Outagamie County, Wisconsin
Died: May 26, 1995 in Kaukauna, Outagamie County, Wisconsin
Buried at: St. John Catholic Cemetery, Little Chute, WI, section 11, row 1
Married: October 19, 1949 in Appleton, Outagamie County, Wisconsin

Elaine E. VanRooy
Born: April 15, 1927 in Appleton, Outagamie County, Wisconsin
Died: February 14, 2013 in Neenah, Winnebago County, Wisconsin
Buried at: St. John Catholic Cemetery, Little Chute, WI, section 11, row 1
Parents: Clarence M. VanRooy (1903-1973) and Elvira Kipp (1906-1998)

    3   Clarence Henry Weyenberg
Born: February 19, 1931 in Town of Vandenbroek, Outagamie County, Wisconsin
Died: July 03, 1984 in Kaukauna, Outagamie County, Wisconsin
Buried at: St. John Catholic Cemetery, Little Chute, WI, section 11, row 1
Married: Unknown
Shirley A. Werschem
Born: 1936
Died: Living
Buried at:
Parents: Unknown

2   William Verhagen
Born: June 08, 1898 in Wisconsin
Died: January 02, 1903
Buried at: St. John Catholic Cemetery, Little Chute, WI, sec 1A, row 4
Married: n/a

2   John H. Verhagen, Jr.
Born: 1901 or 1902 in Wisconsin
Died: Unknown
Buried at:
Married: Unknown

2   Martin Verhagen
Born: September 13, 1902 in Grand Chute, Outagamie County, Wisconsin
Died: July 15, 1966 in Milwaukee, Milwaukee County, Wisconsin
Buried at: Wood National Cemetery, Milwaukee, WI., Sec. 36A, Row 20, Site 5
Married: Unknown
Margaret Rose Verhagen
Born: February 17, 1903
Died: November 23, 1992 in Milwaukee, Milwaukee County, Wisconsin
Buried at: Wood National Cemetery, Milwaukee, WI., Sec. 36A, Row 20, Site 5
Parents: Unknown

2   Mary K. Verhagen
Born: November 04, 1905 in Appleton, Outagamie County, Wisconsin
Died: June 05, 1992 in Outagamie County, Wisconsin
Buried at: St. John Catholic Cemetery, Little Chute, WI, sec 2, row 26
Married: May 28, 1929 in Little Chute, Outagamie County, Wisconsin
John N. Hietpas
Born: May 28, 1902 in Little Chute, Outagamie County, Wisconsin
Died: November 20, 1957 in Little Chute, Outagamie County, Wisconsin
Buried at: St. John Catholic Cemetery, Little Chute, WI, sec 2, row 26
Parents: Nicholas Hietpas (1874-1949) and Christena Weyenberg (1872-1926)

3　Christine E. Hietpas
Born: March 05, 1930 in Appleton, Outagamie County, Wisconsin
Died: January 14, 2014 in Little Chute, Outagamie County, Wisconsin
Buried at: St. Joseph Catholic Cemetery, Appleton, WI
Married: 1958 or 1959 in Little Chute, Outagamie County, Wisconsin
Daniel L. Mayer
Born: 1926 in Wisconsin
Died: Living
Buried at:
Parents: Unknown

3　Orville J. Hietpas
Born: 1932 or 1933 in Wisconsin
Died: Living
Buried at:
Married: Unknown
Toni Hietpas
Born: Unknown
Died: Before January 2014
Buried at:
Parents: Unknown

3　Judith E. Hietpas
Born: June 30, 1934 in Appleton, Outagamie County, Wisconsin
Died: August 15, 2014 in Kaukauna, Outagamie County, Wisconsin
Buried at: St. Joseph Catholic Cemetery, Appleton, WI
Married: July 05, 1958
Patrick E. Kenney
Born: 1935
Died: Living
Buried at:
Parents: Unknown

❧ Chapter Eight ❧

Jane Hermens

J ane Margaret was welcomed into this life by her parents on March 31, 1870, and was Joseph and Nellie's first child born on their farm in Grand Chute, WI. She was the fifth child, and daughter number five. Jane broke the series of births occurring in June and December. She also went by the name "Jennie". Jane attended school, which ended early by today's standards after the fourth grade. With 99-acres to farm, I am certain that since Jane was now the age of 10 she was old enough to take on some of the responsibility to help out her parents running the farm.

By the time Jane reached her later teen years she had already made the trip out west to Oregon with her parents and three other sisters. Toward the end of the 1880s she met a nice man by the name of Cornelius Hermens. Their romance grew and they were married on November 30, 1889 at the Visitation Catholic Church in Verboort, OR; just five months after Anna's marriage to Antone, who is Cornelius' older brother. Cornelius was born on April 25, 1867 in Lawrence, Brown County, WI. He was the sixth child of eleven born to his parents William and Catherine (Meulemans) Hermens.

Jane and Cornelius were blessed with their first of ten children on February 11, 1891, and named her Wilhelmina Petronella. Then over the next seven and a half years another four children were welcomed into this growing family. They are Martin Joseph born in 1893, Catherine Mary in 1895, Margaret Mary in 1896, and Joseph William in 1898. During the turn of the new century the Hermens family was living in the Columbia precinct in Washington County, which I believe was near the Verboort and Roy communities. A Hermens Family story I read reveals the family moved onto a 28-acre farm one mile east of

Image 8.01-, Cornelius & Jane (Joosten) Hermens Wedding Photo. Taken 1889.

Verboort in 1900, though there is uncertainty whether this was before or after the census was taken. Cornelius and Jane were captured in the 1900 census where they were operating a farm they were renting. One of their neighbors was the Fred Lepschat family, whose son William would marry into the Bernards family, and became a son-in-law to Frances Bernards. Peter Vandehey was listed as their servant, and probably the hired hand on the farm.

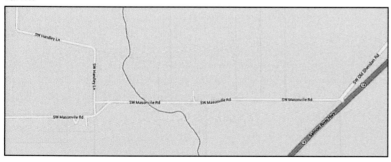

Image 8.02- Map of Masonville Rd., McMinnville, OR

Nearly four and a half years after the fifth child Joseph was born, Elizabeth Natalia came into this world in 1903. The following year (1904) Francis Henry was born, and then Edward Anthony in 1906. In 1908, Jane and Cornelius decided to move 25 miles south to the town of McMinnville, OR. On October 10th, they purchased a 100-acre farm from O.D. Scott for $5,500 near what today is the intersection of SW

Masonville Rd. and SW Handley Ln., which is situated at the south end of McMinnville. There must have been a good deal on farm land down in McMinnville and around the same area because three of Cornelius' siblings also lifted their roots to move south. They were his brother Louis and his wife Wilhelmina (Krieger), sister Rosalie Bernards and her husband John, and another sister Pauline Krieger and her husband Peter.

Named by its founder William Newby, McMinnville became a city in 1882, and is the county seat of Yamhill County. It is located 26 miles northwest of Salem, and 50 miles east of the beautiful Oregon Coast. Oregon's Highway 99 runs right through the middle of this town. Many of Oregon's flourishing wine vineyards are found near McMinnville giving the town claim to the capital of Oregon's wine industry. Today the population is just over 32,000 residents. McMinnville's claim to fame came in June 1950 when a farmer and his wife saw a UFO; a flying saucer. The photos they took made front page headline news in the local McMinnville News-Register (then known as the "Telephone-Register"), and The Oregonian (Oregon's largest newspaper). Within a month this rousing tale made it into Life Magazine, and into McMinnville folklore. And although many have said this was a hoax, no one has been able to discern or disprove whether the sighting was a hoax or not. It is evident this town fully believes an extraterrestrial took a peek at their town by celebrating the event in their annual "UFO Alien Costume Parade and Festival."

Image 8.03- Marriage Certificate of William Evers and Catherine Hermens from Yamhill County, OR

Just one month after the family settled into their new home Jane and Cornelius welcomed their ninth child, Ann Julianna, into the world; born in 1908. And then 19 months later their tenth and last child Jeanette Rosalia was born in 1911. So now the family was set with four boys and six girls. At this time in 1911 Cornelius was 44 years old, and Jane was a young 41.

In 1914, Jane and Cornelius enjoyed the planning and festivities of the first wedding of one of their children. On January 28, 1914, at age 18 daughter Catherine married William A. Evers, son of Peter and Antonia (Vandehey) Evers. According to their marriage certificate I acquired, they were married in the St. James Catholic Church in McMinnville by Fr. Charles Raymond, and Albert J. Evers (William's brother) and Margaret Hermens (Catherine's sister) were the witnesses. If you are wondering if there are others from the Evers family who married into our family, you are correct. Two of William's brothers, Antone and Albert, married Petronella Hermens and Mary Hermens, respectively. Both are daughters of Anna and Antone Hermens; all of whom are mentioned in chapter six. William resided in Lebanon, OR, which is located in Linn County, and the newlyweds spent the first few years of their life together in this small town situated about 64 miles southeast of McMinnville. It is here in Lebanon the first two grandchildren of Jane and Cornelius were born; Janet Antonia on November 14, 1914 and Genevieve Josephine on March 3, 1916.

An interesting fact about Catherine, unfortunately her husband William passed away in 1963, and then she married a second time to William's brother Antone Evers in 1964. As I mentioned in a previous chapter, Antone's first wife Petronella died in 1937. Petronella is Catherine's first cousin.

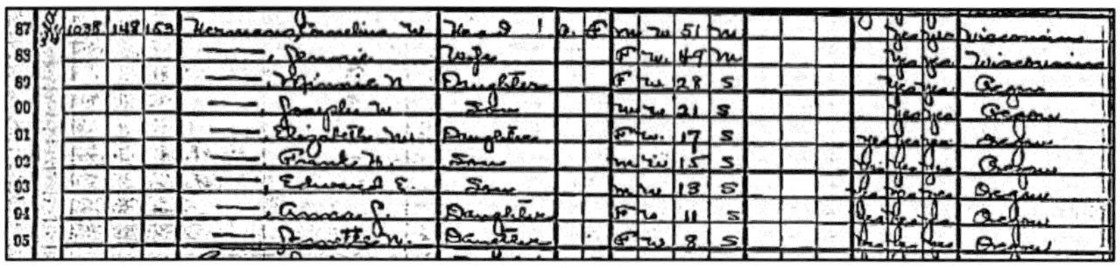

In 1920 the Hermens family was captured in the McMinnville census. Cornelius was earning his living as a highway laborer, and I am sure was still operating a farm too. Seven of their ten children were living at home. They were Minnie, Joseph, Elizabeth, Frank, Edward, Anna, and Jeanette.

Image 8.04- 1920 McMinnville, Yamhill County, OR Census ED 452, sheet 14B

Martin, Catherine, and Margaret were all married and out on their own. Interestingly enough, Joseph was also listed with Antone and Anna Hermens (uncle and aunt) in the Verboort census. He was listed as a farm laborer with both families.

Toward the end of 1921, Elizabeth married Albert ("Bert") J. Vandehey on October 5th in McMinnville with Joseph Hermens (Elizabeth's brother) and Catherine Vandehey (Albert's sister) as the couple's witnesses. A little less than two years later Joseph and Catherine were married on June 6, 1923 in Roy, OR. Here is another instance where siblings married siblings from another family. Albert and Elizabeth welcomed their first child into the world a little more than one year following their marriage. Little Norbert was born on November 26, 1922 in Roy.

Albert and Elizabeth moved to the Roy area, and it has been said that Albert was farming the Chalmers farm. Then an unbelievable accident happened. On December 5, 1923, Albert and his brother Peter were at Joe Moore's store in Roy, finished their purchase, and headed home in their car. There are railroad tracks running east-west right next to the store. As reported in the Hillsboro Argus on December 6th (see an image of the story in the photo gallery below), as the car Albert and Peter were in crossed the tracks it was struck by a westbound Portland-Tillamook Railroad train headed for Tillamook. Albert was the driver of the car. Two theories emerged as to the cause. The first was Albert, after hearing the train's whistle, was confused as to which direction the train was actually coming from, assuming it was headed east toward Portland when in fact it was heading west toward Tillamook. He proceeded over the tracks without looking the other direction. The second theory was the car's engine stalled on the tracks. Whatever the cause, the crushing impact threw both men from the car. Albert was thrown into the path of the moving train and was killed almost instantly. He was just 25 years old. Peter was thrown away from the tracks and wreckage, and sustained injuries to his head and arms. He luckily survived.

The St. Francis Catholic School is within a couple hundred yards of the tracks, and the school children heard the horrific accident. Bert Vanderzanden and Leonard VanDomelen were allowed to run over to check out the scene to see who was hurt, and both witnessed the aftermath of the destruction and the fate of both men. Both went back to the school to inform the teachers what had happened. Coincidently, the Bert Vanderzanden who witnessed this accident is my great uncle, the brother of my grandmother Minnie Shaw (Vanderzanden). At this time in 1923 my grandmother worked for Joe Moore at his store on occasion before working at the store full time in 1927. This leaves me to wonder if she also witnessed this tragedy.

An investigation into the accident ensued which exonerated the railroad from any wrongdoing, and pointed toward Albert's lack of alertness at the railroad crossing. The findings of the investigation were printed in the Hillsboro Argus on December 23, 1923. A real unfortunate set of circumstances for Elizabeth and their young child, now widowed and fatherless. And to top it off Elizabeth was pregnant with their second child who was born just 24 days after the heartbreaking day. Albert was buried in the St. Francis Catholic Cemetery in Roy, OR.

Elizabeth moved back to McMinnville to live with her parents. Alberta Marie was born on December 29, 1923 in McMinnville. Elizabeth did not remarry. Around 1927, Elizabeth was able to rent a place of her own. The family had a boarder by the name of William E. "Earl" Osborn who lived with them. In 1930, the young family of three and Earl were documented in the McMinnville census renting a residence on First Street for $12 per month. Elizabeth was not employed, and Earl (age 29) was employed at the milk company. In 2013, I had a wonderful conversation with Norbert, who was living in McMinnville at the time after living in Eugene, OR for decades. He remembers his mother earned money by doing laundry for folks around the area. Norbert said he would take his little wagon around picking up and delivering laundry. Interestingly, Elizabeth also cooked meals for the prisoners who were in jail to earn extra income. The Yamhill County jail was just a couple of blocks away, and the prisoners came to pick up the food. Elizabeth did not drive and had no car. Earl owned a Ford coupe and would at times provide transportation for the family when other family members could not.

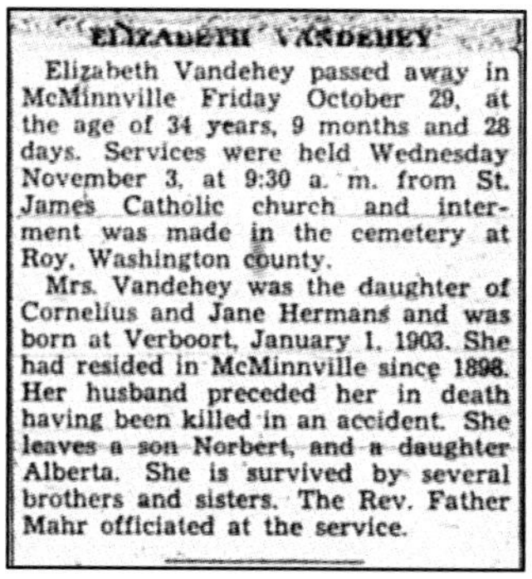

ELIZABETH VANDEHEY

Elizabeth Vandehey passed away in McMinnville Friday October 29, at the age of 34 years, 9 months and 28 days. Services were held Wednesday November 3, at 9:30 a. m. from St. James Catholic church and interment was made in the cemetery at Roy, Washington county.

Mrs. Vandehey was the daughter of Cornelius and Jane Hermans and was born at Verboort, January 1, 1903. She had resided in McMinnville since 1896. Her husband preceded her in death having been killed in an accident. She leaves a son Norbert, and a daughter Alberta. She is survived by several brothers and sisters. The Rev. Father Mahr officiated at the service.

Image 8.05- Obituary of Elizabeth Vandehey (Hermens), McMinnville News-Reporter, 11/14/1937, page 4

Then in 1937 more heartbreak came to the Vandehey family. Elizabeth passed away on October 29, 1937 at the young age of 34 from cancer. And now sadly Norbert (14) and Alberta (13) were orphans. Norbert revealed to me that prior to Elizabeth's death, he and Alberta were called into the hospital as their mother was lying on her death bed. Elizabeth told them William E. Bernards (1880-1959), affectionately known as "Uncle Bill", agreed to take them into his home, and to also send them to college. Both Norbert and Alberta moved into Uncle Bill's McMinnville home following Elizabeth's death. At the time he would have been 57 years old, and taking in two teenagers was an enormous undertaking. Uncle Bill was a single man who never married, and had no children. Norbert calls him a saint for doing such a selfless act. There is no family relation between Elizabeth and Bill Bernards. Elizabeth was buried next to her husband in the St. Francis Catholic Cemetery.

When the United States entered into World War II, Norbert was drafted into the Navy on November 26, 1943, his 21st birthday. He served in the Pacific Theater, and achieved the rank of Radio Technician Petty Officer 2nd Class. He was discharged in 1946. He married Phyllis ("Peggy") Patrick on December 29, 1947 at St. James Catholic Church in McMinnville, OR.

Another member of the Hermens family was taken early too. Jane and Cornelius' oldest daughter Wilhelmina passed away on December 15, 1924 in Portland, OR at the young age of 33. Before she passed, Wilhelmina married Edward J. Vandehey on May 2, 1922 in McMinnville, OR, and three daughters were added to this family. She was laid to rest in the Visitation Catholic Cemetery. You may have noticed Wilhelmina and Elizabeth both married into the Vandehey family. Edward and Albert Vandehey are related too; they are first cousins, their fathers were brothers.

When the 1930s rolled around and another census was taken it reveals some interesting facts about Jane and Cornelius, and some of their children who were out on their own now raising families. First of all, Jane and Cornelius are listed as living in Verboort instead of the McMinnville area, though this may have been a mistake; maybe they were just visiting. There would have been no reason for them to move to Verboort and then back to Yamhill by 1940. Cornelius is employed as a carpenter and Jane is listed as "Johanna". They own their property with a value of $2,500. In September 1930 they purchased 54.61 acres lying near what today is NW McSween Ln. in

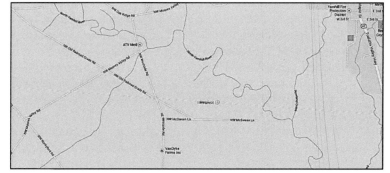

Image 8.06- Map of Yamhill NE Westside Rd & NW McSween Ln. in Yamhill, OR.

Yamhill, OR from George and Eugenia Robinson for, as the land deed indicates, $10 although additional money may have been exchanged and not recorded. This medium sized farm bordered the Carlton & Coast Railroad tracks on the west side, NW McSween Ln. on the north side. For those interested in knowing the legal description of this farm, it laid in the northwest corner of the Samuel McSween Donation Land Claim (#80) Township Three South, Range Four West (T3S, R4W).

An interesting story was told to me by Josephine Garst (Hermens) about the birth of Theodore and Margaret Bernards' twin babies Jane and John. The twins were the last two of ten children in the family, and were born on November 3, 1934. Ida Hermens (Wagner), Josephine's mother and Margaret's sister-in-law, was going to be the mid-wife and deliver the babies at Margaret's home. Ida and her husband Martin Hermens were late to the birth of Jane, the first child to come into the world, because Martin had accidently backed their Ford Model T car into the ditch, and it had to be pulled out by a tractor. Meanwhile, Theodore delivered his daughter. Martin and Ida made it in time for Ida to deliver John some time later.

Just before this country was thrust into World War II, Jane and Cornelius were still living in Yamhill, and both were retired now. Interestingly, the census reveals both only had 4th grade educations. It's amazing how early in life back in the 1870s kids had to leave school to help out at home and on the farm. Jane and Cornelius owned their property, which was worth $500. In 1935, their son Frank and his wife Julia (Kindel) moved their family from Forest Grove to the farm and purchased Frank's parent's big house for $4,500, and built a smaller house for the parents to live in, which is why the home value shown in the census is much lower. According to the census the larger home and farm was valued at $1,500. Frank was a milk dryer at the Farmers' Cooperative Creamery, and earned $600 in 1939 while working only 44 weeks of the year, and received other non-wage income. What was nice was the 1940 census listed the income earned in 1939. This gives us a nice perspective what the family members were earning during the recovery following the Depression. Both Frank and Julia had an 8th grade education. Margaret and Theodore Bernards were also living in Yamhill on their 205-acre farm, which was located across Westside Rd. from the Hermens farm. They had purchased the first two adjoining properties totaling 146 acres in 1935. Theodore was as a farmer, and the couple's home and farm were valued at $2,000. Theodore and Margaret obtained 7th grade educations, and had no income for 1939, but received other non-wage income, which must have been from farming.

Our widower Edward Vandehey was in Verboort living with his daughter Eunice and her husband Clarence VanDyke. Oddly enough, Eunice and Clarence have an interesting family link. Clarence is a son of Margaret VanDyke (Joosten). Eunice's step mother (Wilhelmina Vandehey) is a daughter of Jane, and of course Margaret and Jane are sisters, making Wilhelmina and Clarence first cousins. Edward was a farmer and both Clarence and Eunice worked at the cannery. Joseph and Catherine Hermens lived in Verboort too, and rented their home for $7 per month. All nine of their children born and living at the time were still at home. Looks like Joseph was a feed grinder owning his own hammermill, the purpose of which was more than likely to mill grain into smaller pieces for cattle feed. Joseph and Catherine both were educated up to the 7th grade.

Mrs. Hermans Dies

ROY—Mrs. C. W. Hermans of Yamhill, sister of Mrs. Walter Van Dyke of Verboort and an aunt of Mrs. J. M. Vanderzanden, died last Wednesday evening and funeral services were held Saturday at the McMinnville church with interment in the McMinnville Catholic cemetery. Many relatives and friends from Roy and Verboort attended the funeral.

Image 8.07- Obituary of Jane Hermens (Joosten), Hillsboro Argus, 10/24/1940.

You will remember Jane's sister Frances had diabetes for many years, and this disease wielded its power over Jane too. So it looks as though diabetes ran through the Joosten sisters. Jane suffered from diabetes for three years. According to her obituary, she was living with her daughter Margaret Bernards in Yamhill since 1935. Sadly toward the end of 1940 she passed away from a diabetic coma and gangrene for five days prior to her death on October 16, 1940. She lived to age 70, and had celebrated 50 years of marriage with Cornelius the year before. Jane was known as a very outgoing person and loved life. She was very funny, and had a joke for almost everything. Her hair was a dark sandy red in color, which she never cut and it went down to her waist. As most women of the time, she rolled her hair up into a bun. She is buried in row 11 of the northeast section of the St. James Catholic Cemetery in McMinnville, OR.

During this time Cornelius was in his late 70s, and his health was declining too. He was having heart and kidney problems, and to top it off he had developed dementia and Alzheimer's disease. Without the skilled nursing homes or "memory care" facilities we have today, his family took care of him. He went to live with Martin and Ida in McMinnville, and then later back to Yamhill with Frank and Julia. His Alzheimer's became an issue and bad enough where Cornelius had to be locked in his bedroom at night for his safety because he was known to leave the house, walk away, and get lost. Heartbreaking news came to the Hermens family five and a half years following their mother's death, Cornelius succumbed to his failing heart and kidney complications on April 9, 1946 in Yamhill. He reached 78 years of age after, I am sure, working his body so hard for so many years. Cornelius was known as a very quiet man, and stood around five and a half feet tall, and an inch or two shorter than Jane. He was buried next to his life partner in St. James Catholic Cemetery.

CORNELIUS WM. HERMENS

Funeral services were held today at St. James church for Cornelius William Hermens, of Yamhill who passed away April 9 at Yamhill at the age of 78 years. He had lived in Oregon since 1893 and in McMinnville and at Yamhill.

Mr. Hermens was born in Wisconsin April 25, 1867. His wife Jane Joosten Hermens preceded him in death on Oct. 16, 1940. He leaves four sons, Martin, Joseph, Frank of Yamhill and Edward of San Francisco; also four daughters, Mrs. Catherine Evers of Dayton, Mrs. Margaret Bernards of Yamhill, Mrs. Anna Bride of McMinnville and Jeanette Kelly of Idaho; also two sisters Elizabeth and Minnie Van Dehey.

The Rev. Father Maken officiated. Interment was in the St. James cemetery.

Image 8.08- Obituary of Cornelius Hermens, McMinnville News-Reporter, 04/1946, page 4.

Jane and Cornelius left quite a legacy who follow them. From their 10 children came 65 grandchildren. Long marriages were also a primary value of this family too. As previously mentioned, Jane and Cornelius reached 50 years, and three of their children celebrated 50 years or more. Frank and Julia were married 60 years, Martin and Ida 59 years, and Joseph and Catherine at 56 years.

There were a large number of good men and women of the Hermens Family who served our fine country in the military. They are:

- ❖ Hubert J. Bernards – Served in the U.S. Navy during World War II. He was stationed on a tanker ship in the South Pacific that delivered supplies to his fellow servicemen.
- ❖ Robert E. Bernards - Served as a flight engineer with the Army Air Force during World War II.
- ❖ Lee D. Emery – Served as a TEC4 in the US Army during World War II.
- ❖ Eugene "Gene" T. Hamilton - Served for the US Army in the 508th Airborne Paratrooper Division and later in the 11th Airborne Division.
- ❖ Forrest L. Henry - Served as a Private First Class in Company D of the 145th Infantry in the US Army during World War II. Discharged 12/22/1945 out of Ft. Lewis, WA.
- ❖ Gene E. Hermens – Served in the US Army.
- ❖ Nolan J. Hermens – Served as a Private First Class in the US Army during the Korean War.
- ❖ Norbert J. Hermens – Served as a Sergeant in the US Army during the Korean War.
- ❖ Robert F. Hermens - Served as a Sergeant in the 50th Engineer Port Construction Company during the Korean War.
- ❖ Wilfred I. Hermens – Served in the US Navy during World War II.
- ❖ Norbert J. Vandehey – Served in the US Navy during World War II as a Radio Technician Petty Officer 2nd Class. He was discharged in 1946.
- ❖ Robert G. Van Domelen – Served as a Corporal in the US Army during World War II. Stationed in Africa and Italy where he was wounded and received a Purple Heart. He was honorably discharged after four years of service.
- ❖ Max F. Wade - Served as a Corporal in the US Marines during World War II.
- ❖ Robert W. Wade - Served as a Sergeant in the Army Air Forces in World War II.

Jane & Cornelius Hermens

Image 8.09- Jane M. Hermens (Joosten) Death Certificate

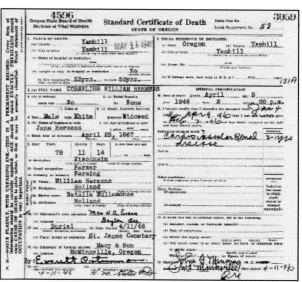

Image 8.10- Cornelius W. Hermens Death Certificate

*Image 8.11- Cornelius W & Jane M Hermens Gravesite Headstone,
St. James Catholic Cemetery, McMinnville, OR.*

*Image 8.12- Cornelius & Jane (Joosten)
Hermens Golden Anniversary Photo-Nov 1939*

*Image 8.13- Cornelius & Jane (Joosten) Hermens Golden
Anniversary Family Photo-Nov 1939*

*Image 8.14- Cornelius & Jane (Joosten) Hermens Golden Anniversary Family Photo
with Grandchildren-Nov 1939*

Image 8.15- Albert Vandehey Obituary, Hillsboro Argus, 12-06-1923, page 1

Image 8.16- William & Catherine (Hermens) Evers

Image 8.17- Cornelius & Jane (Joosten) Hermens Family Photo with Frank Tillman

Image 8.18- Hermens Sisters with Wisc. Cousin. Front: Unknown cousin from WI and Catherine M. Evers (Hermens). Back: and Minnie Hermens (Vandehey) and Mag Hermens (Evers).

Image 8.19- Cornelius & Jane (Joosten) Hermens Family Photo. Top row: Catherine, Martin, Margaret, & Joseph. Middle row: Cornelius, Jeanette, Jane, Wilhelmina, & Edward. Bottom row: Frank, Elizabeth, and Ann. Taken about 1913.

Image 8.20- Albert & Elizabeth (Hermens) Vandehey Wedding Photo 1921

Image 8.21- Martin J & Ida F (Wagner) Hermens Gravesite Headstone, St. James Catholic Cemetery, McMinnville, OR.

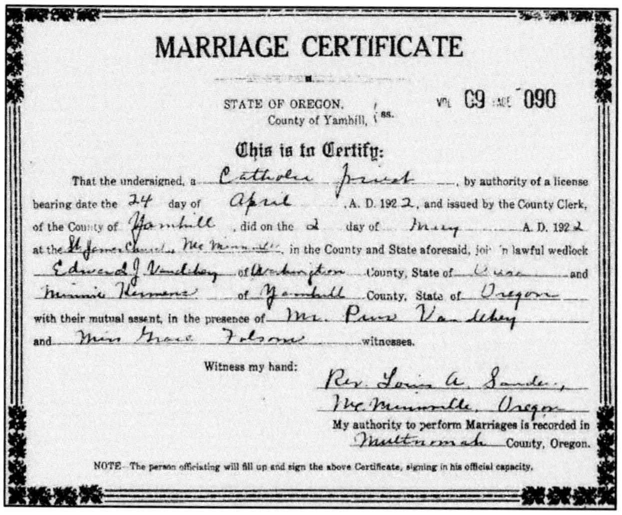

MARRIAGE CERTIFICATE

STATE OF OREGON,
County of Yamhill, ss.

This is to Certify:

That the undersigned, a _Catholic priest_ , by authority of a license bearing date the _24_ day of _April_ , A.D. 192_2_, and issued by the County Clerk, of the County of _Yamhill_ , did on the _2_ day of _May_ A.D. 192_2_ at the _St. James Church, McMinnville_ , in the County and State aforesaid, join in lawful wedlock _Edward J. Vandehey_ of _Washington_ County, State of _Oregon_ and _Minnie Hermens_ of _Yamhill_ County, State of _Oregon_ with their mutual assent, in the presence of _Mr. Pius Vandehey_ and _Miss Grace Folsom_ witnesses.

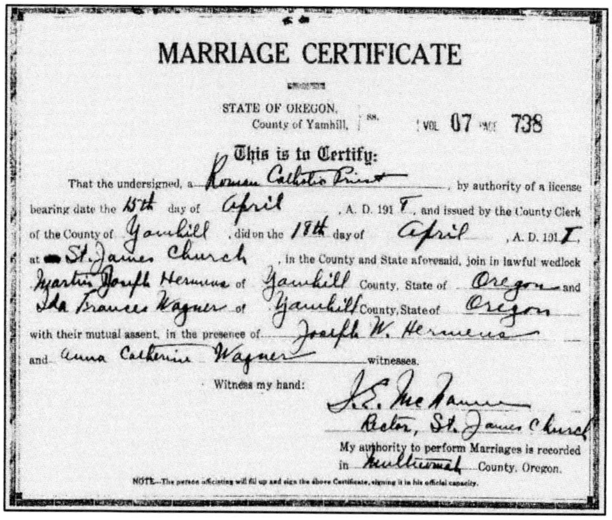

Witness my hand: _Rev. Louis A. Sander,_
McMinnville, Oregon
My authority to perform Marriages is recorded in _Multnomah_ County, Oregon.

NOTE- The person officiating will fill up and sign the above Certificate, signing in his official capacity.

Image 8.22- Edward J. Vandehey & Minnie Hermens Marriage Certificate

MARRIAGE CERTIFICATE

STATE OF OREGON,
County of Yamhill, ss.

This is to Certify:

That the undersigned, a _Roman Catholic Priest_ , by authority of a license bearing date the _15th_ day of _April_ , A.D. 191_7_, and issued by the County Clerk, of the County of _Yamhill_ , did on the _18th_ day of _April_ , A.D. 191_7_ at _St. James Church_ , in the County and State aforesaid, join in lawful wedlock _Martin Joseph Hermens_ of _Yamhill_ County, State of _Oregon_ and _Ida Frances Wagner_ of _Yamhill_ County, State of _Oregon_ with their mutual assent, in the presence of _Joseph W. Hermens_ and _Anna Catherine Wagner_ witnesses.

Witness my hand: _J.C. McNamee_
Rector, St. James Church
My authority to perform Marriages is recorded in _Multnomah_ County, Oregon.

NOTE- The person officiating will fill up and sign the above Certificate, signing in his official capacity.

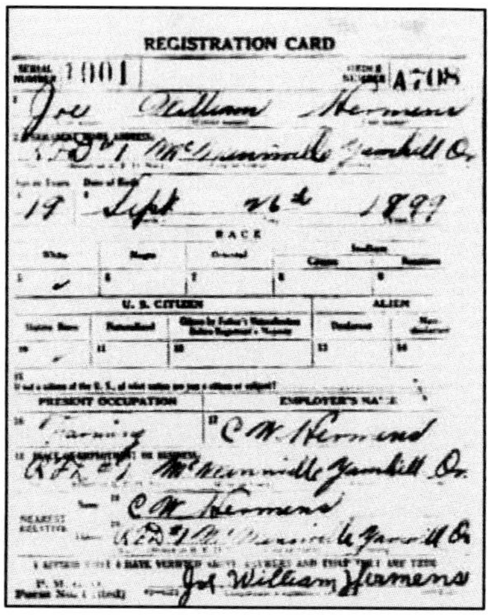

Image 8.23- Martin J. Hermens & Ida F. Wagner Marriage Certificate

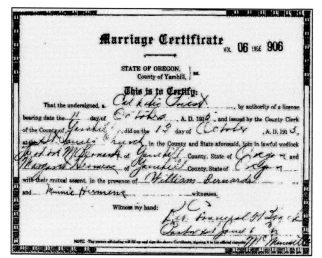

Image 8.24- Margaret Hermens & Theodore Bernards Marriage Certificate

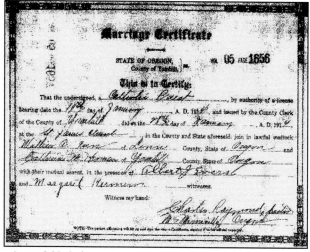

Image 8.25- Catherine Hermens & William Evers Marriage Certificate

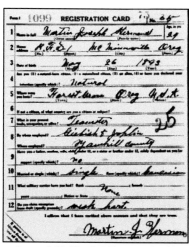

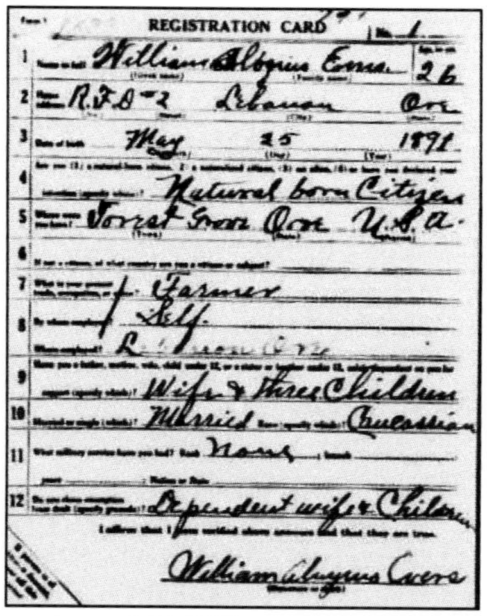

Image 8.26- Martin J. Hermens World War 1 Draft Card

Image 8.27- Joseph W. Hermens World War 1 Draft Card

Image 8.28- William A. Evers World War 1 Draft Card

❧ Descendants of Jane and Cornelius Hermens ❧

Notes: 1= 1st generation, 2= 2nd generation, 3= 3rd generation.
The year of birth is only given for individuals still living, if known.

1   Jane Margaret Joosten
Born: March 31, 1870 in Grand Chute, Outagamie County, Wisconsin
Died: October 16, 1940 in Yamhill, Yamhill County, Oregon
Buried at: St. James Catholic Cemetery, McMinnville, OR., northeast section, row 11
Married: November 30, 1889 in Verboort, Washington County, Oregon
Cornelius William Hermens
Born: April 25, 1867 in Lawrence, Brown County, Wisconsin
Died: April 09, 1946 in Yamhill, Yamhill County, Oregon
Buried at: St. James Catholic Cemetery, McMinnville, OR., northeast section, row 11
Parents: William Hermens, Sr. (1830-1916) and Catharine N. Meulemans (1840-1911)

    2   Wilhelmina Petronella Hermens
Born: February 11, 1891 in Verboort, Washington County, Oregon
Died: December 15, 1924 in Portland, Multnomah County, Oregon
Buried at: Visitation Catholic Cemetery, Verboort, OR, NE row 5
Married: May 02, 1922 in McMinnville, Yamhill County, Oregon
Edward Joseph Vandehey
Born: January 17, 1891 in Cornelius, Washington County, Oregon
Died: March 11, 1968 in Hillsboro, Washington County, Oregon
Buried at: Visitation Catholic Cemetery, Verboort, OR, NE row 5
Parents: Theodore Vandehey (1863-1956) and Bernadina Smith (1867-1936)

        3   Eunice Marie Vandehey (step daughter of Wilhelmina)
Born: 1917 in Oregon
Died: Living
Buried at:
Married: November 29, 1939 in Verboort, Washington County, Oregon
Clarence George VanDyke
Born: December 11, 1914 in Verboort, Washington County, Oregon
Died: October 29, 2005 in Forest Grove, Washington County, Oregon
Buried at: Visitation Catholic Cemetery, Verboort, OR, SE row 7
Parents: Walter VanDyke (1876-1940) and Margaret J. Joosten (1880-1960)

        3   Eileen Mary Vandehey
Born: February 10, 1923 in Banks, Washington County, Oregon
Died: September 01, 2012 in Verboort, Washington County, Oregon
Buried at: Visitation Catholic Cemetery, Verboort, OR, NE row 6
Married: January 18, 1940 in Verboort, Washington County, Oregon
Lawrence Joseph Jansen
Born: July 16, 1920 in Verboort, Washington County, Oregon
Died: October 10, 2009 in Verboort, Washington County, Oregon
Buried at: Visitation Catholic Cemetery, Verboort, OR, NE row 6
Parents: Albert Jansen (1883-1943) and Theodora VanDyke (1886-1955)

        3   Martha J. Vandehey
Born: April 06, 1924 in Verboort, Washington County, Oregon
Died: June 19, 1980 in Portland, Multnomah County, Oregon
Buried at: Visitation Catholic Cemetery, Verboort, OR
Married: January 25, 1944 in Verboort, Washington County, Oregon

Leslie Joseph Verboort
Born: April 28, 1921 in Verboort, Washington County, Oregon
Died: October 03, 1976 in Portland, Multnomah County, Oregon
Buried at: Visitation Catholic Cemetery, Verboort, OR
Parents: William A. Verboort (1876-1940) and Petronella M. VanDyke (1883-1954)

2   Martin Joseph Hermens
Born: May 26, 1893 in Verboort, Washington County, Oregon
Died: March 08, 1978 in Portland, Multnomah County, Oregon
Buried at: St. James Catholic Cemetery, McMinnville, OR., northeast section, row 11
Married: April 18, 1918 in McMinnville, Yamhill County, Oregon
Ida Francis Wagner
Born: November 21, 1897 in Antelope, Wasco County, Oregon
Died: December 21, 1990 in McMinnville, Yamhill County, Oregon
Buried at: St. James Catholic Cemetery, McMinnville, OR., northeast section, row 11
Parents: Joseph Wagner (1867-1952) and Sarah F. Good (1870-1956)

   3   Stanley Joseph Hermens, Sr.
Born: January 04, 1919 in McMinnville, Yamhill County, Oregon
Died: April 15, 2002 in Portland, Multnomah County, Oregon
Buried at: St. James Catholic Cemetery, McMinnville, OR., west section, row 13
Married (1): August 31, 1940 in Newberg, Yamhill County, Oregon
Married (2): April 08, 1989 in McMinnville, Yamhill County, Oregon
Erma Agnes Versteeg (1)
Born: September 07, 1918 in Newberg, Yamhill County, Oregon
Died: February 10, 1974 in McMinnville, Yamhill County, Oregon
Buried at: St. James Catholic Cemetery, McMinnville, OR., west section, row 13
Parents: Arie A. Versteeg (1875-1951) and Agnes W. Vanderbeck (1892-1948)
Joyce Copeland (2)
Born: 1926
Died: Living
Buried at:
Parents: Unknown

   3   Clair Ignatius Hermens
Born: March 31, 1920 in McMinnville, Yamhill County, Oregon
Died: March 14, 1936 in McMinnville, Yamhill County, Oregon
Buried at: St. James Catholic Cemetery, McMinnville, OR., northeast section, row 11
Married: n/a

   3   Josephine Marie Hermens
Born: 1921 in McMinnville, Yamhill County, Oregon
Died: Living
Buried at:
Married: August 31, 1945 in Portland, Multnomah County, Oregon
Samuel Leander Garst, Jr.
Born: November 22, 1914 in Westhope, Bottineau County, North Dakota
Died: December 03, 1984 in Eugene, Lane County, Oregon
Buried at: Rest Haven Cemetery, Eugene, OR
Parents: Samuel L. Garst, Sr. (1873-1947) and Lilly M. Maxfield (1872-1948)

3　Julia Marie Hermens
Born: May 23, 1922 in McMinnville, Yamhill County, Oregon
Died: 2005 in Butte, Jefferson County, Montana
Buried at: Sunset Memorial Park, Gregson, MT
Married: Unknown
William Franklin Setzer
Born: June 19, 1915 in Butte, Silver Bow, Montana
Died: February 18, 1979 in Mesa, Maricopa County, Arizona
Buried at: Sunset Memorial Park, Gregson, MT
Parents: Martin L. Setzer (1869-1949) and Maud O. Metzger (1875-1958)

3　Frederick Martin Hermens
Born: September 19, 1924 in McMinnville, Yamhill County, Oregon
Died: March 14, 1943 in Portland, Multnomah County, Oregon
Buried at: Mount St. Michael Cemetery, Spokane, WA
Married: n/a

3　Martha Frances Hermens
Born: 1927 in McMinnville, Yamhill County, Oregon
Died: Living
Buried at:
Married: July 02, 1954 in Los Angeles County, California
Paul Byron Bixby
Born: October 19, 1926 in Sparta, Randolph County, Illinois
Died: July 20, 2011 in Burbank, Los Angeles County, California
Buried at: St. James Catholic Cemetery, McMinnville, OR.
Parents: John W. Bixby (1887-1978) and Essie A. Lively (1888-1936)

3　Louis Dean Hermens
Born: 1930 in Yamhill, Yamhill County, Oregon
Died: Living
Buried at:
Married: Unknown

3　Patricia Ann Hermens
Born: March 17, 1933 in Yamhill, Yamhill County, Oregon
Died: February 20, 2010 in McMinnville, Yamhill County, Oregon
Buried at: Yamhill-Carlton Pioneer Cemetery, Carlton, OR.
Married: April 28, 1951 in Yamhill County, Oregon
Albert Laughlin Jr.
Born: 1932
Died: Living
Buried at:
Parents: Unknown

3　Frances Jane Hermens
Born: 1935 in Yamhill, Yamhill County, Oregon
Died: Living
Buried at:
Married: September 08, 1951 in Yamhill County, Oregon

George Sampson
Born: Unknown
Died: Living
Buried at:
Parents: Unknown

3   Joseph Cornelius Hermens
Born: 1937 in Yamhill, Yamhill County, Oregon
Died: Living
Buried at:
Married: Unknown

2 Catherine Mary Hermens
Born: February 25, 1895 in Verboort, Washington County, Oregon
Died: August 20, 1971 in Washington County, Oregon
Buried at: St. James Catholic Cemetery, McMinnville, OR., west section, row 4
Married (1): January 28, 1914 in McMinnville, Yamhill County, Oregon
Married (2): October 1964
William Aloysius Evers (1)
Born: May 25, 1891 in Verboort, Washington County, Oregon
Died: August 24, 1963 in McMinnville, Yamhill County, Oregon
Buried at: St. James Catholic Cemetery, McMinnville, OR., west section, row 4
Parents: Peter Evers (1851-1937) and Antonia Vandehey (1858-1891)
Antone Henry Evers (2)
Born: September 16, 1886 in Verboort, Washington County, Oregon
Died: November 20, 1978 in Beaverton, Washington County, Oregon
Buried at: Visitation Catholic Cemetery, Verboort, OR, SW row 2
Parents: Peter Evers (1851-1937) and Antonia Vandehey (1858-1891)

3   Janet Antonia Evers
Born: November 14, 1914 in Lebanon, Linn County, Oregon
Died: October 06, 2002
Buried at: Visitation Catholic Cemetery, Verboort, OR., SW row 4
Married: June 01, 1937 in McMinnville, Yamhill County, Oregon
Arthur Joseph Verboort
Born: February 08, 1911 in Verboort, Washington County, Oregon
Died: February 17, 1991 in Hillsboro, Washington County, Oregon
Buried at: Visitation Catholic Cemetery, Verboort, OR., SW row 4
Parents: William A. Verboort (1876-1940) and Petronella M. VanDyke (1883-1954)

3   Genevieve Josephine Evers
Born: March 03, 1916 in Lebanon, Linn County, Oregon
Died: December 05, 1999
Buried at: St. Matthew Catholic Cemetery, Hillsboro, OR
Married: July 21, 1936 in McMinnville, Yamhill County, Oregon
Henry John Van Domelen
Born: July 03, 1912 in Banks, Washington County, Oregon
Died: September 29, 1990 in Portland, Multnomah County, Oregon
Buried at: St. Matthew Catholic Cemetery, Hillsboro, OR
Parents: William Van Domelen (1883-1974) and Wilhelmina Vanderzanden (1887-1981)

3   Clair Peter Evers
     Born: March 22, 1917 in Crabtree, Linn County, Oregon
     Died: July 27, 1989 in Monroe, Benton County, Oregon
     Buried at: St. Rose Catholic Cemetery, Monroe, OR
     Married: October 03, 1938
     Marie Agnes Vanderzanden
     Born: January 31, 1917 in Roy, Washington County, Oregon
     Died: September 01, 2003 in McMinnville, Yamhill County, Oregon
     Buried at: St. Rose Catholic Cemetery, Monroe, OR
     Parents: Albert Vanderzanden (1882-1959) and Elizabeth Cornelia Van Domelen (1888-1977)

3   Howard Corneal Evers
     Born: February 14, 1919 in Crabtree, Linn County, Oregon
     Died: January 04, 1975 in Portland, Multnomah County, Oregon
     Buried at: St. Mary Cemetery, Arcata, CA
     Married: June 01, 1940
     Loretta Bertha Wagner
     Born: July 04, 1918 in Yankton, Yankton County, South Dakota
     Died: November 15, 1965 in Orick, Humboldt County, California
     Buried at: St. Mary Cemetery, Arcata, CA
     Parents: George C. Wagner (1886-1961) and Marie C. Wagner (1895-1980)

3   Mary Jane Evers
     Born: December 29, 1920 in Dayton, Yamhill County, Oregon
     Died: May 07, 2002 in Oregon City, Clackamas County, Oregon
     Buried at: St. John Catholic Cemetery, Oregon City, OR
     Married: 1939
     Raymond P. Ritter
     Born: 1916 or 1917 in Minnesota
     Died: 1967
     Buried at:
     Parents: Unknown

3   Charles William Evers
     Born: August 12, 1923 in Dayton, Yamhill County, Oregon
     Died: October 29, 2004 in Dayton, Yamhill County, Oregon
     Buried at: St. James Catholic Cemetery, McMinnville, OR., southeast section, row 6
     Married: June 07, 1945 in McMinnville, Yamhill County, Oregon
     Anna Ellen Cantlon
     Born: March 18, 1923 in Sparks, Washoe County, Nevada
     Died: June 08, 2012 in McMinnville, Yamhill County, Oregon
     Buried at:
     Parents: John E. Cantlon (1883-1930) and Anna R. Brooks

3   Lawrence Joseph Evers
     Born: May 10, 1925 in Dayton, Yamhill County, Oregon
     Died: June 19, 1947 in Hillsboro, Washington County, Oregon
     Buried at: St. James Catholic Cemetery, McMinnville, OR., southeast section, row 6
     Married: n/a

3   <u>Raymond E. Evers</u>
    Born: August 30, 1927 in McMinnville, Yamhill County, Oregon
    Died: August 07, 2011 in Springfield, Lane County, Oregon
    Buried at: St. James Catholic Cemetery, McMinnville, OR.
    Married (1): March 04, 1970 in Lane County, Oregon
    Married (2): 1978 in Springfield, Lane County, Oregon
    <u>Norma Jeane Evers (1)</u>
    Born: December 10, 1929
    Died: October 18, 2007 in Oregon
    Buried at: Willamette National Cemetery, Portland, OR
    Parents: Unknown
    <u>Eileene Marie Chambers (2)</u>
    Born: March 20, 1919
    Died: March 13, 2008 in Lane County, Oregon
    Buried at:
    Parents: Unknown

2   <u>Margaret Mary Hermens</u>
   Born: March 08, 1896 in Verboort, Washington County, Oregon
   Died: December 27, 1989 in Hillsboro, Washington County, Oregon
   Buried at: St. James Catholic Cemetery, McMinnville, OR., west section, row 16
   Married: October 13, 1915 in McMinnville, Yamhill County, Oregon
   <u>Theodore Matthias Bernards</u>
   Born: December 05, 1888 in Verboort, Washington County, Oregon
   Died: April 08, 1956 in Yamhill, Yamhill County, Oregon
   Buried at: St. James Catholic Cemetery, McMinnville, OR, west section, row 16
   Parents: Hubert Bernards (1849-1923) and Johanna Cop (1853-1912)

    3   <u>Martha Frances Bernards</u>
      Born: February 22, 1917 in Yamhill, Yamhill County, Oregon
      Died: September 23, 1983 in McMinnville, Yamhill County, Oregon
      Buried at: St. James Catholic Cemetery, McMinnville, OR., west section, row 16
      Married: November 23, 1939 in Yamhill, Yamhill County, Oregon
      <u>Walter Wenzel Juenemann</u>
      Born: September 01, 1913 in New Ulm, Brown County, Minnesota
      Died: April 12, 2011 in Hillsboro, Washington County, Oregon
      Buried at: St. James Catholic Cemetery, McMinnville, OR., west section, row 16
      Parents: Frederick W. Juenemann (1891-1960) and Margaret Helget (1888-1973)

    3   <u>Robert Edward Bernards</u>
      Born: January 11, 1919 in Yamhill, Yamhill County, Oregon
      Died: January 30, 2006 in Benton County, Oregon
      Buried at: St. James Catholic Cemetery, McMinnville, OR., west section, row 16
      Married: December 01, 1956 in McMinnville, Yamhill County, Oregon
      <u>Patricia Clare Connell</u>
      Born: May 05, 1923 in Portland, Multnomah County, Oregon
      Died: November 07, 2006 in Benton County, Oregon
      Buried at: St. James Catholic Cemetery, McMinnville, OR., west section, row 16
      Parents: Francis Connell (1892-?) and Adelaide M. Kasberger (1899-1964)

3   <u>Donald Theodore Bernards</u>
Born: January 20, 1921 in Yamhill, Yamhill County, Oregon
Died: June 16, 1991 in Salem, Marion County, Oregon
Buried at: City View Cemetery, Salem, OR
Married: September 25, 1946 in Yamhill County, Oregon
<u>Kathleen Ora Wade</u>
Born: June 30, 1924 in Yamhill, Yamhill County, Oregon
Died: May 13, 1975 in Salem, Marion County, Oregon
Buried at: City View Cemetery, Salem, OR.
Parents: Guy Wade (1889-1971) and Meda Z. Goodrich (1893-1943)

3   <u>Hubert James Bernards</u>
Born: September 28, 1923 in Yamhill, Yamhill County, Oregon
Died: October 24, 2012 in Newberg, Yamhill County, Oregon
Buried at: St. James Catholic Cemetery, McMinnville, OR.
Married: September 14, 1949 in Roy, Washington County, Oregon
<u>Lucille Marie Vanderzanden</u>
Born: 1931 in Roy, Washington County, Oregon
Died: Living
Buried at:
Parents: Francis M. Vanderzanden (1903-1982) and Hermina H. Vandecoevering (1902-1951)

3   <u>Theodore Cornelius Bernards</u>
Born: November 07, 1925 in Yamhill, Yamhill County, Oregon
Died: May 04, 1996 in Polk County, Oregon
Buried at: St. James Catholic Cemetery, McMinnville, OR., west section, row 16
Married: May 18, 1947 in Yamhill, Yamhill County, Oregon
<u>Margaret Jean Hacker</u>
Born: December 01, 1927 in Casper, Natrona County, Wyoming
Died: January 20, 2015 in Oregon
Buried at: St. James Catholic Cemetery, McMinnville, OR., west section, row 16
Parents: Clifford E. Hacker (1901-1986) and Marlene E. Lea (1905-1983)

3   <u>Mary Theresa Bernards</u>
Born: October 15, 1927 in Yamhill, Yamhill County, Oregon
Died: April 14, 1983 in Dallas, Polk County, Oregon
Buried at:
Married: November 21, 1948 in McMinnville, Yamhill County, Oregon
<u>Harland Anderson</u>
Born: December 04, 1916 in Almont, Morton County, South Dakota
Died: Unknown
Buried at:
Parents: Unknown

3   <u>Lawrence William Bernards</u>
Born: 1929 in Yamhill, Yamhill County, Oregon
Died: Living
Buried at:
Married: May 01, 1951 in Roy, Washington County, Oregon

Dorothy Louise Vanderzanden
Born: 1929 in Roy, Washington County, Oregon
Died: Living
Buried at:
Parents: Francis M. Vanderzanden (1903-1982) and Hermina H. Vandecoevering (1902-1951)

3   Norman Eugene Bernards
Born: November 07, 1931 in Yamhill, Yamhill County, Oregon
Died: March 23, 2014 in McMinnville, Yamhill County, Oregon
Buried at: St. James Catholic Cemetery, McMinnville, OR.
Married: December 27, 1954 in Yamhill County, Oregon
Louise Marie Ricke
Born: 1935 in Sharon, Barber County, Kansas
Died: Living
Buried at:
Parents: Henry E. Ricke (1904-1990) and Florence L. Leonard (1910-2005)

3   Jane Margaret Bernards
Born: 1934 in Yamhill, Yamhill County, Oregon
Died: Living
Buried at:
Married: November 11, 1953 in McMinnville, Yamhill County, Oregon
Ervin Aloysius VanDyke
Born: November 03, 1915 in Forest Grove, Washington County, Oregon
Died: November 26, 1990 in Forest Grove, Washington County, Oregon
Buried at: Visitation Catholic Cemetery, Verboort, OR, SW row 6
Parents: William A. VanDyke (1877-1942) and Alice C. Evers (1884-1959)

3   John Theodore Bernards
Born: November 03, 1934 in Yamhill, Yamhill County, Oregon
Died: Living
Buried at:
Married: May 05, 1962 in Verboort, Washington County, Oregon
Marilyn Anne Herinckx
Born: September 19, 1939 in Verboort, Washington County, Oregon
Died: July 22, 1986 in Hillsboro, Washington County, Oregon
Buried at: Visitation Catholic Cemetery, Verboort, OR, SE row 6
Parents: Joseph J. Herinckx (1912-1978) and Gladys F. Kindel (1912-1995)

2 Joseph William Hermens
Born: September 26, 1898 in Verboort, Washington County, Oregon
Died: March 17, 1980 in McMinnville, Yamhill County, Oregon
Buried at: St. Francis of Assisi Catholic Cemetery, Roy, OR, south row 7
Married: June 06, 1923 in Roy, Washington County, Oregon
Catherine J. Vandehey
Born: October 25, 1904 in Roy, Washington County, Oregon
Died: March 08, 1994 in Forest Grove, Washington County, Oregon
Buried at: St. Francis of Assisi Catholic Cemetery, Roy, OR, south row 7
Parents: Antone Vandehey (1870-1934) and Mary Anna Smith (1870-1955)

3   Patricia A. Hermens
     Born: 1924 in Roy, Washington County, Oregon
     Died: Living
     Buried at:
     Married: June 27, 1946 in Yamhill County, Oregon
     Robert George Van Domelen
     Born: November 03, 1917 in Banks, Washington County, Oregon
     Died: March 06, 2011 in Banks, Washington County, Oregon
     Buried at: St. Francis of Assisi Catholic Cemetery, Roy, OR
     Parents: William Van Domelen (1883-1974) and Wilhelmina Vanderzanden (1887-1981)

3   Wilfred Ignacious Hermens
     Born: October 19, 1925 in Roy, Washington County, Oregon
     Died: August 25, 2008 in McMinnville, Yamhill County, Oregon
     Buried at:
     Married: November 11, 1947 in Yamhill, Yamhill County, Oregon
     Aileen Ann Thayer
     Born: May 28, 1929 in Yamhill, Yamhill County, Oregon
     Died: July 12, 2012 in McMinnville, Yamhill County, Oregon
     Buried at:
     Parents: Lynol H. Thayer (1896-1949) and Beulah M. Funk (1898-1965)

3   Gerald A. Hermens
     Born: 1927 in Oregon
     Died: Living
     Buried at:
     Married: November 09, 1948 in Yamhill County, Oregon
     Zelma J. Van Schaack
     Born: 1930 in Concord, Contra Costa County, California
     Died: Living
     Buried at:
     Parents: Ralph Van Schaack (1902-?) and Margaret Van Schaack (1907-?)

3   Ethel Hermens
     Born: 1929 in Oregon
     Died: Living
     Buried at:
     Married: April 24, 1954 in Yamhill County, Oregon
     Alvin Reed
     Born: Unknown
     Died: Living
     Buried at:
     Parents: Unknown

3   James Hermens
     Born: 1931 in Oregon
     Died: Living
     Buried at:
     Married: August 18, 1951 in Yamhill County, Oregon

Wilma G. Smith
Born: 1931
Died: Living
Buried at:
Parents: Unknown

3   Rita Hermens
Born: 1932 in Verboort, Washington County, Oregon
Died: Living
Buried at:
Married: September 03, 1952 in Yamhill County, Oregon
Bernard Arthur Van Domelen
Born: 1931 in Banks, Washington County, Oregon
Died: Living
Buried at:
Parents: William Van Domelen (1883-1974) and Wilhelmina Vanderzanden (1887-1981)

3   Irvin F. Hermens
Born: 1933 in Verboort, Washington County, Oregon
Died: Living
Buried at:
Married: August 04, 1956 in Yamhill, Yamhill County, Oregon
Hildegard G. Dambacher
Born: July 10, 1936 in Ulm, Baden-Württemberg, Germany
Died: July 26, 2005 in Yamhill, Yamhill County, Oregon
Buried at: St. James Catholic Cemetery, McMinnville, OR., west section, row 4
Parents: Robert Dambacher and Rosa Neft

3   Lawrence Cornelius Hermens
Born: 1935 in Verboort, Washington County, Oregon
Died: Living
Buried at:
Married: September 03, 1956 in Roy, Washington County, Oregon
Elaine Dorothy Herb
Born: 1935 in Oregon
Died: Living
Buried at:
Parents: William P. Herb (1904-1991) and Alfreda DeVlaeminck (1911-1991)

3   Eldon F. Hermens
Born: 1937 in Verboort, Washington County, Oregon
Died: Living
Buried at:
Married: November 23, 1963 in Multnomah County, Oregon
Mary Jane Van Schaack
Born: April 15, 1939 in Concord, Contra Costa County, California
Died: September 03, 2011 in Milwaukie, Clackamas County, Oregon
Buried at:
Parents: Ralph Van Schaack (1902-?) and Margaret Van Schaack (1907-?)

3 David A. Hermens
Born: 1940 in Verboort, Washington County, Oregon
Died: Living
Buried at:
Married: August 10, 1963 in Santa Clara County, California
Ann C. Schirle
Born: 1940 or 1941
Died: Living
Buried at:
Parents: Unknown

3 Marie Hermens
Born: 1942 in Verboort, Washington County, Oregon
Died: Living
Buried at:
Married: October 06, 1962 in Yamhill County, Oregon
Thomas Jorgenson
Born: Unknown
Died: Living
Buried at:
Parents: Unknown

2 Elizabeth Natalia Hermens
Born: January 01, 1903 in Verboort, Washington County, Oregon
Died: October 29, 1937 in McMinnville, Yamhill County, Oregon
Buried at: St. Francis of Assisi Catholic Cemetery, Roy, OR, south row 6
Married: October 05, 1921 in McMinnville, Yamhill County, Oregon
Albert Joseph Vandehey
Born: August 04, 1898 in Roy, Washington County, Oregon
Died: December 05, 1923 in Roy, Washington County, Oregon
Buried at: St. Francis of Assisi Catholic Cemetery, Roy, OR, south row 6
Parents: Antone Vandehey (1870-1934) and Mary Anna Smith (1870-1955)

3 Norbert Joseph Vandehey
Born: 1922 in Roy, Washington County, Oregon
Died: Living
Buried at:
Married: December 29, 1947 in McMinnville, Yamhill County, Oregon
Phyllis Ann Patrick
Born: 1926 in Klamath Falls, Klamath County, Oregon
Died: Living
Buried at:
Parents: Roy L. Patrick (1901-1978) and Phyllis M. Patison (1923-1985)

3 Alberta Marie Vandehey
Born: December 29, 1923 in McMinnville, Yamhill County, Oregon
Died: May 28, 1980 in Portland, Multnomah County, Oregon
Buried at: Willamette National Cemetery, Portland, OR., sec O, site 3960
Married: Unknown

Lee Duane Emery
Born: February 12, 1923 in Klamath Falls, Klamath County, Oregon
Died: July 11, 2008 in LaPine, Deschutes County, Oregon
Buried at: Willamette National Cemetery, Portland, OR., sec O, site 3960
Parents: Lee E. Emery (1889-1973) and Rosalie A. Rossman (1892-1989)

2   Francis Henry Hermens
Born: October 21, 1904 in Verboort, Washington County, Oregon
Died: October 27, 1992 in McMinnville, Yamhill County, Oregon
Buried at: St. James Catholic Cemetery, McMinnville, OR., west section, row 17
Married: June 28, 1927 in Verboort, Washington County, Oregon
Julia J. Kindel
Born: July 20, 1906 in Verboort, Washington County, Oregon
Died: October 22, 1987 in Yamhill, Yamhill County, Oregon
Buried at: St. James Catholic Cemetery, McMinnville, OR., west section, row 17
Parents: John H. Kindel III (1881-1956) and Anna J. Jansen (1881-1955)

    3   Robert Francis Hermens
Born: December 25, 1927 in Portland, Multnomah County, Oregon
Died: November 21, 1951 in Portland, Multnomah County, Oregon
Buried at: Mount Calvary Catholic Cemetery, Portland, OR
Married: January 28, 1950 in Yamhill County, Oregon
Viola M. Burk
Born: Unknown
Died: Living
Buried at:
Parents: Unknown

    3   Nolan John Hermens
Born: September 06, 1929 in Yamhill, Yamhill County, Oregon
Died: November 30, 2003 in McMinnville, Yamhill County, Oregon
Buried at: St. James Catholic Cemetery, McMinnville, OR., west section, row 16
Married (1): April 19, 1952 in Yamhill County, Oregon
Married (2): July 27, 1984 in Vancouver, Clark County, Washington
Delores Maxine Sampson (1)
Born: February 09, 1930 in Geddes, Charles Mix County, South Dakota
Died: February 07, 1999 in McMinnville, Yamhill County, Oregon
Buried at:
Parents: Unknown
Virginia S. Smith (2)
Born: April 11, 1932 in Clayton, Union County, New Mexico
Died: January 14, 2002 in McMinnville, Yamhill County, Oregon
Buried at: Alamosa Municipal Cemetery, Alamosa, CO.
Parents: William Smith and Dorothy Sellers

    3   Margaret Ann Hermens
Born: July 09, 1931 in Oregon
Died: May 07, 2006 in Fresno, Fresno County, California
Buried at: Belmont Memorial Park, Fresno, CA
Married: July 18, 1950 in Yamhill County, Oregon

Arthur L. Jorgensen
Born: October 06, 1924
Died: December 26, 1998
Buried at:
Parents: Unknown

3   Norbert Joseph Hermens
Born: March 25, 1933 in Verboort, Washington County, Oregon
Died: April 27, 1995 in Yamhill, Yamhill County, Oregon
Buried at: St. James Catholic Cemetery, McMinnville, OR., west section, row 18
Married: December 30, 1954 in Stevenson, Skamania County, Washington
Gloria Milne
Born: 1937 in Oregon
Died: Living
Buried at:
Parents: Robert C. Milne (1913-1972) and Winifred R. Turner (1915-2009)

3   Gene Edward Hermens
Born: November 17, 1934 in Verboort, Washington County, Oregon
Died: June 21, 1994 in McMinnville, Yamhill County, Oregon
Buried at: St. James Catholic Cemetery, McMinnville, OR., west section, row 17
Married: August 20, 1955 in McMinnville, Yamhill County, Oregon
Patricia Ferger
Born: 1937 in Iowa
Died: Living
Buried at:
Parents: Parents: James G. Ferger (1913-1999) and Bertha L. Ferger (1911-1972)

3   Ralph J. Hermens
Born: February 08, 1938
Died: July 31, 2000 in Bend, Deschutes County, Oregon
Buried at: Pilot Butte Cemetery, Bend, OR
Married: October 06, 1956 in Yamhill County, Oregon
Rosalie M. Ferger
Born: 1938 in Iowa
Died: Living
Buried at:
Parents: James G. Ferger (1913-1999) and Bertha L. Ferger (1911-1972)

2   Edward Anthony Hermens
Born: April 12, 1906 in Verboort, Washington County, Oregon
Died: November 05, 2001 in McMinnville, Yamhill County, Oregon
Buried at: St. James Catholic Cemetery, McMinnville, OR., northeast section, row 11
Married (1): January 21, 1928 in Oakland, Alameda County, California
Married (2): April 12, 1944 in San Francisco, San Francisco County, California
Juanita Marie Hepner (1)
Born: July 06, 1909 in Shaw, Marion County, Oregon
Died: June 1979 in Florence, Pinal County, Arizona
Buried at:
Parents: John A. Hepner (1880-1928) and Ella I. Barrows (1881-1958)

<u>Irene E Stover (2)</u>
Born: January 19, 1915 in Brooks, Marion County, Oregon
Died: July 01, 2006 in McMinnville, Yamhill County, Oregon
Buried at: St. James Catholic Cemetery, McMinnville, OR.
Parents: Guy R. Stover (1872-1943) and Rosa Koontz (1878-1965)

3   <u>Gerald E. Hermens</u>
Born: 1928 in Contra Costa County, California
Died: Living
Buried at:
Married: Unknown

3   <u>Richard J. Hermens</u>
Born: May 23, 1929 in Oregon
Died: April 08, 1937
Buried at: St. James Catholic Cemetery, McMinnville, OR., northeast section, row 11
Married: n/a

3   <u>William Hermens</u>
Born: 1930 or 1931 in Oregon
Died: Living
Buried at:
Married: Unknown

3   <u>Joan K. Hermens</u>
Born: 1933 in Oregon
Died: Living
Buried at:
Married: Unknown
<u>James H. Sims</u>
Born: 1928
Died: Living
Buried at:
Parents: Unknown

3   <u>Elizabeth Hermens</u>
Born: December 01, 1935 in The Dalles, Wasco County, Oregon
Died: February 20, 2014 in Rocky Mount, Edgecombe County, North Carolina
Buried at:
Married: 1955 or 1956
<u>Grady Ray Tart, Sr.</u>
Born: March 26, 1933
Died: January 11, 2014 in Rocky Mount, Edgecombe County, North Carolina
Buried at:
Parents: Unknown

3   <u>Mary Hermens (Castle)</u>
Born: 1937 or 1938 in Oregon
Died: Living
Buried at:
Married: Unknown

2   Ann Julianna Hermens
Born: November 18, 1908 in McMinnville, Yamhill County, Oregon
Died: April 30, 1956 in McMinnville, Yamhill County, Oregon
Buried at: St. James Catholic Cemetery, McMinnville, OR., west section, row 4
Married: May 10, 1927 in McMinnville, Yamhill County, Oregon
Leo Clifford Bride
Born: December 14, 1905 in Oconto Falls, Oconto County, Wisconsin
Died: July 23, 1960 in McMinnville, Yamhill County, Oregon
Buried at: St. James Catholic Cemetery, McMinnville, OR., west section, row 4
Parents: Owen D. Bride (1856-1938) and Elsie A. Coy (1865-1926)

   3   Barbara Ann Bride
Born: 1928 in Monterey County, California
Died: Living
Buried at:
Married (1): August 03, 1947 in Yamhill County, Oregon
Married (2): Unknown
Max Fielding Wade (1)
Born: January 30, 1926 in Yamhill, Yamhill County, Oregon
Died: August 02, 2002 in Grand Junction, Mesa County, Colorado
Buried at: Veterans Memorial Cemetery, Grand Junction, CO
Parents: Guy Wade (1889-1971) and Meda Z. Goodrich (1893-1943)
Arthur Franklin Inman (2)
Born: May 8, 1932
Died: May 01, 2003 in Multnomah County, Oregon
Buried at: Fall City Cemetery, Fall City, OR
Parents: Unknown

   3   Lois M. Bride
Born: 1932 in Contra Costa County, California
Died: Living
Buried at:
Married: February 01, 1952 in Salem, Marion County, Oregon
Robert W. Wade
Born: September 20, 1922 in Yamhill, Yamhill County, Oregon
Died: June 14, 2002 in Portland, Multnomah County, Oregon
Buried at: North Yamhill Cemetery, Yamhill, OR
Parents: Guy Wade (1889-1971) and Meda Z. Goodrich (1893-1943)

   3   Joan Marie Bride
Born: December 04, 1934 in Martinez, Contra Costa County, California
Died: August 09, 2012 in Cornelius, Washington County, Oregon
Buried at: Visitation Catholic Cemetery, Verboort, OR, SE row 3
Married: January 19, 1952 in McMinnville, Yamhill County, Oregon
Cecil N. Heynderickx
Born: 1930
Died: Living
Buried at:
Parents: Cecil W. Heynderickx (1899-1989) and Anna M. Heynderickx (1900-1988)

3   Sandra L. Bride
Born: 1945
Died: Living
Buried at:
Married: July 08, 1969 in Washington County, Oregon
Douglas E. Shook
Born: 1946
Died: Living
Buried at:
Parents: Unknown

2 Jeanette Rosalia Hermens
Born: August 23, 1911 in McMinnville, Yamhill County, Oregon
Died: December 10, 1989 in Gresham, Multnomah County, Oregon
Buried at: Sunset Memorial Park, Twin Falls, ID
Married (1): October 16, 1929
Married (2): September 18, 1943 in Vancouver, Clark County, Washington
Harry Theodore Hamilton (1)
Born: April 21, 1910 in Saint Joseph, Buchanan County, Missouri
Died: October 12, 1967 in Portland, Multnomah County, Oregon
Buried at: Park Hill Cemetery, Vancouver, WA
Parents: William L. Hamilton (1884-1936) and Daisey M. South (1884-1943)
Lloyd Foster Kelley (2)
Born: May 16, 1907 in Kalispell, Flathead County, Montana
Died: May 31, 1995 in Gresham, Multnomah County, Oregon
Buried at: Sunset Memorial Park, Twin Falls, ID
Parents: Arthur D. Kelley (1869-1946) and Phoebe J. Thomas (1871-1948)

3   William Wayne Hamilton
Born: May 11, 1930 in Portland, Multnomah County, Oregon
Died: June 15, 1979 in Twin Falls, Twin Falls County, Idaho
Buried at:
Married: September 21, 1950
Darlene Sangster
Born: 1934 or 1935 in California
Died: Living
Buried at:
Parents: William A. Sangster (1908-1971) and Mildred A. Lee (1907-?)

3   Isla M. Hamilton
Born: 1931 in Oregon
Died: Living
Buried at:
Married (1): June 18, 1948 in Malheur County, Oregon
Married (2): December 10, 1965 in Vancouver, Clark County, Washington
Forrest Laverne Henry (1)
Born: January 21, 1924 in Grover, St Louis County, Missouri
Died: September 07, 1994 in Portland, Multnomah County, Oregon
Buried at: Forest Lawn Memorial Park, Gresham, OR
Parents: Alexander F. Henry and Dovie A. Henry (1902-1977)

Roy Elmood Halligan (2)
Born: June 11, 1929 in Hot Springs, Fall River County, South Dakota
Died: April 17, 1999 in Portland, Multnomah County, Oregon
Buried at: Forest Lawn Memorial Park, Gresham, OR
Parents: Roy Halligan (1891-1972) and Reva L. Halligan (1900-1977)

3   Eugene Theodore Hamilton
Born: November 05, 1933 in Portland, Multnomah County, Oregon
Died: July 08, 2012 in Twin Falls, Twin Falls County, Idaho
Buried at Sunset Memorial Park, Twin Falls, ID
Married: May 21, 1954 in Payette, Payette County, Idaho
Gloria Mae Cutler
Born: Unknown
Died: Living
Buried at:
Parents: Delbert L. Cutler (1901-1968) and Helen Judd (1911-1995)

3   Darrell James Hamilton, Sr.
Born: September 14, 1937 in Portland, Multnomah County, Oregon
Died: July 29, 1995 in Twin Falls, Twin Falls County, Idaho
Buried at:
Married: March 24, 1958 in Ada County, Idaho
Karen Jean Lanphear
Born: September 28, 1939 in Northfield, Dakota County, Minnesota
Died: October 30, 2013 in Northfield, Dakota County, Minnesota
Buried at:
Parents: Edgar C. Lanphear (1891-1956) and Ruth E. Parker (1904-1989)

3   Jane Loree Kelley
Born: September 18, 1948 in Ontario, Malheur County, Oregon
Died: March 25, 2003 in Caldwell, Canyon County, Idaho
Buried at: Canyon Hill Cemetery, Caldwell, ID
Married: February 19, 1966 in Twin Falls, Twin Falls County, Idaho
Lynn M. Owens
Born: 1946
Died: Living
Buried at:
Parents: William H. Owens (1910-1995) and Helen B. Savell (1910-1985)

✑ Chapter Nine ✑

Catherine Weyenberg

By the time Catherine came into the world, her parents Joseph and Nellie and older sisters had been on the farm in Grand Chute for four and a half years now. Catherine was born on February 27, 1872, the sixth child and girl born to her parents. And since 1872 was a leap year, just two days after her birth a significant event occurred in United States history. Both chambers of the US Congress passed the "Act of Dedication" to establish Yellowstone Park as the first national park of the United States. President Ulysses S. Grant was on board with this bill, and signed the act into law on March 1, 1872.

Image 9.01- Catherine Weyenberg (Joosten), ca. 1915

As we know, Catherine and her family were documented in the 1880 census in Grand Chute. Catherine's name was written down as "Katie", listed as age 8, and shows her attending school. The 1880 census likewise captured whether individuals could read or write. Though not totally surprising, Catherine's parents were educated and had the ability to read and write. What might be surprising though is how they both obtained an education in The Netherlands during a time of economic difficulty from famine and the Catholic Reformation period.

Image 9.02- St. John Catholic Church, Little Chute, WI in 1898

Around the year of 1892, Catherine, also known as "Kate", had met and fell in love with a fine gentleman by the name of William Weyenberg. Then on September 27, 1892 the happy couple was married. Fr. Theodore Knegtel performed the Sacrament of Matrimony at the St. John Nepomucene Catholic Church in Little Chute. The ceremony was witnessed by Simon Joosten, a first cousin of Kate's, and Ellen Weyenberg, whom we can assume is related to Willie in some way. The beautiful St. John's Church would be the home of many weddings for the Joosten, Weyenberg, VanHandel and many other Catholic families of the Little Chute village.

William Henry Weyenberg was the fifth of seven children born to Martin and Ellen (Hayden) Weyenberg, and was the only boy among many sisters, just like Kate's family with a household full of girls and only one boy. He was born on February 26, 1865 in Grand Chute, WI, one day before Kate's birthday. The Weyenberg family lived in Little Chute where William and his family are recorded in the 1870 and the 1880 censuses. In the 1880 census, William's mother was not recorded. Sadly she passed away on June 13, 1874 at the very young age of 37, leaving six children under the age of 12, including William, for Mr. Weyenberg to care for. This meant William's oldest sisters Mary & Elizabeth, who were only in their mid-teens at the time, would be the ones to fill the role of mother and homemaker. As revealed in the same census, William was 15 years old, out of school helping on the farm, and listed as a "farmhand" as his occupation.

Outagamie County was also home to a famous magician and escape artist, but he was not well known for living in Appleton, WI. Harry Houdini lived in Appleton early in his life with his parents. Harry was born in Budapest, Hungary as Erik Weisz on March 24, 1874. His family came to the United States 1878, and was enumerated in the 1880 census living on Appleton Street. His father, Mayer Samuel Weisz, was the Rabbi at the Zion Reform Jewish Congregation. The Weisz name had a Hungarian spelling, but after coming to America they changed their name to Weiss (the German spelling), and Erik's first name to Ehrich (also German spelling). He gained the nickname "Harry". My guess is the Weiss family feared being Jewish as a reason for the name change. The family's stay in Appleton was a short one, and they moved to New York City in 1887. At age 17, Ehrich changed his name to Harry Houdini, which was inspired by his French magician idol Jean Eugene Robert Houdin. Harry became famous for his illusions, escapes, and magic. His most famous illusions or stunts, such as escaping from the Chinese Water Torture Cell, hanging upside-down in a strait jacket, or jumping from a bridge into a hole cut into the frozen river ice in shackles, dazzled millions of people. In 1894, Harry married Wilhelmina Beatrice ("Bess") Rahner (1876-1943). They did not have any children. Harry and Bess traveled the world performing together.

Image 9.03- Harry Houdini in 1899.

Harry had a very strong abdomen, and loved to challenge those who were brave enough to punch him in the stomach. For years he endured numerous heavy blows to the abdominal area, trained heavily to take the punches, and boasted he felt no pain. It is widely believed it was a sucker punch to the stomach that ultimately led to his death. In October 1926, Houdini was performing at the Princess Theater in Montreal. In his dressing room he was posing for two university students who were drawing a portrait of him. A third student from McGill University, named J. Gordon Whitehead, entered the room uninvited to voice his displeasure about remarks Houdini had made regarding a particular physic (Houdini was very skeptical of physics and mediums, and labeled them as frauds). It has been written Mr. Whitehead surprised Houdini with numerous blows to the stomach. The severity of these punches ruptured Houdini's appendix, but Harry never sought medical attention until it was too late, and the pain was too unbearable for him to even stand. He was too proud to show pain to anyone, let alone any weakness. He finally was admitted to the Grace Hospital in Detroit. His ruptured appendix caused a massive infection leading to peritonitis, which ended his life on October 31, 1926 at age 52. He is buried at the Machpelah Cemetery in Glendale, Queens in New York City.

In 1911, an author by the name of Thomas Henry Ryan wrote a huge book named the "History of Outagamie County, Wisconsin" profiling many people of the County. On page 1088 of this masterpiece, Mr. Ryan eloquently dedicates a page to William, part of which I have included here. Although the profile written about William mentions "his father having left the farm," the author may have meant Martin may have turned over the farming responsibilities to William. In the same sketch the

"William Weyenberg attended the public schools of Little Chute township, to which he went until ten years of age, when, his mother having died the year before, and his father having left the farm, he took charge of the home place, and continued to operate it until 1906, at which time he purchased the old homestead of Mrs. Weyenberg's father, in Grand Chute township, and here he has continued to operate successfully ever since. He has 100 acres in a fine state of cultivation, and gives most of his attention to dairy farming, retailing his product in Appleton. He keeps on an average of twenty-five head of thoroughbred Holstein cows, which are pastured in excellent feeding fields. Mr. Weyenberg is a democrat, but he has never aspired to public office, his farming operations demanding all of his time and attention. He is a member of the Roman Catholic Church at Little Chute, and holds membership in the Catholic Order of Foresters. On September 27, 1892, Mr. Weyenberg was married to Katie Joosten, born on the farm where she now resides, February 27, 1872, daughter of Joseph and Nellie (Van Laanen) Joosten, natives of Holland."

author writes about Martin, William's father, and that he specialized in the saw mill business, having worked his way up to head sawyer in a job he had as a teenager. While the year is not mentioned, the author writes that Martin "entered the employ of Peter Rider Hub & Spoke Company, at Kaukauna, and after the lumber was exhausted at that point he was transferred to Rice Lake for the same company." Many people may interpret the author as saying Martin may have left the family to work in Kaukauna. I am not so sure Martin would have left his family to seek work elsewhere, especially with his children's mother gone. Even though in the 1880s and 1890s it would have been a long commute, Kaukauna is only two to three miles from Little Chute and Martin may have walked or ridden a horse to cover this distance, or maybe Martin had an adult family member move into the house with his children. Of course these are just guesses on my part, and I have no existing evidence to prove one way or the other.

As indicated earlier, William and Kate were married at the St. John Parish in 1892. Just a short time later the stork took flight for the first time landing at the Weyenberg home and presenting James William to his parents on July 23, 1894. Almost two years to the day, little James would welcome his little sister named Ellen Marie on July 21, 1896, and then later a younger brother named Joseph Peter on August 24, 1898. The 1900 Kaukauna census shows William, Kate, and the three youngsters on the farm, presumably the Weyenberg family farm once owned by William's father, since Mr. Weyenberg (Martin) is enumerated with the family, as seen in the census sheet pictured.

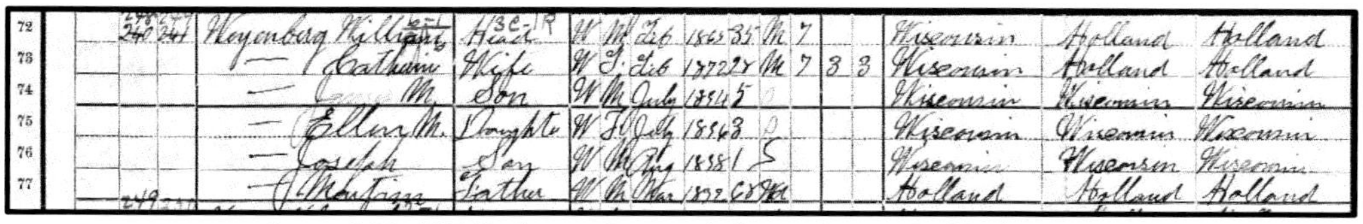

72	240	241	Weyenberg William	Head	W	M	Feb	1865	35	M	7			Wisconsin	Holland	Holland
73			— Catharine	Wife	W	F	Feb	1872	28	M	7	3	3	Wisconsin	Holland	Holland
74			— [illegible] M.	Son	W	M	July	1894	5					Wisconsin	Wisconsin	Wisconsin
75			— Ellen M.	Daughter	W	F	July	1896	3					Wisconsin	Wisconsin	Wisconsin
76			— Joseph	Son	W	M	Aug	1898	1					Wisconsin	Wisconsin	Wisconsin
77			— Martin	Father	W	M	Mar	1832	68	Wd				Holland	Holland	Holland

Image 9.04- 1900 Kaukauna, Outagamie County Census, ED 89, sheet 15B

Two more children would be blessed to William and Kate. Their fourth child, named Albert, was born on September 15, 1900, and their fifth and final child, a son, Francis was delivered on August 12, 1902. A very interesting coincidence can be realized by looking at all five dates of birth of the children. All of them occurred within a three month period from July to September, and all are two years apart. Now that is planning.

As I wrote back in chapter three, in October 1906, William and Kate purchased the 99-acre Joosten family farm in Grand Chute from Kate's parents Joseph and Nellie, which was located on what today is French Road. The huge farm was sold to the Weyenbergs for $9,500 with $2,000 cash down; therefore a loan was taken out in the amount of $7,500. It appears Joseph and Nellie carried the loan, which was for 15 years at 4% interest. According to the deed, interest payments were due in January on an annual basis separate from the principal payments that were $500 per year. Loan payments were to be made to Farmers and Merchant Bank of Forest Grove, OR. When Nellie passed away in 1911, I am uncertain what happened to the remaining balance of this loan. It is more than likely the Weyenbergs refinanced the $6,656 remaining loan balance because this amount was collected as part of Nellie's total estate that was distributed to her heirs. And the Weyenbergs continued to live on the property for many more years.

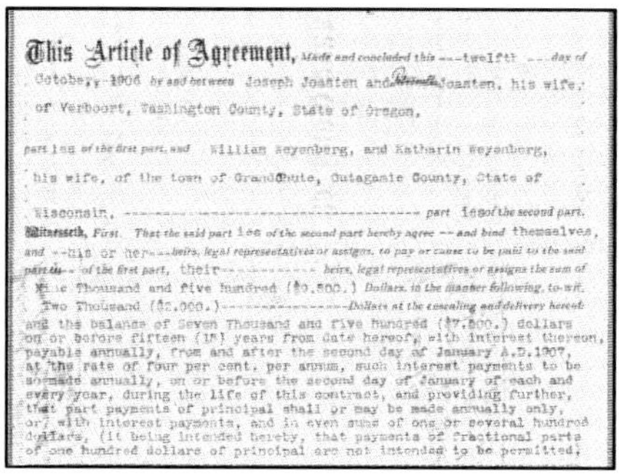

This Article of Agreement, Made and concluded this ---twelfth --- day of October, 1906 by and between Joseph Joosten and [illegible] Joosten, his wife, of Verboort, Washington County, State of Oregon,

part ies of the first part, and William Weyenberg, and Katharin Weyenberg, his wife, of the town of GrandChute, Outagamie County, State of Wisconsin, ------------------------------------ part ies of the second part.

Witnesseth, First. That the said part ies of the second part hereby agree -- and bind themselves, and --his or her---heirs, legal representatives or assigns, to pay or cause to be paid to the said part ies -- of the first part, their ----------- heirs, legal representatives or assigns the sum of Nine Thousand and five hundred ($9,500.) Dollars, in the manner following, to-wit. Two Thousand ($2,000.)----------------Dollars at the ensealing and delivery hereof and the balance of Seven Thousand and five hundred ($7,500.) dollars on or before fifteen (15) years from date hereof, with interest thereon, payable annually, from and after the second day of January A.D.1907, at the rate of four per cent. per annum, such interest payments to be so made annually, on or before the second day of January of each and every year, during the life of this contract, and providing further, that part payments of principal shall or may be made annually only, or with interest payments, and in even sums of one or several hundred dollars, (it being intended hereby, that payments of fractional parts of one hundred dollars of principal are not intended to be permitted;

Image 9.05- Land Deed of Grand Chute Farm from the Joostens to the Weyenbergs

By the mid-1910s, William and Kate's first son James was now nearing 20 years old. He met a nice lady by the name of Agatha West. She also was from Grand Chute, and they married in 1916. The happy couple settled down in Grand Chute where they rented some property. On May 31, 1917 they welcomed William and Kate's first grandchild into the world who was given the name of Robert. Within 22 months, James and Agatha were blessed with their second child Dorothy on March 4, 1919. According to the 1920 census, James made a living owning his own business in the retail milk trade and making deliveries to area homes. In addition to their two children in the household, James and Agatha also had a young man living with them, noted as a servant, but he probably helped James with the milk deliveries by driving the delivery wagon. His name was Herman Langenberry, and he was age 17 at this time. Also during 1919, Ellen welcomed her first child, and the third grandchild, into the greater Weyenberg family. Ellen named him Robert George and he was born on June 11.

In May 1924, family from Oregon traveled east to visit the Wisconsin folks. Ann Vanderzanden (Bernards) wrote her mother Frances a letter in May 1924 while in Wisconsin visiting Kate and William. I possess this letter in its original paper form, which I acquired from my grandmother's house following her passing, and my grandmother must have obtained it from her mother (Ann). This letter reveals many interesting names and facts she encountered during her stay. She took the train across the country landing in DePere, WI and then went to Little Chute to visit her Aunt Kate. Since this was a surprise visit, Ann must not have known exactly where Kate and William lived because she stopped by the butcher shop who directed her to "Mary VanHandel's house" (I am assuming this is the home of Mary (Berghuis) and Martin VanHandel, who is a 1st cousin of Ann). But when Ann went to the wrong house, the lady who opened the door immediately recognized her as a Joosten, and thought Ann was Frances (Joosten) Bernards. This charming lady invited Ann into her home and they chatted for a while. Ann indicated in her letter it was "Mrs. Hermsen" and "Kate Joosten". This must have been Kate (Joosten) Hermsen, daughter of Christian and Johanna Joosten, a 1st cousin of Joseph Joosten.

I have mentioned numerous times throughout this book how the diabetes disease plagued so many members of the Joosten family. Well, Ann reveals in her letter another family member who contracted the disease, though this time at a younger age, this time it was James. In the letter she wrote *"they got Jim home from the hospital yesterday where he had been for a month doctoring for diabetes. He gained 10 lbs while he was there. He has to diet and is using the same medicine as you are."*

Included with Ann's letter was a note from Kate herself to her sister Frances. She referred to Frances as "Frank", apparently her nickname, and wishes she could have come along in the visit. Frances was not able to go along due to her poor health. She would pass away just one month after the letter was written.

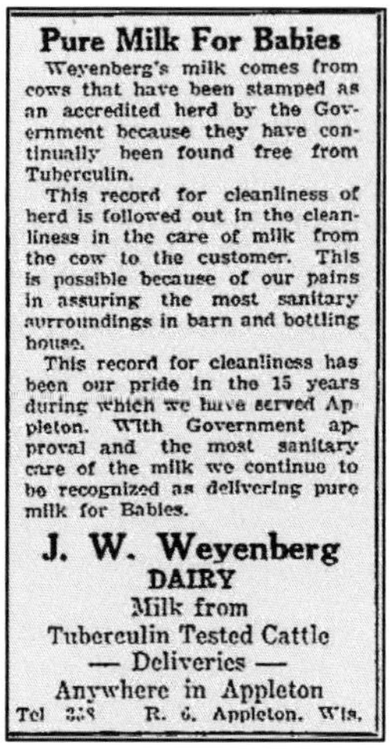

Pure Milk For Babies
Weyenberg's milk comes from cows that have been stamped as an accredited herd by the Government because they have continually been found free from Tuberculin.
This record for cleanliness of herd is followed out in the cleanliness in the care of milk from the cow to the customer. This is possible because of our pains in assuring the most sanitary surroundings in barn and bottling house.
This record for cleanliness has been our pride in the 15 years during which we have served Appleton. With Government approval and the most sanitary care of the milk we continue to be recognized as delivering pure milk for Babies.

J. W. Weyenberg
DAIRY
Milk from
Tuberculin Tested Cattle
— Deliveries —
Anywhere in Appleton
Tel 318   R. 6. Appleton. Wis.

Image 9.06- James Weyenberg Dairy Ad Appleton Post-Crescent 09-13-1924, page 16

In September 1924, James ran this ad in the Appleton Post-Crescent newspaper to let people know about his pure milk for babies. His dairy cows and milk processing were accredited by the government as free from tuberculin. Prior to the pasteurization process people drank raw milk straight from cows. It was widely believed tuberculosis was easily transmitted from cows to humans who consumed the nutritious drink. A test known as "Tuberculin" was discovered to ensure unpasteurized milk was free from the tuberculosis bacteria. It appears James used this test to give his customers and the public assurance his milk was safe and healthy to drink. And from what the ad reveals, it seems as though he went to great lengths to make sure his cows and bottling house were very sanitary.

The 1920 census reveals William and Kate are shown living in Grand Chute, more than likely still on French Rd. Living with them were Ellen (23) and her son Robert (1), Joseph (21), Bert (19), and Frank (17). William was 54 now and continuing his work on the farm, and Kate was 47. Their property is shown as mortgaged, meaning they must have obtained another loan to pay off the loan to Kate's parents. Also living in Grand Chute near the Weyenbergs were Kate's brother-in-law John Verhagen and his new wife Anna; Martin Joosten and his wife Hattie, a first cousin of Kate's; and one of Kate's nephews, Martin VanHandel and his wife Mary.

During the Roaring 20s, the rest of William and Kate's children were married. First up was Frank who married Catherine DeGroot on November 28, 1922 in Little Chute. Then Joseph married Wilhelmina Hooyman on April 4, 1923, and Albert to Lucille Forster on September 20, 1927. And lastly, Ellen married Leander Deiler, Jr. on September 27, 1928 and ended up moving to Evanston, Illinois. Therefore with Ellen and her son Robert moved out of the house, William and Kate welcomed Frank and Catherine and their three children into the house, and all are shown in the 1930 census.

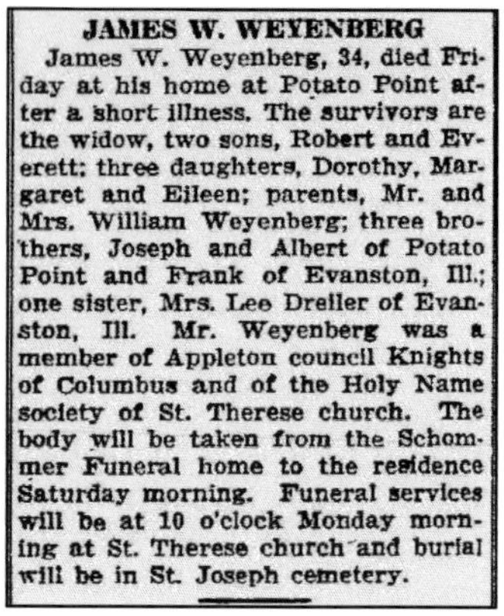

Heartbreak came to the Weyenberg family with the passing of James. According to his obituary from the Appleton Post-Crescent, he died after a short illness on February 15, 1929. As previously mentioned he had come down with diabetes just four years ago. I am left to wonder if he too died from complications of diabetes. He was laid to rest in the first row of section H in St. Joseph Catholic Cemetery in Appleton, WI. Agatha was now left with five children to raise on her own. She lived on Appleton Rd. in Grand Chute, and would marry again on September 01, 1930 to Arnold Derks, and together they had one child, Arnold Derks, Jr.

JAMES W. WEYENBERG
James W. Weyenberg, 34, died Friday at his home at Potato Point after a short illness. The survivors are the widow, two sons, Robert and Everett; three daughters, Dorothy, Margaret and Eileen; parents, Mr. and Mrs. William Weyenberg; three brothers, Joseph and Albert of Potato Point and Frank of Evanston, Ill.; one sister, Mrs. Lee Dreiler of Evanston, Ill. Mr. Weyenberg was a member of Appleton council Knights of Columbus and of the Holy Name society of St. Therese church. The body will be taken from the Schommer Funeral home to the residence Saturday morning. Funeral services will be at 10 o'clock Monday morning at St. Therese church and burial will be in St. Joseph cemetery.

Image 9.07- James W. Weyenberg Obituary, Appleton Post-Crescent, 02/15/1929, page 23.

In 1930, William was 65 and Kate was 57, and the value of their farm was now worth $1,500. William and Frank both were listed as farmers, and Frank was helping his father on the farm. Living near them were their neighbors the Raymond Bissing and Edward Brockman families.

As for some of the other children, Joseph and Minnie were also living on Appleton Rd. in Grand Chute with a property valued at $4,200. He was shown in the census working as a milkman on a dairy route. I think it is likely he could have taken over his brother James' milk business. Ironically, their neighbors are also part of the Brockman family. Also living on the same street a couple of doors down was Joseph's uncle John Verhagen with his wife Anna, and cousin Mary Hietpas' family. Albert and his wife Lucille also lived on Appleton Rd. in Grand Chute, and rented a farm for $30 per month. With no children at this time, they had two servants on the farm; Arthur West, age 17, a nephew of Agatha, and Dorothy Brinkleman, age 18. And as mentioned earlier Ellen moved to Evanston, IL and was still living there.

At some point in the 1930s, Frank and Catherine moved off of family farm and into Little Chute buying a home on Grand Ave., which was valued at $4,000. The 1940 census makes known Frank owns a tavern and is listed as a bartender. Catherine's brother, Theodore DeGroot (1906-1974), who was age 33 at this time, boarded with them and worked in the tavern also as a bartender. Agnes Jansen, age 17, was working as a maid for the family.

I came across a copy of the 1936 city directory of Appleton, and it gives many interesting facts and a glimpse into life in the Fox Cities. Appleton was founded in 1848 when the first settlers built their shacks around the Lawrence Institute (today known as Lawrence University). The estimated population was 27,500 residents, but what's interesting is only 7,947 of the residents had a telephone in service. Appleton is at an elevation of 795 feet above sea level, and at the time sat on 6.5 square miles of land; today that number is 25 square miles. 6700 children attended 20 schools including one high school, three junior high, eight public elementary, and seven parochial schools. Homeownership was near 70%, and there were virtually no foreign residents. The major industry was paper from the paper mills, which thrived in the area, and benefited from the Fox River for two main reasons. First, the river dropped 33 feet in elevation within Appleton's city limits, therefore generating a potential 40,000 horsepower of electricity to run the paper mills. The second advantage was the cleanliness of the river's water from certain chemicals enabling successful pulping and sheeting of clean, high-quality paper products. Other industries popped up to support the paper mills, such as the big papermaking machinery, wire cloth, beaters, woolen paper machine felts, paper roll plugs, and other mechanical devices important in the paper making process. Secondary industries included toys, soft drinks, canned vegetables, ornamental iron and brass, and other products.

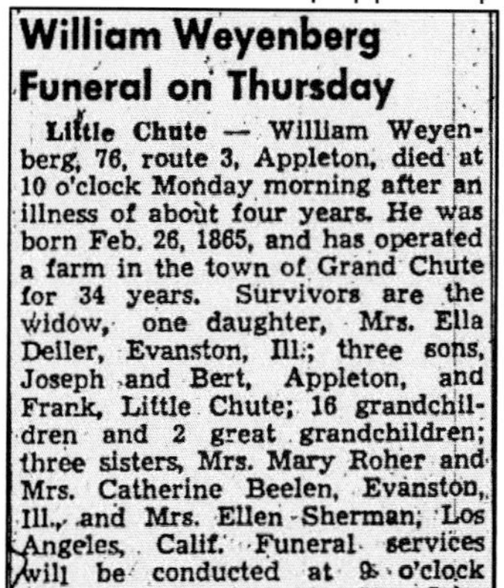

William Weyenberg Funeral on Thursday

Little Chute — William Weyenberg, 76, route 3, Appleton, died at 10 o'clock Monday morning after an illness of about four years. He was born Feb. 26, 1865, and has operated a farm in the town of Grand Chute for 34 years. Survivors are the widow, one daughter, Mrs. Ella Deller, Evanston, Ill.; three sons, Joseph and Bert, Appleton, and Frank, Little Chute; 16 grandchildren and 2 great grandchildren; three sisters, Mrs. Mary Roher and Mrs. Catherine Beelen, Evanston, Ill., and Mrs. Ellen Sherman, Los Angeles, Calif. Funeral services will be conducted at 9 o'clock Thursday morning at St. John church, Little Chute, by the Rev. John J. Sprangers and burial will take place in the parish cemetery.

Image 9.08- William Weyenberg Obit APC 11-04-1941, pg 16

By the time 1940 rolled around, William was now 75 years old, and Kate 68. At some point they must have sold the farm to someone, because they rented some part of it for $12 per month. The 1940 census reveals both William and Kate achieved only 4th grade educations. Now their son Joseph and his wife Minnie and family were living next to his parents, and renting their residence for $10 per month. In 1941, William's health was hampered by an illness his body was holding onto for a few years now. Sadly he passed away on November 03, 1941 at the age of 76. He lived a full life, and four of his five children survived him. William's funeral service was celebrated by Fr. John Sprangers at St. John Church in Little Chute, and he was laid to rest in the church cemetery in row 17 of section one.

In 1942, William Hermens, son of Anna and Antone and a nephew of Kate, purchased a new car from the factory, and went back east to take possession of it. On his way back he picked up Kate and drove five days back to Verboort. Kate visited her sister Margaret VanDyke, and other relatives and friends.

Soon after our country came out of World War II, the baby boom generation began, and the extended Weyenberg family experienced another loss. Frank's wife Catherine was called home to the eternal life early at the young age of 42. Catherine passed away in Little Chute on October 14, 1946, and left behind her husband, and two sons and two daughters. Her sister was Christina (DeGroot) Verhagen, the wife of Joseph Verhagen (son of Mary (Joosten) Verhagen). She is buried in the 17th row of section one at St. John Catholic Cemetery; same row as William and Kate. Frank was married a second time to Rose M. Hopfensperger.

Almost 13 years after the passing of her husband William, sadly Kate passed away into the next life on August 2, 1954 following an extended illness. She lived a long and full life of 82 years, and witnessed incredible changes to the American way of life and culture. At some point prior to her death, Kate moved in with Joseph and Minnie at their home at 1328 S. Monroe St. in Appleton, and this is where she spent her final days. She outlived all of her siblings except for her youngest sister Margaret VanDyke. Kate and William were married a long love-filled 58 years, the longest of all of her siblings. The Weyenbergs were blessed to have enjoyed many healthy years together where, as we know, her sibling's marriages were unfortunately cut short by their early deaths. Nonetheless a remarkable achievement by two wonderful people. She was laid to rest beside her life partner where they could spend eternal life together.

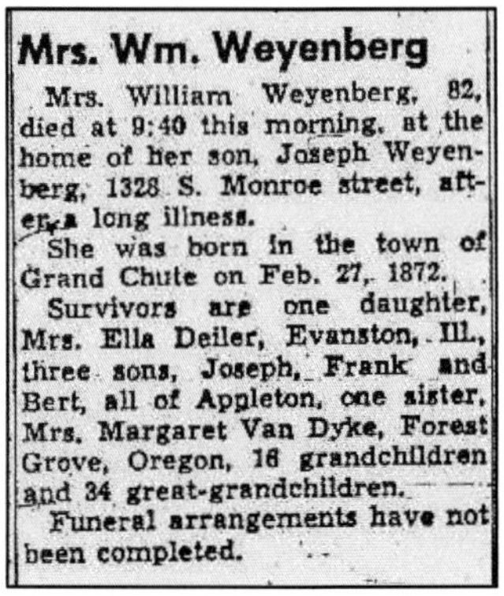

Mrs. Wm. Weyenberg

Mrs. William Weyenberg, 82, died at 9:40 this morning, at the home of her son, Joseph Weyenberg, 1328 S. Monroe street, after a long illness.

She was born in the town of Grand Chute on Feb. 27, 1872.

Survivors are one daughter, Mrs. Ella Deiler, Evanston, Ill., three sons, Joseph, Frank and Bert, all of Appleton, one sister, Mrs. Margaret Van Dyke, Forest Grove, Oregon, 16 grandchildren and 34 great-grandchildren.

Funeral arrangements have not been completed.

Image 9.09- Catherine Weyenberg (Joosten) Obituary, Appleton Post-Crescent, 08-02-1954, page 26.

From Kate and William's five children came 20 grandchildren overall. Although Kate's obituary mentions only 16, this is due to the unfortunate passing of four grandkids during infancy. By the time of Kate's passing in 1954 there were 34 great-grandchildren, and many more to come.

Catherine & William Weyenberg

There were a large number of good men and women of the Weyenberg Family who served our fine country in the military. They are:

- ❖ Leander B. Deiler Jr. – Served during World War I.
- ❖ Raymond T. Schumacher – Served as a Sergeant with the 8th Air Force in World War II.
- ❖ Melvin J. Sutheimer - Served his country in Iceland as a Supply Sergeant in the U.S. Army's 232D Engineer Company, 74th Regiment, during the Korean Conflict.
- ❖ Everett J. Weyenberg - Served in the Air Corp in North Africa during World War II.
- ❖ Richard J. Weyenberg – Served as an EN3 in the US Navy during the Korean War.
- ❖ Robert A. Weyenberg - Served as a photographer in the US Navy in World War II.

Image 9.10- Gravesite Headstone of William & Catherine Weyenberg, and Ellen Deiler (Weyenberg) at St. John Catholic Cemetery, Little Chute, WI

Mrs. Ellen Deiler

Mrs. Ellen Deiler, 62, Evanston, Ill., died at 5:45 a.m. today in Appleton. She had been staying in Appleton during a short illness.

Mrs. Deiler was born July 21, 1896, in Appleton.

The Verkuilen Funeral Home, Little Chute is in charge of funeral arrangements.

Survivors include one son Robert, Appleton; three brothers, Bert, Joseph and Frank Weyenberg, all of Appleton, and three grandchildren.

Image 9.11- Obituary of Ellen M. Deiler (Weyenberg), Appleton Post-Crescent, 03/16/1959, page A16.

ELLEN WEYENBERG AND LEE DEILER ARE MARRIED

Special to Post-Crescent

Little Chute — The marriage of Miss Ellen Weyenberg, daughter of Mr. and Mrs. W. Weyenberg, Route 6, Appleton, and Lee Deiler, Evanston, took place at 8 o'clock Thursday morning at St. John church. The Rev. J. J. Sprangers performed the ceremony. Mr. and Mrs. Frank Weyenberg, Evanston, attended the couple. A wedding breakfast was served after the ceremony to about 70 guests at the Weyenberg home, and in the evening a dance will be held at Apple Creek. Mr. and Mrs. Deiler will make their home in Evanston.

Image 9.12- Wedding News Article of Ellen Weyenberg & Lee Deiler, Appleton Post-Crescent, 09/27/1928, page 19.

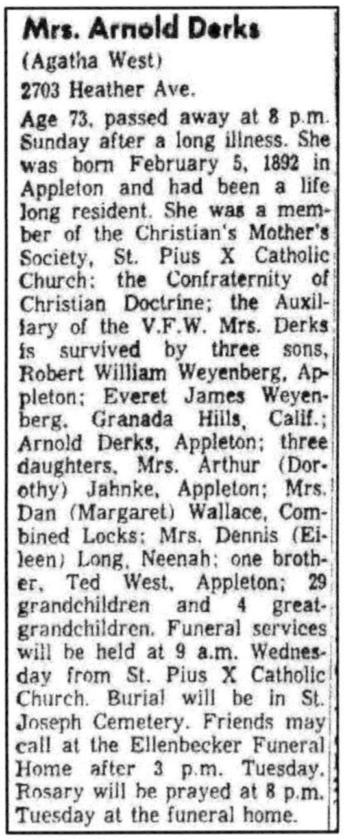

Mrs. Arnold Derks

(Agatha West)

2703 Heather Ave.

Age 73, passed away at 8 p.m. Sunday after a long illness. She was born February 5, 1892 in Appleton and had been a life long resident. She was a member of the Christian's Mother's Society, St. Pius X Catholic Church; the Confraternity of Christian Doctrine; the Auxiliary of the V.F.W. Mrs. Derks is survived by three sons, Robert William Weyenberg, Appleton; Everet James Weyenberg, Granada Hills, Calif.; Arnold Derks, Appleton; three daughters, Mrs. Arthur (Dorothy) Jahnke, Appleton; Mrs. Dan (Margaret) Wallace, Combined Locks; Mrs. Dennis (Eileen) Long, Neenah; one brother, Ted West, Appleton; 29 grandchildren and 4 great-grandchildren. Funeral services will be held at 9 a.m. Wednesday from St. Pius X Catholic Church. Burial will be in St. Joseph Cemetery. Friends may call at the Ellenbecker Funeral Home after 3 p.m. Tuesday. Rosary will be prayed at 8 p.m. Tuesday at the funeral home.

Image 9.13- Obituary of Agatha Weyenberg-Derks (West), Appleton Post-Crescent, 05/03/1965, page A6

Image 9.14- Gravesite Headstone of Agatha M. Weyenberg-Derks (West), St. Joseph Catholic Cemetery, Appleton, WI

Image 9.15- Gravesite Headstone of James W. Weyenberg, St. Joseph Catholic Cemetery, Appleton, WI

Frank M. Weyenberg

1120 N. Division St., Appleton

Age 71, passed away Saturday, at 11 a.m. after an extended illness. He was born August 12, 1902 in Little Chute, Wisconsin. He operated a tavern business in Little Chute, from 1937 to 1950 with bowling operations from 1939 to 1946. He moved to Appleton in 1951 and was formerly employed by the City of Appleton Park Department. He retired six years ago. He was a member of St. Therese Catholic Church. Survivors are his wife, Rose; two daughters, Mrs. John (Betty) Grafmeier, Kimberly and Mrs. Duane (Frances) Baker, Marinette, Wisconsin; two sons, Gene, Darboy and Dick, of Kimberly; a step-son Vincent J. Foster, Saukville, Wisconsin; a brother, Bert, Appleton; and twenty-one grandchildren and five great-grandchildren. Also survived by two step-grandchildren. Complete funeral services will be held at 11 o'clock Tuesday at St. Therese Catholic Church, with Rev. Joseph Bestler officiating. Burial will be in St. John Cemetery in Little Chute. Friends may call at the Brettschneider-Trettin Funeral Home from 4 to 9 on Monday and after 8 a.m. on Tuesday until the time of services. The prayer service will be held at 8 p.m. Monday at the funeral home.

Image 9.16- Weyenberg, Francis M Obit Appleton Post-Crescent, 11/26/1973, page B11

Image 9.17- Gravesite Headstone of Joseph P. & Minnie H. Weyenberg, St. John Catholif Cemetery, Little Chute, WI.

WEDDINGS

The marriage of Joseph P. Weyenberg of Grand Chute and Miss Wilhelmina M. Hooyman of Freedom, took place at the Catholic church at Freedom at 9 o'clock Wednesday morning. The ceremony was performed by the Rev. F. G. Peeters. The attendants were Bert Weyenberg and Miss Ida Hooyman.

A reception was held after the ceremony at the home of the bride's parents, Mr. and Mrs. John Hooyman. The couple left on a trip, after which they will make their home on the bridegroom's farm in Grand Chute.

Image 9.18- Marriage News Article of Joseph Weyenberg & Minnie Hooyman, Appleton Post-Crescent, 04/05/1923, page 5

Image 9.21- Gravesite Headstone of Albert & Lucille Weyenberg, St. Joseph Catholic Cemetery, Appleton, WI.

Joseph P. Weyenberg

1328 S. Monroe St.

Age 63, passed away at 8:45 a.m. Friday after a short illness. He was born August 24, 1898 in the Town of Vanden Broek and lived in this vicinity all of his life. For the past 11 years he was the janitor at Sacred Heart Catholic Church. He was a member of Sacred Heart Catholic Church; the Holy Name Society and the Peoples Eucharistic League of Sacred Heart Church. Mr. Weyenberg is survived by his wife; four daughters, Mrs. Raymond (Marion) Schumacher; Mrs. Maurice (Florus) Schumacher and Mrs. Melvin (Marlene) Sutheimer, all of Appleton; Mrs. Donald (Lucille) Jacobs, Neenah; two brothers, Bert and Frank, both of Appleton; 11 grandchildren. Funeral services will be held at 11 a.m. Monday from Sacred Heart Catholic Church, the cortege forming at 10:30 a.m. at the Brettschneider Funeral Home. Burial will be in St. Joseph Cemetery. Friends may call at the funeral home after 2 p.m. Sunday. The rosary will be prayed at 8 p.m. Sunday at the funeral home.

Image 9.19- Obituary of Joseph P. Weyenberg, Sr., Appleton Post-Crescent, 06/22/1962, page B9.

Bert Weyenberg

2501 E. Northland Ave.

Age 81, died at 11:15 p.m. Wednesday following a brief illness. He was born September 15, 1900 in Outagamie County, and was a life long resident of Appleton. From 1930 until 1940, he owned and operated the Weyenberg Dairy. After that time, he was involved in dairy farming until his retirement. Mr. Weyenberg was a member of St. Thomas More Catholic Church, a past President of the Dairy Bottle Exchange, on the Board of Directors of the Outagamie County Equity Coop and Credit Union, and was associated for many years with the Agricultural Stabilization and Conservation (ASC) Office. He was involved with various square dance groups in the "Valley." Survivors include a daughter, Mrs. Lawrence "Butch" (Roberta) "Babe" Plach, Menasha; a son, James W. Weyenberg, Neenah; seven grandchildren; eight great-grandchildren. He was preceded in death by his wife, Lucille Forster Weyenberg, three brothers and a sister. The complete concelebrated mass will be at 11 a.m. Saturday at St. Thomas More Catholic Church, with Fr. Paul Feider, and Fr. Gerald Falk concelebrating. Interment will be in St. Joseph Cemetery. Friends may call at the Wichmann Funeral Home, 537 N. Superior St., from 4 to 9 p.m. Friday, and after 8 a.m. Saturday until the cortege leaves for the church. The prayer and scripture service will be at 7:30 p.m. Friday. A memorial fund is being established.

Image 9.22- Albert J. Weyenberg Obituary, Appleton Post-Crescent, 06/03/1982, page B16.

Minnie Weyenberg

(Hooyman)
515 W. First St., Kimberly

Formerly of Appleton, age 87, died unexpectedly 11 a.m. Thursday, November 24, 1988, at St. Elizabeth Hospital. She was born July 13, 1901, in Freedom, daughter of the late John J.A. and Anna (Verhoeven) Hooyman. Minnie was united in marriage to Joseph P. Weyenberg April 4, 1923, sharing 39 years together, before his death in 1962. She had served as housekeeper to Rev. Norbert VandeLoo for many years. She was a member of Holy Name Catholic Church, Kimberly. Survivors include four daughters and sons-in-law: Marion (Raymond) Schumacher, Appleton; Lucille (Donald) Jacobs, Neenah; Florus (Maurice) Schumacher and Marlene (Melvin) Sutheimer, all of Appleton; four sisters: Frances Krieg, Neenah; Ida Jahnke, Appleton; *Margaret (Clem) Vandenberg,* Freedom; Sr. Marianne SSND, Milwaukee; a sister-in-law: Gladys Hooyman, Freedom; 18 grandchildren, 36 great-grandchildren. Besides her husband, Minnie was preceded in death by three infant sons, an infant-granddaughter, four brothers: Al, Clarence, Art and Stanley Hooyman; three sisters: Regina Friebel, Bernice Rickert and Hazel Powell. The Mass of Resurrection will be 10:30 a.m. Saturday at Holy Name Catholic Church, Kimberly, with the Rev. Norbert VandeLoo, Rev. Leander Nickel, Msgr. Karl Steiner, Rev. Wilbert Staudenmaier, co-celebrating. Interment will be in St. Joseph Cemetery. Friends may call at the Brettschneider-Trettin-Lederer Funeral Chapel, 606 N. Oneida St. from 4 until 9 p.m. Friday (today) and until 10 a.m. Saturday at which time the cortege will leave for the church. A prayer service will be held at 7:30 p.m. Friday. A memorial fund has been established.

Image 9.20- Obituary of Wilhelmina M. Weyenberg (Hooyman) Appleton Post-Crescent, 11/25/1988, page C4.

Mrs. Bert Weyenberg

(Lucille Forster)
2501 East Northland Ave.

Age 65, passed away at 7:50 a.m. Tuesday morning following a six-month illness. She was born September 20, 1905 in Appleton and had been a life long resident of Appleton. Survivors are her husband; one daughter, Mrs. Lawrence (Roberta) Plach, Appleton; one son, James W., Neenah; one brother, Matt W. Forster, Appleton; three sisters, Mrs. Irene Flynn, and Mrs. Gertrude Hoffman, both of Appleton, Mrs. Arthur Wolfgram, Kaukauna; 7 grandchildren. Funeral services will be held Thursday at 10 a.m. at St. Thomas More Catholic Church with burial in St. Joseph Cemetery. Friends may call at the Wichmann Funeral Home after 3 p.m. Wednesday. There will be a rosary-prayer service at 8 p.m. Wednesday evening.

Image 9.23- Obituary of Lucille E. Weyenberg (Forster), Appleton Post-Crescent, 09/22/1970, page B10.

Image 9.24- William & Catherine (Joosten) Weyenberg Family Photo.
Front row left to right: Minnie (Hooyman), Agatha (West), Lucille (Forster), Kate (DeGroot), Ella, and Catherine. Back row left to right: Joe, Jim, Bert, Frank, Lee Deiler, and William.

Image 9.25- Joseph & Minnie (Hooyman) Weyenberg Wedding Photo, April 1923

Image 9.26- Joseph & Albert Weyenberg Photo, taken about 1901

Image 9.27- Gravesite Headstone of Frank & Catherine Weyenberg, St. John Catholic Cemetery, Little Chute, WI.

✂ Descendants of Catherine and William Weyenberg ✂

Notes: 1= 1st generation, 2= 2nd generation, 3= 3rd generation.
The year of birth is only given for individuals still living, if known.

1   Catherine Joosten
Born: February 27, 1872 in Grand Chute, Outagamie County, Wisconsin
Died: August 02, 1954 in Appleton, Outagamie County, Wisconsin
Buried at: St. John Catholic Cemetery, Little Chute, WI, sec 1, row 17
Married: September 27, 1892 in Little Chute, Outagamie County, Wisconsin
William Henry Weyenberg
Born: February 26, 1865 in Grand Chute, Outagamie County, Wisconsin
Died: November 03, 1941 in Grand Chute, Outagamie County, Wisconsin
Buried at: St. John Catholic Cemetery, Little Chute, WI, sec 1, row 17
Parents: Martin Weyenberg (1834-1908) and Ellen Maria Hayden (1837-1874)

   2   James William Weyenberg
   Born: July 23, 1894 in Grand Chute, Outagamie County, Wisconsin
   Died: February 15, 1929 in Grand Chute, Outagamie County, Wisconsin
   Buried at: St. Joseph Catholic Cemetery, Appleton, WI, section H, row 1
   Married: May 31, 1916 in Appleton, Outagamie County, Wisconsin
   Agatha Mary West
   Born: February 05, 1892 in Appleton, Outagamie County, Wisconsin
   Died: May 02, 1965 in Appleton, Outagamie County, Wisconsin
   Buried at: St. Joseph Catholic Cemetery, Appleton, WI, section H, row 1
   Parents: Albert J. West (1864-1938) and Anna M. Meyer (1864-1941)

      3   Robert A. Weyenberg
      Born: May 31, 1917 in Appleton, Outagamie County, Wisconsin
      Died: November 30, 2007 in Auburndale, Polk County, Florida
      Buried at: St. Joseph Catholic Cemetery, Appleton, WI
      Married (1): January 10, 1941
      Married (2): April 30, 1977 in Outagamie County, Wisconsin
      Leona Mary Jochman (1)
      Born: May 06, 1916 in Mackville, Outagamie County, Wisconsin
      Died: February 21, 1975 in Appleton, Outagamie County, Wisconsin
      Buried at: St. Joseph Catholic Cemetery, Appleton, WI
      Parents: Henry J. Jochman (1882-1982) and Anna Dietz
      June A. (Ohm) Sehloff (2)
      Born: 1931
      Died: Living
      Buried at:
      Parents: Unknown

      3   Dorothy Ann Weyenberg
      Born: March 04, 1919 in Appleton, Outagamie County, Wisconsin
      Died: December 07, 1995 in Winnebago County, Wisconsin
      Buried at:
      Married: January 24, 1940 in Appleton, Outagamie County, Wisconsin
      Arthur Frederick Jahnke
      Born: May 20, 1920 in Appleton, Outagamie County, Wisconsin
      Died: May 28, 2004 in MacClenny, Baker County, Florida
      Buried at: Highland Memorial Park Cemetery, Appleton, WI.
      Parents: William Jahnke (1897-?) and Wilhelmina A. Wundrow (1900-1968)

3   Everett James Weyenberg
     Born: July 15, 1920 in Appleton, Outagamie County, Wisconsin
     Died: June 20, 2007 in Granada Hills, Los Angeles County, California
     Buried at: Oakwood Memorial Park, Chatsworth, CA
     Married: Unknown
     Wanda Friend
     Born: 1927 in Neosho, Newton County, Missouri
     Died: February 1994 in Canoga Park, Los Angeles County, California
     Buried at:
     Parents: Unknown

3   Margaret Catherine Weyenberg
     Born: July 21, 1923 in Appleton, Outagamie County, Wisconsin
     Died: September 08, 2013 in Little Chute, Outagamie County, Wisconsin
     Buried at: St. Paul Catholic Cemetery, Combined Locks, WI
     Married: January 21, 1941 in Appleton, Outagamie County, Wisconsin
     Daniel Mathias Wallace II
     Born: June 23, 1916 in Darboy, Calumet County, Wisconsin
     Died: November 09, 1993 in Combined Locks, Outagamie County, Wisconsin
     Buried at: St. Paul Catholic Cemetery, Combined Locks, WI
     Parents: Daniel Wallace (1860-1946) and Helena Grode (1882-1869)

3   Eileen Ellen Weyenberg
     Born: December 19, 1924 in Appleton, Outagamie County, Wisconsin
     Died: September 21, 2012 in Neenah, Winnebago County, Wisconsin
     Buried at: St. Mary Catholic Cemetery, Menasha, WI
     Married: January 19, 1943
     Dennis J. Long Sr.
     Born: October 24, 1909 in Grand Chute, Outagamie County, Wisconsin
     Died: January 30, 1982 in Neenah, Winnebago County, Wisconsin
     Buried at: St. Mary Catholic Cemetery, Menasha, WI
     Parents: Richard Long (1862-?) and Catherine Long (1870-?)

3   James Weyenberg
     Born: 1927 in Appleton, Outagamie County, Wisconsin
     Died: 1927 in Appleton, Outagamie County, Wisconsin
     Buried at:
     Married: n/a

2 Ellen Marie Weyenberg
   Born: July 21, 1896 in Grand Chute, Outagamie County, Wisconsin
   Died: March 16, 1959 in Appleton, Outagamie County, Wisconsin
   Buried at: St. John Catholic Cemetery, Little Chute, WI, sec 1, row 17
   Married: September 27, 1928 in Little Chute, Outagamie County, Wisconsin
   Leander B. Deiler, Jr.
   Born: July 31, 1896 in Wisconsin
   Died: July 18, 1941 in Cook County, Illinois
   Buried at: St. Patrick Catholic Cemetery, Halder, WI
   Parents: Leander B. Deiler, Sr. (1861-1930) and Magy Delier (1864-1908)

3   Robert George Weyenberg
Born: June 11, 1919 in Appleton, Outagamie County, Wisconsin
Died: October 15, 2003 in Appleton, Outagamie County, Wisconsin
Buried at: Highland Memorial Park Cemetery, Appleton, WI.
Married: August 29, 1942 in Appleton, Outagamie County, Wisconsin
Virginia M. Burke
Born: July 04, 1921 in Wisconsin
Died: July 25, 1999 in Appleton, Outagamie County, Wisconsin
Buried at: Highland Memorial Park Cemetery, Appleton, WI.
Parents: James J. Burke (1897-1933) and Freda Hoppe (1899-1936)

2   Joseph Peter Weyenberg Sr.
Born: August 24, 1898 in Grand Chute, Outagamie County, Wisconsin
Died: June 22, 1962 in Appleton, Outagamie County, Wisconsin
Buried at: St. Joseph Catholic Cemetery, Appleton, WI, Lady of Fatima section, row 5
Married: April 04, 1923 in Freedom, Outagamie County, Wisconsin
Wilhelmina Mary Hooyman
Born: January 13, 1901 in Freedom, Outagamie County, Wisconsin
Died: November 24, 1988 in Appleton, Outagamie County, Wisconsin
Buried at: St. Joseph Catholic Cemetery, Appleton, WI, Lady of Fatima section, row 5
Parents: John Jacob Anton Hooyman (1874-1941) and Anna Verhoeven (1878-1907)

3   Joseph Peter Weyenberg Jr.
Born: January 05, 1924
Died: January 05, 1924
Buried at: St. Joseph Catholic Cemetery, Appleton, WI
Married: n/a

3   Marion Catherine Weyenberg
Born: 1925 in Wisconsin
Died: Living
Buried at:
Married: Unknown
Raymond Theodore Schumacher
Born: November 07, 1918 in Town of Vandenbroek, Outagamie County, Wisconsin
Died: November 22, 2000 in Neenah, Winnebago County, Wisconsin
Buried at: St. Joseph Catholic Cemetery, Appleton, WI, Lady of Fatima section, row 5
Parents: John P. Schumacher (1889-1961) and Henrica N. Williamsen (1896-1986)

3   Lucille M. Weyenberg
Born: 1927 in Appleton, Outagamie County, Wisconsin
Died: Living
Buried at:
Married:
Donald A. Jacobs
Born: 1924 in Wisconsin
Died: Living
Buried at:
Parents: Leonard O. Jacobs (1898-1990) and Helen Schwab (1899-1993)

3   William Lee Weyenberg
     Born: July 07, 1929 in Little Chute, Outagamie County, Wisconsin
     Died: February 26, 1933 in Madison, Dane County, Wisconsin
     Buried at: St. John Catholic Cemetery, Little Chute, WI
     Married: n/a

3   Floris Ann Weyenberg
     Born: 1931 in Grand Chute, Outagamie County, Wisconsin
     Died: Living
     Buried at:
     Married:
     Maurice Justin Schumacher
     Born: 1926 in Wisconsin
     Died: Living
     Buried at:
     Parents: John P. Schumacher (1889-1961) and Henrica N. Williamsen (1896-1986)

3   Daniel John Weyenberg
     Born: February 08, 1933 in Grand Chute, Outagamie County, Wisconsin
     Died: February 09, 1933 in Grand Chute, Outagamie County, Wisconsin
     Buried at: St. John Catholic Cemetery, Little Chute, WI
     Married: n/a

3   Marlene T. Weyenberg
     Born: 1936 in Grand Chute, Outagamie County, Wisconsin
     Died: Living
     Buried at:
     Married: September 16, 1954 in Appleton, Outagamie County, Wisconsin
     Melvin J. Sutheimer
     Born: December 03, 1929 in Elderon, Marathon County, Wisconsin
     Died: June 22, 2012 in Appleton, Outagamie County, Wisconsin
     Buried at: Highland Memorial Park Cemetery, Appleton, WI.
     Parents: Carl E. Sutheimer (1905-2003) and Viola J. Massey (1907-2001)

2 Albert J. Weyenberg
   Born: September 15, 1900 in Little Chute, Outagamie County, Wisconsin
   Died: June 02, 1982 in Winnebago County, Wisconsin
   Buried at: St. Joseph Catholic Cemetery, Appleton, WI, Lady of Fatima section, row 4
   Married: September 20, 1927 in Evanston, Cook County, Illinois
   Lucille E. Forster
   Born: September 20, 1905 in Appleton, Outagamie County, Wisconsin
   Died: September 22, 1970 in Appleton, Outagamie County, Wisconsin
   Buried at: St. Joseph Catholic Cemetery, Appleton, WI, Lady of Fatima section, row 4
   Parents: John Forster and Elizabeth Sturm (1869-1928)

3   James W. Weyenberg
     Born: 1930 in Appleton, Outagamie County, Wisconsin
     Died: Living
     Buried at:
     Married: 1953

Ethel M. Flenz
Born: 1930 in Wisconsin
Died: Living
Buried at:
Parents: Ferdinand F. Flenz (1892-1971) and Henrietta A. Harder (1889-1975)

3   Roberta Lou Weyenberg
Born: February 27, 1933 in Appleton, Outagamie County, Wisconsin
Died: March 31, 1987 in Phoenix, Maricopa County, Arizona
Buried at: St. Joseph Catholic Cemetery, Appleton, WI
Married: February 03, 1951 in Appleton, Outagamie County, Wisconsin
Lawrence Raymond Plach
Born: August 14, 1931 in Appleton, Outagamie County, Wisconsin
Died: May 31, 2010 in Grand Chute, Outagamie County, Wisconsin
Buried at: St. Joseph Catholic Cemetery, Appleton, WI
Parents: John L. Plach (1904-1992) and Rosannah K. VanGompel (1906-1990)

2   Francis M. Weyenberg
Born: August 12, 1902 in Little Chute, Outagamie County, Wisconsin
Died: November 24, 1973 in Appleton, Outagamie County, Wisconsin
Buried at: St. John Catholic Cemetery, Little Chute, WI, sec 1, row 17
Married (1): November 28, 1922 in Little Chute, Outagamie County, Wisconsin
Married (2): Unknown
Catherine DeGroot (1)
Born: April 04, 1904 in Town of Vandenbroek, Outagamie County, Wisconsin
Died: October 15, 1946 in Little Chute, Outagamie County, Wisconsin
Buried at: St. John Catholic Cemetery, Little Chute, WI, sec 1, row 17
Parents: Joseph DeGroot and Allegonda Vandenheuvel
Rose Mary Hopfensperger (2)
Born: September 08, 1896 in Appleton, Outagamie County, Wisconsin
Died: January 03, 1982 in Port Washington, Ozaukee County, Wisconsin
Buried at: St. Joseph Catholic Cemetery, Appleton, WI
Parents: Andrew Hopfensperger (1847-1917) and Elizabeth Geiger (1856-1944)

3   Eugene William Weyenberg
Born: June 08, 1924 in Appleton, Outagamie County, Wisconsin
Died: October 02, 1981 in Appleton, Outagamie County, Wisconsin
Buried at: St. John Catholic Cemetery, Little Chute, WI, sec 7, row 1
Married: February 21, 1946 in Little Chute, Outagamie County, Wisconsin
Germaine E. Hinkens
Born: June 11, 1926 in Appleton, Outagamie County, Wisconsin
Died: April 11, 2009 in Kimberly, Outagamie County, Wisconsin
Buried at: St. John Catholic Cemetery, Little Chute, WI, sec 7, row 1
Parents: John L. Hinkens (1887-1932) and Henrietta Dreel (1888-1983)

3   Elizabeth Jane Weyenberg
Born: January 04, 1927 in Wisconsin
Died: August 29, 2005
Buried at: Holy Cross Catholic Cemetery, Kaukauna, WI
Married: October 02, 1946 in Little Chute, Outagamie County, Wisconsin

John Peter Grafmeier
Born: July 30, 1920 in Kaukauna, Outagamie County, Wisconsin
Died: June 27, 1995 in Kimberly, Outagamie County, Wisconsin
Buried at: Holy Cross Catholic Cemetery, Kaukauna, WI
Parents: John F. Grafmeier (1879-1937) and Margaret Klein (1881-1965)

3   Richard J. Weyenberg
Born: March 27, 1930 in Appleton, Outagamie County, Wisconsin
Died: September 20, 2003 in Kimberly, Outagamie County, Wisconsin
Buried at: Holy Name Catholic Cemetery, Kimberly, WI, sec 2, row 4
Married: March 05, 1957
Elizabeth Jane Meulemans
Born: September 20, 1927 in Appleton, Outagamie County, Wisconsin
Died: November 04, 1996 in Kimberly, Outagamie County, Wisconsin
Buried at: Holy Name Catholic Cemetery, Kimberly, WI, sec 2, row 4
Parents: Felix A. Meulemans (1889-1971) and Adell M. Appleton (1907-1995)

3   Frances Ann Weyenberg
Born: July 22, 1933 in Appleton, Outagamie County, Wisconsin
Died: July 06, 1977 in Porterfield, Marinette County, Wisconsin
Buried at: Winesville Cemetery, Porterfield, WI
Married:
Duane Baker
Born: Unknown
Died: Living
Buried at:
Parents: Unknown

✃ Chapter Ten ✄

Martin Joosten

The seventh child and only son blessed to Joseph and Nellie was Martin. Martin was born on September 07, 1874 on his parent's farm in Grand Chute, WI. Martin came into this world two and a half years after his sister Catherine (Kate), and seems likely he was named after his grandfather Martin Joosten (1799-1889). Joseph was now 36, and Nellie 34 with a house full of seven children, but I am sure the oldest two girls were helping out with "mothering" type duties with the babies, and domestic work. By the time Martin was five years old, he was the only boy among a houseful of eight sisters (imagine that!), and when he was nine his oldest two sisters Elizabeth and Frances were married and out of the house. Once the 1890s decade came Martin was at home with his three youngest sisters. All the others were married, with three of them (Frances, Anna and Jane) moving out to Oregon. My guess is Martin finished his formal education before the 8th grade, and went to work on his parent's farm helping out his dad at a very early age.

Image 10.01- Martin Joosten about 1920.

In his early 20s, Martin met and fell in love with a lovely lady named Anna Marie VanDomelen. He married his sweetheart two weeks following his 23rd birthday on September 21, 1897 at the St. John Catholic Church in Little Chute becoming the fifth Joosten child to celebrate nuptials at this wonderful church. Annie was born July 2, 1872 to her parents William and Anna Marie (VenRooy) VanDomelen in Oconto Falls, WI, which is 52 miles away from Little Chute and about 30 miles north of Green Bay. The VanDomelen family, just like the Joostens, originated from North Brabant Province, Holland. They moved to the Little Chute area in the early 1880s from Oconto Falls.

Image 10.02- Martin Joosten and Anna Marie VanDomelen Wedding Day 1897.

Following their marriage the happy couple moved onto his parent's farm, and began farming the 99-acres. In a little more than a year later, Martin and Annie welcomed their first child into the world. Mamie was born on November 19, 1898 on the farm in Grand Chute. As you will remember from chapter three, it was about this time that Joseph and Nellie moved west out to Verboort, OR. Then only ten months following the birth of their first daughter, their 2nd daughter Wilhelmina was born on September 8, 1900.

When the 1900 census was taken, Martin and Annie were still living in Grand Chute and renting Martin's parent's farm. As mentioned back in chapter three, Joseph was included in the Verboort and Grand Chute censuses. Joseph and Nellie were listed in the Verboort census with their daughter Margaret, and only Joseph was shown living with his son Martin in Grand Chute. In the Verboort census, Joseph is noted as owning his farm, which was located on the corner of Verboort and Porter roads. Martin and Annie's first child Mamie (listed as "Mary") is written in with them, and is one and a half years old. Also living with Martin and Annie at the time was Frank Shultz, who was the hired hand for helping out with the farming duties. He was 39 years old, and born in Germany in February 1861. Living near Martin and Annie was his brother-in-law John Verhagen and his 2nd wife Elizabeth (Schumacher), and their four children Henry (8), Joseph (6), Hattie (3), and Willie (1).

Terrible heartbreak came to the Joosten family when news that Martin & Annie's daughter Mamie had tragically passed away on May 5, 1902. Her obituary in the May 10th edition of the Appleton Post-Crescent mentioned convulsions led to her death. Losing your first child in this manner must have been very difficult for Martin and Annie to bear, but their faith brought them through. Mamie was laid to rest in the 5th row of the old section of the St. John Catholic Cemetery in Little Chute.

At the time of Mamie's death, Annie was about six months pregnant with Joseph William, who came into this world on August 31, 1902. Then nearly two years later they welcomed another daughter into the young family. Maymie was born on July 5, 1904 in Grand Chute, and would be the last born on the Joosten family farm. And although her name had a Y added to it, she was named after her deceased older sister. Usually, if you see two children with the same name in a family, it meant the oldest one died before the youngest one was born. Dutch tradition embraced naming newly born children after a predeceased sibling. So if a female passed away, the next born girl was given the same name.

In 1905, Martin and Annie made a life changing decision, and picked up their family roots from the farm and moved west to Rudolph, WI, which is 84 miles west of Grand Chute. As previously written, the 99-acre farm was later sold to Kate and William Weyenberg in 1906, Martin's sister and brother-in-law. Martin had a couple of relatives who already lived in Rudolph. John and Rosa Joosten and their children moved to Rudolph from Nebraska in 1898 and purchased 176-acres of farmland. He was a first cousin of Martins, and 13 years older. The other relative was another first cousin by the name of Simon Joosten and his wife Minnie (Molitor) who were both born and raised in Little Chute. Maybe it was the two of them who attracted Martin and Annie to Rudolph. Martin purchased two farms totaling 133-acres just west of Rudolph and about ½ mile north of the Rudolph station on the Chicago, Milwaukee & St. Paul Railroad. To move their possessions, it has been written Martin shipped his cattle by train from Grand Chute, and made two trips with a team of horses back to Grand Chute to move the machinery and belongings.

John Joosten was a central figure in organizing the Farmers & Merchants Bank of Rudolph, and was the bank's first president. The Bank was founded in February 1918 on $15,000 in capital, and was housed in a 24ft. x 36ft. one-story brick building on Main Street. John's son, Louis, was the Cashier in 1923. The Bank still exists today at 1680 Main St. in Rudolph, and has grown to $28 million in assets. It is very impressive how a small community bank has survived for nearly 100 years amid the huge mega banks who have been gobbling up the community banks for years.

Image 10.03- Farmers & Merchants Bank, Rudolph Photo

So we can learn a little more about Rudolph, here's a brief history. Rudolph, the second town to be established in Wood County, is located about seven miles to the north of Wisconsin Rapids, and 14 miles west of Stevens Point. It was named after Rudolph Hecox, the first Caucasian boy born there among the Native American people. Reed's Sawmill and plenty of farm land drew many men into the area in the early 1860s. The region was full of great white pine trees measuring four feet in diameter, which were cut down and burned to clear land for agriculture. The Chicago, Milwaukee & St. Paul Railroad and the Post Office were established in 1874, and Charles Fileottreau was the first Postmaster, who housed the post office in his general store. The village was incorporated in 1960, and now has a population of 439 residents.

Image 10.04- Rudolph Train Station

Another large business in Rudolph was the Creamery. According to the *"History of Wood County"* by George O. Jones, in 1921 the creamery was operated by the Rudolph Central Cooperative Creamery Company in a steam-operated 36 x 56 foot brick structure on the west side of town, and had 75 shareholders at the time. The Creamery produced 289,024 pounds of cheese in 1921.

Martin & Annie Joosten

Following the birth of Maymie, William was the next born nearly three years later on April 15, 1907, and then their brother Richard Simon came along on August 6, 1909. Prior to Richard being born, you probably noticed the last four children were a girl, then a boy, a girl, and another boy. With the new baby this brought the Joosten household to seven.

On Wednesday November 25, 1908, the day before Thanksgiving, a large thunder and lightning storm passed over the Wood County area. It would turn out to be a huge devastating storm after a tornado touched down in Rudolph wreaking destruction on its citizens, including the Joosten family. As told by the December 3rd issue of the Wood County Reporter, the Joosten farm took a direct hit from the tornado. All of the structures from the house, to the barns, sheds, and granary were leveled. When the tornado struck the family was inside the house unaware of the sudden change of the weather. The family was cut and bruised by the flying debris, but all escaped major injury. The newspaper story reveals the tornado rose from the ground at the Joosten place, and hit the ground again on the Cornelius VanAsten place 1¼ miles away inflicting enormous damage to his house and barn. Miraculously no one was killed by this tornado. Unfortunately for Martin though, he had no insurance and suffered losses estimated at $3,000.

Image 10.05- Joosten Farm Tornado Damage Nov 1908

Helen Zubella (Kempen), daughter of Maymie, documented her mother's version and memory of that harrowing night. She tells of how her parents were unaware of the sudden change in the weather because of the noise level of the cream separator running in the kitchen (farmers separated the cream from the cow's milk). When the noise from the tornado rose above the separator, it was too late to take cover. Joseph and Maymie were already in bed asleep. The doors were blown open and the windows began to shatter. This is when the tornado swept the house off of its foundation and ripped the roof off of the house, Joseph and Maymie were thrown about 150 feet from the house out into the field, but somehow incredibly landed upright still in their bed unharmed. After the two children were found, Martin and Annie were able to gather the frightened family together and take shelter in an old cellar where they raised their chickens. Once the storm quieted down, Martin emerged from the cellar and the destruction became very apparent, it was everywhere. The family headed to the Krommenachers' place for shelter for the rest of the night. Martin and his neighbors worked all night to save cows and horses as some were trapped in the mangled barn debris. Some were saved, others were found dead or too injured to salvage, and had to be put down. This storm destroyed everything the Joosten family had, but in the end everyone was unharmed and ok, and there was a lot to be thankful for on Thanksgiving Day.

Martin and Annie were enumerated in the 1910 Rudolph census with their five children Minnie (9), Joseph (7), Maymie (5), William (3), and newborn son Richard, listed as Simon, (eight months old) when the census was taken in April 1910. As we know,

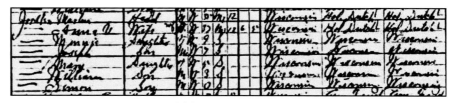

Image 10.06- 1910 Rudolph, Wood County, WI Census, ED 204, sheet 7A

Annie had given birth to six children by this time, but only five were still living. They were living next door to John Joosten (first cousin of Martin and son of Walter Joosten) and his wife, and their nine children living with them at the time.

Over the next four years two more beautiful children came into the family. And consistent with the boy and girl pattern Annie and Martin had established, first was Rosella on September 23, 1911, followed by George on June 25, 1914. In between these two births the family was still living in temporary housing following the 1908 tornado. In 1912, Martin built a three-story (including basement), five-bedroom house made of cement blocks and most likely strong enough to withstand another tornado. When looking at pictures of this house it is clear memories of the tornado were front and center in Martin's mind when he built this house; he did not want to lose everything ever again. There was a lovely family picture taken about 1915 of the entire family out in front of their new home. The house had a huge porch on the front side to sit in a nice rocking chair and rock away an easy afternoon or evening. The chimney rose through the middle of the roof, and there must have been a nice fireplace in the center of the house for the family and visitors to enjoy. Pictured in this portrait from left to right are: Richard, Rosella, William, Maymie, Joseph, Minnie, Anna (holding George), and Martin.

Image 10.07- Martin J. Joosten Family Photo in front of new house about 1915

When Congress enacted, and with the stroke of President Woodrow Wilson's pen, the second war draft of World War I required those men who had turned age 21 since the first draft registration, and the third draft for men ages 18 to 21 and 31 to 45 to register for the war by September 12, 1918. At this time Martin had just turned 44 years old, and was old enough to be required to register. He and his cousin Simon both went down to the draft center in Grand Rapids and registered. The World War I draft cards reveal interesting details about the men who filled them out and signed them. Besides basics such as date of birth, address and occupation, Martin's height, weight, hair and eye color were also recorded. He was determined to be "tall" with a "medium" build with blue eyes and black hair.

RUDOLPH

The sympathy of the community is extended to the Martin Joosten family in the loss of their little 7 year-old girl Rosella, who died Friday afternoon after a weeks illness of pneumoia. Everything was done that loving hands could do and Fr. Wagner was so good to do everything he could to save her but she was too good for this earth, she was always so good and saintly for a child of her age. At the home and church and school she will be greatly missed. The funeral was held Monday morning from the Catholic church.

Image 10.08- Rosella Joosten Obituary from Wood County Reporter 12-12-1918

In addition to the war draft occurring in 1918, the flu pandemic swept across the country and also descended upon Rudolph and tragically entered the Joosten home claiming Rosella as one of its victims. Rosella contracted the flu, then pneumonia, and succumbed to the deadly disease on November 29, 1918. This would be the second child lost for Martin and Annie; what a terrible burden to bare. The Good Lord called Rosella to Heaven at the young age of seven years old. She was laid to rest in the 12th row of the St. Philip Catholic Cemetery in Rudolph.

When the end of the 1910s decade was coming to a close happy times were celebrated with the marriage of Minnie to Leo VanAsten in Rudolph on January 20, 1919, most likely at St. Philomena Catholic Church. Leo is the son of Cornelius and Antonia, and surprisingly enough this family also experienced massive damage to their home and property from the same Thanksgiving Eve tornado in 1908, which Minnie and Leo shared in common. Leo was employed with the Rudolph Telephone Company and then the Wood County Telephone Company with a career spanning 41 years.

At the turn into the roaring twenties decade, Martin and Annie and their six remaining children are enumerated in the 1920 Rudolph census. Martin continues to run his successful dairy farm. Minnie and Joseph were ages 19 and 17 respectively, and not attending school, therefore had finished their education through the 8th grade. The other four children, Maymie (15), William (13), Richard (10), and George (5) were all attending school. Besides having Hollander families as neighbors, the family was also friendly neighbors with the Crotteau and Ratille families who were of French Canadian descent.

The year 1922 was a good year. In July, Annie celebrated her milestone 50th birthday. Then more than two and a half years following Minnie's nuptials to Leo, the Joostens celebrated two more weddings. First up was Maymie and Anton Kempen who married on September 21, 1922 in Rudolph, most likely at St. Philomena Catholic Church. Anton is the son of Peter and Wilhelmina (Vanderloop) Kempen. Anton was raised in Calumet County, WI, and as a young man was employed as a cheese maker for the Lodgeville Cheese Company in Wrightstown. In 1921, he moved west to Rudolph just as his bride did many years earlier. They began their early married life in Portage County, WI, and then moved back to Rudolph where they raised their seven daughters. He owned and operated Rudolph Oil Company for many years until his retirement in 1946. Then just three months after his sister's wedding, Joseph married Beulah Fountain in Rudolph on January 9, 1923. She is the daughter of Exeous and Phillette (Beau) Fountain and came from Portage County, WI. After living in Gurnee, IL for a few years they returned to Wood County where they raised their ten children.

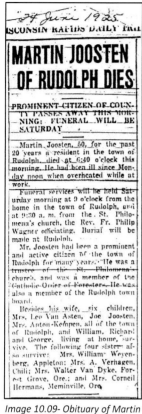

Image 10.09- Obituary of Martin Joosten from Wisc. Rapids Daily Tribune 06-24-1925.

In 1925, Martin celebrated his milestone 50th birthday. The ensuing year Martin fell ill on Monday June 22nd, and by Wednesday the 24th he unfortunately passed away. On Saturday morning the funeral services started at the family home, and moved to St. Philomena Church (today St. Philip) for the funeral mass. Martin was an original trustee of the church, and was a member of the Catholic Order of Foresters. He was laid to rest in the 12th row of the St. Philip Catholic Cemetery.

The sadness this family endured did not fade. Only three months after his father passed, William had an attack of appendicitis and tragically passed away September 23, 1925 following an operation. This means the death of a third child at such a young age. I am sure you have noticed now how Annie and the rest of the family had to endure the death of three of her eight children before they reached adulthood, and her husband. Such tragic events. William was laid to rest in the same 12th row as this father in the St. Philip Catholic Cemetery. Annie was left with only two children to raise on her own in the house, Richard and George.

It was another nine years before another Joosten child would tie the knot. When Richard was 23 years old, he married Theresa Jackan on September 15, 1932 in Wisconsin Rapids. She was the daughter of Mr. and Mrs. Michael Jackan. Theresa was born on December 30, 1912 and raised in Rudolph. Richard and Theresa lived in numerous cities in Wisconsin and Illinois, and settled in Wonder Lake, IL later in life. Richard worked as a maintenance man for General Telephone. Last but not least, George married his bride Margaret Hilgers on March 16, 1943 in Rudolph, presumably at St. Philomena Catholic Church. Margaret was born on August 18, 1921 in neighboring Wisconsin Rapids, WI. George served our country in World War II as a mechanics instructor, and achieved a rank of Sergeant. He must have been discharged from the military prior to his marriage, and the happy couple started their family, raising four girls. He enjoyed a long career as a truck driver for CW Transport Company, which was unfortunately cut short in 1968 due to his poor health.

The 1940 census gives a great glimpse into our Joosten families in Rudolph. First of all, Annie is shown living next door to her daughter Minnie and family, and renting her home for $8 per month. Annie is noted as having achieved a 5th grade education. As for Minnie and her family, they were renting their home for $10 per month. Leo was a manager for the phone company and earned a very respectable $1,500 in 1939. Their daughter Lorraine was 18 years old at this time, was finished with school after the 8th grade, and worked as a housekeeper for a local resident receiving $100 in wages in 1939. Their son Aloysius was in his 3rd year of high school, presumably a junior, Armella was in the 5th grade at age 12, and the youngest Donald, age 8, was shown as not yet in school, but very well could have been in the 1st grade. The Joostens and VanAstens had the Fred Piltz and the Louis and Eulalia Joosten families as neighbors; as previously mentioned Louis was the son of John Joosten.

Maymie was also living in Rudolph with her husband Anton and their seven daughters. Anton was a gas truck driver, and it appears his typical work week was 60 hours. They owned their home, which was valued at $2,000 at the time. All of the girls were attending school with the oldest Lucille in her first year of high school. The Kempens lived near the St. Philomena Catholic Church and their neighbors were Fr. Philip Wagner, pastor of the church, and four nuns who lived in the Church's convent. Three of the nuns were school teachers, while the fourth was the housekeeper.

After the passing of another decade, Annie was well into her 70s, and it had been 25 years since Martin passed away; she had never remarried. During the summer of 1950, Annie was living with her daughter Minnie. Her health was declining, and she experienced a heart attack, which took her from this life and into the next in Heaven. She passed away on June 29, 1950 at the age of 77. Four days later on Monday, Fr. Philip celebrated her funeral mass. After a full life of happiness she was laid to rest next to her life partner in the St. Philip Catholic Cemetery. May she continue to rest in peace.

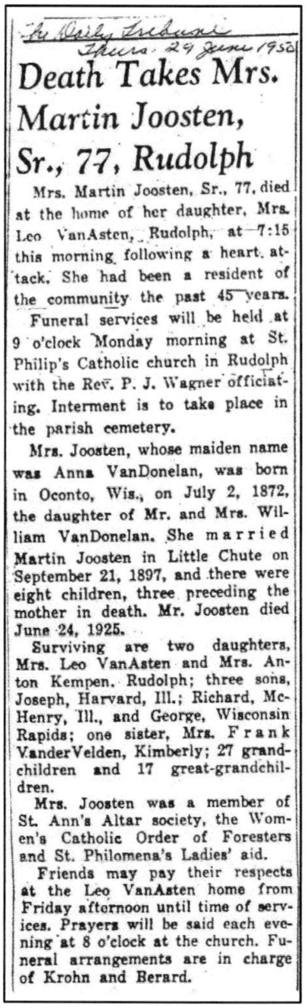

The legacy Martin and Annie leave behind continues to grow. From their eight children there came 33 grandchildren, although sadly four of the grandbabies did not make it out of infancy. So by 1950, just after Annie's passing 27 grandchildren survived her, and an additional two grandchildren were born after their grandparents passing, bringing the total to 29.

Now it is time to talk about some fun facts related to the longest married and the longest living of the Martin Joosten family. The longest living was Maymie who lived to age 89, and of the in-laws Beulah was 90. The longest marriage belongs to Joseph and Beulah with 65 happy years. Both lived long lives.

First grandchild born was Lorraine VanAsten (Jagodzinski) in 1921, and the last was Sally Joosten (Kissner) born in 1954; a span of 33 years between first cousins.

Death Takes Mrs. Martin Joosten, Sr., 77, Rudolph

Mrs. Martin Joosten, Sr., 77, died at the home of her daughter, Mrs. Leo VanAsten, Rudolph, at 7:15 this morning following a heart attack. She had been a resident of the community the past 45 years.

Funeral services will be held at 9 o'clock Monday morning at St. Philip's Catholic church in Rudolph with the Rev. P. J. Wagner officiating. Interment is to take place in the parish cemetery.

Mrs. Joosten, whose maiden name was Anna VanDonelan, was born in Oconto, Wis., on July 2, 1872, the daughter of Mr. and Mrs. William VanDonelan. She married Martin Joosten in Little Chute on September 21, 1897, and there were eight children, three preceding the mother in death. Mr. Joosten died June 24, 1925.

Surviving are two daughters, Mrs. Leo VanAsten and Mrs. Anton Kempen, Rudolph; three sons, Joseph, Harvard, Ill.; Richard, McHenry, Ill., and George, Wisconsin Rapids; one sister, Mrs. Frank VanderVelden, Kimberly; 27 grandchildren and 17 great-grandchildren.

Mrs. Joosten was a member of St. Ann's Altar society, the Women's Catholic Order of Foresters and St. Philomena's Ladies' aid.

Friends may pay their respects at the Leo VanAsten home from Friday afternoon until time of services. Prayers will be said each evening at 8 o'clock at the church. Funeral arrangements are in charge of Krohn and Berard.

Image 10.10- Obituary of Anna M. (VanDomelen) Joosten from Wisc. Rapids Daily Tribune 06-29-1950

There were a large number of good men and women of the Joosten Family who served our fine country in the military. They are:

- ❖ Wilton Hebert - Served as a Boatswain's Mate 3rd Class (BM3) in the US Navy during World War II.
- ❖ Harold J. Jagodzinski - Served in a Seaman 1st Class for the US Navy during World War II.
- ❖ George A. Joosten – Served as a Sergeant in US Army during World War II.
- ❖ James K. Joosten - Served as a medic in the US Army during World War II in the 108th Evacuation Hospital Unit during the Normandy invasion at Utah Beach. Purple Heart recipient.

✃ **Photo and Image Gallery** ✃

Image 10.11- Joosten Family Photo about 1927. Back: Minnie, Richard, Joseph. Front: Maymie, Anna, George

Image 10.12- Martin & Anna Joosten Headstone. St. Phillip Catholic Cemetery, Rudolph, WI., row 12.

Image 10.13- Joseph W. & Beulah (Fountain) Joosten Marriage Photo with William Joosten & Mildred Kuntjis-1923

Image 10.14- Maymie (Joosten) & Anton Kempen Wedding Photo-1922

Image 10.15- George A. & Margaret (Hilgers) Joosten Wedding Photo-1943

Image 10.16- Maymie (Joosten) & Anton Kempen Family Photo abt 1935. Girls L to R: Lucille, Bernadine, Clarabell, Janet, Marjory, Irene, & Helen.

Image 10.17- Richard & Theresa (Jackan) Joosten Wedding Photo. L to R: Olive Peters, George Joosten, Richard Joosten, Theresa Jackan, Edward Jackan, Elenora (Bushmaker) Jackan, Margaret Kempen-1932

H. J. WAGNER, N. KAUKAUNA, WIS.

Image 10.18- Mamie Joosten (#1)

DEATHS

RICHARD S. JOOSTEN

Richard S. Joosten, 59, of 7412 Cedar drive, Wonder Lake died Sunday, Aug. 11 in his Wonder Lake home.

Mr. Joosten was born Aug. 4, 1909, in Wisconsin. He was employed as maintenance man for the General Telephone Co.

His wife, Theresa, died Aug. 12, 1967. He leaves three daughters, Mrs. Donald (Marlene) Malo of Wonder Lake, Mrs. Lawrence (Joan) Freund of Fond du lac, Wis., and Mrs. Tony (Mary Jane) Mogdans of McHenry; one son, Richard, of Orlando, Fla; a sister, Mrs. Mamie Kampen, of Rudolph, Wis.; two brothers, George of Wisconsin Rapids and Joseph of California; also ten grandchildren.

The body rests at the George R. Justen & Son funeral home until 10 o'clock Wednesday morning, when a Mass will be offered in Christ the King Catholic church, Wonder Lake. Burial will be in the church cemetery.

Image 10.22- Richard S. Joosten Obituary

Mrs. Leo Van Asten

23 april 19, 1964.

RUDOLPH—Mrs. Leo Asten, 63, died at 4:50 a.m. today at her home here. Cause of death was a lingering illness.

Funeral services will be held at 10 a.m. Monday in St. Philip's Catholic Church, the Rev. G. J. Muller officiating. Burial will be in All Soul's Cemetery here.

The former Minnie Joosten daughter of Mr. and Mrs. Martin Joosten, was born in Little Chute Sept. 8, 1900, coming to this area at the age of 5. She was married to Leo Van Asten on Jan. 20, 1920, in Rudolph.

Surviving in addition to her husband are two sons, Alois and Donald, both of Rudolph; two daughters, Mrs. Harold Jagodzinski, Rudolph, and Mrs. Larry Berard, Wisconsin Rapids; three brothers, Joe Joosten, Las Alamedas, Calif.; Richard Joosten, Wonder Lake, Ill., and George Joosten, Wisconsin Rapids, and a sister, Mrs. Anton Kempen, Rudolph.

There are 16 grandchildren and two great-grandchildren.

A son, two brothers and two sisters preceded her in death.

Mrs. Van Asten was a member of the Christian Mothers of St. Philip's Church and St. Mary's Court, Women's Catholic Order of Foresters.

Friends may call at the Ritchay Funeral Home after 4 p.m. Saturday.

The Christian Mothers and men and women Foresters will join in a rosary at 8 p.m. Saturday. The general rosary will be at 8 p.m. Sunday.

Image 10.19- Wilhelmina VanAsten (Joosten) Obituary printed in Wisconsin Rapids Daily-Tribune on 04-23-1964

Mamie Kempen-Smrz

Mamie Kempen-Smrz

RUDOLPH — Mamie Kempen-Smrz, 89, of 6976 Grotto Ave., died Friday, June 24, 1994, at her home.

Services will be at 11 a.m. Monday at St. Philip's Catholic Church, Rudolph. The Rev. Richard Herrmann will officiate. Burial will be in All Souls Cemetery.

Mrs. Kempen-Smrz was born July 5, 1904, in Grand Chute, to Martin and Anna (Van Domelen) Joosten. She married Anton J. Kempen Sept. 21, 1922, in Rudolph. He died Jan. 15, 1969. She married Ernest Smrz April 20, 1974, in Rudolph. He died June 14, 1976.

She was a cook for Edgewater Haven Nursing Home, Port Edwards, retiring in 1966. She was a life member of the National Catholic Society of Foresters, a charter member of Rudolph Senior Citizens and a member of Philip's Christian Mothers.

Survivors include seven daughters, Lucille O'Shasky, Bernadine Jagodzinski, Marjory (John) Schenk, Irene Van Asten and Helen (Robert) Zubella, all of Rudolph; Clarabell (James) See, Sheboygan, and Janet (Gregory) Van Asten, Krakow; eight step-children; 49 grandchildren; 104 great-grandchildren; and three great-great-grandchildren. She was predeceased by one daughter, two grandchildren, two great-grandchildren, four brothers and three sisters.

Friends may call at Ritchay Funeral Home from 3-8 p.m. Sunday, and at the church from 10-11 a.m. Monday. Christian Mothers and general rosary services will be at 4 and 7 p.m. Sunday, respectively, at the funeral home.

Image 10.20- Maymie Kempen (Joosten) Obituary, Wisconsin Rapids Daily-Tribune, 06-25-1994

George A. Joosten

11 December 1972

George A. Joosten, 58, 421 7th St. S., died at 2:45 a.m. Sunday at Riverview Manor, where he had been a patient for 10 days. Death followed a lingering illness.

Services will be 10 a.m. Wednesday at St. Vincent de Paul Catholic Church, the Rev. Earl Dockendorff officiating. Burial will be in Restlawn Memorial Park with military rites by the American Legion.

Mr. Joosten was born June 25, 1914, in Rudolph, son of Mr. and Mrs. Martin Joosten, and had resided in the area all his life. He was employed by CW Transport as a truck driver until his retirement in 1966 due to poor health. He was the recipient of the 20-year Safe Driving award. He married Peggy Hilgers in Rudolph March 16, 1943.

Surviving are his wife; four daughters, Mrs. Larry Frank, Mrs. Gary Giebels and Mrs. Michael Joosten, all of Wisconsin Rapids, and Sally Joosten, at home; a brother, Joseph Joosten, Illinois; a sister, Mrs. Mamie Kempen, Rudolph; and three grandchildren. He was preceded in death by a daughter, three sisters and two brothers.

Mr. Joosten served in World War II as a mechanics instructor and attained the rank of sergeant.

Friends may call at Higgins Funeral Home from 7 to 9 p.m. today and after 10 a.m. Tuesday. A wake service will be held at 7:30 p.m. Tuesday.

The Daily Tribune

Image 10.21- George A Joosten Obituary, Wisconsin Rapids Daily-Tribune 12-11-1972

Image 10.23- Joseph W. & Beulah M. Joosten Headstone, St. Joseph Cemetery, Harvard, IL.

Image 10.24- Anton & Maymie Kempen Headstone, All Souls Catholic Cemetery, Rudolph, WI.

Image 10.25- Leo & Minnie VanAsten Headstone, All Souls Catholic Cemetery, Rudolph, WI.

❧ Descendants of Martin and Anna (VanDomelen) Joosten ❧

Notes: 1= 1st generation, 2= 2nd generation, 3= 3rd generation.
The year of birth is only given for individuals still living, if known.

1   Martin J. Joosten
     Born: September 07, 1874 in Grand Chute, Outagamie County, Wisconsin
     Died: June 24, 1925 in Rudolph, Wood County, Wisconsin
     Buried at: St. Philip Catholic Cemetery, Rudolph, WI., row 12
     Married: September 21, 1897 in Little Chute, Outagamie County, Wisconsin
     Anna Marie Van Domelen
     Born: July 02, 1872 in Oconto Falls, Oconto County, Wisconsin
     Died: June 29, 1950 in Rudolph, Wood County, Wisconsin
     Buried at: St. Philip Catholic Cemetery, Rudolph, WI., row 12
     Parents: William Van Domelen (1839-1893) and Anna Marie VenRooy (1845-1926)

     2   Mamie Joosten
          Born: November 19, 1898 in Grand Chute, Outagamie County, Wisconsin
          Died: May 05, 1902 in Grand Chute, Outagamie County, Wisconsin
          Buried at: St. John Catholic Cemetery, Little Chute, WI, sec 1A, row 5

     2   Wilhelmina Joosten
          Born: September 08, 1900 in Grand Chute, Outagamie County, Wisconsin
          Died: April 23, 1964 in Rudolph, Wood County, Wisconsin
          Buried at: All Souls Catholic Cemetery, Rudolph, WI, row 1
          Married: January 20, 1919 in Rudolph, Wood County, Wisconsin
          Leo VanAsten
          Born: November 22, 1898 in Carson, Portage County, Wisconsin
          Died: September 27, 1978 in Rudolph, Wood County, Wisconsin
          Buried at: All Souls Catholic Cemetery, Rudolph, WI, row 1
          Parents: Cornelius VanAsten (1865-1949) and Antonia Hartjes (1869-1941)

          3   Lorraine A. VanAsten
               Born: April 26, 1921 in Little Chute, Outagamie County, Wisconsin
               Died: June 10, 2010 in Wisconsin Rapids, Wood County, Wisconsin
               Buried at: All Souls Catholic Cemetery, Rudolph, WI.
               Married: August 21, 1940 in Rudolph, Wood County, Wisconsin
               Harold J. Jagodzinski
               Born: November 02, 1917 in Wisconsin Rapids, Wood County, Wisconsin
               Died: September 17, 2000 in Wisconsin Rapids, Wood County, Wisconsin
               Buried at: All Souls Catholic Cemetery, Rudolph, WI.
               Parents: John W. Jagodzinski (1889-1951) and Rosa E. Schmick (1886-1967)

          3   Aloysius C. VanAsten
               Born: 1923 in Wisconsin Rapids, Wood County, Wisconsin
               Died: Living
               Buried at:
               Married: September 04, 1948 in Wisconsin Rapids, Wood County, Wisconsin
               Eleanor C. Honkomp
               Born: 1928 in Sheldon, O'Brien County, Iowa
               Died: Living
               Buried at:
               Parents: Charles A. Honkomp (1887-1966) and Margaret A. Honkomp (1898-1985)

3   Gregory VanAsten
Born: July 22, 1925 in Wisconsin Rapids, Wood County, Wisconsin
Died: July 22, 1925 in Wisconsin Rapids, Wood County, Wisconsin
Buried at:
Married: n/a

3   Armella VanAsten
Born: April 18, 1928 in Marshfield, Wood County, Wisconsin
Died: May 02, 2007 in Wisconsin Rapids, Wood County, Wisconsin
Buried at:
Married: June 30, 1956 in Rudolph, Wood County, Wisconsin
Lawrence Jon Berard
Born: February 02, 1930 in Wisconsin Rapids, Wood County, Wisconsin
Died: January 02, 1995 in Marshfield, Wood County, Wisconsin
Buried at:
Parents: George A. Berard (1881-1936) and Theresia K. Berard (1887-1956)

3   Donald VanAsten
Born: 1933 in Wausau, Marathon County, Wisconsin
Died: Living
Buried at:
Married: June 17, 1953 in Rudolph, Wood County, Wisconsin
Virginia Pillsbury
Born: 1932 in Tomahawk, Lincoln County, Wisconsin
Died: Living
Buried at:
Parents: Unknown

2 Joseph William Joosten
Born: August 31, 1902 in Grand Chute, Outagamie County, Wisconsin
Died: June 23, 1988 in Los Alamitas, Orange County, California
Buried at: St. Joseph Cemetery, Harvard, IL
Married: January 09, 1923 in Rudolph, Wood County, Wisconsin
Beulah Mae Fountain
Born: August 16, 1904 in Linwood, Portage County, Wisconsin
Died: July 23, 1996 in Los Angeles County, California
Buried at: St. Joseph Cemetery, Harvard, IL
Parents: Exos Fountain (1860-?) and Phillette Bean (1885-1971)

3   James Kenneth Joosten, Sr.
Born: 1924 in Port Edwards, Wood County, Wisconsin
Died: April 04, 2015 in Colorado Springs, El Paso County, Colorado
Buried at: St. Joseph Catholic Cemetery, Harvard, IL
Married (1): January 08, 1949 in Woodstock, McHenry County, Illinois
Married (2): December 31, 1992 in Clark County, Nevada
Edna Kumm (1)
Born: 1930
Died: Living
Buried at:
Parents: Unknown

Nell Sue Paxton (2)
Born: 1937
Died: Living
Buried at:
Parents: Unknown

3   Geraldine Joosten
Born: 1925 in Carson, Portage County, Wisconsin
Died: Living
Buried at:
Married (1): March 24, 1943 in Lake Geneva, Walworth County, Wisconsin
Married (2): November 29, 1963 in Clark County, Nevada
Marvin L. Swance (1)
Born: February 03, 1922
Died: October 28, 1986 in Cook County, Illinois
Buried at: Oak Hill Cemetery, Lake Geneva, WI
Parents: Unknown
Wilton Hebert (2)
Born: April 05, 1924 in Louisiana
Died: May 06, 1997 in Riverside County, California
Buried at: Riverside National Cemetery, Riverside, CA
Parents: Unknown

3   Joseph William Joosten, Jr.
Born: 1927 in Gurnee, Lake County, Illinois
Died: Living
Buried at:
Married (1): October 10, 1955 in DeKalb County, Illinois
Married (2): November 17, 1992 in Clark County, Nevada
Marie A. Adams (1)
Born: Unknown
Died: Living
Buried at:
Parents: Unknown
Agnes Sandra Kruger (2)
Born: Unknown
Died: Living
Buried at:
Parents: Unknown

3   Charles Lewis Joosten
Born: 1929 in Gurnee, Lake County, Illinois
Died: Living
Buried at:
Married: Unknown
Perle Kleckner
Born: Unknown
Died: Living
Buried at:
Parents: Unknown

3   Orville Clarence Joosten
    Born: September 27, 1931 in Rudolph, Wood County, Wisconsin
    Died: August 21, 1948 in Freeport, Stephenson County, Illinois
    Buried at: St. Joseph Cemetery, Harvard, IL
    Married: n/a

3   Delores F. Joosten
    Born: 1934 in Carson, Portage County, Wisconsin
    Died: Living
    Buried at:
    Married (1): December 22, 1951 in Los Angeles County, California
    Married (2): Unknown
    Gaylen Baker (1)
    Born: 1928 or 1929
    Died:
    Buried at:
    Parents:
    Alvin Jacobs (2)
    Born: Unknown
    Died: Living
    Buried at:
    Parents: Unknown

3   Charlotte Joosten
    Born: 1935 in Rudolph, Wood County, Wisconsin
    Died: Before April 2015
    Buried at:
    Married: Unknown

3   Duane F. Joosten
    Born: 1937 in Rudolph, Wood County, Wisconsin
    Died: Living
    Buried at:
    Married: June 11, 1960, DeKalb County, Illinois
    Georgia K. Whiting
    Born: Unknown
    Died: Living
    Buried at:
    Parents: Unknown

3   Beverly Joosten
    Born: 1939 in Sigel, Wood County, Wisconsin
    Died: Living
    Buried at:
    Married: Unknown

3   Judith Jean Joosten
    Born: October 27, 1940 in Wisconsin Rapids, Wood County, Wisconsin
    Died: June 02, 1971
    Buried at: St. Joseph Cemetery, Harvard, IL
    Married: n/a

2   Maymie Joosten
Born: July 05, 1904 in Grand Chute, Outagamie County, Wisconsin
Died: June 24, 1994 in Rudolph, Wood County, Wisconsin
Buried at: All Souls Catholic Cemetery, Rudolph, WI, row 1
Married (1): September 21, 1922 in Rudolph, Wood County, Wisconsin
Married (2): April 20, 1974 in Rudolph, Wood County, Wisconsin
Anton Joseph Kempen (1)
Born: June 13, 1891 in Woodville, Calumet County, Wisconsin
Died: January 15, 1969 in Rudolph, Wood County, Wisconsin
Buried at: All Souls Catholic Cemetery, Rudolph, WI, row 1
Parents: Peter Martin Kempen (1859-1909) and Wilhelmina Vanderloop (1859-1927)
Ernest J. Smrz (2)
Born: January 03, 1900 in Johnson County, Iowa
Died: June 14, 1976 in Rudolph, Wood County, Wisconsin
Buried at: St. Michael Cemetery, Junction City, WI
Parents: Joseph F. Smrz (1870-1954) and Rosalie Rihacek (1873-1958)

     3   Lucille A. Kempen
Born: October 26, 1923 in Carson, Portage County, Wisconsin
Died: July 15, 2014 in Rudolph, Wood County, Wisconsin
Buried at: All Souls Catholic Cemetery, Rudolph, WI.
Married: June 09, 1945 in Rudolph, Wood County, Wisconsin
Edward S. O'Shasky
Born: September 20, 1923 in Rudolph, Wood County, Wisconsin
Died: January 03, 1992 in Wisconsin Rapids, Wood County, Wisconsin
Buried at: All Souls Catholic Cemetery, Rudolph, WI.
Parents: Peter J. O'Shasky (1879-1956) and Frances O'Shasky (1888-1959).

     3   Bernadine K. Kempen
Born: 1925 in Carson, Portage County, Wisconsin
Died: Living
Buried at:
Married: July 14, 1943 in Rudolph, Wood County, Wisconsin
William F. Jagodzinski
Born: January 06, 1919 in Wisconsin Rapids, Wood County, Wisconsin
Died: December 25, 1988 in Marshfield, Wood County, Wisconsin
Buried at: All Souls Catholic Cemetery, Rudolph, WI.
Parents: John Walter Jagodzinski (1889-1951) and Rosa Elizabeth Schmick (1886-1967)

     3   Clarabell Kempen
Born: 1927 in Rudolph, Wood County, Wisconsin
Died: Living
Buried at:
Married: November 22, 1947 in Rudolph, Wood County, Wisconsin
James See
Born: 1925 in Wisconsin
Died: Living
Buried at:
Parents: Peter See (1898-1970) and Othilia "Tillie" Schulhauser (1902-1977)

3   Janet Kempen
    Born: 1928 in Rudolph, Wood County, Wisconsin
    Died: Living
    Buried at:
    Married: May 29, 1948 in Rudolph, Wood County, Wisconsin
    Gregory C. VanAsten
    Born: November 27, 1927 in Rudolph, Wood County, Wisconsin
    Died: December 27, 2013 in Seymour, Outagamie County, Wisconsin
    Buried at: St. Casimir Catholic Cemetery, Krakow, WI.
    Parents: Simon VanAsten (1903-1996) and Marie K. Bushmaker (1905-1993)

3   Marjory Kempen
    Born: 1929 in Rudolph, Wood County, Wisconsin
    Died: Living
    Buried at:
    Married: August 21, 1948 in Rudolph, Wood County, Wisconsin
    John Cyril Schenk
    Born: October 08, 1925 in Wisconsin Rapids, Wood County, Wisconsin
    Died: November 28, 1997 in Wisconsin Rapids, Wood County, Wisconsin
    Buried at: All Souls Catholic Cemetery, Rudolph, WI.
    Parents: Karl Schenk (1893-?) and Oral Schenk (1893-1966)

3   Irene E. Kempen
    Born: 1931 in Rudolph, Wood County, Wisconsin
    Died: Living
    Buried at:
    Married: October 21, 1950 in Rudolph, Wood County, Wisconsin
    Marvin G. VanAsten
    Born: July 22, 1929 in Rudolph, Wood County, Wisconsin
    Died: August 16, 1984 in Rudolph, Wood County, Wisconsin
    Buried at: All Souls Catholic Cemetery, Rudolph, WI, row 3
    Parents: Simon VanAsten (1903-1996) and Marie K. Bushmaker (1905-1993)

3   Helen L. Kempen
    Born: 1932 in Rudolph, Wood County, Wisconsin
    Died: Living
    Buried at:
    Married: August 27, 1952 in Rudolph, Wood County, Wisconsin
    Robert J. Zubella
    Born: January 15, 1931 in Bevent, Marathon County, Wisconsin
    Died: May 16, 1998 in Rudolph, Wood County, Wisconsin
    Buried at: All Souls Catholic Cemetery, Rudolph, WI.
    Parents: John Zubella (1905-1981) and Marie Boschuetz (1912-1988)

3   Baby Kempen
    Born: December 23, 1934 in Marshfield, Wood County, Wisconsin
    Died: December 23, 1934 in Marshfield, Wood County, Wisconsin
    Buried at:
    Married: n/a

2   William Joosten
    Born: April 15, 1907 in Rudolph, Wood County, Wisconsin
    Died: September 23, 1925 in Rudolph, Wood County, Wisconsin
    Buried at: St. Philip Catholic Cemetery, Rudolph, WI., row 12
    Married: n/a

2   Richard Simon Joosten
    Born: August 06, 1909 in Rudolph, Wood County, Wisconsin
    Died: August 11, 1968 in Wonder Lake, McHenry County, Illinois
    Buried at: Christ the King Catholic Cemetery, Wonder Lake, IL
    Married: September 15, 1932 in Wisconsin Rapids, Wood County, Wisconsin
    Theresa Jackan
    Born: December 30, 1912 in Rudolph, Wood County, Wisconsin
    Died: August 12, 1967 in Woodstock, McHenry County, Illinois
    Buried at: Christ the King Catholic Cemetery, Wonder Lake, IL
    Parents: Michael J. Jackan (1882-1956) and Janet Filipkowski (1887-1966)

    3   Marlene Joosten
        Born: 1935 in Rudolph, Wood County, Wisconsin
        Died: Living
        Buried at:
        Married: Unknown
        Donald Malo
        Born: Unknown
        Died: Living
        Buried at:
        Parents: Unknown

    3   Richard Michael Joosten
        Born: July 03, 1937 in Chicago, Cook County, Illinois
        Died: January 15, 2010 in Orlando, Brevard County, Florida
        Buried at:
        Married: Unknown
        Debra Joosten-Tagliaferri
        Born: Unknown
        Died: Living
        Buried at:
        Parents: Unknown

    3   Dennis M. Joosten
        Born: November 24, 1941 in Wisconsin Rapids, Wood County, Wisconsin
        Died: April 23, 1944 in Racine, Racine County, Wisconsin
        Buried at: Holy Family Catholic Cemetery, Racine, WI.
        Married: n/a

    3   Joan Joosten
        Born: 1945 in Racine, Racine County, Wisconsin
        Died: Living
        Buried at:
        Married: November 06, 1965 in McHenry, McHenry County, Illinois

Lawrence Freund
Born: Unknown
Died: Living
Buried at:
Parents: Unknown

3   Mary Jane Joosten
Born: 1946 in Woodstock, McHenry County, Illinois
Died: Living
Buried at:
Married: October 21, 1967 in Wonder Lake, McHenry County, Illinois
Anthony A. Mogdans
Born: 1944
Died: Living
Buried at:
Parents: Unknown

2   Rosella Joosten
Born: September 23, 1911 in Rudolph, Wood County, Wisconsin
Died: November 29, 1918 in Rudolph, Wood County, Wisconsin
Buried at: St. Philip Catholic Cemetery, Rudolph, WI., row 12
Married: n/a

2   George A. Joosten
Born: June 25, 1914 in Rudolph, Wood County, Wisconsin
Died: December 10, 1972 in Wisconsin Rapids, Wood County, Wisconsin
Buried at: Restlawn Memorial Park, Wisconsin Rapids, WI
Married: March 16, 1943 in Rudolph, Wood County, Wisconsin
Margaret Hilgers
Born: August 18, 1921 in Wisconsin Rapids, Wood County, Wisconsin
Died: May 02, 2003 in Wisconsin Rapids, Wood County, Wisconsin
Buried at: Restlawn Memorial Park, Wisconsin Rapids, WI
Parents: Frank Hilgers (1892-1967) and Mary Langer (1897-1969)

3   Shirley Ann Joosten
Born: 1943 in Wisconsin Rapids, Wood County, Wisconsin
Died: Living
Buried at:
Married (1): Unknown
Married (2): October 14, 2006
Lawrence Frank (1)
Born: January 01, 1940
Died: April 23, 2000
Buried at:
Parents: Unknown
Robert Exner (2)
Born: Unknown
Died: Living
Buried at:
Parents: Unknown

3   Mary Jean Joosten
     Born: July 10, 1945 in Chicago, Cook County, Illinois
     Died: July 11, 1945 in Chicago, Cook County, Illinois
     Buried at: St. Joseph Catholic Cemetery, River Grove, IL
     Married: n/a

3   Sharon Joosten
     Born: 1946 in Chicago, Cook County, Illinois
     Died: Living
     Buried at:
     Married: October 01, 1966 in Wisconsin Rapids, Wood County, Wisconsin
     Gary F. Giebels
     Born: Unknown
     Died: Living
     Buried at:
     Parents: Unknown

3   Susan M. Joosten
     Born: 1951 in Wisconsin Rapids, Wood County, Wisconsin
     Died: Living
     Buried at:
     Married (1): January 02, 1971
     Married (2): January 17, 1987 in St. Paul, Hennepin County, Minnesota
     Norman Michael Joosten (1)
     Born: 1949 in Wisconsin Rapids, Wood County, Wisconsin
     Died: Living
     Buried at:
     Parents: Norman S. Joosten (1922-2010) and Shirley L. Smith
     Donald L. Stein (2)
     Born: 1957
     Died: Living
     Buried at:
     Parents: Unknown

3   Sally Marie Joosten
     Born: 1954 in Wisconsin Rapids, Wood County, Wisconsin
     Died: Living
     Buried at:
     Married: September 08, 1973 in Wisconsin Rapids, Wood County, Wisconsin
     Stephen John Kissner
     Born: 1953
     Died: Living
     Buried at:
     Parents: Anton P. Kissner (1925-2012) and Eva M. Truchinski (1929-2011)

⁊ **Chapter Eleven** ⁊

Christina Verhagen

I n the middle of the summer of 1876, Christina was the eighth child and seventh daughter blessed to Joseph and Nellie. She was born on August 6, 1876 on the family farm in Grand Chute, of course, just like most of her siblings, and one month following the Centennial celebration of the founding of our great country. She was first captured in the 1880 census at the young tender age of three.

A couple of major US historical events happened in the year Christina was born. On February 14, 1876, Alexander Graham Bell and Elisha Gray applied separately for telephone patents. The Supreme Court eventually ruled Bell as the rightful inventor. And then two days following her birth, on August 8th, Thomas Edison receives his US patent for his mimeograph invention. The mimeograph was a low-cost printing press which forced ink through a stencil onto paper. What was interesting was the term mimeograph became known as a "generic" word just like Xerox and Google, where company names (nouns) also became verbs.

Image 11.01- Christina J. Verhagen

Christina attended school through the eighth grade, and then at the age 19 met, fell in love with, and married Adrian Verhagen in Little Chute on November 6, 1895. More than likely, the ceremony took place at St. John Catholic Church just as her older siblings who remained in Wisconsin did. Adrian was 23 years old at the time, and was the brother of John Verhagen, the husband of Mary, Christina's sister. Adrian was born on September 22, 1871 in Little Chute to Henry and Henriette (VanHammond) Verhagen. Adrian's father, and his first wife Catherine (Joosten), like many other Little Chute families, emigrated from Holland and landed in the Port of New York on the Ship Mississippi in 1854 before settling in Little Chute. An interesting fact is Catherine is the sister of our Joseph Joosten.

Image 11.02- Adrian H. & Christina J. (Joosten) Verhagen Wedding Photo Taken 1895

After spending two years in Little Chute, the young couple moved west to the small farming community of Chili, WI, which is in the Fremont Township in Clark County. Chili, WI is about 40 miles west of Rudolph where Christina's brother Martin was living. It is unknown what drew Christina and Adrian to Clark County other than the possibility of a job opportunity for Adrian. As far as I know, there was no other family in the vicinity. They purchased a farm and put down roots that would grow for decades to come.

To shine a little history on Fremont, it is said it was named after John Charles Fremont (1813-1890) when it was created by the County Board of Supervisors on March 11, 1874. Mr. Fremont was a General during the Civil War, explorer of the West, and politician who served as one of the first U.S. Senators from California (1850–51). In 1856, the Republican Party chose him as their first presidential candidate to run for the presidency of the United States of America. He died in New York City on July 13, 1890.

Just before the end of the 19th century, happiness and joy came to the young couple with the birth of their first child. Edward Henry was born on June 4, 1899, and this would begin a wonderful family journey of raising twelve children. When the 20th century began, Christina and Adrian were enumerated in the 1900 Fremont census. Christina was 23, Adrian 27, and little Edward 11 months. They also had a 24 year old boarder who lived with them by the name of Henry Mernelson (first letter of his last name is illegible from the hand written census sheet) who was also of Dutch decent, and was Adrian's hired hand for the farm work. Many of the residents of Chili descended from Holland, Germany, and Canada, or moved to Chili from the New England region.

Over the next 10 years, six more children were born to this growing family. The second child born was Ellen on February 24, 1901, next came Joseph Albert on November 20, 1902, then Harriet Alice born April 3, 1904. The fifth child that came into the family was Paul Martin on September 14, 1905, then 26 months later Marie Mathilda came into the world on December 23, 1907. Lastly, Louise Elizabeth was born in November 1909 before the close of the first 20th century decade.

In 1920 when the next census was taken, the Verhagen family was still living in Chili at this time with nine of their eleven children living with them. Ellen and Harriet were 18 and 15 years old, respectively, and were finished with their formal education and not attending school, and more than likely assisting on the farm. All the

other children were attending school working toward their eighth grade education, which was the normal duration. Edward and Joseph were both out of the house, but it is unknown where they were living at this time. Joseph was 17, and could have very well been a boarder with another local family working as a farmhand. Edward was 21 now, and it looks like he moved east to Wood County for a short time because this is where he met his future wife, Irene F. Gourlie, and married her on November 23, 1926 in Bakerville, which is close to the city of Marshfield and about 10 miles from Chili. Very soon the young couple packed their belongings and moved further away west to Polk County near the western Wisconsin border and the Mississippi River.

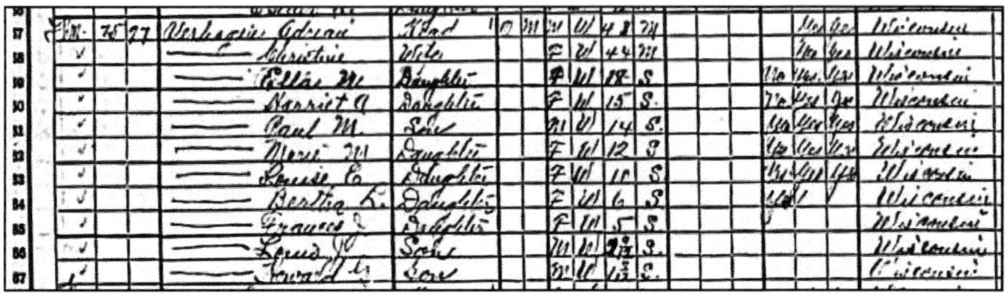

Image 11.03- Verhagen Family in the 1920 Fremont, Clark County, WI Census, ED18, sheet 4B.

Later in 1920 joy came to the family one more time with the birth of the twelfth and last child. Mabel Phyllis was born on May 04, 1920. You might be thinking twelve children are quite a few, and it is by today's culture, but 12 kids in the Joosten family was only second best. The most children prize goes to Christina's younger sister Margaret VanDyke who had 14 children, which chapter twelve is dedicated to covering.

Similar to how some of Christina's sibling's families lost children at a very young age, Christina and Adrian would experience this same heartbreak as sadness entered the Verhagen family upon the death their second son Joseph who passed away on November 9, 1921, just shy of his 19th birthday. He was laid to rest in the St. Stephen Catholic Cemetery in Chili.

Just before the 1930s, joy came to Christina (age 51) and Adrian (age 56) as their first grandchild was born. Norma Christine came into the world on March 04, 1928 in Clam Falls, WI to her happy parents Edward and Irene. When the 1930s did finally roll around Christina and Adrian were up in their years now at 53 and 58 respectively, and half of the kids were out of the house. Paul was age 24 and lived on the farm helping out his father with the

Image 11.04- St. Stephen Catholic Church in Chili, WI

farm work. Louise, Bertha, and Francis were all out of school, while Louis, Howard, and Mabel were attending school. When reviewing the occupations from the census most of the residents of Chili were farmers, but there were some others, such as the local dentist who was Louis Lindow, and probably related to Louise's future husband Roy Lindow. Edward and Irene were living in Clam Falls, Wisconsin, which lies in the Lorain Township in Polk County. At this time they were renting their farm for $10 per month, and operating a cheese factory. Norma and Lester were their only two children in the family at this time, but also living with Edward's family was a 17 year old boarder by the name of Harry Taylor, who was born in North Dakota, and helping out in the cheese factory.

The 1930 federal census revealed the population in the Fremont Township was 1079, which was one of the more populated townships in Clark County. And of course the census proved that Wisconsin was the largest producer of milk in the United States. There were more than 125,000 dairy farms in the state with 63% of all land in Wisconsin designated as farmland, and 71% of the farmland was used for dairy farming. In Clark County, there were 4,510 dairy farms, which represented 89% of all farms in the county. Then the Great Depression came and with it falling milk prices. Since some members of the Verhagen family were dairy farmers this must have hit them hard, especially those who produced milk for butter, cheese, and other foods. In 1933, the famous Wisconsin Milk Strike occurred during three separate months of the year. Members of the Wisconsin Cooperative Milk Pool went on strike by not selling their milk. It seems as though some of the Cooperative members were selling their milk at reduced prices; probably those who produced milk for bottling, who were not affected as much with the falling prices. This activity angered the other members who then resorted to forming roadblocks to prevent trucks from entering milk processing plants. During a strike in February 1933, it was reported violence broke out in the Fox Valley near Appleton. Milk convoy guards threw heavy objects at a group of 100 strikers hurting some of them. When it was over the toll was heavy on those who took part in the strike. These farmers lost a reported $10 million.

During the 1920s and 1930s, the Verhagen family experienced more of the Verhagen kids getting married. Although I do not have all the marriage dates, I do know Ellen married Clarence W. Livingston, Harriet married Richard C. Donner, Paul was wedded to Irma R. Schuster, and Marie married Roland W. Braun on June 27, 1930. On October 22, 1936 Louise married Roy J. Lindow in Bakerville located in Wood County, Wisconsin. They operated a dairy in Chili for many decades, and then at the age of 64, Louise passed away on December 12, 1973. It was not long after that when Roy moved out to Oregon and took up his residence in Verboort. Bertha married William H. Nebel on September 30, 1931; both were a young 18 years old then. Frances married Edwin A. Fait on June 30, 1945 with Mary Ellen Petersen as the maid of honor and Howard Verhagen, Frances' brother, as best man. Howard's spouse was Vera E. Steltenpohl, and finally Mabel married Alvord H. Selk in Chili on April 4, 1940.

Image 11.05- Train Rolling Through Chili, WI

In 1940, Louis moved out to Verboort, Oregon where a lot of his Joosten cousins, and brother-in-law Roy Lindow already lived in. He was drafted into World War II, and served our country in the US Army. When the war was over he married Marjorie C. Vandervelden on October 30, 1945 at Visitation Catholic Church in Verboort. Marjorie was born and raised in the Verboort area. Following Louis' unfortunate and untimely passing on March 17, 1974, Marjorie married Roy Lindow on May 29, 1976. And as we know, Roy's first wife was Louis' sister Louise.

In 1931 Christina was now 55 years old, a little young to be experiencing health problems. But at 55 she had outlived most of her siblings. During what would be agreeably one of worst times of the year to experience a death in the family, Christina passed away two days before Christmas on December 23rd. Her obituary states her death resulted from paralysis, which may have meant she experienced a stroke from which she did not recover. Christina lived longer than most of her siblings with only three of her sisters living longer. Her funeral Mass was held at St. Stephen Catholic Church in Chili, and she was buried in the third row of the parish cemetery. Her obituary was printed in the Neillsville Press on December 31, 1931, and contributed this wonderful tribute about Christina:

"The large attendance at the funeral, the beautiful flowers and the many spiritual bouquet cards offered told of the high esteem in which she was held. She was a very devoted wife and mother, a wonderful well-meaning friend and neighbor, never missing an opportunity of helping in time of need. She will be sadly missed by the members of her family and a host of friends and neighbors. Heartfelt sympathy is extended to the bereaved husband and children."

So where was the Verhagen family at the beginning of the 1940s decade? Most of the Verhagen kids still lived in Chili while four of the kids moved away and two returned. The 1940 federal census reveals very interesting details about the family. As we know, Adrian was now widowed, and at age 68 was still living in Chili. He was captured in the census residing with his son Howard and his wife Vera. In addition to Adrian, this household included the newly wedded Selks, Mabel and Alvord. The Verhagens were renting their home and farm for $10 per month, and they all farmed the land. Interestingly enough Adrian finished his formal education after completing the 5th grade, after which time he more than likely stayed at home to help with farming duties. Howard reached the 8th grade, both Mabel and Vera completed the 9th grade, and Alvord finished the 11th grade.

In the mid-1930s, Edward and Irene moved their family back to Chili from Lorain in Polk County. They owned their farm they were living on, which was valued at $600 and located on Highway H.

Ellen and Clarence moved to Toledo, Ohio following their marriage in the early 1930s. It is in Toledo where they were enumerated in the census with their three children, and Clarence's father Thomas who was age 79 at the time and a widower. Their address was 418 Segur Ave. in Toledo, which was about a mile west of the Maumee River. Clarence was employed as a Weatherstrip Mechanic for a home builder, and earned $400 in 20 weeks of work during 1939. The Livingston's three children were all born in Ohio, and all with birthdays within four days of each other in the month of January; a rare occurrence.

Harriet and Richard also lived in Chili, and owned the farm they lived on valued at $900. All three of their children, who were all born in the 1930s, Oren (age 8), Jerry (age 5), and Richard Jr. (age 2) were part of the household.

In the mid-1930s, Paul and his wife Irma moved their family from Chili to Warner, which was also in Clark County about 27 miles northwest of Chili. Paul and Irma were renting the farm they lived on and paying $8 per month in rent.

Marie and Roland were living near their other Verhagen relatives in Chili with their first two children June Marie (age 8), and Marlene Joy (age 4), and were renting their home for $5 per month. The Brauns had recently moved to Chili from Wood County. Roland was employed at the local creamery as the Buttermaker's Helper, and had earned $835 from this job in 1939.

Bertha and William were living in Chili (Fremont Township), and owned their home, which was valued at $1,500. At this time, their first two sons were born, William Jr. was 7 years old, and James was age 4. William (Sr.) was a farmer, and his uncle Herman Schilling, age 54, lived with the Nebel family, and had been for a few years prior to this time. Herman was a carpenter. As far as education level achieved, Bertha completed the 7th grade, and William the 8th grade.

Frances was age 25 at this time, and not yet married. She moved east to Wisconsin Rapids in Wood County to work in the hospital. She worked as a maid and earned $340 during 1939. Another wonderful person worked at the hospital too, Edward Fait, who was 27 years old, worked there as a janitor. I bet this is where Frances met her future husband and began their work romance. As we know they were married in 1945. Like most of her siblings, Frances' formal education ended after the 8th grade.

And as mentioned earlier Louis moved out to Oregon and was a farming hired man in Verboort. He was a boarder with the Peter ("George") and Rose Hermens family. Peter's parents are Anna and Antone Hermens making the two first cousins. Also living near Louis was another first cousin Josephine Lepschat, and his aunt Maggie VanDyke.

In 1943, when our country was in the middle of World War II, Adrian was in his early 70s now, and his health was starting to fade. He experienced a slight stroke, and a short time later he passed away peacefully in his sleep on October 14, 1943. His son Howard, who was 25 years old at the time, thought Adrian was sleeping during the morning and eventually discovered his father had died. A doctor and a coroner were called out to the

Christina & Adrian Verhagen

house, and they determined Adrian had a heart attack late in the night. Howard mentioned to them he remembered hearing Adrian snoring as he slept late the night before. A funeral Mass was celebrated in his honor, and then he was placed next to his wife in the St. Stephen Catholic Cemetery to rest in peace.

Christina and Adrian leave behind a vast legacy. From their 12 children came 36 grandchildren. The first grandchild born was Norma Christine Verhagen in 1928, and the last was Mary Kay Fait (Peschke) born in 1956; a span of 28 years between cousins.

Now it is time to talk about some fun facts related to the longest married and the longest living of the Verhagen family. The longest living was Mabel who lived to age 88, and of the in-laws, Marjorie was 93. The average length of life for the 12 Verhagen children was 62.92 years, and the sisters definitely lived longer than their brothers. Although I do not have all of the marriage dates, of the dates I do have the longest marriage belongs to Marie and Roland at 58 happy years. Both lived long lives.

* * *

There were a large number of good men and women of the Verhagen Family who served our fine country in the military. They are:

- ❖ Ronald W. Kitzhaber - Served in the U.S. Army from 1956-1958.
- ❖ William A. Nebel Sr. - Joined the U.S. Air Force on May 3, 1949 and served in the Korean War. Honored with the Korean Service Medal and the United Nations Medal. He was honorably discharged on November 14, 1952.
- ❖ Donald Ruhl – Served in the U.S. Air Force as an Airman 2nd Class.
- ❖ Lawrence E. Verhagen, Sr. - Served in the U.S. Army as a military police officer in Germany for five years. Honorably discharged in 1990.
- ❖ Louis J. Verhagen – Served in US Army during World War II.

Image 11.06- Verhagen Family Photo with VanHandel Siblings, circa 1914. Back (L to R): Martin VanHandel (1892), Adrian, Edward (on wagon). Front (L to R): Paul, Harriet, Joseph, Marie, Ellen, Louise, Christine, Bertha (in mom's arms), Christine VanHandel (Vandenheuvel), and Cora Hammen (VanHandel).

Image 11.07- Adrian & Christina Verhagen Headstone, St. Stephen Catholic Cemetery, row 3

Verhagen, Adrian
(September 22, 1870-October 14, 1943)

Adrian Verhagen, 73, was found dead in his bed at 2 p.m. Thursday at the farm home just west of Chili where he had lived since coming to Clark County in 1897.

The body was discovered by his son, Howard, who had come home from helping a neighbor. The son said that his father had suffered a slight stroke a short time ago, and although still able to do some work about the farm, had been in the habit of sleeping as long as he wished and often did not rise before noon. Consequently other members of the family assumed that he was sleeping.

Dr. V. M. Overman, Granton, and Coroner H. L. Brown, Neillsville, were called and decided that Mr. Verhagen had suffered a heart attack and died in his sleep during the night. Young Verhagen said he had heard his father snoring at midnight, establishing the fact that he was living at that hour. A small granddaughter of the stricken man had been in the room during the morning but thought that he was asleep.

Mr. Verhagen was born at Little Chute, Wis., on Sept. 22, 1870, and was married there on Nov. 6, 1895, to Christine Joosten, who died in 1931. They came to Clark County in 1897 and settled on the present Verhagen farm.

Surviving are 11 of their 12 children: Edward H., Chili; Mrs. Clarence (Ella) Livingston, Toledo, Ohio; Mrs. Richard (Harriet) Donner, Oshkosh; Paul, Richmond, Ill.; Mrs. Roland (Marie) Brown, Waukegan, Ill.; Mrs. Ray (Louise) Lindow, Spencer; Mrs. William (Bertha) Nebel, Waukegan, Ill; Louis, Forest Grove, Ore.; Miss Frances, Wisconsin Rapids; Howard, on the home farm; and Mrs. Everett (Mabel) Selk, Chili. One son, Joseph, died in 1921. Also surviving are 25 grandchildren, a brother, Albert Verhagen, Kaukauna; a sister, Mrs. Katherine Vandenberg, Little Chute; and a half-brother, Anton, Green Bay.

Funeral rites will be conducted at St. Stephen's Catholic Church of Chili at 10 a.m. Tuesday.

Image 11.08- Obituary of Adrian H. Verhagen

Verhagen, Christina
(6 Aug. 1876 - 23 Dec. 1931)

Mrs. Adrian Verhagen passed away at her home in the town of Fremont near Chili, Dec. 23, 1931, death resulting from paralysis.

Christina Joosten was born at Little Chute, Wis., Aug. 6, 1876, being one of nine children born to Mr. and Mrs. Joseph Joosten. She was married to Adrian Verhagen, Nov. 6, 1895. After living at Little Chute two years they came to the town of Fremont; buying the farm that has since been her home.

To this union were born 12 children: Joseph preceding her in death 10 years ago; the other 11 with the husband survive. They are: Edward of Clam Falls, Wis.; Ella, Mrs. Clarence Livingstone, Toledo, Ohio; Harriet, Mrs. Richard Downer; Marie, Mrs. Roland Braun, Bertha, Mrs. W. Nebel all of the town of Fremont; Paul, Louise, Frances, Lewis, Howard and Mabel at home; also three sisters -- Mrs. Wm. Weyenberg of Appleton; Mrs. Corneal Hermens and Mrs. Walter Vandyke of Forest Grove, Oregon.

The funeral was held from the St. Stephen's church at 10 o'clock on Saturday, Rev. Fr. Willitzer of Bakerville officiating, burial being near the church. The large attendance at the funeral, the beautiful flowers and the many spiritual bouquets cards offered told of the high esteem in which she was held. She was a very devoted wife and mother, a wonderful well meaning friend and neighbor, never missing an opportunity of helping in time of need. She will be sadly missed by the members of her family and a host of friends and neighbors. Heartfelt sympathy is extended to the bereaved husband and children.

Image 11.09- Obituary of Christina J. Verhagen, Neillsville Press (Neillsville) 12/31/1931

Edward Verhagen

Ver Hagen, Edward (4 June 1899 – 6 June 1953)

Edward Ver Hagen, 54, Route 3, Granton, died of a heart attack June 6 at his home.

Funeral services were held June 10 in St. Stephen's Catholic Church in Chili with Fr. Carl Wohlmuth officiating. The body, in charge of the Bergemann Funeral Home of Neillsville, reposed at the family home until time of burial. A general rosary service was said at 9 p.m. Monday and Tuesday.

Edward Ver Hagen was born June 4, 1899, to Adrian and Christine (Joosten) Ver Hagen at Chili. He spent most of his life in Clark County. His marriage to Irene Gourlie took place November 23, 1926, at Bakerville, Wis. He worked for 10 years as a cheesemaker in Polk County, returning to a farm north of Chili where he farmed for another 10 years, moving then to a farm south of Lynn, where he resided until his death.

He was a member of the Holy Name Society of St. Stephen's Catholic Church of Chili.

Survivors include his wife and the following ten children: Mrs. Ralph (Norma) Tauschek, Wisconsin Rapids; Sgt. Lester Ver Hagen, stationed in Germany; Mrs. Clarence (Joyce) Gilbertson, Rockford, Ill.; Mrs. Donald (Eleanor) Kapusta, Marshfield; Mrs. Alvin (Edna) Kapusta, Wichita, Kans.; Howard, Harlow, Margie, Louis and Larry, all at home.

He is also survived by seven grandchildren; three brothers, Paul of Long Beach, Cal.; Louis of Forest Grove, Ore.; Howard of Willard; and seven sisters: Mrs. Clarence (Ella) Livington, Clear Lake, Ind.; Mrs. Richard (Harriet) Donner, Long Beach, Cal.; Mrs. Ronald (Marie) Brown, Waukegan, Ill.; Mrs. Roy (Louise) Lindow, Spencer; Mrs. William (Bertha) Nebel, Lake Villa Ill.; Mrs. Edwin (Frances) Fait, Wisconsin Rapids; and Mrs. Alvord (Mabel) Selk, Chili. One brother is deceased.

Image 11.10- Obituary of Edward H. Verhagen, Clark County Press (Neillsville), June 11, 1953

48-5-6 C REGISTRATION CARD

4/391

Edward Henry Ver Hagen

Chili Clark Wis

19 June 4 1899

Farmer Adrian Ver Hagen

Chili Clark Wis

Christine Ver Hagen

Chili Clark Wis

Edward Henry Ver Hagen

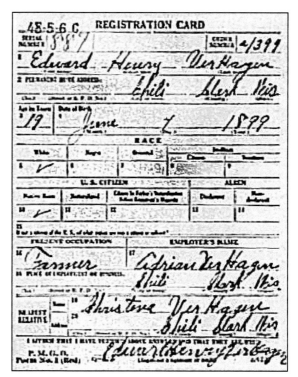

Image 11.11- Edward H. Verhagen World War 1 Draft Card

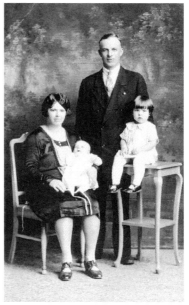

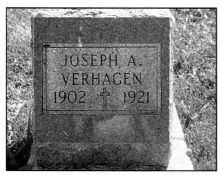

Image 11.12- Joseph A. Verhagen Headstone, St. Stephen Catholic Cemetery, row 3

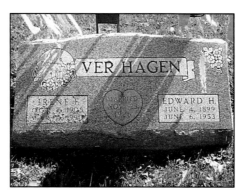

Image 11.13- Edward H & Irene F Verhagen Headstone, St. Stephen Catholic Cemetery, row 4

Image 11.14- Edward & Irene (Gourlie) Verhagen, Norma & Lester, about 1929

BERHAGEN—Paul M., 59, shiprigger, of 2882 Elm Ave., died Sunday. Surviving are son, Paul E.; daughter, Mrs. Dale Christensen; brothers, Louis, Howard; sisters, Mrs. Ella Livingston, Mrs. Harriet Donner, Mrs. Marie Braun, Mrs. Louise Lindow, Mrs. Bertha Nebel, Mrs. Frances Fait, Mrs. Mabel Selk. Rosary Tuesday, 8 p.m. Requiem Mass Wednesday, 10 a.m., St. Cornelius Church. Lakewood Mortuary in charge.

Image 11.15- Paul M. Verhagen Obituary, Long Beach Independent, 12/21/1964, page D3

Louis J. VerHagen

FOREST GROVE — Louis J. VerHagen, 57, died Sunday at a Portland hospital following an extended illness.

Recitation of Holy Rosary will be tonight at 7:30 at Visitation Catholic Church at Verboort with Requiem Mass at the church at 10 a.m. Wednesday. The Very Rev. Father Paul Malyszko will officiate with vault interment at Visitation Cemetery.

Funeral arrangements were made by Fuiten Mortuary in Forest Grove.

Mr. VerHagen was born at Chili, Wis., the son of Adrian and Christine Joosten VerHagen. He spent his early life there and came to Verboort in 1940, where he has lived since. He served a short time in the U.S. Army during World War II and was a truck driver for the McCready Lumber Co. in Forest Grove for 20 years. He was on the custodial staff at Pacific University until his health forced his retirement. He was a member of Visitation Catholic Church.

He was married at Verboort to Marjorie Vandervelden on Oct. 30, 1945. She survives at the family home. Also surviving are five sisters, Mrs. William (Bertha) Nevel of Lake Villa, Ill.; Harriett Donner of Bellflower, Cal.; Mrs. Roland (Marie) Braun of Waukegan, Ill.; Mrs. Eddie (Frances) Fiat of Wisconsin Rapids and Mabel Selk of Marshfield, Wis.

Image 11.16- Louis J Verhagen Obituary, Hillsboro Argus, 03/19/1974, page 11

Roy J. Lindow, 80, ex-dairy farmer

VERBOORT—Recitation of the Holy Rosary and a Mass of Christian Burial were held Saturday morning for Roy John Lindow, 80, Verboort.

Mr. Lindow died March 14, 1991, at his home.

The Rev. Francis J. Walsh was celebrant at Saturday's mass, with the Very Rev. James H. Harris as co-celebrant. The services were at Visitation Roman Catholic Church in Verboort.

Vault interment was this morning in Spencer Cemetery in the Township of Sherman, Clark County, Wisc., with the Rev. Randy E. Olson of St. John's Roman Catholic Church in Marshfield, Wisc., officiating.

Mr. Lindow was born Aug. 29, 1910, in Chili, Wisc., a son of John and Ida Luckow Lindow. He was raised in the Chili area and attended Pine Circle Grade School and Marshfield High School.

On Oct. 22, 1936, he married Louise E. VerHagen in Bakerville, Wisc. and they lived in Chili. His wife died Dec. 12, 1973 in Marshfield, Wisc.

On May 29, 1976, he married Marjorie C. Vandervelden VerHagen in Verboort. They had lived in Verboort since.

Mr. Lindow owned and operated a dairy in Chili, Wisc., until 1973, when he retired. Since moving to Verboort, he had been working with the Oregon State University Extension Office in the certification of seed varieties.

He was a 55-year member of the Roman Catholic Church and since moving to Verboort had been a member of Visitation Parish.

Among his special interests were gardening and playing cards, especially pinochle.

Survivors include his wife, Marjorie C. Lindow, Verboort; a sister, Clara Gerber, Marshfield, Wisc.; and numerous nieces and nephews.

The family suggests memorial contributions to the Alzheimer's Disease Association, Inc., 1015 SW 22nd Ave., Portland 97210.

Fuiten-Rose Mortuary Chapel of Forest Grove was in charge of arrangements.

Image 11.17- Roy J Lindow Obituary, Hillsboro Argus, 03/19/1991, page 10A

Image 11.18- Alvord H. & Mable P. Selk Headstone, St. Stephen Catholic Cemetery, row 4

Christina & Adrian Verhagen

❧ Descendants of Christina & Adrian Verhagen ❧

Notes: 1= 1st generation, 2= 2nd generation, 3= 3rd generation.
The year of birth is only given for individuals still living, if known.

1   Christina J. Joosten
Born: August 06, 1876 in Grand Chute, Outagamie County, Wisconsin
Died: December 23, 1931 in Fremont, Clark County, Wisconsin
Buried at: St. Stephen Catholic Cemetery, Chili, WI., row 3
Married: November 06, 1895 in Little Chute, Outagamie County, Wisconsin
Adrian Henry Verhagen
Born: September 22, 1871 in Little Chute, Outagamie County, Wisconsin
Died: October 14, 1943 in Chili, Clark County, Wisconsin
Buried at: St. Stephen Catholic Cemetery, Chili, WI., row 3
Parents: Henry Verhagen (1829-1873) and Henriette VanHammond (1846-1871)

   2   Edward Henry Verhagen
Born: June 04, 1899 in Chili, Clark County, Wisconsin
Died: June 06, 1953 in Chili, Clark County, Wisconsin
Buried at: St. Stephen Catholic Cemetery, Chili, WI., row 4
Married: November 23, 1926 in Bakerville, Wood County, WI
Irene Florence Gourlie
Born: October 07, 1905 in Spencer, Marathon County, Wisconsin
Died: March 11, 1990 in Dane County, Wisconsin
Buried at: St. Stephen Catholic Cemetery, Chili, WI., row 4
Parents: Walter J. Gourlie (1879-1954) and Verna B. Gourlie (1888-1974)

      3   Norma Christine Verhagen
Born: March 04, 1928 in Clam Falls, Polk County, Wisconsin
Died: June 01, 1980 in Wisconsin Rapids, Wood County, Wisconsin
Buried at: Calvary Cemetery, Wisconsin Rapids, WI.
Married: May 10, 1946 in Bakerville, Wood County, WI.
Ralph Francis Tauschek
Born: February 22, 1922 in Marshfield, Wood County, Wisconsin
Died: November 1977 in Wisconsin Rapids, Wood County, Wisconsin
Buried at: Calvary Cemetery, Wisconsin Rapids, WI.
Parents: John F. Tauschek (1887-1978) and Theresa T. Tauschek (1894-1975)

      3   Lester Joseph Verhagen
Born: 1929 in Clam Falls, Polk County, Wisconsin
Died: Living
Buried at:
Married (1):
Married (2): September 23, 1967 in Los Angeles County, California
Twyla Hamilton (1)
Born: 1931
Died: Living
Buried at:
Parents: Unknown
Barbara Carol Rudolph (2)
Born: 1947 in Washington
Died: Living
Buried at:
Parents: Unknown

3   Joyce Verna Verhagen
Born: 1930 in Clam Falls, Polk County, Wisconsin
Died: Living
Buried at:
Married: June 19, 1948 in Chili, Clark County, Wisconsin
Clarence Leslie Gilbertson
Born: June 20, 1926 in Black River Falls, Jackson County, Wisconsin
Died: January 29, 1993
Buried at:
Parents: Unknown

3   Elnor Florence Verhagen
Born: November 03, 1931 in Clam Falls, Polk County, Wisconsin
Died: October 24, 2002 in Oregon, Dane County, Wisconsin
Buried at: St. Mary Catholic Cemetery, Oregon, WI.
Married: January 1950 in Clark County, WI.
Donald John Kapusta
Born: 1926 in Lynn, Clark County, Wisconsin
Died: Living
Buried at:
Parents: Martin A. Kapusta (1884-1965) and Marie Hurtuk (1890-1951)

3   Edna Minnie Verhagen
Born: December 30, 1933 in Clam Falls, Polk County, Wisconsin
Died: June 09, 2010 in Oregon, Dane County, Wisconsin
Buried at: St. Mary Catholic Cemetery, Oregon, WI.
Married: January 27, 1951 in Chili, Clark County, Wisconsin
Alvin J. Kapusta
Born: March 01, 1931 in Lynn, Clark County, Wisconsin
Died: March 11, 2006
Buried at: St. Mary Catholic Cemetery, Oregon, WI.
Parents: Martin A. Kapusta (1884-1965) and Marie Hurtuk (1890-1951)

3   Howard Everett Verhagen
Born: June 21, 1935 in Chili, Clark County, Wisconsin
Died: January 24, 1991
Buried at: Belvidere Cemetery, Belvidere, IL.
Married: June 30, 1956 in Rockford, Winnebago County, Illinois
Lillian S. Diebold
Born: August 09, 1937 in Rockford, Winnebago County, Illinois
Died: March 24, 2013 in Belvidere, Boone County, Illinois
Buried at: Belvidere Cemetery, Belvidere, IL.
Parents: Joseph E. Diebold (1903-1942) and Emma W. Payton (1919-1995)

3   Harlow Robert Verhagen
Born: June 21, 1935 in Chili, Clark County, Wisconsin
Died: September 26, 2008 in Belvidere, Boone County, Illinois
Buried at: Belvidere Cemetery, Belvidere, IL.
Married: April 16, 1955 in Rockford, Winnebago County, Illinois

Christina & Adrian Verhagen

Laura Anna Gump
Born: November 28, 1938 in Milwaukee, Milwaukee County, Wisconsin
Died: December 28, 2004 in Belvidere, Boone County, Illinois
Buried at: Belvidere Cemetery, Belvidere, IL.
Parents: George J. Gump (1911-1952) and Martha L. Reisner (1914-2004)

3   Margie Ann Verhagen
Born: December 04, 1940 in Neillsville, Clark County, Wisconsin
Died: October 27, 2012
Buried at:
Married: February 07, 1959 in Neillsville, Clark County, Wisconsin
Allen Lyle Meier
Born: 1939 in Neillsville, Clark County, Wisconsin
Died: Living
Buried at:
Parents: William H. Meier (1913-1998) and Lillian G. Meier (1916-2006)

3   Louis Henry Verhagen
Born: 1944 in Neillsville, Clark County, Wisconsin
Died: Living
Buried at:
Married: May 30, 1970 in Long Beach, Los Angeles County, California
Charlota Borsa
Born: 1943 in Orange, Orange County, California
Died: Living
Buried at:
Parents: Unknown

3   Lawrence Edward Verhagen Sr.
Born: September 04, 1948 in Neillsville, Clark County, Wisconsin
Died: June 28, 2010 in Fitchburg, Dane County, Wisconsin
Buried at:
Married: June 19, 1966 in Rockford, Winnebago County, Illinois
Elizabeth Ann Camp
Born: 1950 in Peoria, Peoria County, Illinois
Died: Living
Buried at:
Parents: Unknown

2   Ellen N. Verhagen
Born: February 24, 1901 in Chili, Clark County, Wisconsin
Died: April 25, 1955 in Chili, Clark County, Wisconsin
Buried at:
Married: Unknown
Clarence William Livingston
Born: October 21, 1909 in Ohio
Died: September 02, 1991
Buried at:
Parents: Thomas G. Livingston (1860-1950) and Emma L. Stair (1862-1925)

3   Robert Duane Livingston
    Born: 1935 in Swanton, Fulton County, Ohio
    Died: Living
    Buried at:
    Married: September 02, 1958 in Lafayette, Georgia
    Nancy Lou Miller
    Born: 1942 in Archbold, Fulton County, Ohio
    Died: Living
    Buried at:
    Parents: Unknown

3   David Lee Livingston
    Born: 1936 in Toledo, Lucas County, Ohio
    Died: Living
    Buried at:
    Married: January 10, 1959 in Rockford, Winnebago County, Illinois
    Sharon Lee McBain
    Born: 1936 in Toledo, Lucas County, Ohio
    Died: Living
    Buried at:
    Parents: Unknown

3   Patricia Ann Livingston
    Born: 1939 in Toledo, Lucas County, Ohio
    Died: Living
    Buried at:
    Married: Unknown
    Anthony J. Vella
    Born: September 09, 1918 in Rockford, Winnebago County, Illinois
    Died: July 11, 1986 in Rockford, Winnebago County, Illinois
    Buried at:
    Parents: Unknown

2   Joseph Albert Verhagen
    Born: November 20, 1902 in Chili, Clark County, Wisconsin
    Died: November 09, 1921 in Chili, Clark County, Wisconsin
    Buried at: St. Stephen Catholic Cemetery, Chili, WI., row 3
    Married: n/a

2   Harriet Alice Verhagen
    Born: April 03, 1904 in Chili, Clark County, Wisconsin
    Died: February 18, 1987 in Madera, Madera County, California
    Buried at:
    Married: Unknown
    Richard Christopher Donner
    Born: August 11, 1898 in Nekimi, Winnebago County, Wisconsin
    Died: January 25, 1966 in Long Beach, Los Angeles County, California
    Buried at:
    Parents: Christian Donner and Valeria Donner

3   <u>Oren Leonard Donner</u>
    Born: 1931 or 1932 in Wisconsin
    Died: Living
    Buried at:
    Married (1): September 07, 1952 in Los Angeles County, California
    Married (2): Unknown
    <u>Elizabeth A. Stewart (1)</u>
    Born: 1931 or 1932
    Died: Living
    Buried at:
    Parents: Unknown
    <u>Martha Hilda Veldhuizen (2)</u>
    Born: Unknown
    Died: Living
    Buried at:
    Parents: Unknown

3   <u>Gerald Joseph Donner</u>
    Born: September 24, 1934 in Wisconsin
    Died: November 22, 1980 in Riverside County, California
    Buried at:
    Married: n/a

3   <u>Richard Russell Donner</u>
    Born: 1937 or 1938 in Wisconsin
    Died:
    Buried at:
    Married: Unknown

2   Paul Martin Verhagen
    Born: September 14, 1905 in Chili, Clark County, Wisconsin
    Died: December 20, 1964 in Los Angeles, Los Angeles County, California
    Buried at:
    Married: Unknown
    <u>Irma Margaret Schuster</u>
    Born: March 28, 1912 in Wisconsin
    Died: June 13, 1993 in Long Beach, Los Angeles County, California
    Buried at:
    Parents: Charles E. Schuster (1868-?) and Mary A. Madler (1874-?)

3   <u>Evelyn Christine Verhagen</u>
    Born: 1932 in Neillsville, Clark County, Wisconsin
    Died: Living
    Buried at:
    Married: September 20, 1952 in Yuma, Yuma County, Arizona
    <u>Dale Robert Christensen</u>
    Born: February 20, 1926 in Manassa, Conejos County, Colorado
    Died: October 23, 2004
    Buried at: Forest Lawn Memorial Park, Cypress, CA
    Parents: Peter Christensen (1896-1965) and Ettie McKenzie (1900-1945)

3   Paul Edward Verhagen
    Born: October 25, 1934 in Chili, Clark County, Wisconsin
    Died: November 08, 1980 in Thurston County, Washington
    Buried at: Grand Mound Cemetery, Rochester, WA
    Married: August 08, 1969 in Los Angeles, Los Angeles County, California
    Myrtle M. Rogers
    Born: May 02, 1931 in Signal Hill, Los Angeles County, California
    Died: November 27, 2000 in Lewis County, Washington
    Buried at: Grand Mound Cemetery, Rochester, WA
    Parents: Unknown

2   Marie Mathilda Verhagen
    Born: December 23, 1907 in Chili, Clark County, Wisconsin
    Died: June 10, 1989 in Waukegan, Lake County, Illinois
    Buried at: Ascension Catholic Cemetery, Libertyville, IL
    Married: June 27, 1930 in Wisconsin
    Roland William Braun
    Born: October 25, 1906 in Granton, Clark County, Wisconsin
    Died: December 08, 1992 in Gurnee, Lake County, Illinois
    Buried at: Ascension Catholic Cemetery, Libertyville, IL
    Parents: Henry C. Braun (1867-1953) and Marie C. Winkler (1868-1950)

    3   June Marie Braun
        Born: 1931 in Neillsville, Clark County, Wisconsin
        Died: Living
        Buried at:
        Married: June 06, 1953 in Waukegan, Lake County, Illinois
        Charles William Druba, Jr.
        Born: 1931 in North Chicago, Lake County, Illinois
        Died: Living
        Buried at:
        Parents: Charles W. Druba, Sr. (1900-1942) and Agnes Druba (1903-1978)

    3   Marlene Joy Braun
        Born: 1935 in Marshfield, Wood County, Wisconsin
        Died: Living
        Buried at:
        Married: May 11, 1957 in Waukegan, Lake County, Illinois
        Russell F. Constantino
        Born: May 04, 1935 in Waukegan, Lake County, Illinois
        Died: May 20, 2008
        Buried at:
        Parents: Gregory Constantino (1914-?) and Beatrice Constantino (1915-?)

    3   Donald Lee Braun
        Born: May 01, 1940 in Marshfield, Wood County, Wisconsin
        Died: April 24, 1992 in Waukegan, Lake County, Illinois
        Buried at:
        Married: Unknown

Nikki S. Tew
Born: 1944
Died: Living
Buried at:
Parents: Unknown

3   Gary Roland Braun
Born: 1948 in Waukegan, Lake County, Illinois
Died: Living
Buried at:
Married: November 26, 1983
Janette L. Pearson
Born: 1945 in Chicago, Cook County, Illinois
Died: Living
Buried at:
Parents: Unknown

2   Louise Elizabeth Verhagen
Born: August 19, 1909 in Wisconsin
Died: December 12, 1973 in Marshfield, Wood County, Wisconsin
Buried at:
Married: October 22, 1936 in Bakerville, Wood County, WI
Roy John Lindow
Born: August 29, 1910 in Chili, Clark County, Wisconsin
Died: March 14, 1991 in Verboort, Washington County, Oregon
Buried at: Spencer Cemetery, Sherman, WI
Parents: John F. Lindow (1868-1949) and Ida J. Luckow (1875-1936)

2   Bertha Lucille Verhagen
Born: February 11, 1913 in Chili, Clark County, Wisconsin
Died: October 30, 1985 in Antioch, Lake County, Illinois
Buried at:
Married: September 30, 1931
William Henry Nebel
Born: March 25, 1913 in Wisconsin
Died: February 20, 1978 in Antioch, Lake County, Illinois
Buried at:
Parents: Ferdinand Nebel (1885 -1975) and Elizabeth M. Nebel (1887-1972)

3   William Adrian Nebel, Sr.
Born: April 22, 1932 in Chili, Clark County, Wisconsin
Died: December 01, 2001 in Hayward, Sawyer County, Wisconsin
Buried at: St. Francis Catholic Cemetery, Reserve, WI
Married: September 01, 1955 in Waukegan, Lake County, Illinois
Verona Wolfe
Born: December 03, 1930 in Hayward, Sawyer County, Wisconsin
Died: June 19, 2011 in Stillwater, Washington County, Minnesota
Buried at: St. Francis Catholic Cemetery, Reserve, WI
Parents: Charles Wolfe (1901-?) and Lillian DeMarr (1906-?)

3 James Willard Nebel
   Born: July 24, 1935 in Chili, Clark County, Wisconsin
   Died: March 30, 2013
   Buried at: Transfiguration Catholic Cemetery, Wauconda, IL
   Married: September 25, 1954 in Chicago, Cook County, Illinois
   Joan Annette Angellotti
   Born: 1935 in Chicago, Cook County, Illinois
   Died: Living
   Buried at:
   Parents: Unknown

3 Salene Louise Nebel
   Born: 1940 in Chili, Clark County, Wisconsin
   Died: Living
   Buried at:
   Married: October 03, 1959 in Antioch, Lake County, Illinois
   Donald J. Ruhl
   Born: May 14, 1938 in Chicago, Cook County, Illinois
   Died: May 06, 2009 in Merrill, Lincoln County, Wisconsin
   Buried at: St. Francis Xavier Catholic Cemetery, Merrill, WI
   Parents: Jacob J. Ruhl (1915-1962) and Mary Riegenborne (1919-1970)

3 Kathleen Mary Nebel
   Born: 1947 in Waukegan, Lake County, Illinois
   Died: Living
   Buried at:
   Married: January 20, 1968
   Paul George Hameau
   Born: 1944 in Racine, Racine County, Wisconsin
   Died: Living
   Buried at:
   Parents: Unknown

3 Ralph Charles Nebel
   Born: 1948 in Waukegan, Lake County, Illinois
   Died: Living
   Buried at:
   Married: Unknown
   Casey Nebel
   Born: Unknown
   Died: Living
   Buried at:
   Parents: Unknown

2 Frances Josephine Verhagen
   Born: May 10, 1914 in Chili, Clark County, Wisconsin
   Died: October 22, 1994 in Wisconsin Rapids, Wood County, Wisconsin
   Buried at: Restlawn Memorial Park, Wisconsin Rapids, WI
   Married: June 30, 1945 in Wisconsin Rapids, Wood County, Wisconsin

Edwin Arthur Fait
Born: September 16, 1912 in Milladore, Wood County, Wisconsin
Died: December 22, 1996 in Marathon County, Wisconsin
Buried at: Restlawn Memorial Park, Wisconsin Rapids, WI
Parents: Edward Fait (1878-1957) and Mary Fait (1879-1973)

3   Dennis Edwin Fait
     Born: 1946 in Wisconsin Rapids, Wood County, Wisconsin
     Died: Living
     Buried at:
     Married: December 28, 1974 in Milwaukee, Milwaukee County, Wisconsin
     Luann Listman
     Born: 1952 in Milwaukee, Milwaukee County, Wisconsin
     Died: Living
     Buried at:
     Parents: Unknown

3   Thomas Arthur Fait
     Born: 1951 in Wisconsin Rapids, Wood County, Wisconsin
     Died: Living
     Buried at:
     Married: August 09, 1986 in Bowman Lake, Minnesota
     Susan L. Ahlin
     Born: 1949 in Sioux Falls, Minnehaha County, South Dakota
     Died: Living
     Buried at:
     Parents: Unknown

3   Mary Kay Fait
     Born: 1956 in Wisconsin Rapids, Wood County, Wisconsin
     Died: Living
     Buried at:
     Married: October 17, 1981 in Wisconsin Rapids, Wood County, Wisconsin
     Scott Robert Peschke
     Born: 1956 in Milwaukee, Milwaukee County, Wisconsin
     Died: Living
     Buried at:
     Parents: Unknown

2 Louis John Verhagen
   Born: February 10, 1917 in Chili, Clark County, Wisconsin
   Died: March 17, 1974 in Forest Grove, Washington County, Oregon
   Buried at: Visitation Catholic Cemetery, Verboort, OR, SW row 5
   Married: October 30, 1945 in Verboort, Washington County, Oregon
   Marjorie Clara Vandervelden
   Born: February 16, 1920 in Forest Grove, Washington County, Oregon
   Died: March 03, 2013 in Portland, Multnomah County, Oregon
   Buried at: Visitation Catholic Cemetery, Verboort, OR, SW row 5
   Parents: Edward J. Vandervelden (1896-1947) & Mary C. Kemper (1896-1997)

2   <u>Howard George Verhagen</u>
Born: May 22, 1918 in Chili, Clark County, Wisconsin
Died: April 01, 1965 in Waukegan, Lake County, Illinois
Buried at: Ascension Catholic Cemetery, Libertyville, IL.
Married: Unknown
<u>Vera E. Steltenpohl</u>
Born: November 11, 1921 in Chili, Clark County, Wisconsin
Died: May 31, 1975 in Gurnee, Lake County, Illinois
Buried at: Ascension Catholic Cemetery, Libertyville, IL.
Parents: William H. Steltenpohl (1895-1966) and Rosa A. Duchow (1899-1964)

     3   <u>Bonita Marie Verhagen</u>
       Born: August 01, 1941 in Chili, Clark County, Wisconsin
       Died: June 08, 2013 in Owen, Clark County, Wisconsin
       Buried at: St. Mary Catholic Cemetery, Greenwood, WI
       Married: April 11, 1959 in Antioch, Lake County, Illinois
       <u>Ronald William Kitzhaber</u>
       Born: February 21, 1936 in Greenwood, Vernon County, Wisconsin
       Died: October 20, 2003 in Marshfield, Wood County, Wisconsin
       Buried at: St. Mary Catholic Cemetery, Greenwood, WI
       Parents: Lawrence A. Kitzhaber (1885-1965) and Mabel McDowell (1888-1970)

     3   <u>Virginia Mae Verhagen</u>
       Born: 1942 in Marshfield, Wood County, Wisconsin
       Died: Living
       Buried at:
       Married: September 29, 1962 in Waukegan, Lake County, Illinois
       <u>Howard Donald Opal</u>
       Born: 1938 in Waukegan, Lake County, Illinois
       Died: Living
       Buried at:
       Parents: Arthur A. Opal (1906-?) and Alma Opal (1910-?)

     3   <u>Eugene Verhagen</u>
       Born: Unknown
       Died: Living
       Buried at:
       Married: Unknown
       <u>Geri Verhagen</u>
       Born: Unknown
       Died: Living
       Buried at:
       Parents: Unknown

     3   <u>Gary H. Verhagen</u>
       Born: February 13, 1946 in Neillsville, Clark County, Wisconsin
       Died: December 27, 2003 in Zion, Lake County, Illinois
       Buried at: Ascension Catholic Cemetery, Libertyville, IL.
       Married: Unknown

                 Christina & Adrian Verhagen

3   Cheryl R. Verhagen
Born: 1951 in Neillsville, Clark County, Wisconsin
Died: Living
Buried at:
Married: June 21, 1986 in Minneapolis, Hennepin County, Minnesota
Alan J. Mathews
Born: 1946 in Minneapolis, Hennepin County, Minnesota
Died: Living
Buried at:
Parents: Unknown

2   Mabel Phyllis Verhagen
Born: May 04, 1920 in Chili, Clark County, Wisconsin
Died: August 13, 2008 in Medford, Taylor County, Wisconsin
Buried at: St. Stephen Catholic Cemetery, Chili, WI., row 4
Married: April 04, 1940 in Fremont, Clark County, Wisconsin
Alvord Harriman Selk
Born: December 13, 1917 in Chili, Clark County, Wisconsin
Died: September 11, 1967 in Marshfield, Wood County, Wisconsin
Buried at: St. Stephen Catholic Cemetery, Chili, WI., row 4
Parents: George C. Selk (1889-1967) & Effie R. Harriman (1891-1982)

3   Alvord Adrian Selk
Born: February 21, 1942 in Chili, Clark County, Wisconsin
Died: May 04, 2013 in Medford, Taylor County, Wisconsin
Buried at: Holy Rosary Catholic Cemetery, Medford, WI
Married: June 15, 1963 in Chili, Clark County, Wisconsin
Billie Lee Binning
Born: June 03, 1944 in Unity, Clark County, Wisconsin
Died: Living
Buried at:
Parents: Unknown

Christina & Adrian Verhagen

❧ Chapter Twelve ❧

Margaret VanDyke

The baby of the family came into this world on April 8, 1880. Margaret was born on the family farm in Grand Chute just as her previous three sisters and only brother. Margaret came to be known as "Maggie", and by the time she was two years old her two oldest sisters, Elizabeth and Frances, were married and out of the house. Maggie became an aunt for the first time at age three to Anna Marie Bernards (my great-grandmother); yes, age three, imagine that. She had six nieces and nephews by the time she turned 10 years old. Toward the late 1880s three of her older sisters, Frances, Anna, and Jane, moved out to Oregon, and by 1890 only she, Catherine, Martin and Christina remained in the farmhouse.

Image 12.01- Margaret Joosten in 1895.

In the mid-1890s, Maggie and her parents packed their bags, and more, and followed her three older sisters, for the promise of better soil for crops, and moved west to Verboort. Maggie's obituary states the trek west occurred in 1896 when she was 16. When the century turned to the 1900s, Maggie was 20 years old and shown in the census with her parents in Verboort.

Image 12.02- Walter & Margaret (Joosten) VanDyke Wedding Day Photo-1901

Within the first few years after arriving in Verboort, Maggie at age 21 married Walter VanDyke on May 9, 1901 at the Visitation Catholic Church in Verboort. Walter was the third of ten children born to his parents Theodore and Mary Ann (Bernards). He was born on September 27, 1876 in DePere, WI, which lies just west of Green Bay. Walter came to Oregon as a young boy in the early 1880s. He was a farmer by trade, and a very good one.

Two months following their first year of marriage, Maggie and Walter welcomed their first child into the world. Joseph Theodore was born on July 17, 1902 on the family farm. And then over the next eight years five more children would be added to the young family. First came George Theodore on November 12, 1903, then Wilhelmina Mary on March 29, 1905. Next was Albert Martin on July 6, 1906, and Theodore August on February 14, 1908. At the close of the decade Cecilia Josephine was born on November 16, 1909. Maggie and Walter had their hands full with four boys and two girls all under the age of eight, but this was only the beginning of an amazing journey of creating their legacy.

In the beginning, the VanDykes made their home in Verboort, and more than likely rented land to live on and farm. Credible stories have been written and told that in 1904 Maggie's parents assisted the young couple with the purchase of 40-acres of what was known as Firwood Farm on Porter Rd. near Cornelius. A few years later in 1907 Walter's parents deeded Maggie and Walter 40-acres of the lot next to the one they already owned in Firwood Farm.

When the 1910 census was taken, Maggie and Walter had been married for nine years now, and had four boys and two girls in their rapidly growing family. They lived near Maggie's second oldest sister Frances Bernards and her family who lived on Martin Rd., the next road over to the east from the road on which the church was located. Walter was a farmer, and as mentioned earlier they owned the farm they grew crops on. As we know,

Joseph is the oldest and was probably in the 1st grade at Visitation Catholic School at this time. Of course the rest of his brothers and sister were all at home. During the 1910s, another five children were added to the VanDyke family. The seventh child born was Raymond Wilfred who came into the world on September 11, 1911. Numbers eight and nine were Christine Margaret and Clarence George born on May 29, 1913 and December 11, 1914, respectively. Next were Loretta M. born on December 7, 1916 and Howard Walter born October 20, 1918 who became children numbers 10 and 11. Of these eleven kids this brought a total to six boys and five girls. Whoa!

When the roaring 1920s decade began, Maggie was now in her late 30s and Walter in his early 40s. They still resided on the same farm they have owned now for many years. Joseph is age 17 now and attending school, most likely high school in Forest Grove. It was fairly uncommon for kids to go onto high school at this time in history. Usually the children of the family ended their formal education after the 8th grade and began full time work on the farm. At age 16, George is out of school, and working on the farm helping his father. The rest of the children, except for the youngest, were attending school. The VanDykes lived near the John and Cornelia Peters family and the Jacob and Amelia Sonnen family; both likewise were farmers.

The year 1920 was very historic when it came to ending limitations of voter's rights, especially those against women, across America. This was a decades long passionate effort began by Susan B. Anthony and Elizabeth Cady Stanton who first drafted a constitutional amendment, which was first introduced in the Senate in 1878 by Republican California Senator Aaron A. Sargent, who was a devoted women's rights advocate. Proposals went to vote numerous times through the years, only to be defeated. Toward the end of the 1910s there was considerable bipartisan desire to pass a Constitutional Amendment prior to the 1920 general election. Finally, under the leadership of President Woodrow Wilson, who called a special session of the Congress, a proposal was brought before the House again. On May 21, 1919, it passed the House, and on June 4, 1919, it passed the Senate. When amendments to the Constitution are proposed it becomes part of the Constitution as soon as three-fourths of the States have ratified it. Our beloved State of Wisconsin was one of the first three states to ratify the amendment on June 10, 1919. Our other favorite State of Oregon was the 25th state who ratified on January 13, 1920.

Image 12.03- Elizabeth Cady Stanton (seated) and Susan B. Anthony about 1900

With the new decade ringing in, the next child to come along was Florence, who was born about two and a half years following her brother Howard on February 13, 1921. The 13th child was Leona Ida who came next on July 15, 1922, and then two years later the 14th and final child born to the very large VanDyke family was Ralph John who was born on June 24, 1924. Interestingly enough Maggie was 44 years old following the birth of Ralph, and she was 22 years old when her first child, Joseph, was born. Ralph was also the last grandchild to Joseph and Nellie, whom they were not privileged to meet. He was born an incredible forty-one years later than his oldest cousin, Anna Vanderzanden (maiden name Bernards). And as we know the fourteen children, eight boys and six girls, came in a span of 22 years, which is simply amazing given there were no twins born into the family.

After all the children were born, Maggie and Walter were not only busy raising children, but now had their hands full with planning weddings. The three oldest boys, now men, were married over the next few years. Joseph was the first to get married. His nuptials to Theresa H. Cop occurred on February 16, 1926 at the St. Francis of Assisi Catholic Church in Roy, OR. More than two years later George married Ethel M. Kummer on December 29, 1928 in Forest Grove, OR, and before the close of the 1920s decade, Albert was joined in matrimony with Marian C. Miller on May 28, 1929 at Visitation Catholic Church in Verboort.

Maggie and Walter's first of many grandchildren came from the proud parents of Joseph and Theresa. Elizabeth Jean VanDyke was born on May 9, 1927 in Verboort. What this also meant was Maggie and Walter's youngest child Ralph became an uncle for the first time at the young tender age of two. A couple of years after Elizabeth was born, Joe and Theresa purchased a 100-acre dairy farm in Gaston, OR in 1928, and moved onto the property in 1929. Gaston is located about ten miles south of Verboort on Hwy 47. In a Rural Living feature story in the Hillsboro Argus on May 12, 1981, Joe reveals to the reporter he developed a love affair working with horse teams, and often worked with horses to plow fields beginning at a young age when he *"worked my folks' team after school and on weekends when I had to reach up to the handles on the walking plow."* Joe also used horse teams to drive a wagon filled with milk cans to a milk processing plant on the south edge of Hillsboro. Their dairy farm included 65 head of Jersey and Holstein cows, which they sold in 1966 when Joe went into active retirement. At this point, Joe purchased his first team of registered Belgian draft horses from a well-known expert in Prineville, OR. Belgian draft horses are very big horses, getting upwards of 1,900 pounds and 17 hands (68 inches) high. Joe and Theresa enjoyed their Belgian draft horses so much they worked together as a team to show them in horse shows around the state; often pulling a show wagon. Joe and Theresa led a busy retirement, and were active members of several farming related associations, including the Washington County Sherriff's Posse for 35-plus years, the Oregon Draft Horse Association, and the Oregon Dairy Breeders Association. Joe even found time for civic duty and served as Washington County Commissioner from 1963-1967.

VanDyke Walter	Head	0		R	yes	M	W	53	M	24	No	yes	[illegible]
— Margaret	Wife H				x	F	W	60	M	31	No	yes	[illegible]
— Minnie	Daughter				x	F	W	25	S		No	yes	Oregon
— Theodore	Son				x	M	W	22	S		No	yes	Oregon
— Cecilia	Daughter				x	F	W	20	S		No	yes	Oregon
— Raymond	Son				x	M	W	18	S		No	yes	Oregon
— Christine	Daughter				x	F	W	16	S		yes	yes	Oregon
— Clarence	Son				x	M	W	15	S		[illegible]	yes	Oregon
— Loretta	Daughter				x	F	W	13	S		yes	yes	Oregon
— Howard	Son				x	M	W	11	S		yes	yes	Oregon
— Florence	Daughter				x	F	W	9	S		yes	yes	Oregon
— Leona	Daughter				x	F	W	7	S		yes	yes	Oregon
— Ralph	Son				x	M	W	[illegible]	S		No		Oregon

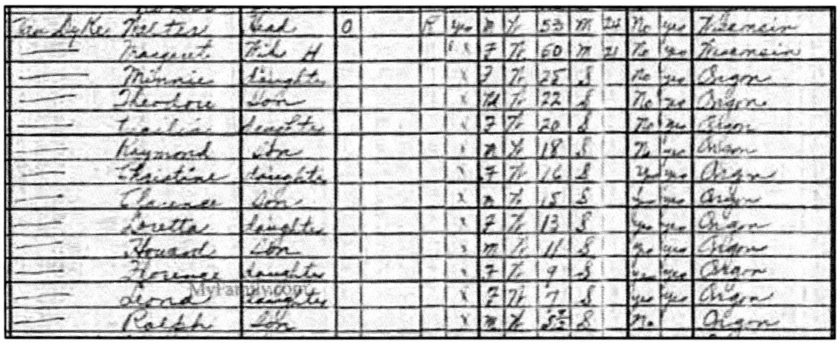

Image 12.04- Walter and Maggie VanDyke Family in the 1930 Verboort, Washington County, OR Census, sheet 1B

At the turn into the 1930s decade, Maggie and Walter were found in the 1930 census with 11 of their children still living at home. Minnie (25), Theodore (22), Cecilia (20), and Raymond (18) were all out of school, and had jobs while living at home. Minnie was a laborer at a local greenhouse, Theodore was a hardware salesman, Cecilia was a housekeeper for a local family, and Raymond worked at home as a farmer. All the other children were attending school with the exception of young Ralph. How about the older kids? Joseph and Theresa, as we know, were living on their farm in Gaston. George, his wife Ethel, and their new born son George Wayne were living in Verboort and renting their home. George was employed as a Foreman with a refrigeration business. Albert, his wife Marian, and their first child Burton are living in Forest Grove. They were renting their home, and Albert ("Bert") was employed at the cannery as a Foreman. Bert worked for B.E. Maling at his fruit and vegetable cannery on West Baseline in Hillsboro on the same property where the Washington County Jail is located today. Bert was promoted to Plant Superintendent. Following Mr. Maling's early death, the plant was sold to Birdseye Frozen Foods. At some point in the late 1930s or early 1940s, Bert was transferred to Walla Walla, WA. So he and Marian moved their family there where Bert continued to work for Birdseye as Plant Manager. He retired in 1964 after an impressive 40 year career. Minnie had a long career early in her life at the cannery too. She spent 12 years working for Mr. Maling starting at age 16, spanning from about 1921 to 1933.

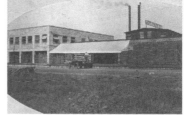

Image 12.05- B.E. Maling Cannery in Hillsboro, OR.

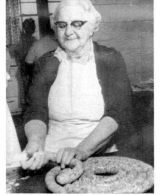

Image 12.06- Margaret (Joosten) VanDyke preparing sausage for Sausage & Kraut Dinner.

Church fundraisers have been around for decades, and normally consisted of chicken or turkey dinners back in the day, and these campaigns at Visitation Catholic Church were no different. In November 1934, the first annual dinner was held with a traditional menu. After four years of the same thing, Maggie offered a suggestion for a menu change to sausage and sauerkraut; no other church served a delicious sausage dinner. The dinner committee bought into the idea, and the first sausage and kraut dinner took place on Tuesday November 5, 1938 in the parish hall of the Visitation Church. Maggie and Walter offered the group of ladies the use of their kitchen to prepare the dinner menu, and even donated the beef for the sausage. All of the food on the menu was grown and hand-prepared by the church community. Along with the sausage and kraut there were green beans, mash potatoes, salad, applesauce, a roll, and apple and lemon meringue pies for dessert. Dinners were priced at 50 cents, and 25 cents for schoolchildren. The first year 150 dinners were served with 198 pounds of sausage and ten gallons of sauerkraut, and it was still not enough to feed everyone. This new idea started an amazing tradition that is still flourishing today. In 1974, the 40th anniversary of the dinner, the number of guests served had ballooned to 5,000. Dinners were priced at $5.00 for adults and $2.50 for children. Six tons of sausage, eight tons of sauerkraut, 150 gallons of applesauce, 800 dozens rolls, and other large amounts of food were on the menu for patrons. Today the popularity of this amazing event continues to grow with the 80th anniversary to be celebrated in 2014. Now 8,000 to 10,000 guests are served who consume 15 tons of sausage and 2,000 pounds of sauerkraut at $15 per adult; do the math and this fundraiser brings in the cash. And the menu has remained the same all these years.

There are some interesting facts about some people who have been involved in the Sausage & Kraut Dinner. In the early days the dinner was held in the basement at the Catholic Order of Foresters Hall. The large two-story white structure, built in 1930, sitting about 100 yards down the road from the church, and across Heesacker Road from the church property. For many years Ed Kindel was asked by the dinner's sausage committee to use his smokehouse located on his farm a couple miles north of the church. Ed operated his "Kindel's Verboort Sausage, Inc." business on his farm too. In 1969, Ed built a brand new building to expand production of his famous sausage. The 3,900 square foot structure was built across the street from the church. Today, Duyck Machine Inc. occupies the building. Sausage making and smoking continued from Ed's new building for many more years to come, which was good because more and more people were coming to the dinner. The Oregonian printed stories seemingly every year promoting the famous local dinner. In the October 30, 1973 edition, Ralph VanDyke, the youngest son of Maggie, who was on the sausage making committee, mentioned to the story reporter the sausage recipe was much the same his mother used. It called for a ratio of 120 pounds of beef and 80 pounds of pork. George VanHandel, whose wife Frances (maiden name VanDyke) was Maggie's niece, was in charge of the smokehouse for the previous 15 years, 1943 to 1958. He revealed there was enough cabbage produced and shredded to fill 34 barrels, which was set aside six weeks prior to the dinner event to cure. The sausage was smoked with vine maple, which turned the sausage into a deep red color. In the same story Margaret Bernards, another niece of Maggie's and daughter of Maggie's older sister Frances, was interviewed too. She mentioned the different booths available for visitors to shop at (which today is in the school gym), and that she was part of the group of older ladies who made the patchwork quilt to be raffled off.

What Maggie first suggested, and helped create and build into an awesome dinner has turned out to be one of the most successful annual fundraisers in the Archdiocese. Proceeds from these dinners have produced wealthy results, which have funded tuition for children to attend the school, major capital expenditures, and construction projects like rebuilding the church after it burned to the ground in February 1941. For decades the dinner has been a single day event always held on the first Saturday in November. If you have not been to this tremendous event, you should make plans to go.

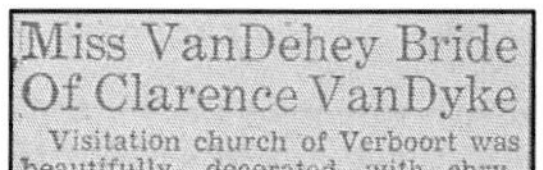

Maggie & Walter's ninth child Clarence married Eunice Marie Vandehey, daughter of Edward and Angeline (Hermens) Vandehey, on November 29, 1939 at the Visitation Catholic Church in Verboort. They started their early married life living with Eunice's father in Verboort since he was living on his own at this time. He had been married twice, and both of his wives passed away at an early age in the 1920s. The 1940 census reveals Clarence completed one year of high school and Eunice obtained an 8th grade education. Interestingly enough, Clarence and Eunice are pretty closely related. Eunice's step mother Wilhelmina (her father Edward's 2nd wife) and her husband Clarence are first cousins. Clarence's mother is Maggie VanDyke, and Wilhelmina's mother Jane Hermens, of course, were sisters; an interesting connection.

Miss VanDehey Bride Of Clarence VanDyke

Visitation church of Verboort was beautifully decorated with chrysanthemums, streamers of blue and white and lighted candles on November 29, when Miss Eunice Vandehey, daughter of Edward Vandehey, became the bride of Mr. Clarence VanDyke, son of Mr. and Mrs. Walter VanDyke. Rev. Father Jonas officiated at the nuptial mass.

A wedding gown of white satin with insets of lace extending from shoulder to the hem of her long train was worn by the bride. Her full-length veil was held in place with a coronet of lilies and pearls. She carried her mother's prayerbook with corsages of orchid and bouvardia with white streamers.

Miss Eileen Vandehey was bridesmaid for her sister and wore a dress of blue taffeta with hoop skirt. She carried an old fashioned bouquet of roses, sweet peas and bouvardia.

Raymond VanDyke of Dallas was best man for his brother and Howard VanDyke was usher.

Mr. and Mrs. VanDyke will make their home in Sheridan.

Image 12.07- Clarence VanDyke and Eunice Vandehey Wedding Announcement, Hillsboro Argus; 12/07/1939

Clarence and Eunice purchased a 135-acre parcel of land in 1940, and operated a dairy farm there for decades on NW Evers Rd. in Verboort just down the road from the Visitation Cemetery. They retired from farming in 1976. Today their daughter Vicki, her husband Charles, and their children operate the same farm, nowadays known as Sun Gold Farms, raising crops of organic fruits, vegetables, and flowers. On August 1, 2011, Ed Langolis of the Catholic Sentinel wrote a wonderful article about a day in the life of Vicki and the farm.

Clarence was a longtime director of the famed Verboort Sausage Dinner, taking it over from his mother, and he was also choir director at Visitation Church while Eunice played the organ. They must have been quite the musical duo. Clarence passed away on October 29, 2005 at the age of 90, and after celebrating 65 years of marriage with Eunice. Wow! That is an amazing legacy. As of 2015, Eunice is still living.

When the calendar turned into the new decade of the 1940s, another census was taken. And of course Maggie and Walter were still living on their Verboort farm, but now with only the five youngest children at home. Loretta was 23; Howard age 21; Florence was 19, and all three of them out of high school. Leona was 17 and a senior in high school, and Ralph age 15 and a sophomore. Howard was doing the majority of the farming, as his parents were now age 60 and older.

As for the older kids who were out of the house, Joseph and Theresa remained on their farm in Gaston, now listed in the census with their first five children, Elizabeth (age 12), Alvin (age 11), Vernon (age 8), Beverly (age 5), and Janice (age 1). Their farm was valued at $1,500. George and Ethel were living on Haynes Rd. in Forest Grove with all of their five children. They owned their home valued at $2,000. George now employed as a Foreman at the cannery. It could be possible he was working with his brother Albert at the same cannery in Hillsboro. Minnie and her husband Henry were living in the Purdin District, which is near the Verboort and Roy communities, with Henry's father Casper; both of whom were full-time farmers. Minnie had a four-year high school education, and Henry had an 8th grade level education.

In the early 1930s, Albert and his wife Marian moved into Hillsboro from Forest Grove where he was closer to his job as the Superintendent at the Maling Cannery. The census reveals he earned a very respectable $3,275 during 1939. They owned their home, which was valued at $4,500. Albert had a 10th grade education, and Marian finished after 8th grade. Theodore and his wife Frances were living in Verboort with their five children, and owned their home. Theodore continued to work as a salesman for the hardware store, in addition to doing some farming. He earned $1,200 in 1939, and both of them had 8th grade educations. The family had Leon Nackers (age 15) living with them as their farmhand. They lived near Theodore's first cousin Ernest Hermens and his wife Ida.

Thursday, October 10, 1940

Walter VanDyke, County Resident 60 Years, Dies

Walter VanDyke, 64, resident of Washington county virtually all his life, died Tuesday at his farm home on Forest Grove route 2, after an illness of over two years. Funeral services will be held at 9:30 a. m. Friday in the Visitation church at Verboort, Father Jonas officiating, with interment in the Visitation church cemetery. Forest Grove Undertaking company is in charge of arrangements.

Surviving are the widow, Margaret, Forest Grove route 2, and fourteen children, George Theodore and Clarence, all at Forest Grove; Howard and Ralph, Forest Grove route 2; Joseph, Gaston; Bert, Hillsboro, and Raymond, Dallas; Mrs. Henry Holsmeyer, Forest Grove; Mrs. George Duyck, Roy; Mrs. Ed Sahlfeld, Hillsboro, and Loretta, Florence and Leona, all of Forest Grove route 2; three brothers, John, Henry, and William, and three sisters, Mrs. William Verboort, Mrs. William Vanderveiden and Mrs. Albert Jensen, all of Forest Grove.

Walter VanDyke was born on September 27, 1876, in Wisconsin. He came to this county with his parents at the age of four years and had been a resident continuously since that time. He was married at Verboort in 1901 and at that time started farming. He had been retired for the past few years.

Two of his sons are employed at the R. L. Maling plant here. Bert is plant superintendent and George is night foreman. Rosary was held at the Forest Grove Undertaking company chapel Wednesday evening and another will be held tonight (Thursday) at 8 o'clock in the family home.

Image 12.08- Obituary of Walter VanDyke Obit, Hillsboro Argus, 10/10/1940

Cecilia and her husband George were living in the Roy community with their first seven children, and renting some farm land for $15 per month, which they were farming. Cecilia completed four years of high school, and George obtained an 8th grade education. Raymond lived with Donald & Matilda Gabbert (age 29 & 27) as a boarder in Dallas, OR, which is west of Salem. Donald was a high school teacher in Dallas. Raymond obtained his Bachelor's Degree, and worked as a part-time teacher at the high school, and earned $540 in 1939. The Gabbert's also had another boarder by the name of Charles Hubber (age 24), who was a full-time teacher at the high school.

More marriages happened during the war years, five in fact. At the start of the decade Raymond married Edna E. Meihoff on August 17, 1940 in Seattle, WA. Next Howard was wedded to Evelyn M. Plass on November 13, 1941 in Hillsboro just before the USA was pulled into World War II. On November 29, 1945, Florence married Clarence J. Waibel in Hillsboro following his return from the War. Loretta married Aloysius R. Vanderzanden on January 3, 1946 in Roy, OR after he returned from serving in the War, and six months later Leona married Edward L. Puncochar on June 3, 1946 in Verboort.

In the fall of 1940, and 11 days following his 64th birthday, sad news came to the community with the passing of Walter. He had not been doing so well for the past couple of years. According to his death certificate, he had recently been diagnosed with pernicious anemia, in addition to suffering from asthma. Webster's defines *"pernicious"* as *"highly injurious or destructive: deadly."* Pernicious anemia is a condition in which the body cannot make enough healthy red blood cells because it doesn't have enough vitamin B12. And back in the 1940s this condition was often deadly from of the lack of vitamin B12 treatments. Today this illness is easily treatable with vitamin B12 supplements. Walter passed away on October 8, 1940, one day following the birth of my father, Gilbert J. Shaw. He was a man who truly made a difference in people's lives he touched, and brought value to the community in which he lived in. Walter was laid to rest in the third row of the southwest section of the Visitation Catholic Cemetery in Verboort. May he rest in peace.

Remains of Fire-Gutted Church

As I mentioned earlier, the Visitation Church burned to the ground. The awful news hit the VanDyke household and greater Verboort area very hard with the tragic loss of their beloved church to fire. On February 9, 1941, a blaze in the middle of the night leveled the 58 year old church, which was the historic site of the first mass said in Washington County. Although the cause was unknown, the fire was suspected to have started near the furnace, and destroyed everything inside the church including the memorial stained glass windows. Area residents and firemen from the Forest Grove and Cornelius fire departments did luckily manage to save numerous priests vestments, twelve statues, and a large crucifix. According to a newspaper article, the firemen saved the other church buildings on the property, including the rectory, school, and nun's convent with the help of their "pumper" fire trucks. More gracious help came from area residents who brought more water in milk cans to refill the pumper truck tanks. Although the church had fire insurance coverage for $9,000, it only amounted to a fraction of the rebuilding costs. So the parishioners were asked to donate the rest, and to do so without the Archdiocese going into debt. A newspaper reported the parish raised $30,000 in one week's time,

Image 12.09- Fire Ravaged Visitation Church in Verboort (Feb 1941)

a very noteworthy beginning to the fundraising effort. To save money, it was decided to eliminate the plastering of the inside walls, and the brick exterior.

The groundbreaking ceremony took place on October 7, 1948 for the new church on the original spot of the previous church building lost in the fire. In December 1948, it was reported the church was about half way completed when a 1,000 pound bell was ordered for the 71-foot bell tower, which featured a state-of-the-art electrical bell ringing system. The new church was formally dedicated by Archbishop Edward D. Howard on Thanksgiving Day November 24, 1949. The Catholic Sentinel reported the dedication Mass was celebrated by the Archbishop, Pastor Fr. Robert S. Neugebauer, Fr. Edmund Vanderzanden, and Fr. Ervin Vandehey. The new church is a Romanesque style in the shape of a crucifix with a beautiful arched ceiling. The alter and communion rail were made of marble imported from Italy and France. And to top off the perfect church, the large life-size crucifix, saved from the fire, hung above the alter.

Image 12.10- Visitation Catholic Church (2004)

The total cost of the new church came to $134,730 with many parishioners donating money for the beautiful stained glass windows, Stations of the Cross, Confessionals, the Estey electric organ, and other cherished items. Maggie and her sister-in-law Alice (Evers) VanDyke purchased the organ and dedicated it to the memory of their husbands. As we know Walter passed away in 1940, his brother William died in 1942.

There are many members of the family who served our country during World War II, and all are heroes for their sacrifice and valor. I would like to draw special attention to one such war hero. Clarence Waibel, the husband of Florence, served our country for 22 months with the 106th Calvary Reconnaissance Squadron of the US Army. Clarence was part of the troops who landed on Omaha Beach in Normandy, France shortly after the major invasion on June 6, 1944, and what history would call D-Day. This is where he worked on reconnaissance and as a radio operator. What is remarkable is he was awarded the coveted Silver Star for his bravery while he saw action against the Germans in Forret de Parroy, France. A Hillsboro Argus newspaper article details the story about this fateful day. On October 4, 1944, Clarence was a Technician Fourth Grade when his platoon was attacked with heavy machine gun fire by the Germans, who were entrenched, and concealed in their position. The attack pinned down the platoon, and then Clarence noticed his Sergeant was seriously wounded. As written in the newspaper story and as quoted from his award citation, Clarence "*without* hesitation and with complete disregard for his own safety, exposed himself to direct fire to reach the wounded soldier, and administer first aid that saved his life. Realizing that the balance of the men were in grave danger of being killed and that the entire mission would be lost unless this key position was eliminated, Technician Fourth Grade Waibel crawled under the withering, enemy machine gun fire to within twenty yards of the positon, threw a hand grenade, which destroyed the gun and crew. Then with heroic fortitude, he rushed a German bazooka position, forcing their surrender and flushed the remaining enemy riflemen from their concealment." Wow, what a story! But it does not end here. The French Government also awarded Clarence with their prestigious Croix de Guerre decoration. The Croix de Guerre (English translation: Cross of War) is a military decoration of France. It was first created in 1915 and consists of a square-cross medal on two crossed swords, hanging from a ribbon with various degree pins. The Croix de Guerre was also commonly bestowed on foreign military forces allied to France, and awarded to those soldiers who distinguish themselves by acts of heroism involving combat with the enemy. Clarence graciously accepted these awards, and then modestly said "a lot of boys did a lot more than I did without getting medals." Thank you Clarence for your service.

Image 12.11- Obituary of Margaret (Joosten) VanDyke

As the 1950s turned into the 1960s decade, Maggie was in her late 70s. It was now nineteen years following Walter's passing. And following a short illness she was hospitalized for, she sadly passed away at age 79 on January 12, 1960. She was a true legend who led a full and happy life, and was most well-known for her decades of dedication to the Verboort Sausage & Kraut Dinner and Visitation Church. She was laid to rest next to her husband in the third row of the southwest section of the Visitation Catholic Cemetery in Verboort. May she rest in eternal peace.

Now for some amazing fun facts. The most impressive and one I have never seen before is the number of grandchildren that came from the VanDyke's 14 children. Maggie and Walter had 91 grandchildren, yes 91! But by the time Maggie passed away in 1960 she had 85 grandchildren to keep track of and birthdays to remember. I bet she had a great tracking system too that did not involve computers!

After looking at the marriages of Margaret and Walter's 14 children, there is amazing longevity. The average length of marriage is a remarkable 57 years! And eight of these marriages lasted 60 years or longer. The longest marriage is 65 happy years. And there are three couples holding the title of longest marriage. They are Raymond and Edna, Clarence and Eunice, and Leona and Edward, but Ralph and Virginia are both still living and are at 63 years of marriage and going strong in 2015.

There is also great longevity in the genes when it comes to length of life, especially with the females. Minnie held the record for many years living 101 years, 10 months, but now her sister Christine holds the record at 101 years, 11 months and still going strong in April 2015.

***

There were a large number of good men and women of the VanDyke Family who served our fine country in the military. They are:

- ❖ Roland H. Duyck - Served in the US Army from 1954-1955, and then US Army Reserves for 8 years.
- ❖ Walter R. Duyck - Enlisted in US Army and served in Germany during the Cold War.
- ❖ Joseph A. Hertel - Served in the U.S. Army as a Corporal during the Korean conflict and was discharged in 1954.
- ❖ Aloysius R. Vanderzanden - Served in the US Army as a Staff Sergeant with the 38th Bomb Squad in the South Pacific during World War II.
- ❖ Anthony E. VanDyke – Currently serving in the US navy as a Colonel. Served in Kuwait during Operation Desert Storm in the 13th Marine Expeditionary Unit (MEU).
- ❖ Clarence J. Waibel - Served as a Technician 4th Grade in the US Army during World War II. Silver Star and Croix de Guerre award given for heroism.

Image 12.12- Walter & Margaret (Joosten) VanDyke Family Photo - about 1910.

Image 12.13- Walter VanDyke Death Certificate

Image 12.14- Margaret VanDyke Verboort Sausage Dinner Photo

Image 12.15- Walter & Margaret VanDyke Headstone Visitation Catholic Cemetery, SW section, row 3

Image 12.16- Christine (VanDyke) & Edward Sahlfeld 50th Anniversary News Article, Hillsboro Argus, 04-25-1989

Image 12.17- Clarence G. & Eunice M. (Vandehey) VanDyke 60th Anniversary News Article, Hillsboro Argus, 12-21-1999

Joseph VanDyke, horse enthusiast

Joseph T.
VANDYKE
1902-1987

GASTON—Joseph T. VanDyke, 84, Gaston, a former member of the Washington County Board of Commissioners, died June 2, 1987, at Camelot Care Center in Forest Grove following a long illness.

Recitation of the Holy Rosary and Mass of Christian Burial will be Friday at 7:30 p.m. at St. Anthony's Roman Catholic Church in Forest Grove, with the Rev. Dennis O'Donovan officiating.

Vault entombment will be in Mt. View Memorial Gardens in Forest Grove. A family service will be held Saturday at 9:30 a.m.

Mr. VanDyke was born July 17, 1902, in Forest Grove, a son of Walter and Margaret Joosten VanDyke. On Feb. 16, 1926, he married Theresa Cop in St. Francis Catholic Church in Roy and they celebrated their 61st wedding anniversary earlier this year.

Mr. VanDyke received his education at Verboort Grade School and Forest Grove High School. He farmed his entire life and had lived on the same farm in Gaston since 1929.

He was an avid lover of Belgian draft horses and was well-known in the area for his participation with his horses in the Oregon State Fair, Washington County Fair, Portland Rose Parade, Forest Grove Gay 90s Parade and Hillsboro Happy Days Parade.

He also drove the hay wagon at the Forest Grove Corn Feed.

He was a past Washington County Commissioner, a committee member of ASC and a member of the Washington County Planning Commission.

Mr. VanDyke was a member of St. Anthony's Catholic Church, a charter member of the Washington County Sheriff's Posse and a charter member of the Oregon Draft Horse Association.

Survivors include his wife, Theresa VanDyke, Gaston; three sons, Alvin VanDyke, Gaston, Vernon VanDyke, Forest Grove, and John VanDyke, Woodbridge, Va.; three daughters, Betty Meiwes, Springfield, Beverly Meeuwsen, Forest Grove, and Janice Matias.

Also surviving are 21 grandchildren, 10 great-grandchildren; six brothers, George VanDyke, Clarence VanDyke and Ralph VanDyke, all of Forest Grove, Albert VanDyke, Walla Walla, Wash., Raymond VanDyke, Gales Creek, and Howard VanDyke, Cornelius; and six sisters, Minnie Holzmeyer, Forest Grove, Cecilia Duyck, Roy, Christine Sahlfeld, Florence Waibel and Leona Pun-

Image 12.18- Joseph T. VanDyke, Obituary, Hillsboro Argus, 06-04-1987, page 8A

Theresa VanDyke, life-long resident

FOREST GROVE—A Mass of Christian Burial was Monday morning for Theresa Helen VanDyke, 93, Forest Grove.

Mrs. VanDyke, a former resident of Gaston, died July 8, 1998, at Tuality Community Hospital in Hillsboro.

VanDYKE

Monday's services were at St. Anthony's Catholic Church, with Father Ed Coleman as celebrant.

Vault entombment was in Mountain View Memorial Gardens.

A reception was held at the parish center and vigil services were Sunday evening at Forest Grove Memorial Chapel.

Mrs. VanDyke was born Jan. 27, 1905, in Greenville, a daughter of Henry and Elizabeth Spierng Cop. She was educated at St. Francis School in Roy and St. Mary's School in Beaverton.

On Feb. 16, 1926, she married Joseph T. VanDyke in Roy. They moved to a farm in Gaston in 1929. She was a homemaker and helped her husband on the farm.

Her husband died in 1987 after 61 years of marriage.

Mrs. VanDyke was a life-long member of the Catholic Church and a member of St. Anthony's Church. She also was a member of the Altar Society.

She enjoyed going to Reno and playing bingo.

Mrs. VanDyke was a member of the Oregon Draft Horse Association and Washington County Sheriff's Posse Auxiliary.

She drove horses at both the Washington County Fair and Oregon State Fair and earned numerous awards for participation in cart and team classes.

She also was a member of the Forest Grove Senior Center.

Survivors include three sons and two daughters-in-law, Alvin VanDyke, Cornelius, Vernon and Doreen VanDyke, Gaston, and John and Nancy VanDyke, Woodbridge, Va.; three daughters and sons-in-law, Betty and Bill Meiwes, Springfield, Beverley and Lyle Meeuwsen, Forest Grove, and Janice and Eugene Matias, Cornelius; 21 grandchildren; 27 great-grandchildren; one great-great-grandson; her caregivers, Shannon and Larry Baker, Forest Grove; and numerous nieces and nephews.

She was preceded in death by five brothers and five sisters.

The family suggests memorial contributions to St. Anthony's Catholic Church, 1660 Elm St., Forest Grove, OR 97116, or to Forest Grove Senior Center, P.O. Box 784, Forest Grove, OR 97116.

Forest Grove Memorial Chapel was in charge of arrangements.

Image 12.19- Theresa H (Cop) VanDyke Obituary, Hillsboro Argus, 07-14-1998, page 10A

Ethel VanDyke

11-17-83

Ethel
VANDYKE
1906-1983

VERBOORT—Funeral Mass for Ethel Mary VanDyke was Monday at Visitation Catholic Church with the Rev. James Harris of Visitation Church officiating. Mrs. VanDyke died Thursday, Nov. 17, 1983, in Forest Grove Community Hospital. She was 76.

Vault interment was in Visitation Cemetery. Recitation of the Holy Rosary was held Sunday, Nov. 20, at the church.

Mrs. VanDyke was born Dec. 8, 1906, in McCook, Neb., the daughter of Joseph C. and Luzetta Wilson Kummer. She was married to George T. VanDyke on Dec. 29, 1928, in St. Anthony's Roman Catholic Church, Forest Grove, and lived in Verboort for 55 years.

She moved to Oregon from Nebraska as a small child. She attended St. Paul School and graduated from Hillsboro High School. She attended Monmouth Normal School (Western Oregon State College), earning a teaching certificate. At age 19 she taught at Jacktown and Springhill Schools.

After she was married, she moved to Verboort, where she lived until her death. She was a member of the Visitation Church, Visitation Altar Society and the Archdiocese Council of Catholic Women.

She and Mr. VanDyke celebrated their 50th wedding anniversary in December 1978.

She is survived by her husband, George, of Verboort; sons Wayne of Mt. Angel, Gene of Forest Grove, James of Hillsboro, and David of Chehalis, Wash.; daughter Joanne Scabery of Portland; brothers Harold Kummer of Hillsboro and Lawrence Kummer of Tigard; 19 grandchildren and one great-grandchild.

Forest Grove Memorial Chapel is in charge of arrangements.

The family suggests contributions to the Visitation Church Parish Center Building Fund.

Image 12.21- Ethel M. (Kummer) VanDyke Obituary, Hillsboro Argus, 11-22-1983

George VanDyke, life-long resident

FOREST GROVE—George T. VanDyke, 87, Forest Grove, died Jan. 5, 1991, at his home of causes related to aging.

A Mass of Christian Burial was celebrated this morning at Visitation Roman Catholic Church in Verboort, with the Rev. Frank Walsh and the Rev. (retired) James Harris officiating.

Interment followed in Visitation Cemetery in Verboort.

Mr. VanDyke was born Nov. 12, 1903, in Verboort, a son of Walter and Margaret Joosten VanDyke. He was educated at Visitation School and on Dec. 29, 1928, he married Ethel Kummer in Forest Grove. She died Nov. 17, 1983.

Mr. VanDyke lived on the family property his entire life. He built a new home in 1932 across from the family home and had lived there since.

He worked at Birds Eye Cannery for 37 years and retired in 1954 as assistant manager.

Mr. VanDyke was a member of Visitation Catholic Church and the Knights of Columbus.

Survivors include four sons, Wayne VanDyke, Mt. Angel, Gene VanDyke, Forest Grove, James VanDyke, Rock Creek and David VanDyke, Chehalis, Wash.; a daughter, Mrs. Charles (Joanne) Scabery, Portland; 19 grandchildren; and five great-grandchildren.

Also surviving are four brothers, Clarence VanDyke and Ralph VanDyke, both of Forest Grove, Howard VanDyke, Cornelius, and Raymond VanDyke, Gales Creek; and six sisters, Minnie Holzmeyer, Forest Grove, Cecilia Duyck and Loretta Vanderzanden, both of Roy, and Christine Sahlfeld, Florence Waibel and Leona Puncochar, all of Hillsboro.

The family suggests memorial contributions to the Visitation Parish Cemetery Fund.

Forest Grove Memorial Chapel was in charge of arrangements.

Image 12.20- George T. VanDyke Obituary, Hillsboro Argus, 01-08-1991

Image 12.22- George T. & Ethel M. VanDyke Headstone, Visitation Catholic Cemetery, SE section, row 5

'Bert' Van Dyke, former resident

Hillsboro Argus 7-25-89

WALLA WALLA, Wash.—Albert M. "Bert" Van Dyke, 83, Walla Walla, died July 18, 1989, at a convalescent center.

Mr. Van Dyke was born in Forest Grove and had lived in Verboort. He was manager of the Ray Maling Cannery in Hillsboro before moving to Walla Walla about 1946.

A funeral mass was held Friday at St. Patrick Roman Catholic Church in Walla Walla, with the Rev. Kevin Codd officiating.

Burial was in Mountain View Cemetery in Walla Walla.

Mr. Van Dyke was born July 6, 1906, in Forest Grove, a son of Walter and Margaret Joosten Van Dyke. He attended school in Verboort and graduated from Adcock Mechanics School in Portland.

He married Marian C. Miller May 28, 1929, in Verboort and they celebrated their 60th wedding anniversary this spring.

After being transferred to Walla Walla as manager of the Birdseye Frozen Food Plant, he also managed a plant for General Foods in Nampa, Idaho. He retired in 1964 after more than 40 years of duty with Birdseye-General Foods.

After retiring, he acted as a consultant for several companies, including Cedar Green Food at Wenatchee, Wash., the University of Alaska (Palmer) Experiment Station and Heinz Co. in Cuidad, Mexico.

Mr. Van Dyke enjoyed golf, fishing and gardening. He was a member of St. Patrick Catholic Church and the Walla Walla Country Club.

He had served on the city planning commission, and was a member of Walla Walla Area Chamber of Commerce and Rotary International of Walla Walla.

Survivors include his wife, Marian Van Dyke, Walla Walla; two daughters, Delores Bennington, Walla Walla, and Joyce King, Bothell, Wash.; two sons, Burton Van Dyke and Jack Van Dyke, both of Walla Walla; 14 grandchildren; and eight great-grandchildren.

Also surviving are six sisters, Minnie Holsmeyer, Forest Grove, Cecelia Duyck and Loretta Vanderzanden, both of Banks, and Christine Sahlfeld, Leona Punchochar and Florence Waibel, all of Hillsboro; five brothers, George Van Dyke, Raymond Van Dyke, Clarence Van Dyke, Howard Van Dyke and Ralph Van Dyke, all of Forest Grove; and numerous nieces and nephews.

He was preceded in death by a grandson, Bob King, and two brothers, Ted Van Dyke, 1960, and Joseph Van Dyke, 1988.

The family suggests memorial contributions to Christian Aid Center in Walla Walla or a charity of choice through the funeral home.

Herring Funeral Home of Walla Walla was in charge of arrangements.

Image 12.23- Albert M. VanDyke Obituary, Hillsboro Argus, 07-25-1989

'Minnie' Holzmeyer, 101, life-long resident

FOREST GROVE - Wilhelmina Mary "Minnie" Holzmeyer, 101, Forest Grove, died Jan. 25, 2007, at her home. Recitation of the rosary and a funeral mass were Monday morning at Visitation Catholic Church in Verboort. Interment was in Mountain View Cemetery, followed by a reception at the Harris Center in Verboort.

Mrs. Holzmeyer was born March 29, 1905, on the family farm in Verboort, the oldest of 14 children of Walter and Margaret Joosten VanDyke. She was raised and educated in Verboort.

Beginning at age 16, she worked at Ray Maling Cannery in Hillsboro for 12 years.

On July 9, 1935, she married Henry Holzmeyer. They lived on the Holzmeyer farm and raised prunes and nuts and operated a prune and nut dryer.

Mrs. Holzmeyer tended to her garden and flower beds and raised ducks, chickens and orphaned pigs. She enjoyed digging for clams and traveling and had visited the 1933 World's Fair in Chicago, Holland, Australia, New Zealand, Alaska, Hawaii and Germany.

Survivors include three children and their spouses, Richard and Bea Holzmeyer, Forest Grove, Gilbert and Pat Holzmeyer, Edmonds, Wash., and Mary Jo and Bob Vandehey, Banks; 10 grandchildren; 18 great-grandchildren; and four sisters, Christine Sahlfeld, Loretta Vanderzanden, Florence Waibel and Leona Puncochar.

She was preceded in death by her husband, Henry; a son, Carl; and eight siblings, Joe, Ted, George, Burt, Raymond, Clarence and Howard VanDyke and Cecelia Duyck.

Memorial contributions are suggested to St. Anthony Catholic Church, 1660 Elm St., Forest Grove, OR 97116.

Duyck and VanDeHey Funeral Home was in charge of arrangements.

Image 12.24- Wilhelmina M. (VanDyke) Holzmeyer Obituary Hillsboro Argus, January 30, 2007

Henry Holzmeyer lifelong farmer

FOREST GROVE—Henry F. Holzmeyer, 87, Forest Grove, died Sept. 15, 1988, at his home.

A funeral mass was held Monday at St. Anthony's Roman Catholic Church in Forest Grove, with Father Dennis O'Donovan officiating. Recitation of the Holy Rosary was Sunday evening.

Vault interment was in Mt. View Memorial Gardens in Forest Grove.

Mr. Holzmeyer was born Dec. 27, 1900, in Forest Grove, a son of Casper and Johanna Cramer Holzmeyer. On July 9, 1935, he married Minnie VanDyke in Verboort and they celebrated their 53rd wedding anniversary earlier this summer.

Mr. Holzmeyer received his education at the Purdin School.

He farmed all his life and raised prunes, grain and filberts. He also owned and operated a prune and nut dryer on Thatcher Road.

He retired in 1985.

Mr. Holzmeyer was active in the refurbishing of Mt. View Memorial Gardens and was a member of the Union Cemetery Association and a member of its board of directors.

He also was a member of St. Anthony's Catholic Church, the Farm Bureau and Forest Grove Grange.

Survivors include his wife, Minnie M. Holzmeyer, Forest Grove; two sons, Richard Holzmeyer, Forest Grove, and Gilbert Holzmeyer, Edmonds, Wash.; a daughter, Mary Jo Vandehey, Banks; eight grandchildren; two step-grandchildren; two step-great-grandchildren; and two sisters, Emma Nixon, Forest Grove, and Frieda McCollom, San Diego, Calif.

The family suggests memorial contributions to St. Anthony's Catholic Church Building Fund.

Forest Grove Memorial Chapel was in charge of arrangements.

Image 12.25- Henry F. Holzmeyer Obituary, Hillsboro Argus, 09-20-1988

Theodore Van Dyke

FOREST GROVE — Funeral Mass for Theodore A. (Ted) Van Dyke, Rt. 2, Forest Grove, were held from Visitation Catholic Church in Verboort Saturday *5-5-79*

He died at Forest Grove Community Hospital Wednesday. *5-2-79 1979*

He was born in Verboort Feb. 14, 1908, and attended school there. *71*

He worked as a carpenter before going to work at Fendall Hardware & Appliance in Forest Grove. In 1944 he became a partner and later bought out Dick Fendall to become sole owner.

He owned and operated Van Dyke Appliance from 1952 until 1970, when he sold the store to his son.

Mr. Van Dyke was well known for the free surrey rides given children of the community during Christmas, Gay 90s and parades.

He leaves his wife, Frances Van Dyke, Forest Grove; sons, Glen and Harvey, Forest Grove; daughters, Mrs. Irvin (Diane) Meeuwsen, Hillsboro, and Mrs. Joan Macnab, Salem; brothers, Howard, Cornelius, Raymond, Gales Creek, Joe, Gaston, Bert, Walla Walla, George, Clarence and Ralph, Forest Grove; sisters, Mrs. Henry (Minnie) Holzmeyer, Forest Grove, Mrs. George (Cecelia) Duyck, Roy, Mrs. Edward (Christine) Sahlfeld, Hillsboro, Mrs. Aloysius (Loretta) Vanderzanden, Banks, Mrs. Clarence (Florence) Waibel, Hillsboro, and Mrs. Edward (Leona) Puncochar, Hillsboro, and 17 grandchildren.

Burial was at Visitation Cemetery with Forest Grove Memorial Chapel in charge of arrangements.

Contributions in his memory may be made to the University of Oregon cancer or heart research funds.

Image 12.26- Theodore A. VanDyke Obituary, Hillsboro Argus, May 1979

Frances VanDyke, long-time resident

FOREST GROVE—Recitation of the Holy Rosary and a Mass of Christian Burial were held Wednesday morning for Frances C. VanDyke, 83, Forest Grove.

Mrs. VanDyke died April 7, 1991, at her home of causes related to age.

The Revs. Frank Walsh of Visitation Roman Catholic Church, and James Harris, retired, officiated at Wednesday's services at Visitation Church in Verboort.

Interment followed in Visitation Cemetery in Verboort.

Mrs. VanDyke was born Feb. 3, 1908, in Roy, a daughter of Peter and Pauline Hermens Krieger. She moved to McMinnville in 1911 and was educated there.

On Sept. 6, 1932, she married Theodore A. VanDyke in McMinnville. He died May 2, 1979.

Mrs. VanDyke had worked at the Birdseye Cannery and as a nanny for several families. After her marriage, she moved to Verboort for a short time before they purchased a farm on Evers Road, where she lived until her death.

Her hobbies included gardening and bingo and she spent considerable time visiting the sick.

She was a member of Visitation Catholic Church, Visitation Altar Society and the Forest Grove Garden Club.

Survivors include two sons, Glen VanDyke, Forest Grove, and Harvey VanDyke, Hillsboro; two daughters, Diane Meeuwsen, Hillsboro, and Joan Drescher, Woodburn; 17 grandchildren; seven great-grandchildren; and a brother, Charles Krieger, McMinnville.

Forest Grove Memorial Chapel was in charge of arrangements.

Image 12.27- Frances C. (Krieger) VanDyke Obituary, Hillsboro Argus, 11-04-1991

Cecilia J. Duyck, 96, life-long resident

A mass of Christian burial was Tuesday morning for Cecilia Josephine VanDyke Duyck, 96, a life-long resident of Verboort and Roy.

Mrs. Duyck died Jan. 4, 2006, at Maryville Nursing Home in Beaverton.

Tuesday's services were at St. Francis of Assisi Catholic Church in Roy. Interment was in St. Francis Catholic Cemetery.

Mrs. Duyck was born Nov. 16, 1909, in Verboort, the fifth oldest of 14 children of Walter and Margaret Joosten VanDyke. She was raised on the family farm in Verboort and was in the first class to attend all 12 grades at Verboort High School, graduating in 1928.

On May 7, 1931, she married George Remi Duyck in Verboort. They farmed in Roy and Mr. Duyck died in 1963.

She enjoyed gardening, flowers, baking pies and breads, fishing, digging clams, card games with her sisters and traveling.

She was a life-long member of the Roman Catholic Church and active at St. Francis Parish, where she was a member of the Altar Society and the Grade School Parents Club. She volunteered many hours at Birthright of Washington County and was an avid baseball fan.

Survivors include 11 children and their spouses, Lloyd and Geri Duyck, Gary and Sally Duyck and Walter and Carolyn Duyck, all of Cornelius, Audrey and Joe Hertel, Roy, Marilyn Grover, Portland, Lorraine and Adolf

Image 12.28- Cecilia J. (VanDyke) Duyck Obituary, Hillsboro Argus, 01-12-2006

Edna E. VanDyke, 98
Jan. 06, 1914 Sept. 15, 2012

Edna Van Dyke of Renton, Wash., formerly of Hillsboro, passed away Sept. 15, 2012. A memorial service is planned for Oct. 12 at 2 p.m. at Skyline Memorial Gardens Funeral Home, 4101 NW Skyline Blvd., Portland.

Edna was born in Milton-Freewater to Fred and Hannah Meihoff on Jan. 6, 1914. She was the youngest of six children.

In 1928 the family moved to Orenco and Edna graduated from Hillsboro High School in 1932. Later she attended Behnke-Walker Business College, then worked as a secretary. In 1940 she married Ray Van Dyke. They moved to Dallas, Ore. where Ray was employed as a music teacher and then to Roseburg where Ray owned a logging company. In 1953 they moved to a farm in the Hillsboro area and later retired in Gales Creek. Edna enjoyed reading, traveling, photography and genealogy.

Survivors include a daughter, Cheryl Gustine; two sons, Dr. Alan Van Dyke and Dr. Jack Van Dyke; five grandchildren and three great-grandchildren. Memorial contributions are suggested to a charity of your choice.

Image 12.29- Edna E. VanDyke (Meihoff) Obituary, Hillsboro Argus, October 5, 2012

Edward Henry Sahlfeld
The Oregonian, November 3, 1999

A funeral Mass will be at 10 a.m. Thursday, Nov. 4, 1999, in St. Matthew Catholic Church in Hillsboro for Edward Henry Sahlfeld, who died Nov. 1 at age 88. Recitation of the rosary will be at 7 p.m. Wednesday, Nov. 3, in Bronleewe-Bass Funeral Home.

Mr. Sahlfeld was born Nov. 19, 1910, in Seneca, Kan. He moved to Mount Angel when he was 4 and to Hillsboro when he was 8. During World War II, he was a pipe fitter and inspector in the Portland shipyards. He was a mechanic for 18 years for the Birds Eye cannery and then was a farmer until retiring in 1975. He was an 80-year member of the church. In 1939, he married Christine Margaret VanDyke.

Survivors include his wife; sons August, Theodore and John, all of Hillsboro, and Joseph of Cedar Mill; daughters, Elizabeth Hepler of Hillsboro and Mary Jane Flanagan of Eugene; sisters, Rose Krautscheid, Ann Pranger and Julie Waibel, all of Hillsboro, and Bertha Imholt of Everett, Wash.; 25 grandchildren; and 15 great-grandchildren.

Interment will be in the church cemetery. The family suggests remembrances to the parish school endowment fund or the building fund of his church.

Image 12.30- Edward H. Sahlfeld Obituary, Oregonian, November 3, 1999

'Jeff' VanDyke, 90, retired dairy farmer

VERBOORT Clarence George "Jeff" VanDyke, 90, a life-long resident of Verboort, died Oct. 29, 2005, at The Haven Foster Care Home in Forest Grove.

Recitation of the rosary and a funeral mass were this morning at Visitation Catholic Church. Vault interment was in Visitation Catholic Cemetery, followed by a reception in the parish hall.

Mr. VanDyke was born Dec. 11, 1914, on the family farm in Verboort, one of 14 children of Walter and Margaret Joosten VanDyke. He was raised on the family farm and attended Visitation High School.

On Nov. 29, 1939, he married Eunice Marie Vandehey in Verboort. They operated a dairy farm until retiring in 1976 and were nearing their 66th wedding anniversary at the time of his death.

Mr. VanDyke enjoyed hunting, playing cards, making wine and activities with his grandchildren and great-grandchildren.

He was involved with horses throughout his life. He was a charter member of the Washington County Sheriff's Posse and participated in horse shows and plowing contests.
Mr. VanDyke played the trumpet in several bands and from 1992 to 1993 was the oldest member of the One More Time Around Again Marching Band.

He was a tenor and the director of the Visitation Church Choir until retiring at age 80, was active in Visitation Parish and volunteered at the Verboort Sausage and Kraut Dinner for many years.

Survivors include his wife, Eunice VanDyke, Verboort; six children and their spouses, Charles W. and Judy VanDyke, La Grande, Jacquelyn M. and Don Hanson, Whittier, Calif., Nicholas E. and Sharrie VanDyke, Cornelius, Frederick M. and Laurelen VanDyke, Banks, Vicki and Charles Hertel, Verboort, and Jeffrey Jon VanDyke, Fairview; 12 grandchildren; 10 great-grandchildren; and seven siblings, Ralph VanDyke, Minnie Holzmeyer, Cecelia Duyck, Loretta Vanderzanden, Christine Sahlfeld, Florence Waibel and Leona Puncochar.

He was preceded in death by an infant daughter and six brothers, Ted, George, Bert, Howard, Raymond and Joseph.

Memorial contributions are suggested to Visitation Parish, 4285 NW Visitation Road, Forest Grove, OR 97116.
Duyck and VanDeHey Funeral Home of Forest Grove was in charge of arrangements.

Image 12.33- Clarence G. VanDyke Obituary, Hillsboro Argus, November 01, 2005

Image 12.31- George R & Cecilia J. Duyck Headstone

Image 12.32- Clarence G & Eunice M. & Jeffrey J. VanDyke Headstone

L. Vanderzanden, 92, service Saturday

BANKS - Loretta M. Vanderzanden, 92, Banks, died Jan. 21, 2009, at Marquis Care Center in Forest Grove.

The rosary will be said at 10:30 a.m. Saturday, Jan. 24, at St. Francis Catholic Church, 39135 NW Harrington Road in Roy. A funeral Mass will be celebrated at 11 a.m. Christian burial and interment will follow at St. Francis Catholic Cemetery in Roy, with a reception at St. Francis Grade School in Roy afterward.

Mrs. Vanderzanden was born Dec. 7, 1916, in Verboort, a daughter of Walter and Margaret Joosten VanDyke. She was raised on the family farm in Verboort and attended Visitation Grade School and Visitation High School.

She married Aloysius "Weice" Vanderzanden, Jan. 3, 1946, in Roy. They had lived on their farm in Banks since then.

She helped raise strawberries, wheat, hay and apples. She enjoyed growing flowers and baking bread for her family. Her interests were sewing, dancing, singing and playing a monthly game of cards with her sisters.

She was preceded in death by her parents.

Survivors include her husband, Weise; her sons, Peter, Chuck, Rob, Ed, and Mark Vanderzanden; daughters, Paula McVay, Karen Kemper and Joan Schouweiler; four siblings; and 21 grandchildren and nine great-grandchildren.

An online guest book is at dvfuneralhome.com.
Remembrances: St. Francis of Assisi Catholic Grade School Endowment Fund. Arrangements: Duyck & VanDeHey, Forest Grove.

Image 12.34- Loretta M. Vanderzanden (VanDyke) Obituary, Hillsboro Argus, January 23, 2009

Aloysius Vanderzanden "Weice"

Aloysius "Weice" Vanderzanden, 96, a resident of the Banks community died, Saturday morning, August 1, 2009 at his home.

Recitation of the Holy Rosary will be said on Friday, August 7, 2009 at 10:30 AM held at the St Francis of Assisi Catholic Church; 39135 NW Harrington Rd. in Roy, OR. Funeral Mass will be celebrated at 11:00 AM on Friday August 7, 2009 at the St Francis Catholic Church in Roy. Rite of Christian Burial and Vault interment will follow the Funeral Mass to be held at the St Francis of Assisi Catholic Cemetery in Roy. A reception will follow at the St Francis Grade School.

Weice was born on June 7, 1913 on the family farm in Banks, OR. He was the youngest son of six children born to Peter John and Agnes R (Herb) Vanderzanden. He was raised on the family farm and attended St Francis Grade School. He later attended Banks High School and was a graduate from the Class of 1931. Following high school he started farming with his family and eventually purchased the family farm in 1946.

Weice enlisted in the US Army during WWII. He served his country as a Staff Sgt with the 38th Bomb Squadron in the South Pacific. His duties as power turret and gun sight mechanic involved him in repairs and scheduled maintenance for several ship armories. He was honorably discharged in 1945.

He was united in marriage to Loretta VanDyke on January 3, 1946 in Roy, Oregon. Following their marriage they made their home on the Vanderzanden family farm in Banks. They farmed together and raised eight children on their farm. They raised berries, wheat apples, hay, chickens and eggs. Loretta died in January of this year.

Weice enjoyed farming; he also went hunting and fishing. He traveled with his wife and visited British Columbia in Canada. He was an avid baseball fan and played scrabble and crossword puzzles. Weice visited the Oregon coast to go clam digging and to enjoy the scenery. He was proud of his garden not only to feed his growing family but later in life because he enjoyed raising it.

He is preceded in death by his loving wife Loretta, his parents and five siblings.

Survivors include eight children and their spouses; Peter and Judy Vanderzanden of Hillsboro, OR, Paula and Mike McVay of Hillsboro, OR, Karen Kemper of Banks, OR, Joan and Rick Schouweiler of Cornelius, OR, Chuck and Brenda Vanderzanden of Hillsboro, OR, Rob and Kathi Vanderzanden of Vancouver, WA, Ed and Jane Vanderzanden of Gales Creek, OR, Mark and Lissa Vanderzanden of Banks, OR, 21 grandchildren and ten great grandchildren.

The family wish donations placed in Weice's name to St Francis of Assisi Catholic Grade School Endowment Fund

Image 12.35- Aloysius R. Vanderzanden Obituary from Duyck & Vandehey Funeral Home

'Deke' Van Dyke, services Friday

CORNELIUS – Howard Walter "Deke" Van Dyke, 82, a life-long area resident, died Oct. 8, 2001, at his home.

A funeral mass will be celebrated Friday at 12:30 p.m. at Visitation Catholic Church, 4285 NW Visitation Road, Verboort, with Father Mark Cach as celebrant and the Rev. Joseph Heuberger as co-celebrant. Interment will follow in Visitation Catholic Cemetery in Verboort.

Family and friends are invited to a reception at the Verboort Rod and Gun Club in Verboort immediately following the cemetery rites.

Mr. Van Dyke was born Oct. 20, 1918, in Verboort, the 10th of 14 children of Walter and Margaret Joosten Van Dyke. He lived his entire life within three miles of where he was born.

He was raised in Verboort and graduated from Verboort High School.

On Nov. 13, 1941, he married Evelyn Plass in Hillsboro. They lived in Cornelius since and were nearing their 60th wedding anniversary.

Mr. Van Dyke drove fuel and feed delivery trucks for Tualatin Valley Co-op until 1950, when he purchased the farm where he lived, worked and played the rest of his life.

He was a member of St. Alexander's Catholic Church in Cornelius, a charter member of the Verboort Rod and Gun Club and a 50-year member of the Knights of Columbus.

Mr. Van Dyke enjoyed the outdoors, especially hunting and fishing. He was an avid trapshooter and had won several High Gun trophies in the local trap league.

He also enjoyed playing cards, chopping firewood, raising hunting dogs, playing and watching baseball, listening to all types of music and playing his harmonica. He especially enjoyed watching his grandchildren play sports, listening to their music and being their "Poppa."

Survivors include his wife, Evelyn Van Dyke, Cornelius; seven sons and five daughters-in-law, Douglas J. and Maurine Van Dyke, Vancouver, Wash., Jerome W. Van Dyke, Cornelius, Norman H. and Kay Van Dyke, Reedville, Roger D. and Janet Van Dyke, Scoggin Valley, Wesley F. and Linda Van Dyke, Hillsboro, Timothy J. Van Dyke, Cornelius, and Bradley J. "Luke" and Megan Van Dyke, Hillsboro; a daughter and son-in-law, Jeanna and Jeff Zimmerman, Glenwood; 12 grandchildren; one great-grandchild; three brothers; six sisters; and numerous nieces and nephews.

He was preceded in death by four brothers.

The family suggests memorial contributions to Doernbecher Children's Foundation, 1121 SW Salmon St., Suite 201, Portland, OR 97205-2021.

Forest Grove Memorial Chapel of Forest Grove is in charge of arrangements.

Image 12.36- Howard W. VanDyke Obituary, Hillsboro Argus, 10-11-2001, page 14A

Image 12.37- Howard W. & Evelyn M. (Plass) VanDyke Headstone, Visitation Catholic Cemetery, SE section, row 6

Clarence J. 'Bud' Waibel

A Mass of Christian burial will be at 10:30 a.m. Thursday, Oct. 31, 2002, in St. Matthew Catholic Church in Hillsboro for Clarence J. "Bud" Waibel, who died Oct. 26 at age 85. Recitation of the rosary will precede the Mass at 10 a.m.

Mr. Waibel was born Sept. 20, 1917, in Helvetia. During World War II, he served in the Army in Europe and received a Silver Star and a Croix de Guerre. Before and after the war, he was a salesman and warehouseman for Tualatin Valley Co-op (later Western Farmers Association), totaling 44 years. A lifetime member of the church, he was an usher and served on many committees. He married Florence Van Dyke in 1945.

Survivors include his wife; daughters, Marg Williamson, Sue Cropp and Diane Reding; sons, Bill, Cliff, Gord, Marv and David; brother, Joe; sisters, Frances Denfeld, Bertie Reidweg and Ethel Kaufmann; 23 grandchildren; and 12 great-grandchildren.

Remembrances to the building fund of his church. Arrangements by Wilhelm.

Image 12.38- Clarence J. Waibel Obituary, The Oregonian, October 29, 2002

Evelyn M. Van Dyke, 87, life-long area resident

Tuesday, December 07, 2004

CORNELIUS A funeral mass was Saturday afternoon for Evelyn M. Van Dyke, 87, Cornelius.

Mrs. Van Dyke died Nov. 30, 2004, at her home.

Saturday's services were at Visitation Catholic Church in Verboort. Interment was in Visitation Catholic Cemetery in Verboort, followed by a reception at the Harris Center.

Mrs. Van Dyke was born Nov. 9, 1917, in Roy, the second of eight children of John and Lela Lyda Plass. She was raised in Roy and attended St. Francis Grade School.

On Nov. 13, 1941, she married Howard W. "Deke" Van Dyke in Hillsboro. They lived on a small farm near Verboort until purchasing a Cornelius farm in 1951.

Mr. Van Dyke died in October 2001, after nearly 60 years of marriage.

Mrs. Van Dyke was a member of St. Alexander Catholic Church in Cornelius for more than 50 years and served as a religious education teacher and in the Altar Society.

She found joy in simple things: listening to her children and grandchildren play musical instruments, watching her daughter perform at Theatre in the Grove, playing cards, crossword puzzles or sitting by the fire reading.

Survivors include eight children and their spouses, Douglas, Vancouver, Wash., Jerome, Cornelius, Norman and Kay, Aloha, Jeanna and Jeff Zimmerman, Gales Creek, Roger and Janet, Gaston, Wesley and Linda, Hillsboro, Timothy, Cornelius, and Bradley and Megan, Hillsboro; 12 grandchildren; three great-grandchildren; three siblings, Theresa Lardy, Forest Grove, Francis Plass, Tulelake, Calif., and Mary Ellen Knipe, Rockaway; and numerous nieces and nephews.

She was preceded in death by a daughter-in-law, Maurine; and four siblings.

The family suggests memorial contributions to Forest Grove Senior Center Meals on Wheels, or to St. Francis School in Roy.

Duyck and VanDeHey Funeral Home of Forest Grove was in charge of arrangements.

Image 12.40- Evelyn M (Plass) VanDyke Obituary, Hillsboro Argus, 12-07-2004

Edward Louis Puncochar
(November 22, 1913 - July 6, 2011)

Edward "Ed" Louis Puncochar, 97, a resident of the Hillsboro community died Wednesday morning at the Tuality Community Hospital in Hillsboro.

Recitation of the Holy Rosary and Funeral Mass will be celebrated at 11:00 AM on Tuesday, July 12, 2011 at St Matthew Catholic Church, 475 SE 3rd Ave in Hillsboro. Rite of Christian Burial and vault interment will be held at the St. Matthew Catholic Cemetery. Family and friends are invited to a reception held at the St Matthew Parish Hall.

Ed was born on November 22, 1913 in St Paul, Nebraska. He was one of four children born to Louis and Estella (Svoboda) Puncochar. Ed was raised in Nebraska and attended school there. In 1935 Ed and his family moved to Hillsboro.

He met his future wife, Leona VanDyke, at a lunch box social in Verboort. After a yearlong courtship they were married on June 3, 1946 in Verboort, OR. Following their marriage they moved onto their farm in Hillsboro where they have since been living.

Ed was a truck driver all of his life. He delivered fuel to local businesses, farms and homes. He retired from this occupation at the age of 72. Ed was also a farmer raising crops on their 30-acre farm south of Hillsboro. Ed would often drive truck all day and then farm most of the evening to get all the chores done and the crops in.

He was a family man and loved spending time with his children and grandchildren. Ed also liked to dance with his wife and daughters. Ed was a fourth degree knight with the Knights of Columbus and was a lifetime member of 75 years.

He is preceded in death by his parents and a sister, Evelyn Horlacker.

He is survived by his loving wife, Leona, eight children and their spouses; Dan and Donna Puncochar of Hillsboro, OR, Ralph and Diane Puncochar of Hillsboro, OR, Charlotte and Stan Corliss of Hillsboro, OR, Cindy and Burt Hasey of Vancouver, WA, Janet and Ken Krase of Portland, OR, Joyce Ayers and her companion, Frank Dawson, both of Salem, OR, Russ and Bev Puncochar of Hillsboro, OR, Doris and Jeff Kennedy of Verboort, OR, two siblings: Louis Puncochar and Robert "Bob" Puncochar, 30 grandchildren and 21 great grandchildren.

The family suggests donations in Ed's name to Knights of Columbus Scholarship Fund, Council 1634; In Care of Mike Wanner; 2730 SE Lonny Ct. Hillsboro, 97123-8371 or Macular Degeneration Research PO Box 1952 Clarksburg, MD. 20871

Image 12.39- Edward L. Puncochar Obituary from Duyck & Vandehey Funeral Home

❧ Descendants of Margaret & Walter VanDyke ❧

Notes: 1= 1st generation, 2= 2nd generation, 3= 3rd generation.
The year of birth is only given for individuals still living, if known.

1   Margaret J. Joosten
Born: April 08, 1880 in Grand Chute, Outagamie County, Wisconsin
Died: January 12, 1960 in Verboort, Washington County, Oregon
Buried at: Visitation Catholic Cemetery, Verboort, OR, SW section, row 3
Married: May 09, 1901 in Verboort, Washington County, Oregon
Walter VanDyke
Born: September 27, 1876 in De Pere, Brown County, Wisconsin
Died: October 08, 1940 in Verboort, Washington County, Oregon
Buried at: Visitation Catholic Cemetery, Verboort, OR, SW section, row 3
Parents: Theodore VanDyke (1847-1934) and Mary Ann Bernards (1846-1922)

    2   Joseph Theodore VanDyke
Born: July 17, 1902 in Verboort, Washington County, Oregon
Died: June 02, 1987 in Forest Grove, Washington County, Oregon
Buried at: Mt. View Memorial Gardens, Forest Grove, OR.
Married:
Theresa Helen Cop
Born: February 16, 1926 in Roy, Washington County, Oregon
Died: July 08, 1998 in Hillsboro, Washington County, Oregon
Buried at: Mt. View Memorial Gardens, Forest Grove, OR
Parents: Henry Cop (1856-1944) and Elizabeth Spiering (1863-1911)

        3   Elizabeth Jean VanDyke
Born: 1927 in Verboort, Washington County, Oregon
Died: Living
Buried at:
Married: April 29, 1950 in Washington County, Oregon
William Henry Meiwes
Born: May 29, 1925 in Hartington, Cedar County, Nebraska
Died: December 30, 2005 in Springfield, Lane County, Oregon
Buried at: Mt. View Memorial Gardens, Forest Grove, OR
Parents: Henry Meiwes (1880-1957) and Mathilda A. Uhing (1884-1963)

        3   Alvin Joseph VanDyke
Born: 1928 in Verboort, Washington County, Oregon
Died: Living
Buried at:
Married: October 20, 1956 in Forest Grove, Washington County, Oregon
Elaine Rosequist
Born: 1930
Died: Living
Buried at:
Parents: Unknown

        3   Vernon H. VanDyke
Born: 1932 in Oregon
Died: Living
Buried at:
Married (1): October 06, 1956 in Washington County, Oregon

Married (2): October 31, 1977 in Vancouver, Clark County, Washington
Evelyn Hulit (1)
Born: Unknown
Died: Living
Buried at:
Parents: Unknown
Doreen G. Scott (2)
Born: 1943
Died: Living
Buried at:
Parents: Unknown

3   Beverly VanDyke
Born: 1934 in Gaston, Washington County, Oregon
Died: Living
Buried at:
Married: April 26, 1958 in Forest Grove, Washington County, Oregon
Lyle F. Meeuwsen
Born: 1936 in Roy, Washington County, Oregon
Died: Living
Buried at:
Parents: William A. Meeuwsen (1895-1974) and Mary Ann Vanderzanden (1896-1988)

3   Janice M. VanDyke
Born: 1938 in Gaston, Washington County, Oregon
Died: Living
Buried at:
Married (1): November 28, 1959 in Washington County, Oregon
Married (2): December 01, 1985 in Reno, Washoe County, Nevada
Eldon John Meeuwsen (1)
Born: June 16, 1938 in Oregon
Died: September 27, 1995 in Washington County, Oregon
Buried at: Mt. View Memorial Gardens, Forest Grove, OR
Parents: John W. Meeuwsen (1910-1989) and Eunice M. Spooner (1917-1978)
Eugene Richard Matias (2)
Born: April 25, 1934 in Cleveland, Cuyahoga County, Ohio
Died: November 01, 2001 in Washington County, Oregon
Buried at: Mt. View Memorial Gardens, Forest Grove, OR
Parents: Steven G. Matias (1898-1974) and Anna Puhalla (1902-1989)

3   John R. VanDyke
Born: 1941 in Gaston, Washington County, Oregon
Died: Living
Buried at:
Married: November 29, 1969 in Washington County, Oregon
Nancy K. Smith
Born: 1944
Died: Living
Buried at:
Parents: Unknown

2   George Theodore VanDyke
Born: November 12, 1903 in Verboort, Washington County, Oregon
Died: January 05, 1991 in Forest Grove, Washington County, Oregon
Buried at: Visitation Catholic Cemetery, Verboort, OR, SE row 5
Married: December 29, 1928 in Forest Grove, Washington County, Oregon
Ethel Mary Kummer
Born: December 08, 1906 in McCook, Red Willow, Nebraska
Died: November 17, 1983 in Forest Grove, Washington County, Oregon
Buried at: Visitation Catholic Cemetery, Verboort, OR, SE row 5
Parents: Joseph C. Kummer (1884-1963) and Luzetta Wilson (1886-1966)

    3   George Wayne VanDyke
Born: 1930 in Verboort, Washington County, Oregon
Died: Living
Buried at:
Married: May 01, 1954 in Oregon City, Clackamas County, Oregon
Elizabeth Rosene Mautz
Born: 1928 in Oregon City, Clackamas County, Oregon
Died: Living
Buried at:
Parents: Albert F. Mautz (1885-1974) and Nellie L. Mautz (1890-1978)

    3   Joanne Cecilia VanDyke
Born: 1931 in Verboort, Washington County, Oregon
Died: Living
Buried at:
Married: July 25, 1959 in Verboort, Washington County, Oregon
Charles Albin Scabery
Born: May 19, 1928 in Regina, Saskatchewan, Canada
Died: November 22, 2004
Buried at: Visitation Catholic Cemetery, Verboort, OR
Parents: Unknown

    3   Eugene Marvin VanDyke
Born: 1932 in Verboort, Washington County, Oregon
Died: Living
Buried at:
Married: November 15, 1954 in Tacoma, Pierce County, Washington
Katherine Mae Jensen
Born: 1934 in Seattle, King County, Washington
Died: Living
Buried at:
Parents: Unknown

    3   James Allen VanDyke
Born: 1935 in Hillsboro, Washington County, Oregon
Died: Living
Buried at:
Married: August 12, 1961 in Portland, Multnomah County, Oregon

Carol Ann Mitchel
Born: 1935 in Butte, Jefferson County, Montana
Died: Living
Buried at:
Parents: Unknown

3   David Walter VanDyke
Born: 1937 in Hillsboro, Washington County, Oregon
Died: Living
Buried at:
Married: December 02, 1961 in Sedro-Woolley, Skagit County, Washington
Veronica Martha Janicki
Born: 1938 in Sedro-Woolley, Skagit County, Washington
Died: Living
Buried at:
Parents: Stanley Janicki (1896-1982) and Hedwiga Kurek (1893-1979)

2   Wilhelmina Mary VanDyke
Born: March 29, 1905 in Verboort, Washington County, Oregon
Died: January 25, 2007 in Forest Grove, Washington County, Oregon
Buried at: Mt. View Memorial Gardens, Forest Grove, OR
Married: July 09, 1935 in Verboort, Washington County, Oregon
Henry Frederick Holzmeyer
Born: December 27, 1900 in Forest Grove, Washington County, Oregon
Died: September 15, 1988 in Forest Grove, Washington County, Oregon
Buried at: Mt. View Memorial Gardens, Forest Grove, OR
Parents: Casper Holzmeyer (1867-1945) and Johanna Cramer (1873-1935)

3   Richard Holzmeyer
Born: 1937 in Oregon
Died: Living
Buried at:
Married: December 07, 1974 in Washington County, Oregon
Beatress Shaw
Born: 1933 or 1934 in Oklahoma
Died: Living
Buried at:
Parents: Hose M. Shaw (1888-1960) and Donia A. Story (1913-1962)

3   Mary Jo Holzmeyer
Born: 1939 in Oregon
Died: Living
Buried at:
Married: December 26, 1959 in Washington County, Oregon
Robert C. Vandehey
Born: 1938 in Oregon
Died: Living
Buried at:
Parents: Charles A. Vandehey (1902-1970) and Agnes C. Hermens (1907-1974)

3　Gilbert Walter Holzmeyer
　　Born: 1943 in Oregon
　　Died: Living
　　Buried at:
　　Married: August 02, 1969 in Chelan, Chelan County, Washington
　　Patricia Ann Betcher
　　Born: 1945
　　Died: Living
　　Buried at:
　　Parents: Unknown

3　Carl Holzmeyer
　　Born: July 16, 1946 in Oregon
　　Died: November 24, 1946
　　Buried at: Mt. View Memorial Gardens, Forest Grove, OR
　　Married: n/a

2　Albert Martin VanDyke
　　Born: July 06, 1906 in Verboort, Washington County, Oregon
　　Died: July 18, 1989 in Walla Walla, Walla Walla County, Washington
　　Buried at: Mountain View Cemetery, Walla Walla, WA
　　Married: May 28, 1929 in Verboort, Washington County, Oregon
　　Marian Clara Miller
　　Born: September 16, 1908 in Beaverton, Washington County, Oregon
　　Died: January 04, 2000 in Walla Walla, Walla Walla County, Washington
　　Buried at:
　　Parents: Unknown

3　Burton Clifford VanDyke
　　Born: 1929 in Hillsboro, Washington County, Oregon
　　Died: Living
　　Buried at:
　　Married: May 12, 1988 in Reno, Washoe County, Nevada
　　Peggy Lee Trout
　　Born: 1953 in Walla Walla, Walla Walla County, Washington
　　Died: Living
　　Buried at:
　　Parents: Unknown

3　Delores Marian VanDyke
　　Born: 1931 in Hillsboro, Washington County, Oregon
　　Died: Living
　　Buried at:
　　Married: November 15, 1952 in Walla Walla, Walla Walla County, Washington
　　William Harris Bennington
　　Born: June 22, 1927 in Ritzville, Adams County, Washington
　　Died: August 29, 2001 in Walla Walla, Walla Walla County, Washington
　　Buried at: Mountain View Cemetery, Walla Walla, WA
　　Parents: Virgil Bennington (1889-1983) & Vera Harris (1899-1981)

3   Joyce Susan VanDyke
    Born: February 11, 1934 in Hillsboro, Washington County, Oregon
    Died: January 04, 2005 in Washington
    Buried at:
    Married: July 17, 1955 in Walla Walla, Walla Walla County, Washington
    Gregory Noel King
    Born: December 03, 1931 in Milton-Freewater, Umatilla County, Oregon
    Died: November 08, 1995 in Kirkland, King County, Washington
    Buried at:
    Parents: Unknown

3   John Warren VanDyke
    Born: 1936 in Hillsboro, Washington County, Oregon
    Died: Living
    Buried at:
    Married: August 02, 1980 in Walla Walla, Walla Walla County, Washington
    Lois Ann Jennens
    Born: 1949 in Cleveland, Cuyahoga County, Ohio
    Died: Living
    Buried at:
    Parents: Unknown

2   Theodore August VanDyke
    Born: February 14, 1908 in Verboort, Washington County, Oregon
    Died: May 02, 1979 in Forest Grove, Washington County, Oregon
    Buried at: Visitation Catholic Cemetery, Verboort, OR, SW row 5
    Married: September 06, 1932 in McMinnville, Yamhill County, Oregon
    Frances Catherine Krieger
    Born: February 03, 1908 in Roy, Washington County, Oregon
    Died: April 07, 1991 in Forest Grove, Washington County, Oregon
    Buried at: Visitation Catholic Cemetery, Verboort, OR, SW row 5
    Parents: Peter J. Krieger (1874-1952) and Pauline E. Hermens (1877-1950)

    3   Glen W. VanDyke
        Born: 1933 in Forest Grove, Washington County, Oregon
        Died: Living
        Buried at:
        Married: June 27, 1964 in Multnomah County, Oregon
        Marianne R. Andreotti
        Born: 1935 in Oregon
        Died: Living
        Buried at:
        Parents: Emilio Andreotti (1901-1952) and Louise Cola (1911-2006)

    3   Lois Frances VanDyke
        Born: January 13, 1935 in Forest Grove, Washington County, Oregon
        Died: April 11, 1978 in Lake Oswego, Clackamas County, Oregon
        Buried at: Mt. Calvary Catholic Cemetery, Portland, OR
        Married: September 02, 1957 in Washington County, Oregon

Carl H. Meeuwsen
Born: 1934 in Oregon
Died: Living
Buried at:
Parents: Walter A. Meeuwsen (1899-1953) and Theresa A. Herb (1901-1983)

3   Harvey T. VanDyke
Born: 1936 in Forest Grove, Washington County, Oregon
Died: Living
Buried at:
Married: July 19, 1959 in Multnomah County, Oregon
Valerie R. Mortimer
Born: 1939
Died: Living
Buried at:
Parents: Unknown

3   Diane Margaret VanDyke
Born: 1938 in Forest Grove, Washington County, Oregon
Died: Living
Buried at:
Married: September 19, 1959 in Washington County, Oregon
Irvin Walter Meeuwsen
Born: April 21, 1932 in Forest Grove, Washington County, Oregon
Died: November 12, 2011
Buried at: Visitation Catholic Cemetery, Verboort, OR
Parents: Walter A. Meeuwsen (1899-1953) and Theresa A. Herb (1901-1983)

3   Joan Elizabeth VanDyke
Born: 1940 in Forest Grove, Washington County, Oregon
Died: Living
Buried at:
Married (1): May 08, 1965 in Washington County, Oregon
Married (2): April 25, 1986 in Marion County, Oregon
Lawrence William McNab (1)
Born: October 09, 1937
Died: November 27, 1984 in Multnomah County, Oregon
Buried at:
Parents: Unknown
Frederick Drescher (2)
Born: 1933
Died: Living
Buried at:
Parents: Unknown

2 Cecilia Josephine VanDyke
Born: November 16, 1909 in Verboort, Washington County, Oregon
Died: January 04, 2006 in Beaverton, Washington County, Oregon
Buried at: St. Francis of Assisi Catholic Cemetery, Roy, OR, south row 7
Married: May 07, 1931 in Verboort, Washington County, Oregon

George Remi Duyck
Born: December 18, 1908 in Mountaindale, Washington County, Oregon
Died: June 18, 1963 in Forest Grove, Washington County, Oregon
Buried at: St. Francis of Assisi Catholic Cemetery, Roy, OR, south row 7
Parents: Henry Duyck (1869-1948) and Helen C. Spiering (1882-1970)

3   Lloyd George Duyck
     Born: 1932 in Roy, Washington County, Oregon
     Died: Living
     Buried at:
     Married: May 08, 1954 in Washington County, Oregon
     Geraldine M. Mayer
     Born: 1933 in Oregon
     Died: Living
     Buried at:
     Parents: Carl T. Mayer (1905-1996) and Wilma E. Vandebeck (1905-1996)

3   Leroy Joseph Duyck
     Born: June 03, 1933 in Roy, Washington County, Oregon
     Died: August 31, 1972 in Multnomah County, Oregon
     Buried at: St. Francis of Assisi Catholic Cemetery, Roy, OR, west row 1
     Married: November 23, 1963 in Washington County, Oregon
     Maurine Ann Walsh
     Born: 1931
     Died: Living
     Buried at:
     Parents: Maurice H. Walsh (1904-1975) and Mary F. Walsh (1905-1990)

3   Audrey Margaret Duyck
     Born: 1934 in Roy, Washington County, Oregon
     Died: Living
     Buried at:
     Married: May 30, 1956 in Roy, Washington County, Oregon
     Joseph Anthony Hertel
     Born: December 16, 1931 in Roy, Washington County, Oregon
     Died: June 19, 2006 in Hillsboro, Washington County, Oregon
     Buried at: St. Francis of Assisi Catholic Cemetery, Roy, OR
     Parents: Frank Hertel (1889-1974) and Gertrude M. Gellings (1890-1975)

3   Roland Henry Duyck
     Born: November 13, 1935 in Roy, Washington County, Oregon
     Died: January 07, 2005 in Hillsboro, Washington County, Oregon
     Buried at: Visitation Catholic Cemetery, Verboort, OR
     Married: January 05, 1957 in Roy, Washington County, Oregon
     Judith Estelle Donaldson
     Born: Unknown
     Died: Living
     Buried at:
     Parents: Unknown

3   Gary Walter Duyck
    Born: 1937 in Hillsboro, Washington County, Oregon
    Died: Living
    Buried at:
    Married: October 24, 1959 in Multnomah County, Oregon
    Sally I. Vanderbeck
    Born: 1937 in Oregon
    Died: Living
    Buried at:
    Parents: Clarence J. Vanderbeck (1911-1973) and June G. Hughes (1912-2009)

3   Walter Robert Duyck
    Born: October 02, 1938 in Roy, Washington County, Oregon
    Died: November 06, 2010 in Cornelius, Washington County, Oregon
    Buried at: Visitation Catholic Cemetery, Verboort, OR
    Married: September 02, 1961 in Verboort, Washington County, Oregon
    Carolyn Marie Herb
    Born: May 25, 1937 in Forest Grove, Washington County, Oregon
    Died: March 22, 2007 in West Linn, Clackamas County, Oregon
    Buried at: Visitation Catholic Cemetery, Verboort, OR
    Parents: Francis J. Herb (1906-1993) and Lena G. Crop (1909-1987)

3   Marilyn Cecilia Duyck
    Born: 1940 in Hillsboro, Washington County, Oregon
    Died: Living
    Buried at:
    Married: September 09, 1967 in Washington County, Oregon
    Gerald D. Grover
    Born: 1944
    Died: Living
    Buried at:
    Parents: Unknown

3   Lorraine Ethel Duyck
    Born: 1941 in Hillsboro, Washington County, Oregon
    Died: Living
    Buried at:
    Married: January 27, 1962 in Multnomah County, Oregon
    Adolf C. Klein
    Born: 1937
    Died: Living
    Buried at:
    Parents: Unknown

3   Kenneth John Duyck
    Born: April 10, 1943 in Forest Grove, Washington County, Oregon
    Died: April 06, 1966 in Portland, Multnomah County, Oregon
    Buried at: St. Francis of Assisi Catholic Cemetery, Roy, OR, south row 7
    Married: n/a

3   Sharon Ann Duyck
     Born: 1945 in Hillsboro, Washington County, Oregon
     Died: Living
     Buried at:
     Married (1): October 14, 1967 in Washington County, Oregon
     Married (2): November 24, 2007 in Washington County, Oregon
     Frede D. Bidstrup (1)
     Born: 1943
     Died: Living
     Buried at:
     Parents: Unknown
     Bill Floyd Racine (2)
     Born: Unknown
     Died: Living
     Buried at:
     Parents: Unknown

3   Dorothy Theresa Duyck
     Born: 1947 in Hillsboro, Washington County, Oregon
     Died: Living
     Buried at:
     Married (1): December 22, 1974 in Los Angeles County, California
     Married (2): Unknown
     James Girard (1)
     Born: 1944
     Died: Living
     Buried at:
     Parents: Unknown
     Stanley Umeda (2)
     Born: Unknown
     Died: Living
     Buried at:
     Parents: Unknown

3   Lorna Mary Duyck
     Born: 1949 in Hillsboro, Washington County, Oregon
     Died: Living
     Buried at:
     Married (1): January 24, 1970 in Washington County, Oregon
     Married (2): January 03, 1997 in Washington County, Oregon
     Robert W. Hermens (1)
     Born: 1948
     Died: Living
     Buried at:
     Parents: Vincent L. Hermens (1916-2007) and Mary Ann D. Meeuwsen (1920-2007)
     Lawrence K. Newby (2)
     Born: Unknown
     Died: Living
     Buried at:
     Parents: Unknown

3   Steven James Duyck
    Born: 1952 in Hillsboro, Washington County, Oregon
    Died: Living
    Buried at:
    Married: November 17, 1973 in Washington County, Oregon
    Marie Kathleen Heinrich
    Born: Unknown
    Died: Living
    Buried at:
    Parents: Unknown

3   Mary Sue Duyck
    Born: 1953 or 1954 in Oregon
    Died: Living
    Buried at:
    Married: October 12, 1974 in Washington County, Oregon
    Frederick Petersen
    Born: Unknown
    Died: Living
    Buried at:
    Parents: Unknown

2 Raymond Wilfred VanDyke
   Born: September 11, 1911 in Verboort, Washington County, Oregon
   Died: March 18, 2005 in Woodland, Cowlitz County, Washington
   Buried at:
   Married: August 17, 1940 in Seattle, King County, Washington
   Edna Emma Meihoff
   Born: January 06, 1914 in Milton-Freewater, Umatilla County, Oregon
   Died: September 15, 2012 in Renton, King County, Washington
   Buried at:
   Parents: Fred J. Meihoff (1876-1961) and Hannah M. Meihoff (1878-1953)

3   Alan Ronald VanDyke
    Born: November 04, 1942 in Salem, Marion County, Oregon
    Died: December 12, 2013
    Buried at:
    Married (1): August 16, 1969 in Multnomah County, Oregon
    Married (2): Unknown
    Brenda Hall (1)
    Born: Unknown
    Died: Living
    Buried at:
    Parents: Unknown
    Karla Waterman (2)
    Born: 1949 in Woodstock, McHenry County, Illinois
    Died: Living
    Buried at:
    Parents: Unknown

3   Cheryl Rae VanDyke
Born: 1946 in Salem, Marion County, Oregon
Died: Living
Buried at:
Married: July 26, 1969 in Washington County, Oregon
Timothy Gustine
Born: 1945 in Lebanon, Linn County, Oregon
Died: Living
Buried at:
Parents: Unknown

3   Jack L. VanDyke
Born: 1951 in Roseburg, Douglas County, Oregon
Died: Living
Buried at:
Married: June 26, 1977 in Multnomah County, Oregon
Victoria L. Frisbie
Born: 1952 in Grants Pass, Jackson County, Oregon
Died: Living
Buried at:
Parents: Unknown

2   Christine Margaret VanDyke
Born: 1913 in Verboort, Washington County, Oregon
Died: Living
Buried at:
Married: February 16, 1939 in Verboort, Washington County, Oregon
Edward Henry Sahlfeld
Born: November 19, 1910 in Seneca, Nemaha County, Kansas
Died: November 01, 1999 in Hillsboro, Washington County, Oregon
Buried at: St. Matthew Catholic Cemetery, Hillsboro, OR
Parents: F. August Sahlfeld (1877-1970) and Elizabeth Stegeman (1888-1981)

      3   August Joseph Sahlfeld
Born: 1941 in Hillsboro, Washington County, Oregon
Died: Living
Buried at:
Married: May 11, 1963 in Roy, Washington County, Oregon
Kathleen Alice Peters
Born: 1940 in Verboort, Washington County, Oregon
Died: Living
Buried at:
Parents: Albert W. Peters (1897-1981) and Catherine E. Hillecke (1897-1981)

      3   Theodore Edward Sahlfeld
Born: 1943 in Hillsboro, Washington County, Oregon
Died: Living
Buried at:
Married: February 12, 1966 in Washington County, Oregon

Kathleen Denise Gerrish
Born: 1944 in Del Rio, Val Verde County, Texas
Died: Living
Buried at:
Parents: Unknown

3   Mary Jane Sahlfeld
Born: 1945 in Hillsboro, Washington County, Oregon
Died: Living
Buried at:
Married: March 28, 1974 in Deschutes County, Oregon
Latham Flanagan
Born: 1936 in Lebanon, Wayne County, Pennsylvania
Died: Living
Buried at:
Parents: Unknown

3   Joseph Walter Sahlfeld
Born: 1946 in Hillsboro, Washington County, Oregon
Died: Living
Buried at:
Married: September 14, 1968 in Washington County, Oregon
Constance Huston
Born: Unknown
Died: Living
Buried at:
Parents: Unknown

3   John Francis Sahlfeld
Born: 1950 in Hillsboro, Washington County, Oregon
Died: Living
Buried at:
Married: August 16, 1985 in Hillsboro, Washington County, Oregon
Dorothy Susan Potter
Born: 1955 in Chicago, Cook County, Illinois
Died: Living
Buried at:
Parents: Unknown

3   Elizabeth Margaret Sahlfeld
Born: 1953 in Hillsboro, Washington County, Oregon
Died: Living
Buried at:
Married: July 21, 1990 in Washington County, Oregon
Paul Hepler
Born: Unknown
Died: Living
Buried at:
Parents: Unknown

2   Clarence George VanDyke
Born: December 11, 1914 in Verboort, Washington County, Oregon
Died: October 29, 2005 in Forest Grove, Washington County, Oregon
Buried at: Visitation Catholic Cemetery, Verboort, OR, SE row 7
Married: November 29, 1939 in Verboort, Washington County, Oregon
Eunice Marie Vandehey
Born: 1917 in Oregon
Died: Living
Buried at:
Parents: Edward J. Vandehey (1891-1968) and Angeline C. Hermens (1896-1920)

3   Charles W. VanDyke
Born: 1940
Died: Living
Buried at:
Married: Unknown
Judith L. VanDyke
Born: 1946
Died: Living
Buried at:
Parents: Unknown

3   Jacquelyn VanDyke
Born: Unknown
Died: Living
Buried at:
Married: September 24, 1962 in Washington County, Oregon
Donald Hanson
Born: Unknown
Died: Living
Buried at:
Parents: Unknown

3   Nicholas Edward VanDyke, Sr.
Born: 1945 in Oregon
Died: Living
Buried at:
Married (1): October 21, 1967 in Washington County, Oregon
Married (2): September 23, 1988 in Washoe County, Nevada
Paula Biden (1)
Born: Unknown
Died: Living
Buried at:
Parents: Unknown
Sharrie D. Hollis (2)
Born: Unknown
Died: Living
Buried at:
Parents: Unknown

3   Frederick Michael VanDyke
Born: 1947 in Oregon
Died: Living
Buried at:
Married (1): December 16, 1967 in Washington County, Oregon
Married (2): June 18, 1993 in Columbia County, Oregon
Deborah Ann Clymore (1)
Born: Unknown
Died: Living
Buried at:
Parents: Unknown
Laurelen Sue Jabbour (2)
Born: Unknown
Died: Living
Buried at:
Parents: Unknown

3   Vicki J. VanDyke
Born: 1953 in Oregon
Died: Living
Buried at:
Married: March 03, 1973 in Washington County, Oregon
Charles E. Hertel
Born: 1949 in Oregon
Died: Living
Buried at:
Parents: Francis H. Hertel (1922-2010) and Loretta Vandervelden

3   Jeffrey Jon VanDyke
Born: 1959
Died: Living
Buried at:
Married: Unknown

2   Loretta M. VanDyke
Born: December 07, 1916 in Verboort, Washington County, Oregon
Died: January 21, 2009 in Forest Grove, Washington County, Oregon
Buried at: St. Francis Catholic Cemetery, Roy, OR, north row 11
Married: January 03, 1946 in Roy, Washington County, Oregon
Aloysius Robert Vanderzanden
Born: June 07, 1913 in Banks, Washington County, Oregon
Died: August 01, 2009 in Banks, Washington County, Oregon
Buried at: St. Francis Catholic Cemetery, Roy, OR, north row 11
Parents: Peter J. Vanderzanden (1879-1957) and Agnes R. Herb (1877-1949)

3   Peter Alan Vanderzanden
Born: 1946 in Forest Grove, Washington County, Oregon
Died: Living
Buried at:
Married: August 11, 1973 in Umatilla County, Oregon

Judith R. Shumway
Born: 1951
Died: Living
Buried at:
Parents: Unknown

3   Paula Mary Vanderzanden
Born: 1947 in Forest Grove, Washington County, Oregon
Died: Living
Buried at:
Married: January 19, 1973 in Washington County, Oregon
Michael B. McVay
Born: 1946
Died: Living
Buried at:
Parents: Unknown

3   Karen Agnes Vanderzanden
Born: 1949 in Hillsboro, Washington County, Oregon
Died: Living
Buried at:
Married: December 06, 1969 in Washington County, Oregon
Donald Kemper
Born: Unknown
Died: Living
Buried at:
Parents: Unknown

3   Joan Margaret Vanderzanden
Born: 1951 in Hillsboro, Washington County, Oregon
Died: Living
Buried at:
Married: April 05, 1986 in Washington County, Oregon
Richard A. Schouweiler
Born: 1949
Died: Living
Buried at:
Parents: Unknown

3   Charles John Vanderzanden
Born: 1952 in Hillsboro, Washington County, Oregon
Died: Living
Buried at:
Married: February 02, 1985 in Washington County, Oregon
Brenda Clarno
Born: Unknown
Died: Living
Buried at:
Parents: Unknown

3 Robert Aloysius Vanderzanden
Born: 1956 in Hillsboro, Washington County, Oregon
Died: Living
Buried at:
Married: March 14, 1981 in Washington County, Oregon
Katherine Walters
Born: Unknown
Died: Living
Buried at:
Parents: Unknown

3 Edmund George Vanderzanden
Born: 1959 in Hillsboro, Washington County, Oregon
Died: Living
Buried at:
Married: n/a
Jane Marie Wood
Born: 1960
Died: Living
Buried at:
Parents: Unknown

3 Mark Joseph Vanderzanden
Born: 1960 in Hillsboro, Washington County, Oregon
Died: Living
Buried at:
Married: August 01, 1981 in Washington County, Oregon
Lissa Ferguson
Born: 1960
Died: Living
Buried at:
Parents: Unknown

2 Howard Walter VanDyke
Born: October 20, 1918 in Verboort, Washington County, Oregon
Died: October 08, 2001 in Cornelius, Washington County, Oregon
Buried at: Visitation Catholic Cemetery, Verboort, OR, SE row 6
Married: November 13, 1941 in Hillsboro, Washington County, Oregon
Evelyn Marie Plass
Born: November 09, 1917 in Roy, Washington County, Oregon
Died: November 30, 2004 in Cornelius, Washington County, Oregon
Buried at: Visitation Catholic Cemetery, Verboort, OR, SE row 6
Parents: John Plass (1889-1963) and Lela Lyda (1896-1970)

3 Douglas J. VanDyke
Born: 1943 in Oregon
Died: Living
Buried at:
Married: February 07, 1976 in Washington County, Oregon

Maurine H. Hammond
Born: 1945
Died: Living
Buried at:
Parents: Unknown

3   Jerome W. VanDyke
Born: 1944 in Oregon
Died: Living
Buried at:
Married:
Joanna L. Franzel
Born: 1954
Died: Living
Buried at:
Parents: Unknown

3   Jeanna VanDyke
Born: Unknown
Died: Living
Buried at:
Married: November 23, 1990 in Washington County, Oregon
Jeffrey Zimmerman
Born: Unknown
Died: Living
Buried at:
Parents: Unknown

3   Norman H. VanDyke
Born: 1947 in Oregon
Died: Living
Buried at:
Married: December 20, 1969 in Washington County, Oregon
Christina Kay Goans
Born: 1947
Died: Living
Buried at:
Parents: Unknown

3   Roger D. VanDyke
Born: 1953 in Oregon
Died: Living
Buried at:
Married: January 29, 1977 in Washington County, Oregon
Janet M. Meeuwsen
Born: 1955 in Oregon
Died: Living
Buried at:
Parents: John W. Meeuwsen (1910-1989) and Eunice M. Spooner (1917-1978)

3   Wesley Frederick VanDyke
     Born: 1956 in Oregon
     Died: Living
     Buried at:
     Married: May 04, 1979 in Washington County, Oregon
     Linda K. Moore
     Born: 1957
     Died: Living
     Buried at:
     Parents: Unknown

3   Timothy J. VanDyke
     Born: 1959 in Oregon
     Died: Living
     Buried at:
     Married: Unknown

3   Bradley James VanDyke
     Born: 1961 in Oregon
     Died: Living
     Buried at:
     Married: October 08, 1994 in Washington County, Oregon
     Megan Ann Martz
     Born: 1959
     Died: Living
     Buried at:
     Parents: Unknown

2 Florence Walteria VanDyke
   Born: 1921 in Verboort, Washington County, Oregon
   Died: Living
   Buried at: St. Matthew Catholic Cemetery, Hillsboro, OR
   Married: November 29, 1945 in Hillsboro, Washington County, Oregon
   Clarence Joseph Waibel
   Born: September 20, 1917 in Helvetia, Washington County, Oregon
   Died: October 26, 2002 in Hillsboro, Washington County, Oregon
   Buried at: St. Matthew Catholic Cemetery, Hillsboro, OR
   Parents: William Waibel (1882-1974) and Mary A. Waibel (1886-1957)

3   Margaret Mary Waibel
     Born: 1946 in Hillsboro, Washington County, Oregon
     Died: Living
     Buried at:
     Married: February 17, 1968 in Washington County, Oregon
     Ronald Eldon Williamson
     Born: 1943 in Portland, Multnomah County, Oregon
     Died: Living
     Buried at:
     Parents: Unknown

3   Susan Cecilia Waibel
Born: 1947 in Hillsboro, Washington County, Oregon
Died: Living
Buried at:
Married: November 23, 1968 in Hillsboro, Washington County, Oregon
Michael Victor Crop
Born: 1947 in Hillsboro, Washington County, Oregon
Died: Living
Buried at:
Parents: Unknown

3   William Edward Waibel
Born: 1949 in Hillsboro, Washington County, Oregon
Died: Living
Buried at:
Married: May 12, 1973 in Washington County, Oregon
Pamela Ann Telles
Born: 1953 in New Orleans, Orleans County, Louisiana
Died: Living
Buried at:
Parents: Samuel R. Telles (1925-2000) and Ellen R. Bergeron (1924-2006)

3   Clifford Charles Waibel
Born: 1952 in Hillsboro, Washington County, Oregon
Died: Living
Buried at:
Married: November 16, 1986 in Hillsboro, Washington County, Oregon
Jerlia Rose Sperry
Born: 1952 in Portland, Multnomah County, Oregon
Died: Living
Buried at:
Parents: Unknown

3   Gordon Joseph Waibel
Born: 1956 in Hillsboro, Washington County, Oregon
Died: Living
Buried at:
Married: April 19, 1986 in Washington County, Oregon
Jaleen Elizabeth Canfield
Born: 1962 in Tacoma, Pierce County, Washington
Died: Living
Buried at:
Parents: Unknown

3   Marvin John Waibel
Born: 1958 in Hillsboro, Washington County, Oregon
Died: Living
Buried at:
Married: August 31, 1985 in Washington County, Oregon

Marla D. Rolfe
Born: 1964
Died: Living
Buried at:
Parents: Unknown

3 David Lawrence Waibel
Born: 1961 in Hillsboro, Washington County, Oregon
Died: Living
Buried at:
Married: Unknown

3 Diane Marie Waibel
Born: 1961 in Hillsboro, Washington County, Oregon
Died: Living
Buried at:
Married: November 27, 1982 in Washington County, Oregon
Jeffrey Wayne Reding
Born: 1962 in Portland, Multnomah County, Oregon
Died: Living
Buried at:
Parents: Unknown

2 Leona Ida VanDyke
Born: 1922 in Verboort, Washington County, Oregon
Died: Living
Buried at:
Married: June 03, 1946 in Verboort, Washington County, Oregon
Edward Louis Puncochar
Born: November 22, 1913 in St Paul, Howard County, Nebraska
Died: July 06, 2011 in Hillsboro, Washington County, Oregon
Buried at: St. Matthew Catholic Cemetery, Hillsboro, OR
Parents: Louis J. Puncochar (1887-1970) and Estella L. Svoboda (1893-1988)

3 Daniel Edward Puncochar
Born: 1947 in Hillsboro, Washington County, Oregon
Died: Living
Buried at:
Married: August 15, 1970 in Forest Grove, Washington County, Oregon
Margaret Mary Moore
Born: 1946 in Forest Grove, Washington County, Oregon
Died: Living
Buried at:
Parents: James H. Moore (1904-1990) and Frances A. Murphy (1907-1984)

3 Ralph Louis Puncochar
Born: 1948 in Hillsboro, Washington County, Oregon
Died: Living
Buried at:
Married: April 28, 1973 in Washington County, Oregon

Marlene E. Churchley
Born: 1948
Died: Living
Buried at:
Parents: Unknown

3   Charlotte Ann Puncochar
Born: 1951 in Hillsboro, Washington County, Oregon
Died: Living
Buried at:
Married: March 16, 1979 in Washington County, Oregon
Stanley A. Corliss
Born: 1947
Died: Living
Buried at:
Parents: Unknown

3   Cynthia Marie Puncochar
Born: 1955 in Hillsboro, Washington County, Oregon
Died: Living
Buried at:
Married: January 20, 1979 in Hillsboro, Washington County, Oregon
Burton W. Hasey
Born: Unknown
Died: Living
Buried at:
Parents: Unknown

3   Joyce Elaine Puncochar
Born: 1959 in Hillsboro, Washington County, Oregon
Died: Living
Buried at:
Married: October 22, 1982 in Washington County, Oregon
Charles H. Ayers
Born: 1949
Died: Living
Buried at:
Parents: Unknown

3   Janet Lorraine Puncochar
Born: 1959 in Hillsboro, Washington County, Oregon
Died: Living
Buried at:
Married (1): April 30, 1977 in Washington County, Oregon
Married (2): Unknown
Michael Hartill (1)
Born: Unknown
Died: Living
Buried at:
Parents: Unknown

Kenneth Krase (2)
Born: Unknown
Died: Living
Buried at:
Parents: Unknown

3   Russell W. Puncochar
Born: 1960 in Hillsboro, Washington County, Oregon
Died: Living
Buried at:
Married: May 16, 1987 in Washington County, Oregon
Beverly Ann Howard
Born: 1962
Died: Living
Buried at:
Parents: Unknown

3   Doris Jean Puncochar
Born: 1964 in Hillsboro, Washington County, Oregon
Died: Living
Buried at:
Married: June 15, 1985 in Washington County, Oregon
Jeffrey William Kennedy
Born: 1960
Died: Living
Buried at:
Parents: Unknown

2   Ralph John VanDyke
Born: 1924 in Verboort, Washington County, Oregon
Died: Living
Buried at:
Married: July 02, 1951 in Washington County, Oregon
Virginia J. Huschka
Born: 1928 in North Dakota
Died: Living
Buried at:
Parents: Anton F. Huschka (1873-1973) and Selma T. Knutson (1905-1988)

3   Walter Allen VanDyke
Born: 1952 in Hillsboro, Washington County, Oregon
Died:
Buried at:
Married: June 01, 1985 in Enterprise, Wallowa County, Oregon
Tammy Daggett
Born: 1960 in Enterprise, Wallowa County, Oregon
Died:
Buried at:
Parents: Unknown

3   Patricia Ann VanDyke
Born: 1954 in Hillsboro, Washington County, Oregon
Died: Living
Buried at:
Married: Unknown

3   Anthony Eugene VanDyke
Born: 1955 in Hillsboro, Washington County, Oregon
Died: Living
Buried at:
Married: Unknown

3   Bernard Charles VanDyke
Born: May 13, 1957 in Hillsboro, Washington County, Oregon
Died: July 09, 2003 in Portland, Multnomah County, Oregon
Buried at: Visitation Catholic Cemetery, Verboort, OR
Married: February 12, 2000 in Portland, Multnomah County, Oregon
Tonya Louise Anderson
Born: Unknown
Died: Living
Buried at:
Parents: Mark Anderson and Beverly Anderson

3   Donna Jean VanDyke
Born: 1961 in Hillsboro, Washington County, Oregon
Died: Living
Buried at:
Married: July 29, 1989 in Castro Valley, Alameda County, California
William Cherry
Born: 1946
Died: Living
Buried at:
Parents: Unknown

3   Margaret Mary VanDyke
Born: 1965 in Hillsboro, Washington County, Oregon
Died: Living
Buried at:
Married: Unknown

≈ **Appendix A** ≈

Index of Individuals

Descendants of Joseph & Nellie in **Bold**

Descendants of Joseph & Nellie in **Bold**

Descendants of Joseph & Nellie in **Bold**

Descendants of Joseph & Nellie in **Bold**

Descendants of Joseph & Nellie in **Bold**

VanLoo, Arthur W. Sr.	87, 95	Verbruggen, Henry F.	59
VanLoo, Augustine	95	Verhagen (Borsa), Charlota	189
VanLoo, Clifford A.	87, 96	Verhagen (Camp), Elizabeth A.	189
VanLoo, Donald E.	87, 96	Verhagen (DeGroot), Christina J.	108, 114, 150
VanLoo, Doris E.	96	Verhagen (Dercks), Irene C.	114
VanLoo, Earl J.	98	Verhagen (Diebold), Lillian S.	188
VanLoo, George H.	97	Verhagen (Ducat), Mary M.	114
VanLoo, Maurice A.	95	Verhagen (Gourlie), Irene F.	180, 182, 187
VanLoo, Vernon L.	87, 97	Verhagen (Gump), Laura A.	189
VanLoo, William F.	81-83, 95	Verhagen (Hamilton), Twyla	187
Vanoudenhoven (Joosten), Frances	26	Verhagen (Joosten), Catherine	21-23, 26, 27, 107, 179
Vanoudenhoven, Cornelius	107	**Verhagen (Joosten), Christina**	38, 40, 45, 179-181, 183, 187, 199
VanRooy (Kipp), Elvira	117	**Verhagen (Joosten), Mary**	37, 40, 44, 107, 113, 179
VanRooy, Clarence M.	117	Verhagen (Pynenberg), Theresa	115
VanThiel (Hammen), Elizabeth J.	55, 62	Verhagen (Rogers), Myrtle M.	192
VanThiel (Wydeven), Harriet M.	55	Verhagen (Rudolph), Barbara C.	187
VanThiel, Joseph R.	55	Verhagen (Schumacher), Elizabeth	108, 113, 161
VanThiel, Theodore A.	55	Verhagen (Schuster), Irma M.	182, 191
VanVeghel (VanLanen), Christine	33	Verhagen (Steltenpohl), Vera E.	181, 182, 196
VanVeghel (VanLanen), Mary	32	Verhagen (VandeKerkhof), Elizabeth	25
VanVeghel, Henry	33	Verhagen (VandenBoogart), Johanna	108, 113, 148, 149
VanVeghel, John	32	Verhagen (Vandenheuvel), Christine	108, 113
Vella (Livingston), Patricia A.	190	Verhagen (Vandervelden), Marjorie C.	181, 183, 195
Vella, Anthony J.	190	Verhagen (VanHammond), Henriette	25, 26, 45, 107179
Verberk, Anthony J (Fr.)	6, 47, 61, 107	Verhagen (VanStappen), Cornelia	27
Verberk, Martin	6	**Verhagen, Adrian H.**	45, 179, 180, 182, 183, 187
Verbeten, John Cornelius	31	Verhagen, Blanche B.	114
Verboort (Aerts), Petronella	16	**Verhagen, Earl H.**	110, 114
Verboort (Evers), Janet A.	120, 131	**Verhagen, Edward H**	179, 180, 182, 187
Verboort (Jansen), Antonetta	16	**Verhagen, Eugene**	196
Verboort (Van de Rayt), Theodora	7, 8, 15	**Verhagen, Gary H.**	196
Verboort (Vandehey), Martha J.	128	Verhagen, Geri	196
Verboort (VanDyke), Petronella	16	Verhagen, Gijsbert	27
Verboort (VanDyke), Petronella M.	129, 131	**Verhagen, Harlow R.**	188
Verboort, Albert	8, 9, 16	Verhagen, Henry (1829)	21, 22, 24, 26, 27, 45, 107, 179
Verboort, Arthur J.	131	**Verhagen, Henry J. (1892)**	40107, 113161
Verboort, John (1871)	16	**Verhagen, Howard E.**	188
Verboort, John Jr.	8, 9, 15, 22	**Verhagen, Howard G.**	180-183, 196
Verboort, John Sr.	7-9, 15	**Verhagen, John H. Jr.**	108, 117
Verboort, Leslie J.	129	**Verhagen, John H. Sr.**	45, 107-109, 113, 148, 149, 161, 179
Verboort, William A.	16, 129, 131	**Verhagen, Joseph (1894)**	40, 107, 108, 115, 150, 161
Verboort, William Augustine (Fr.)	1, 7-9, 12, 15, 37	**Verhagen, Joseph A.**	180, 190
Verbrick (Doyle), Grace R.	60	**Verhagen, Joseph J. (1916)**	113
Verbrick (Vandenheuvel), Joan Margaret	59	**Verhagen, Joseph J. (1919)**	109, 110, 114
Verbrick, Joseph W.	60	**Verhagen, Lawrence E. Sr.**	183, 189
Verbrick, Willard C.	60	**Verhagen, Lester J.**	180, 187
Verbruggen (Vandenheuvel), Mary Jane	59	**Verhagen, Louis H.**	189
Verbruggen (VanRhijn), Caroline M.	59		
Verbruggen, Cornelius Anthony	59		

Descendants of Joseph & Nellie in **Bold**

My Family Tree

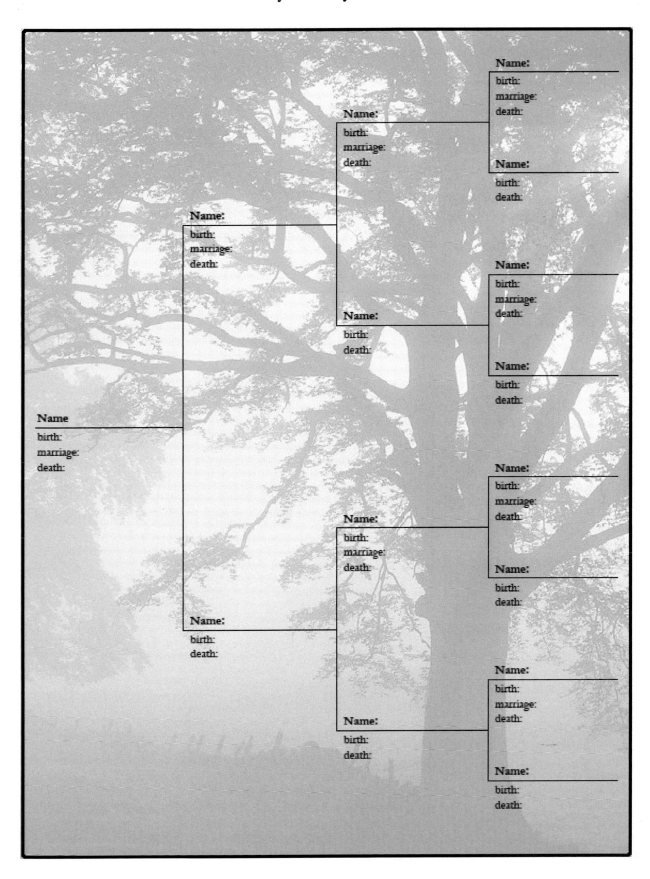

Name:
birth:
marriage:
death:

Name:
birth:
death:

Name:
birth:
marriage:
death:

Name:
birth:
death:

Name
birth:
marriage:
death:

Name:
birth:
marriage:
death:

Name:
birth:
death:

Name:
birth:
marriage:
death:

Name:
birth:
death:

Name:
birth:
marriage:
death:

Name:
birth:
death:

Name:
birth:
marriage:
death:

Name:
birth:
death: